Million Dollar Blackjack

by
Ken
Uston

MILLION DOLLAR BLACKJACK

Published by   SRS Enterprises, Inc.
1018 N. Cole Ave.
Hollywood, CA 90038

Copyright © 1981 by Ken Uston.

Second Printing—June 1981

ISBN: 0-914314-08-4

All material presented in this book is offered as information to the reader. No inducement to gamble is intended or implied.

Printed in the United States of America

TO JERRY FUERLE, "THE ROCK,"

AND ONCE AGAIN,

TO ERROLL GARNER

Acknowledgments

I would first like to thank Dr. Edward Thorp, for his pioneering work in the field of blackjack, and the late Lawrence Revere, who contributed significantly to the player's knowledge of blackjack. My initial blackjack education stemmed directly from the work of these two men.

The person solely responsible for my entering the business bears the pseudonym of Al Francesco. "Al" spent hundreds of hours painstakingly training our first team, and through the years, has been unselfishly supportive of our team operations. Al also introduced me to Dale Crase, the producer of the movie of my first book, *The Big Player.*

This book would not be possible without the expertise of literally dozens of players with whom I have worked over the past six years. While I will not name them all, the primary contributors include Bill E., Ron K., Daryl P., Frank S. and Frank P., whom I consider to be among the strongest blackjack players in the world.

I would like to thank Mark Estes, who generously contributed information on the "Double Exposure" game. Finally, I would like to thank Stanley Roberts, who encouraged the publication of this book, and Bruce Plopper, who painstakingly read and re-read several versions of the manuscript.

Ken Uston

Table of Contents

Table of Contents (continued)

Table of Contents *(continued)*

15   Spooking and Other Hole Card Play   223

16   Cheating   237

17   Getting Barred   255

18   Being the House and Caddy Blackjack (A Peek Inside The Underworld)   269

19   Blackjack Abroad—Where It Is and How To Play It   283

Table of Contents (continued)

List of Tables and Illustrations

Tables and Illustrations (continued)

Tables and Illustrations (continued)

Million Dollar Blackjack

PUBLISHER'S FOREWORD

When Ken Uston came to my office some three years ago with a request that I publish his book, my initial reaction was—does the world really need another blackjack book? Ken had come to me because he knew that my two books on the game, *Winning Blackjack* and *How to Win at Weekend Blackjack,* were both best sellers. In fact, at that particular time, *Winning Blackjack* had grossed more money than the next three or four most popular books on the game combined.

Clearly, Kenny wanted to maximize his possible returns by having me put into the sale of his book the same kind of effort that I had put into the sale of my books in the past. Smart fellow this Uston; he didn't get to be Senior Vice President of the Pacific Stock Exchange by accident! To the many before and since who have wished me to publish their works on the game, my typical response is to be polite and informative even though another blackjack book will be competitive with my own works.

On the other hand, Ken's reputation had preceded his visit to my office. I had read his initial book, *The Big Player,* a narrative on his early playing experiences, and knew that his expertise was solid and unique. I also knew many of the people who had played with Ken. So, I agreed to read the manuscript he proffered.

The original manuscript, which has since been improved and expanded, was impressive even then. It was clear that Ken's experiences playing blackjack were beyond the scope of nearly any other player in the history of the game. You will see that when you read the three chapters in this book devoted to his playing experience. It also was clear that many new techniques of casino play, which were not commonly known, were about to be put into print for the first time. Further, Ken had done some outstanding work on compiling the data on the elementary and well known basic strategies, and had spent the obligatory time and money to derive a new professional level strategy.

I was impressed with Ken's experience and his skills at blackjack, but I was even more impressed by his manuscript. In addition to being a skilled player, Uston also happened to be a skilled writer, as you will find in reading this book. There's an important lesson to be learned from Ken Uston—if one devotes his full energies and capabilities to anything, there is little that human beings cannot accomplish.

Million Dollar Blackjack brings to the reader a broad range of black-jack systems, from a handful of rules for the lazy player, which will surely cut his losses, to the most efficient professional-level system, which should only be undertaken by the serious and experienced player. Included are all basic strategies for major casino areas—depending upon the rules, basic strategy will create a break-even game. The intermediate-level strategy presented here is easy to learn and is the first and simplest of the four levels of winning strategies in this book. Also presented is an advanced-level strategy, the Uston Simple Plus/Minus. This is followed by a beginning professional-level strategy, the Uston Advanced Plus/Minus; and finally, the Uston Advanced Point Count, a professional level strategy, is presented.

The reader is cautioned that he should not expect an instant injection of blackjack wisdom just from reading this book. My ten years in this field dealing with thousands of students have taught me that the worst error you can make is to attempt a more complex strategy than you are able to master at the moment. Like an infant, you must crawl before you walk. So, too, must you learn the simple strategies and use them under casino conditions before you attempt the more complex ones. If you fail with a complex strategy that is too difficult at this stage—but possible after experience—you will destroy the mental attitude that is needed to create the confidence and discipline required in learning to play a winning game of blackjack. Even though the material presented here will appear easy, remember, you are going to risk money on your learned skills and cannot afford to make errors which will negate the small edge you have acquired.

Speaking of small edges, remember that even the best of players, under favorable rules and playing conditions, only has about a two percent edge. This small percentage, however, is very powerful for those players who are prepared to grind down the house. Remember, this edge is greater than that the casino has at the Baccarat table. . .or at the pass line at craps.

Playing winning blackjack requires that you control your greed and exercise caution, or you too may be barred. How to do this and what to do if you are barred are also covered in this book. Now that you possess the most complete book ever published on this fascinating game, read it carefully and study it seriously...that's why we've provided flashcards to help you to learn the material. Cut them out and paste on cardboard as instructed, or order an index card set. But start with the lowest level you are ready to attempt. Then, if you need additional help, there are schools and other books, as well as additional materials described in the last part of this book.

Now as to our "friends" in the casino who will read this book, there is probably no need to panic, as you did in 1964 when Dr. Thorp's book, *Beat the Dealer*, received widespread distribution. At that time, you changed the rules but found the effect on the game hurt the player activity, so within a week, the rules were changed back. The history of the publication of blackjack books shows that the volume of players and gross casino wins increase directly with the publication and distribution of good books on the game. The reason, of course, is that the players do not follow the advice in the books and especially do not heed the warnings recited above.

On the other hand, this is the most comprehensive book and the most powerful book ever published on the game. We cannot predict the results of its impact. Further, both the author and I hereby disclaim any responsibility for any damage caused to casinos or players by virtue of the publication of this work.

The worst thing a casino or player could do is not to become fully conversant with all the material in this book, which takes more than a casual reading. Any casino employee who is involved with the dealing or administration of the game of "21," and does not have his copy of this book, is comparable to a minister without a bible. We recommend that he be instantly defrocked. So, anyone who plays for serious money who has not read and studied this book is like a sinner expecting salvation without repenting the error of his ways.

But enough of my writing; you can read that monthly in *Gambling Times* magazine. It's now time for you to read Ken Uston's *Million Dollar Blackjack*. It's not my habit to wish people "luck" at blackjack, because blackjack is a game of skill. So read, study and go get 'em.

Stanley Roberts

Chapter One

Can You Win at Blackjack?

Man has always been fascinated by gambling—indeed, for centuries gambling has been a popular pastime for many and a livelihood for a few. Today, gambling casinos exist in many countries, including England, France, Germany, Spain, Portugal, Panama, Argentina, Ecuador, Korea, Macao, Australia, Malaysia, Nepal, Swaziland, Egypt, Morocco, throughout the Caribbean, and many more places too numerous to mention.

The American gambling mecca is Las Vegas, where gaming has proliferated for nearly 50 years. Although the city was founded in 1905 and chartered in 1911 by C.P. "Pop" Squires, today's huge gambling palaces owe their existence primarily to the pioneering of Bugsy Siegal, the Chicago mobster, and others who headed West in the early 1940's. Bugsy was convinced that the Las Vegas desert could be transformed into a resort area unprecedented for its gambling, glitter and entertainment, and that is exactly what happened, although Bugsy never lived to enjoy it (he was gunned down by his so-called "partners" before his dream fully materialized).

In May 1978, New Jersey became the second state to allow casino gambling, as Resorts International opened its doors to the Eastern gambling public and immediately became the world's most successful casino, grossing $220 million in its first year of operation. Caesars Boardwalk Regency opened in June 1979, Bally's Park Place during the winter of 1979, and Great Bay Casino's Brighton Hotel in August 1980. Most insiders feel it's just a matter of time before other states will follow suit.

But gambling existed in this country long before Las Vegas was developed. In the East, particularly in Steubenville, Ohio (the hometown of many Las Vegas pitbosses and casino officials), Coventry, Kentucky, New York City, Chicago and other metropolitan areas, illegal gambling was widespread. Standard scales of "ice," or bribes, were paid to local law enforcement officials to ensure that the casinos, usually set up in warehouses, garages or private flats, could operate untouched by the law. Even today, illegal casinos thrive in brownstone houses in Manhattan, apartments on Long Island, in private residences in Odessa and Austin, Texas, and in a surprising number of locations around the country.

Most people who gamble do so to experience the excitement of wagering sums on the green felt tables and because of the possibility, however slim, of doubling their bankroll or even striking it rich and earning thousands. As a rule, these gamblers are fully cognizant of the built-in advantage to the house; however, some are convinced they have a "system" that will ensure steady earnings. Most systems are based on wishful thinking and superstition. Among the most popular are those based on number progressions, but they cannot and do not alter the basic house advantage.

House Advantage At Selected Casino Games

Casino games other than blackjack have a standard, measurable advantage to the house, ranging from about 1-to-25%. Table 1-1 below lists the house advantage in most casino games.

For the Walter Mittys who hope to get rich through a small investment, there is Keno, where as little as 70 cents can win up to $12,500. This Irish Sweepstakes-type game yields the house an overwhelming advantage of about 25%—that is, on average, for every $1,000 in total gambling "action" (the total value of bets placed), the house will earn $250.

The pastime that seems to be favored by most *Li'l Ol' Ladies* is pulling the "one-armed bandits," the slot machines, which can be programmed to yield the house varying odds, but which normally provide the house an advantage of from 10-to-20%. Currently, there are $1 slot machines at the Flamingo Hilton and Harold's Club, and other casinos in Las Vegas and Reno which offer tempting "progressive jackpots" where the jackpot pay-out increases in size each time the machine is played. In late 1979 and early 1980, jackpots of over $300,000 were hit—the largest payouts in Nevada history.

Roulette gives the house an advantage of about 5¼% in the United States. Roulette in Europe, where the wheels have only an "0" instead of both an "0" and "00," and where the rules are slightly more liberal, yields a smaller advantage to the house—less than 1½% on even money bets. Some Nevada casinos, reflecting the competitive pressures for the gamer's dollar, offer single-zero roulette as well.

Craps, or dice, yields the house varying odds. The best player odds (betting the Pass Line and taking the "odds" or betting the Don't Pass

Line and giving "odds") give the house approximately .8% on the total amount bet. With the "double odds" offered by some houses, the player's disadvantage is as little as .6% on the total bet (although the house edge on the Pass Line bet is still 1.4%). Other craps bets, the proposition bets, such as playing the "field," can favor the house more, some in fact up to 16.7%.

Table 1—1

House Advantage—Selected Casino Games

Keno...........Approximately 25%

Slot Machines....3-to-24%, usually closer to the higher figure (17% maximum in Atlantic City)

Big Six..........Approximately 18% (varies with the bet)

Chuck-A-Luck....Approximately 2.78% to 8% (varies with the bet)

Roulette:

Double zero....5.27%
Single zero.... 2.70%
Single zero and
  en prison....1.35%

Craps:

Field, Proposition &
  other bets... From 1.5% to 16.7%
Pass, Don't Pass
Come, Don't Come 1.4%

Odds Bets.....Even, but you give up 1.4% on the Line.
  Line bets with odds: .8% on total bet
  Line bets with double odds: .6% on total bet

Baccarat:
  Player........ 1.36%
  Banker........1.17%

Baccarat is favored by many because of its international mystique, the security-guarded area, the tuxedoed croupiers and the good-looking young lady shills (called "starters" by casino personnel) who are present at most baccarat games, even in the very largest Strip casinos. The Sahara in Las Vegas uses the large, plastic, rectangular

3

chips found in European casinos, an international touch added, no doubt, to stimulate business. Some houses offer "mini-baccarat" games; these games are played on tables slightly larger than blackjack tables which are scattered around the unsecured portion of the casino to make the game available to the dollar bettor. In baccarat, the house has an advantage of 1%—for every $1,000 that is bet by the customers, the house, on average, will pocket $11 to $14.

Thus, there is a significant variation in the house advantage among the different games, and in fact, wide variation depending upon the type of bet made at craps. The worst games for the player are keno, the slot machines, the Big Six Wheel and certain proposition bets at craps. The best games, other than blackjack, are baccarat and the line bets with odds at craps.

Why Blackjack Can Be Beaten

Unlike all other casino games, blackjack is unique in that the house advantage is completely dependent upon the decisions made by the player. The player may choose to hit his hand (taking additional cards), stand pat, double-down, split pairs, take insurance, and in some casinos, surrender his hand, giving up half his bet (these options are described in detail in Chapter 4). The completely self-destructive player theoretically could play at a 100 percent disadvantage, hitting all hands including blackjack until he busted.

Blackjack is unique in another way: it is the only casino game where the odds continually change back and forth during the course of the game. This is because, unlike other casino games, blackjack is not subject to what the statisticians call the "Law of Independent Trials."* This law can best be illustrated as follows:

> The odds of throwing a 7 in craps on an honest pair of dice are 1-out-of-6—of the 36 possible combinations, there are six possible combinations that will yield a 7. If three 7's are thrown consecutively, the odds of a 7 occurring on the fourth roll are exactly the same as they were initially, that is, 1-out-of-6. This is because previous rolls have *no* effect on subsequent rolls, or, as gamblers sometimes say, "The dice have no memory." This law pertains equally to roulette, to slot machines and to keno.

Yet, many gamblers do not understand this law and gamble as if it did not exist. For example, note the *Li'l Ol' Lady* who, after having played one slot machine for two hours without hitting a jackpot, will take a break and ask the attendant to reserve the machine for her. This, she argues, is because the machine is "due" for a jackpot now. In fact, the chances of a jackpot from the slot machine are exactly the same as they were two hours ago when the *Li'l Ol' Lady* began her gambling session. But, it is impossible to convince her of this and the practice of reserving slot machines is widespread throughout Nevada.

---

* This also pertains to baccarat, but in a far less significant way.

The most amazing demonstration of the misconception over the Law of Independent Trials takes place in the casinos in Europe, particularly in France and Monte Carlo. On any given day the chances are that you will see *every* player at the roulette and baccarat tables faithfully recording the outcome of each roll or hand on the score sheets happily provided by the house for this purpose. Even bystanders record the results—slyly waiting to jump in when the game gets "hot."

Far more sophisticated players gambled as if the Law of Independent Trials did not exist. Famous gamblers, such as Harold Smith, Jr. (36)* and the late Nicholas "Nick the Greek" Dandolas, were convinced that the dice or cards ran in "hot" or "cold" streaks, governed by some mystical force. Nick the Greek would "test" the dice with small bets to "see how they were running" and then decide whether to continue playing with larger stakes.

It often appears that streaks occur, but what is overlooked is that there are also many periods when streaks do not occur. For any unpredictable series of events, whether the toss of a die, the flip of a coin, or the turn of a card, the sheer randomness to which the test is subject will result in episodes when, for example, several 7's are thrown consecutively, or will not appear for a long period or will show up fairly close to 1-out-of-6 times. Streaks, of course, do occur, but they cannot be predicted and the beginning of a streak has *no* effect on whether the streak will continue. Many gamblers, however, cannot be convinced of this fact.

How is it that blackjack is not subject to the Law of Independent Trials? It is because, after one hand has been played, subsequent hands *are* influenced by the cards that have already been used. In fact, even during the first hand enough cards may be seen to influence a change in strategy. Let's take an example:

> Assume, to take an extreme case, that three players are playing a single deck blackjack game. The cards are shuffled and, on the first round, all three players and the dealer get a "natural" or blackjack, that is, an ace and a ten-valued card. On the second round, the players' chances of getting another blackjack are nil, since all four aces have been dealt. The *players' advantage* is clearly reduced on the second round, since the house pays 3-to-2 for blackjack, and the possibility of blackjack has been eliminated.

In this case, the content of the deck is now to the players' disadvantage, as compared to a complete 52-card deck. As can be readily surmised, at times the content of the deck also varies the other way, to the benefit of the players.

Basically, when many 10's and aces are played (throughout we will refer to a "10" as any ten-valued card: a 10, jack, queen or king), the

---

*Numbers in ( ) refer to references listed on pages 325 to 329.

5

deck favors the house. When many small cards relative to aces and 10's have been played, the deck tends to favor the player.

The player can use this knowledge to his advantage. When the deck is in his favor, he can bet larger and vary his play based on the fact that there are more 10's and aces in the deck. When the deck is in the house's favor, he can bet smaller and also vary his play to reflect the disproportionately high number of low cards in the deck. The net result of this can yield the player an edge over the house of from 1-1½%.

History of Card Counting

This phenomenon has been known for a number of years. In 1957, it was contained in a technical paper by Baldwin, Cantey, Maisel and McDermott which was published in the *Journal of the American Statistical Association* (21). It was first generally made known to the public in 1962 by Dr. Edward O. Thorp in his first edition of *Beat the Dealer* (1), a book on blackjack that became so popular it eventually was listed on a national best-seller list; over 300,000 copies of this book have been sold. The book was based on exhaustive computer analyses of the game, which produced a "Basic Strategy" (the optimum way to play blackjack hands by the non-counting player) and a card counting system.

One result of Thorp's book was the unfounded suspicion by casino bosses that there was a proliferation of "system" players who would keep track of the content of the deck and vary their bet size and playing strategy accordingly. This belief became so prevalent that the blackjack rules in Las Vegas were changed to provide an additional percentage advantage for the house (splitting aces was forbidden and doubling-down was permitted only on a total of 11). These changes were unpopular and seriously cut into the volume of blackjack play. As a result, they were soon rescinded. The casinos had decided that it was more advantageous to put up with a few card counting players than to reduce the action they received from the vast majority of players who did not count cards.

The second version of Thorp's book (1), published in 1966, introduced a simple "point count" technique similar to the method used in counting points in bridge à la Charles Goren. This made blackjack card counting more practical for large numbers of players because of its simplicity and resulted in the proliferation of even more card counters.

Five years later, in 1971, the late Lawrence Revere (nee Griffith K. Owens, and also known as Specks Parsons) with the assistance of computer runs conducted by Julian H. Braun of IBM Corporation (who had also assisted Dr. Thorp in his earlier calculations), further refined Thorp's methods. Revere developed several systems, the most sophisticated of which is called the "Revere Advanced Point Count," or more simply, the "14 Count."* This method, somewhat more complex than Thorp's, yields the player an impressive advantage over the house if applied properly. Although this system was not made available in his book, *Playing Blackjack As A Business* (3), Revere sold it for $200 to those interested in investing that amount for the potential of large blackjack profits.

In the same year, a simple-to-use system yielding a respectable percentage over the house was developed by Stanley Roberts and published in his book, *Winning Blackjack* (4), which sells for $95 and has grossed over $1,000,000 to date. Roberts subsequently developed a chain of blackjack schools across the U.S. bearing his name.

Later, another simple system, Hi Opt I, was developed by Dr. Lance Humble of Toronto, Canada, in conjunction with Julian Braun. This system claimed to have equal power to the Revere 14 Count, but studies have shown it to be somewhat less powerful, in both betting and playing efficiency. Hi Opt I, however, offered a relatively simple point count method, making it easier for the average player to learn and reducing the likelihood of player error.

Several years later, Humble introduced Hi Opt II, a more complicated "two-level" count, i.e., the maximum card values are plus or minus two. At the time of its introduction, Hi Opt II was in fact more powerful than any other system on the market. It also sold for $200.

Several years ago, I commissioned several computer experts to develop an advanced system for the optimum three-level count. This count, the Uston Advanced Point count, is slightly more powerful than both Hi Opt II and the 14 Count and is currently the most powerful non-parameterized count currently available (non-parameterized refers to counting systems which do not require a side count of specific card denominations, other than aces.)** It had been marketed for $97 and over 1,400 students have been practicing and employing it. The most successful student I know of won $185,000 in Nevada in 1979 and was barred in only one club. The Uston Advanced Point Count is included in complete detail in Chapter 8.

Some students, frankly, found the Uston Advanced Point Count difficult or didn't want to devote the time necessary to master it completely. As a result, I developed the Uston Simple Plus/Minus, a one-level count which can be readily learned by the average person. This system, particularly attractive for the favorable Atlantic City game, is described in complete detail in Chapter 6. An extension of this count, the Uston Advanced Plus/Minus, which is roughly on par with the Hi Opt I, was subsequently developed and also is included in Chapter 6.

Through the years, numerous other systems have been

---

*The count is so named because the card values add to a total of 14.

** A comparative evaluation of the major count systems is included in Chapter 8.

7

developed—some accurate and valuable to the blackjack player, others fraught with inaccuracies. The unknowing blackjack neophyte is in a precarious position. Not only are there all too many poor systems on the market, but, unfortunately, the number of books giving misleading and inaccurate advice on blackjack far exceeds those that can help the prospective player. This situation is particularly regrettable since the student of blackjack not only pays—sometimes dearly—for the poor system, but then he invests many hours of practice and many dollars before he realizes that the system he purchased is worthless. The bibliography at the end of this text evaluates many of the available books on blackjack.

Today, most casino personnel, from casino managers on down to dealers, know that the game of blackjack can be beaten and are quite aware of the existence of card counters. Several years ago, many of the clubs converted to the use of multiple deck games, assuming that this would protect them from card counting players. (It turned out that not only could multiple deck games be beaten, but their very existence led to a lucrative opportunity on which to capitalize now called "team play" and described in both Chapters 2 and 12.) The casino people have taken even more steps to offset the counter's edge, from shuffling the deck to outright barring of players.

Prior to 1978, counters made impressive amounts playing in Nevada casinos. The casinos reacted and in 1978 and 1979, it became difficult to make significant amounts in Las Vegas. At the sight of black ($100) chips, the casino bosses would become wary. Nickel ($5 chip) players and occasionally quarter ($25 chip) players seemed to escape the "heat," however. Then, Atlantic City opened and offered the most favorable blackjack rules in the world (excluding the single deck game at Caesars Palace in Las Vegas), creating a fabulous opportunity for the skillful player. The New Jersey bosses gradually became educated as counters won significant amounts, particularly in 1979 and 1980. Despite this, the favorable New Jersey rules currently lend themselves to unusual approaches whereby the player may enjoy an edge over the house without most bosses being aware of it.

In Las Vegas, in the meantime, with most high-rolling counters in New Jersey and elsewhere in the world, the pendulum once again swung the other way, in favor of the players. As of this writing, a few clubs have reverted to the use of single deck, no doubt concluding that the small risk of attracting counters is offset by the additional "legitimate" business that single deck will lure. In many multiple deck clubs, a greater proportion of the cards is being dealt than was the case several years ago, once again offering an opportunity for the skillful player.

While Vegas and Atlantic City (and in fact the rest of the world) are not the "candy stores" they were several years ago, opportunity does exist. For the serious student of blackjack, who practices long and hard and exercises self-discipline and complete dedication, attractive financial opportunities in blackjack still exist.

Use Of This Book

This book has been organized to be of use to anyone interested in playing blackjack—from the infrequent visitor to casinos in Las Vegas, Reno, Atlantic City, the Bahamas, Europe or elsewhere, who is interested in having an enjoyable vacation and not losing too much at the tables—to the potential full-time professional interested in earning a living from blackjack. Readers with considerably different motivations will benefit from the information contained in the various chapters. Perhaps you are one of the following types:

The Social Player. You don't want to spend any time studying the game. You probably visit casinos a few times a year, play blackjack for the excitement of gambling and you basically just want to have a good time without throwing your money away. Or, perhaps you're the spouse or date of a more serious gambler who likes to get a few hands in during the course of the trip.

Chapter 5 lists seven rules which can be learned in ten minutes, or even written on a card or envelope and kept at the blackjack table (they'll let you). These simple rules can be followed whether you're absolutely sober or have had quite a few drinks. By following them, you cut the house edge to about 1% if you're playing single deck in Las Vegas or multiple deck in Atlantic City.

The Even-With-The-House Player. You don't have the patience or desire to count cards, since you also play for fun, not for profits, often after having had a few drinks or so. You're not interested in all the scientific, mathematical mumbo jumbo, but you like the idea of being able to play essentially even with the house and are willing to spend maybe five-to-ten hours learning about 17 simple rules and put in a half-hour of practice before each trip. The Basic Strategy in Chapter 5 is for you.

The Well-Off But Thrifty Bon Vivant. You have enough means to maintain a $10,000 bank balance and would like to enjoy a free vacation occasionally in Vegas, Aruba, the Bahamas or Monte Carlo—that is, have the casinos pick up your air fare, room (or suite) charges, and restaurant and show tabs. You may be married and want to bring your spouse, or you may be single and want to win over some local lovely by taking her on a trip to Vegas, or some combination of the two. But you don't want to spend a lot of time studying blackjack. Read Chapter 20, "Living The American Fantasy Without Spending A Dime."

The Mafia Bookie. You probably live in New York, Chicago or Detroit and can get into one of the many illegal private "caddy" blackjack games (where the deal rotates from player-to-player) played for high stakes in those areas; or maybe you already play in the game once in a while, but you never win consistently. You don't want to spend time learning to count cards, but the idea of being able to win perhaps $500 or $1,000 per night, on average, from the other guys appeals to you. Read Chapter 18, "Being The House and Caddy Blackjack."

The Curious Pitboss

You Were A Pitboss At:	On or About:	And Wondered How:	Won:	Read About:
The Fremont Hotel	January 14, 1975	That guy who said he was from Connecticut	$27,600	Team 1, Chapter 2
The Desert Inn	January 28, 1975	The red-head who kept bouncing from table to table	$57,000	Team 1, Chapter 2
Carson City Nugget	August 9-11, 1975 March 16, 1976	The guy with the red beard	$30,000	Spooking, Chapter 15
Loews' Monte Carlo	October 24, 1975	The four Americans who didn't seem to know each other	126,000 francs	Blackjack Abroad, Chapter 19
Dieppe, France	Fall, 1974	The two Americans who always bet big toward the end of the shoe	$180,000	Blackjack Abroad, Chapter 19
Harrah's Reno	December 1975 to April 1977	The many high rollers who played with a day shift dealer, Sylvia	$43,000	Front-loading, Chapter 14
Marina	April 1977	The quiet well-dressed black from San Francisco	$16,000	Team 3, Chapter 7
4 Queens	April 1977	The drunk with the New York accent	$22,000	Team 3, Chapter 7
Sahara Tahoe	November 1978	The dark-haired drunk	$23,000	Team 4, Chapter 7
Resorts International	January 1979	Ken, Rob, Jack, Mike, Ty, Peter	$145,000	Team 5, Chapter 13
Oostende, Belgium	July 1979	Two Americans	$80,000	Blackjack Abroad, Chapter 19
Resorts and Boardwalk Regency	December 1979 to March 1980	Eleven Players	Lots and lots	Team 6, Chapter 13
Bally's Park Place	March 1980	The Californian who seemed to like Atlantic City	$75,000	Team 6, Chapter 13

The Disillusioned Counter. You read the books by Dr. Thorp or Lawrence Revere and became really interested in the game. You spent hours learning the point count or tens count and went to Nevada or Atlantic City to play. You won a few times, but then on one trip you lost nearly all your bank—maybe you were even wiped out. You became disillusioned and quit and have been playing only for fun ever since. You fell into the trap that catches probably 90% of card counters. Read Chapter 9, "Determination of Betting Strategy."

The Part-time Card Counter. You're interested in learning all you can about the game, so you can take your stake and go to Nevada or Atlantic City and win money consistently. You probably have a job and will play only on weekends—unless the 1½% edge that you have generates enough profits to tempt you to become a full-time player sometime in the future. Read Chapters 3 through 9.

The Blackjack Professional. You play the game professionally now and have enjoyed some success, but are becoming known in too many of the clubs to suit you. You may even have been barred a few times. You'd like to find a way to continue making a profit. The time has come to consider working through and with other blackjack players to enhance and hopefully perpetuate your profits. Read Chapter 12 on how to form a team operation.

The Card Counter With Good Vision. You can count cards successfully and also have 20/20 vision—or can get glasses to convert you to 20/20 vision. You're interested in a legal way to increase your advantage in the casino to as much as an enticing 5% over the house. Read Chapter 14, "Front-Loading."

The Potential Thief. You have some knowledge of the game and may even be a good card counter. You're down on your luck and are willing to risk doing something that might be against the law (although it's never been tested in court) in order to make some money at blackjack. Read Chapter 15, "Spooking." (I do *not* recommend this approach and in fact advise against it—but it's included since its part of the body of blackjack knowledge.)

The Real Thief. You're really down on your luck—you're desperate and are willing to risk doing something that is definitely against the law—in fact, it's a felony. Read the section of Chapter 15 entitled, "Playing With The Help." (I emphatically advise against this approach, but to make this book a complete text on blackjack, I have included the material.)

The Aspiring Globetrotter. You've got some free time and would like to travel around the world inexpensively, at the same time, staying in top hotels and dining in gourmet restaurants. Read Chapter 19 which (1) tells you how to play in casinos in the foreign countries where blackjack profits are attainable and (2) identifies the factors

11

you should consider in evaluating the profitability of blackjack games around the globe so you can capitalize on a good game when you find one.

The Barred Counter. You've been barred by one or more of the casinos and are contemplating filing a law suit against the house. Or, perhaps you're worried about getting barred in the future and wonder how to react. Read Chapter 17, "Getting Barred."

The Six Teams And Current Opportunities

Blackjack has been my business—indeed the primary component of my life—for the past six years. Most of the time, I've been playing the game and forming and administering teams. I've also written a couple of books on the subject and am now working on the adaptation of the first book, *The Big Player* (37), as a major motion picture (budget: $10 million).

But, despite these ancillary preoccupations, the real kick to me is playing the game. I love the mathematical challenge of playing accurately, putting on the "act" for the pitbosses and the enjoyment of being a high-roller catered to by pitbosses, cocktail waitresses, dealers ... and showgirls. Other fringe benefits from playing blackjack include staying in lavish hotel suites, eating in the best of gourmet restaurants and seeing spectacular shows in Nevada, Atlantic City, Monte Carlo, France and around the world—usually free.

Over the past years, the members of my six teams have actually played over 3,000,000 hands, placed over one half *billion* dollars in action and won over $4,000,000. We did this in a variety of ways, including team play, the use of computers, individual play, and with other techniques. Our experiences have been laughable, frustrating, hilarious, sometimes physically dangerous and often bordering on the unbelievable.

Although this book is intended primarily to teach, I've included a description of some of our exploits—in Chapter 2 (Teams 1 and 2), Chapter 7 (Teams 3 and 4) and Chapter 13 (Teams 5 and 6). I suppose it would have been easy to exaggerate by overstating wins, understating losses or by making up dramatic episodes or enhancing real ones through "poetic license." But I have not. In many cases, it seems that the truth has proven to be more fascinating than fiction. Believe me, the episodes have happened exactly as described herein.

It's been a phenomenal six years. We've had upswings and downturns; successes and frustrations; we've been elated and dejected. But the "Mission Impossible" aspect of what we're doing leads most of us to love every minute of it.

And we're not through. As I write this, we have money on tables in Nevada. Just two weeks ago I was playing up to $1,200 per hand at the Frontier in Vegas. There's still plenty of opportunity out there, although I frankly doubt that we'll win another $4,000,000.

I hope this text will help you to acquire the skills necessary to get a piece of the action too. Everything you need to know—and more—is contained herein. It's really up to you; your practice and training habits, your self-discipline, your persistence, your ability to stay cool under pressure. . . and your positive attitude.

Can You Win At Blackjack?

The opportunity for winning is out there. Games in Nevada, Atlantic City and abroad *can* be beaten. The only real question is WHETHER *YOU* ARE CONVINCED THAT YOU CAN BECOME A WINNING BLACKJACK PLAYER.

Success in blackjack is like success in any other field of endeavor. The man who *knows* he can succeed in business *will* succeed in business. The man who doesn't believe he can succeed, or feels he doesn't deserve to succeed, will not succeed.

"But," you'll say, "I've got to be a mathematical genius." WRONG. That's a cop-out. I've met more people who play blackjack for a living than most. Successful players come from all walks of life: students, real estate people, ex-restaurant employees, an airline stewardess, a music store manager, a bowling professional, an engineer, and a used car salesman. Good, solid, average people.

What did they have in common? A burning desire and the self-confidence that THEY COULD DO IT.

Don't limit yourself. If you don't believe you can achieve your goals, there's NO WAY that you will. If you truly feel that you can, you're well on your way to succeeding.

There's not a player on any of my teams who does not feel that a positive attitude somehow contributes to winning. We don't use parapsychology or mysticism in any way when we play. Yet, somehow, that indefinable winning feeling and winning attitude lead to success.

Many before you have succeeded at blackjack—probably some people with less talent and innate ability than yours. Reach out and grab the opportunity that's in front of you. As you begin to succeed, you'll find your confidence growing, which will lead in turn to greater success—an upward spiral of success.

Think to yourself, "I CAN DO IT. I WILL DO IT."

* * * *

So get to work and go get 'em—and feel free to drop me a line at P.O. Box 1949, Philadelphia, PA 19105, and let me know how you're doing.

13

Chapter Two

How We Won $4,000,000 Part 1 (Teams 1 and 2)

Meeting A Professional Gambler

Back in 1974, my life seemed to be pretty well planned out. I was the Senior Vice President for the Pacific Stock Exchange, administering the roughly 300 people who worked for the Exchange in San Francisco. I'd attended Yale (on scholarship) and Harvard Business School, majoring in finance (I wanted to major in music, but my dad said, "Kenny, there's only one Sammy Kaye," i.e., the competition was too rough). Through 60-hour weeks and a compulsion to succeed which was probably due to my middle class childhood, I'd advanced through the echelons of business to the position of District Manager of the Southern New England Telephone Company, Corporate Planning Manager for American Cement, and Vice President and finally Senior Vice President for the Exchange.

I was a bachelor and had a penthouse apartment in San Francisco overlooking the Bay. I earned about $50,000 a year—and spent every dime of it. Then, a chance dinner party—one which I nearly decided to skip—completely changed my life and eventually the lives of dozens of other people.

The dinner party was given by one of the managers who reported to me at the Exchange. I was introduced to an attractive girl, Joan, and we spent most of the evening engaged in conversation. By chance, the topic turned to blackjack. She told me of a friend of hers, Al Francesco (a pseudonym), who played blackjack on a full-time basis, i.e., a professional gambler. This fascinated me, since I'd read Thorp's book a few years earlier and experimented with his point count system in Lake Tahoe for a few months before abandoning it for the more "serious" pursuits of life.

15

Several days later, Al called me at the Exchange. He was looking for people interested in playing blackjack on a team he had formed. A few days after Al's call, I went to his apartment and met several of his recruits who had been playing blackjack full-time.

The teammates seemed motivated and highly skilled at blackjack. The team's *modus operandi* was based on a concept that is now known as "team play." A card counter employing wide bet variation would most likely encounter "heat" from the pit. The team used several people to allow bet variation of up to 1,000-to-1 and even greater, yet escaped detection by the pitbosses.

The team consists of "counters" and a "big player"(BP). The counters station themselves at various tables throughout the casino and begin counting down a four deck shoe, playing Basic Strategy (the optimum way for a non-counting player to play his hands) and making the minimum allowable bet, generally $2 or $5. The team played only four deck games since counts favorable to the player remained far longer in four deck games than in single or double deck games. At that time, games with more than four decks were not found in the major casinos.

The counter begins card counting immediately after the four decks are shuffled and the deal begins. If the deck becomes sufficiently favorable to the player, the counter gives a predetermined signal to the big player, who then approaches the table and is signalled both the count and the number of aces played by the counter. An example of signals used by team players is given in Chapter 12. The big player then places large bets, which vary in size from $200 to $2,000, depending upon the limit at the casino and the degree to which the deck is favorable to the player.

Counters, of course, pretend that they do not know the big player. Thus, to the dealers and pit bosses, the big player is just another non-counting, high-rolling gambler who likes to make big bets. He obviously is not a counter, they feel, since he often approaches a table well after the shoe has been shuffled and dealt anew. He would appear to have no way of knowing the count since he didn't observe all the cards from the beginning of the shoe.

The team is at a healthy advantage over the house, probably somewhere between 1½—2½%, depending on casino rules. The counters make their minimal bets when the deck is average or unfavorable to the player. The big player makes his large bets only when he has an advantage of at least ½% or more.

In actuality, the percentage advantage to the team could well be significantly higher than 2½%. Since we used an advanced system, the 14 Count, which under ideal conditions theoretically yields a 2.2% advantage to the player with a bet variation of 1-to-4, it would appear that the team advantage had to exceed 2.2%. In effect, since the counters made minimum bets as low as $1, the team was enjoying a bet variation of 1,000-to-1, 2,000-to-1, or even more when, for example, seven hands of $1,000 were played. The percent advantage would be even higher at clubs where doubling-down-on-split-pairs was allowed and where the surrender option was permitted. Thus, in some instances, the team was probably playing at more than a 3% advantage over the house.

Joining Team 1

After Al explained all this to me, I started training in earnest. At that point, I had no intentions of becoming a full-time blackjack player, but was more intrigued with the "Mission Impossible" aspect of the operation, of being able to beat the casinos at their own game. Being a bachelor, the prospect of bringing dates to Vegas and maybe even making a few dollars to boot, appeared attractive.

For four weeks, I counted down decks, memorized Basic Strategy, practiced a side count of aces and generally went through the steps outlined for the potential team counter in Chapter 12. For my first major trip with the team, I took a week off from the Exchange. We had a "bank" (or playing stake) of $50,000, six counters and two big players.

The first time I had a "hot deck" and called in the BP, I was pathetic. My hands shook as I tried to give the signals; I knocked over a drink and the BP left my table for fear I'd give the whole ruse away. After a few sessions, my nervousness subsided and confidence gradually grew.

After five days, the team was up $44,000. The big players earned about $11,000 each. I made $2,100 for five days' work. Since my take-home pay from the Exchange was about $3,000 for an entire month's work, I started becoming more serious about blackjack.

As word of our success spread around the Bay Area, the team grew in size, eventually expanding to three BP's and twenty counters. This was to the benefit of the team as we became aware of the advantages of minimizing statistical fluctuation by playing more hands, just as a casino could minimize its risk of large negative swings by having more tables open to the public. Further, a larger team offered additional flexibility and "cover," since counters could be rotated from one BP to another, further precluding detection by the casino bosses.

After two months with the team, I was promoted to big player. Another round of training was necessitated. I'll never forget that first trip as BP. After three uneventful sessions, we scheduled a noon session at the Fremont in downtown Vegas. A gal counter, Lori, called me into a "hot shoe." I took out five one hundred dollar bills and placed them on the table. I won the hand, put the bills back in my pocket (I had $15,000 with me) and never used my cash again. Another counter called me into a shoe that was so hot I signalled the counter to leave the table. I then spread to seven hands of $500. Forty-five minutes later, I cashed out for $27,600—all winnings since I hadn't dropped a penny of cash. I ran back to the team meeting room at the El Morocco Motel, discovered the other BP's were up over $23,000, and we called off the trip after only two days, $50,000 ahead.

Over the next eight months, we made periodic forays into Las Vegas, playing the four deck shoes at the MGM, Caesars Palace, Tropicana, Sands, Stardust and downtown casinos. The size of our bank grew eventually to $150,000, allowing us to make opening bets of $2,000 (two hands of $1,000 or four hands of $500) if we could get the money out quick enough. On occasion, we would bet as much as seven hands of $1,000.

The $17,000 Card

One particular "hot shoe" led to the most money I've ever had on the table at one time. At that time, the Sands was the only club on the Las Vegas Strip that permitted the player to split pairs indefinitely. Most Vegas clubs permit the player to split pairs only three times for a total of four hands.

The "count" was sky-high, that is, there was a very high proportion of ten-valued cards and aces remaining in the shoe. My count was over +55, an extremely rare and favorable situation for the player.

My initial bet was three hands of $1,000. I drew an A,9 on the first; a "stiff" (or poor) hand of 13, on the second; and a 20, on the third. The dealer showed a 6 upcard.

I doubled down on the A,9, putting out another $1,000 because the count was so high. (This is *not* a Basic Strategy play and the average player should never make this play.) The dealer dealt me a 10, and things looked good. I stood on the stiff.

The count was so high and the remaining part of the shoe so rich in 10's and aces that I split the 10's for another $1,000. I drew another 10. The count was still far beyond that necessary to split 10's versus a dealer's 6. So I split again.

I drew a 4 on the first 10. And then I was dealt another 10. So I put out another $1,000 and split again. Now I had $6,000 on the table.

I drew yet another 10!! I said to the boss, "Can I split them again?"

He smiled, thinking he had a real "sucker" on the line, and said, "Sure, all you want."

I threw out another $1,000. The dealer hit me with a 6 on the second 10, and I stood with the 16. Then I drew another 10 on the next hand. The dealer automatically pushed it off to my left, assuming I would split again. The deck was so high in 10's that I kept drawing more and more 10's until I had split eight times! I had a total of $12,000 on the table.

The hand looked like this:

Figure 2a

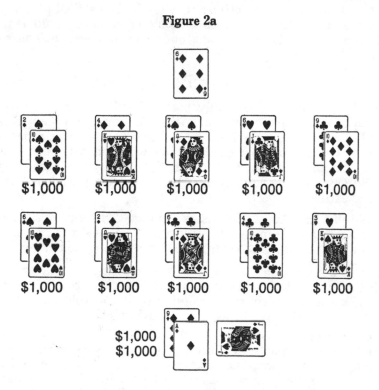

$1,000 $1,000 $1,000 $1,000 $1,000

$1,000 $1,000 $1,000 $1,000 $1,000

$1,000
$1,000

The count was still over +30, and with a dealer 6 upcard, the chances of the dealer busting were well in excess of 60% (with a zero-count, the dealer has a 42% chance of busting with a 6 upcard).

The dealer's hole card was a 4 and my heart sank. Now he had a total of ten. If he hit with another 10 (and there were plenty of them left in the shoe), I'd lose $10,000 (tying the A,9 double-down).

He drew a card. It was a 6!

My spirits soared. If he drew a 10, or a 9,8,7, or 6, I'd win $12,000! And I knew there were still many 10's left in the shoe.

The dealer drew again. I held my breath—and noticed the pitboss doing the same thing. My palms were very damp at that point.

The next card was an ace! The dealer had a total of 17. My heart sank as I watched him collect eight of my huge $100 stacks, pay three of them and wrap his knuckles on the green felt for the "push" (a tie or stand-off) on my 17.

Had that last card been a 6 through 10 (there was a far better than 8-out-of-13 chance of that since the shoe was so rich in 10's), I would have won $12,000 instead of losing $5,000. The value of that one single card to me was $17,000!

But that's the way the game goes. I had made all the correct plays. Sometimes they work; sometimes they don't. The skilled player must always play correctly, as close to the way a computer would as possible. In the long run, he should come out ahead and beat the house consistently.

The Bust

The trips continued successfully, both to Las Vegas and occasionally to Europe. With our larger banks, the wins on the Vegas trips increased—first $49,000, then $57,000, then $89,000. Over a period of six weeks, I continually played the Sands, which soon came to "comp" (provide complimentary hotel services) this strange high-roller to every service they could provide. My senior vice president position provided excellent cover.

I could just imagine the pitbosses talking, "This guy works for the Stock Exchange. He must be a gambler. And he's a big shot—why would he pull any kind of 'scam?' He doesn't need the money."

They liked my action even more after one weekend of horror, during which I dropped $71,000 in a quite normal negative statistical swing. The invitations to celebrity and invitational golf tournaments were coming in hot and heavy to my San Francisco office.

On one weekend, I took the usual 5 P.M. Friday flight to Vegas and checked into my Sands suite, putting $30,000 in the cage and $20,000 in a safety deposit box. Our counters were in the casino and upon entering, I was immediately signalled into a hot deck. As was my custom by now, I instructed, "Give me five."

A pitboss brought over a marker and had the dealer give me $5,000 in black chips. As I played, I noticed a Tropicana pitboss in the Sands lounge. That seemed strange, but I shrugged it off.

After ten minutes, I needed another marker.

"Give me five."

"Ken, check with the cashier."

I was surprised and anxious to play the "hot shoe." "But I want to make a bet *now*. I've got 30 in your cage. Give me 5 of it."

The pitboss shrugged apologetically. "Kenny, you gotta go to the cage."

I went to the cage where the shift boss, Herb Nunaz, asked me to step into the back office. In the office was a plainclothes detective who asked me for identification.

I had none with me and said, "It's in my room."

The cop, decidedly unfriendly, said, "In Nevada you can be arrested for not having ID. Consider yourself under arrest."

I was flabbergasted and becoming more than a bit worried. Several of our counters were herded into the back room as I was photographed and frisked. Then, a security guard read me "The Trespass Act" from a little card, a statement that in effect meant that were I to return to the Sands or any other Hughes club, I would be arrested.

I was given my remaining $45,000 and took a cab to the Dunes. One of our counters, who had no ID, was actually arrested. (The judge later threw the case out, stating, "Apparently you frowned when you should have smiled.") Calls from the Sands were apparently made to the Dunes, as I was locked out of my room and asked to leave there as well. I took several cabs in an evasive move and finally spent the night, unharassed, at the Royal Las Vegas.

In retrospect it was obvious to us that we had played the same club for far too long. I'd played the Sands many weekends over the past two months. I'd lost heavily on the two previous weekends and we'd been lulled into thinking, erroneously, that the losses there would protect us from detection.

We particularly regretted that we had been barred by the only club that would be vindictive enough to go through the questioning and arrest routine which they did. In the past, all other clubs that had suspected our operation merely shuffled up the shoe or, in one instance, politely asked the BP to leave. The incident was even more unfortunate in that the Sands was part of the huge Hughes hotel chain, and I was barred from all the other Hughes hotels, including the Frontier, the Landmark (which was sold by the Hughes organization a few years later), the Desert Inn, the Castaways and the Silver Slipper.

The entire team of twenty people left Vegas in a glum mood. We had earned just under $500,000 in Vegas (some members had earned *over* $500,000 in Europe) since we'd been together and we'd had an exciting time. But the close friendships that had developed and the bi-weekly excitement, it appeared, would come to a close. At our last team meeting in San Francisco, where we distributed our small win from the last trip (about $10,000), it was the last time that many of us would see each other. The team attempted a small trip several months hence, but encountered immediate heat at Caesars, the Tropicana, the Landmark and several other clubs.

The Lawsuits

Back in San Francisco, I secured copies of the Nevada statutes in order to research whether card counting, alone or with a team, was illegal. There were statutes against sleight-of-hand schemes, fraudulent cards, dice or devices, swindling and "banco-steering," but nothing about counting. It appeared that by barring, the casinos were in effect offering a game of skill to the public, permitting the unskillful, drunk, degenerate and compulsive gamblers to play, and arbitrarily excluding the skillful.

I initiated lawsuits against the Sands and the Dunes hotels. The lawyers cited a violation of civil rights and the Public Accommodations statutes. The day after the lawsuits were filed, there was an unexpected explosion of publicity across the country. The San Francisco Chronicle ran a front page story entitled, "Man Who Beat Vegas Sues for $24 Million." Newspapers in Houston, New York City, South Carolina and across the country wrote about the lawsuits. Radio and television stations from Boston, New Orleans and elsewhere called for interviews. Little did I know that this very publicity, ironically, would lead to a continued career in blackjack.

The Formation of Team 2

A few months later, missing the excitement of Vegas, the comped suites, shows and gourmet dinners, I took a trip to see just how bad the "heat" was. The Stardust apparently hadn't gotten the word from the Sands since they obliged me with "RFB" (complimentary room, food and beverage) for the weekend.

I found that Caesars allowed me to draw markers against my credit line and I played a few hands there, betting only $25 to $100, but with no heat. At the MGM, a pitboss, Chuck Wenner, currently casino manager at the Treasury, recognized me and said, "Kenny, where have you been? Haven't seen you in a while. Let me know if you need anything."

I went to the Holiday, the Frontier, the Fremont and other clubs downtown (avoiding the Sands and the Dunes), where I played without incident. All of a sudden the good news hit me: the inter-casino communication network was not nearly as effective as we had thought. I could still play in this town!

I returned to San Francisco, knowing that somehow my blackjack career would be continued. I started growing a beard and moustache to change from the previous image, which was your basic-straight stock exchange executive, complete with three-piece business suit and Rotary pin. (I'd left the Exchange several months prior.)

Because of the publicity, other card counters called me periodically. One fellow, a Phi Beta Kappa from an Ivy League school, impressed me in particular. He was broke; in fact, he had to wash dishes at a bridge club so he could afford the $1 per hour charge to play bridge—but he was also brilliant. Let's call him Rob, his pseudonymn in my second book, *One-Third Of A Shoe* (7).

A few other players, with advanced blackjack expertise but no money, called as well. I decided to form a team. We trained in my San Francisco apartment for three weeks, practicing true count adjustments, ace adjustment, signalling and the many fine points of team play covered in Chapter 12. Finally, I felt we were ready.

There were five of us for the first trip. I was the BP; Rob was a counter, as were Don, Les and Jim. We played to a tiny bank, $15,000—nearly all my money—and the first session was at the Thunderbird (now the Silverbird). We were stuck from the start so I let the session go on for five hours. There was no heat on the play, but the counters were obviously fatigued, so I called the session off, down $2,400.

Team 2 Wins $650,000

We played only clubs where Team 1 hadn't gotten any heat—the Hacienda, California Club, Marina, Aladdin and, cautiously, the MGM. Rob was so obviously competent that he was made a BP on that very trip. After our initial losing session, we had nine straight winners. Our first trip yielded a $12,000 win in only three days, way beyond our expected return. Psychologically, the win was the best thing that could have happened to unify our little group. The other players parlayed their win by adding to our second bank, which was $20,000. We doubled that bank in a week, formed a $30,000 bank and doubled that in nine days.

As I scouted the clubs in Vegas, I was hit with the realization that there wasn't a single club we shouldn't be able to beat. There were fabulous four deck games at many clubs, including the Trop, Caesars, MGM, Stardust and the Landmark, and we now had a totally fresh BP. We were working on training a third BP as well. Further, there were fine single deck games at the Landmark, Horseshoe, Mint, Stardust, and Caesars. Rob and I, and eventually Jim, would play these without the team. We used the team at the fine double deck games at the Riviera, Aladdin and Marina. We'd mix our play up a bit at the clubs that had both single and four deck games. The BP would play single deck and then get called into a shoe by a counter. It made the bosses smile! "How could this guy be counting if he jumps to the middle of a shoe and bets $500 a hand?" The profitable four deck play of the BP took the heat off his single deck counting.

We worked hard, but we also played hard. Frank Fertitta, then General Manager of the Fremont, comped me into his personal "Presidential Suite" at the top of the Fremont, with fully-stocked bar and period furniture. I'd bring some of the pitbosses (yes, and gal dealers), most of whom had never seen the oft-discussed suite, up for a drink on their boss.

I had some trouble with my *nom de jeu* there. I was playing under the name Roger Hughes. A pitboss asked me my name as I was in the middle of a complex calculation. My pseudonym didn't come to mind and I hastily replied, "Bruce." Another boss later questioned me on this. I ad libbed, "My real name is Roger, but my good friends call me Bruce." It seemed to work.

There were many unusual and sometimes humorous incidents. We had three BP's comped simultaneously into the Aladdin on the weekend of its Big Expansion—the July 4, 1976 Neil Diamond opening: Rob, myself and Karen, another BP. As our counters found the hot decks, we would literally compete with each other to get to the table first to place our $1,000 bets. Some of our counters used the HI-OPT strategies and others the Revere APC. Both methods were effective.

That was the very weekend that the *New York Times* put my picture on the front page of their Sunday Magazine Section. I, of course, knew about it in advance and had to get up early Sunday Morning and drive all over town, buying every *Sunday New York Times* I could find—at $3.50 per copy. (I found out later that it didn't work; Harry Wald, a top official at Caesars Palace, had a personal subscription.)

Vic Wakeman, a diminutive MGM pitboss, had given Team 1 much heat. I'd chuckle as I hid behind a row of slot machines watching Rob and our counters playing under his very nose.

I started playing the Dunes and miraculously was comped there (as Roger Hughes). Then the supreme irony—as I was sitting at a blackjack table with perhaps 6 or 7 thousand in front of me, I was paged as Roger Hughes. I was handed a pit phone by a boss. It was my lawyer, John Greenman, informing me that the Dunes was willing to settle the lawsuit for $8,500. Talking loudly so the pit could hear my end of the conversation, I said, "Tell them at least 100 grand." Obviously the pit-bosses didn't know the subject of the conversation, but they must have thought I was a pretty big deal.

At the Landmark, I was Dan Saunders, with a $10,000 credit line and a personal bottle of Chateau Neuf-du-Pape at the casino bar—the General Manager knew I couldn't stand the red wine they normally poured.

The names were starting to get confusing. I was Don Sanders at the Desert Inn; Billy Williams comped to several suites simultaneously at the Marina; Bill Thomas at General Manager Bill Friedman's Castaways; Tommy Rogers at the Hilton.

I arranged Rob's first comp for him at the Riviera. He was too bashful to call himself. They gave him a suite in the tower, but it really ended up costing him money. Instead of 40 cents worth of sunflower seeds for lunch, he'd have a "free" prime rib and French wine on the house. But his tips, at 15% of the tab, would run $4 or $5 per meal. During one month, we all played the Riv; we hit them so hard I believe we literally put them in the red.

For about six months, we played cat and mouse with the Griffin detective people. The Griffin Agency is retained by many Nevada casinos to spot slot cheats, dishonest employees and card counters. The Griffin people followed our group out of the MGM once and actually arranged to have associates they knew on the Las Vegas Metropolitan Police Department stop us and examine our ID's. The Griffin Agency sent pictures of me, with and without beard, to the casinos, noting we had a group of "eight or nine associates, mostly young, including three Chinese members and several girls."

Our people were busted at the Sands, detected at the Hilton, and pulled up at the Mint, the Frontier, the Sahara and the Riviera. But, we kept on playing, convinced we were doing nothing illegal. Miraculously, play continued. One of the Griffin agents, Richard Gonzales, became my personal nemesis. It seemed he would always show up where I was playing—the Holiday, the Silver Slipper, the Sahara—and tell the bosses who I was. He played Captain Ahab to my Moby Dick.

As Team 2 winnings exceeded $500,000, our BP's started getting barred or shuffled up on at an increasingly larger number of casinos. But we trained more and more BP's. As we used to say, "Hell, we can train 'em faster than they can bar 'em."

As our little band continued to make money, one incident happened which infuriated me. I'd met a cute gal who worked at the MGM cashier's cage. We dated a few times; to say we enjoyed each other's company was to put it mildly. I finally told her who I was—our relation was becoming that strong. She then told me her stepfather was the head of security at the Dunes.

The very next day, she phoned me in tears. It seems her stepdad told her that if she were seen with me she'd lose her job on the spot and that, despite his "juice" (connections), he wouldn't be able to help her find a job anywhere on the Strip; no one would hire her.

She was supporting a small child. We had no choice but to stop seeing each other. I think the man's conclusion may have been overstated, but despite that, the fact that the casino hiring policy could be subject to such petty politics made me relish our team wins even more.

Team 2 also grew to over 20 members. As our winnings surpassed $650,000, I received a call from the Bay Area that would lead to one of the most fascinating, and potentially profitable, blackjack endeavors of all time. The call would also provide the undisputed answer to the often-asked question: "Who is the greatest blackjack player in the world?"

The story is continued in Chapter 7.

Chapter Three

Do You Know How to Play Blackjack?

How Well Can The Typical Player Do?

The typical player, I would guess, plays at about a 3% disadvantage to the house. It's difficult to know exactly because, unlike craps or roulette, the odds in blackjack uniquely depend upon the player's skill. Table 3-1 shows the expected results for the typical player, assuming he plays for a weekend, or about 15 hours, at 100 hands per hour (a fairly realistic average).

As shown in the table, the typical "nickel" player (with an average bet of $5 per hand) would lose $225 on average for a weekend. The "quarter" player (average bet: $25) should lose around $1,125. The black chip player (average bet: $100) can expect to lose about $4,500!

Table 3—1

Expected Results of Typical Player, Basic Strategy Player and Good Card Counter

	Typical Player	With Basic Strategy	Good Card-Counter
Edge vs. House:	−3%	0	+ 1-1/2%
Average Bet:			
$5	−$ 225	0	+$ 110
$25	−$1,125	0	+$ 560
$100	−$4,500	0	+$2,300

Assumptions:
- A weekend of play: equaling 15 hours at 100 hands per hour.

- Single deck, Las Vegas Strip rules or multiple deck, Atlantic City Rules.

Notes:
- Long-term averages only; short-term results can fluctuate widely due to random statistical variation.
- Deduct 1/2% for four deck play, 1/2% for Reno-Tahoe single deck play; 2/3% for play in the Bahamas.

Basic Strategy Defined

As we have stated, it has been known for some time, from computer analyses of the game, that, for any given set of rules at blackjack, without counting the cards, there is one optimum way to play the game, called "Basic Strategy." Basic Strategy varies according to the rules of the game, that is, the options offered to the player and the number of decks used.

Please remember that there is *only one* correct Basic Strategy for a given set of rules. Basic Strategy, which has been derived by several blackjack experts through detailed computer analyses, is as exact a science as mathematics. To say, "The player should hit 12 versus a dealer 2 upcard" is similar to saying, "One plus one equals two." The rules herein do not comprise Ken Uston's way of playing the game; they delineate *the way* to play the game and all responsible Basic Strategies are identical. (Thorp's Basic Strategy in his book *Beat the Dealer* differs from the others essentially because he assumed that the double-on-split pairs option was a prevalent rule on the Vegas Strip; today that option is offered by only a few casinos.)

In Chapter 5 we will examine Basic Strategy for the games in Atlantic City, in Las Vegas, in Northern Nevada (Reno and Lake Tahoe) and in the Bahamas. Generally, Basic Strategy allows the player to play even with the house (for single deck Vegas Strip rules). In a few cases, including Caesars Palace single deck and Atlantic City, the Basic Strategy player has a slight advantage over the house.

Do You Know How To Play Blackjack?

Rarely does a day go by without someone saying to me something like, "Oh, I know how to play the 'basics,' " or "I can play the hands correctly." After I've asked only one or two questions about playing strategy, it inevitably turns out that the player does not know Basic Strategy. It is surprisingly easy to learn. Yet a distressingly high proportion of players, many of whom spend hours and hours at the blackjack tables, have not yet learned the strategy.

Why is this so? I suspect there are many players who do not know that there *is* an optimum way of playing or that computer analysis has proven that there is only *one preferred way* to play the hands, for a given set of rules. There are probably other people who have heard, and probably believe, that such a thing as Basic Strategy exists, but who for one reason or another have not been able to find a simple, clear way of learning the strategy. It is for these two categories of players that this chapter will be of most benefit.

There is another group of people who will not believe that an optimum way of playing exists, no matter how much I drone on about computers, probability and statistics. They're convinced that their method, whatever it might be, is the best. Other players prefer to play their hunches, sometimes playing a given hand one way, sometimes another, depending on how lucky they feel, or how "hot" or "cold" the dealer is running. There is no way this book will help them as long as funds to support their losing blackjack are available. To this group, I say, "Good luck! I hope you get a 'good run' of cards."

Table 3—2

Blackjack Quiz—Rate Yourself
Do You Hit, Stand, Double-Down, Split Pairs or Surrender?

| | | You're Playing In: | | |
| | | Atlantic City | Las Vegas Strip | The |
Your Hand	Dealer Shows	(Resorts)	(Single Deck)	Bahamas
9,9	8	H S D P Su	H S D P Su	H S D P Su
2,2	2	H S D P Su	H S D P Su	H S D P Su
A 8	6	H S D P Su	H S D P Su	H S D P Su
7,7	10	H S D P Su	H S D P Su	H S D P Su
10,2	3	H S D P Su	H S D P Su	H S D P Su
A 2	5	H S D P Su	H S D P Su	H S D P Su
A 7	10	H S D P Su	H S D P Su	H S D P Su
A 10	Ace	(Insurance?) (YES NO)	(Insurance?) (YES NO)	(Insurance?) (YES NO)
6,5	Ace	H S D P Su	H S D P Su	H S D P Su
9,9	7	H S D P Su	H S D P Su	H S D P Su
A 6	2	H S D P Su	H S D P Su	H S D P Su
10,6	9	H S D P Su	H S D P Su	H S D P Su
6,6	7	H S D P Su	H S D P Su	H S D P Su
8,8	10	H S D P Su	H S D P Su	H S D P Su
A 3	3	H S D P Su	H S D P Su	H S D P Su
5,4	2	H S D P Su	H S D P Su	H S D P Su
10,6	10	H S D P Su	H S D P Su	H S D P Su
3,2	Ace	H S D P Su	H S D P Su	H S D P Su
4,4	6	H S D P Su	H S D P Su	H S D P Su
2,2	3	H S D P Su	H S D P Su	H S D P Su

Circle the correct choice:

H = Hit   D = Double-Down   Su = Surrender
S = Stand   P = Split Pairs

For those of you interested in assessing your blackjack play, I have included 20 playing situations in Table 3-2. Because of rules variations, the answers may vary depending on whether you play in Atlantic City, in Las Vegas or in the Bahamas. Thus, a separate answer column for each of these locations is provided.

Table 3—3

Answers to Quiz

Atlantic City (Resorts)	Las Vegas Strip (Single Deck)	The Bahamas
P—Split	P—Split	P—Split
P—Split	H—Hit	H—Hit
S—Stand	D—Double	S—Stand
Su—Surrender	S—Stand	H—Hit
H—Hit	H—Hit	H—Hit
D—Double	D—Double	H—Hit
H—Hit	H—Hit	H—Hit
NO	NO	NO
H—Hit	D—Double	H—Hit
S—Stand	S—Stand	S—Stand
H—Hit	D—Double	H—Hit
Su—Surrender	H—Hit	H—Hit
H—Hit	H—Hit	H—Hit
Su—Surrender	P—Split	P—Split
H—Hit	H—Hit	H—Hit
H—Hit	D—Double	H—Hit
Su—Surrender	H—Hit	H—Hit
Su—Surrender	H—Hit	H—Hit
P—Split	D—Double	H—Hit
P—Split	P—Split	H—Hit

Grade yourself against the answers provided in Table 3-3 above. If you have made no errors, you're capable of winning modestly at Caesars Palace single deck and in Atlantic City. If you made one or two errors, you probably play nearly even with the house, although the house does have a slight edge over you.

If you've made from three to six errors, you're about equivalent to the average player who loses from 1-to-3% of the amount bet. Any more than six errors indicates that you should study Basic Strategy to improve your blackjack game, or you should consider switching to one of the games at which the casino does not have a significant edge over the player (these are identified in Table 1-1 in Chapter 1.)

Rating

Scoring—Number Of Wrong Answers	
0	—You're able to win modestly in Atlantic City and a few clubs in Las Vegas.
1 to 2	—You're close to a perfect Basic Strategy player and probably play almost even with the house.
3 to 6	—You're an average player and probably lose 1-to-3% of the amount you bet.
7 to 10	—You're a below-average player and will lose (or have lost) tons in a casino.
More than 10	—You're throwing your money away at the tables. You should either learn to play better or stick to baccarat, roulette or the better bets at craps.

Even after this type of explanation, some players who do not play perfect Basic Strategy will counter, "But I win nearly every time I play."

My only answer to this is, "Either you've been experiencing undeserved statistical good fortune, or there's some other factor that I do not understand, cannot explain and would never let govern my playing, such as para-psychology, ESP and the like."

If you have made two or more errors on the quiz, I would suggest that you should at least study Chapter 5. Learning the strategies therein will enable you to save money in the casinos in the long-run, money I'm sure you could well use for other purposes.

Why Good Players Can Lose And Bad Players Can Win

It is a fact that the worst player in the world and the best player in the world could play at the same table for an hour or so, and the worst player could win and the best player could lose. This is because, in the short run, results can vary widely around mathematical expectation. Thus, the Vegas roulette player, facing 5¼% odds against him, might win for a night or so; but in the long run, the true percentages will prevail and the house will "grind him down." Similarly, in the short term, the typical blackjack player may win and the advanced card counter may lose.

I will repeat a black bean-white bean analogy that I used in my second book *One-Third Of A Shoe*, because so many students have mentioned that it clarifies to them the phenomenon of statistical variation.

Imagine a game in which there are 100 beans in a jar, white beans and black beans. If you pick a white bean, you win the "hand;" if you pick a black bean, you lose the hand. After each draw, the bean is replaced in the jar, the jar is shaken up and you pick another bean for the next hand.

As shown below, the typical player is faced with a game in which he has roughly 48 white beans and 52 black beans (actually this mix gives him a 4% rather than 3% disadvantage, but, is used to avoid "half-beans"). The Basic Strategy player is faced with 50 white beans and 50 black beans. The advanced card counter has roughly 51 white beans and 49 black beans (again rounding to whole beans, which in this case gives him a 2% edge over the house).

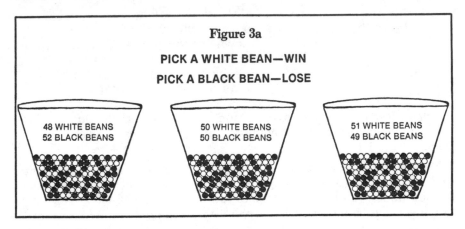

Figure 3a

PICK A WHITE BEAN—WIN

PICK A BLACK BEAN—LOSE

48 WHITE BEANS
52 BLACK BEANS

50 WHITE BEANS
50 BLACK BEANS

51 WHITE BEANS
49 BLACK BEANS

The typical player, faced with only 48 white beans and 52 black ones, might, in the course of a few hours of "bean picking", actually pick more white ones than black ones, thus winning for the session. But if he were to bet on each pick, and pick beans night after night for weeks, eventually the excess of black beans over white ones would be felt and the player would eventually end up a loser.

By the same token, the Basic Strategy player, faced with an even game, could easily win (pick more white beans than black) or lose (pick more black beans than white) in the short term. But over a long period of time, he should pick white beans very close to half the time, thus approximately breaking even.

The good card counter can also pick more black beans than white in the short term. Indeed, there are only two more white beans than black beans. Again, in the long term, after many hours of bean-picking, he should pick more white beans, thus winning. I have had a distressingly high number of "black bean sessions." Just a month before this writing, I lost $15,000 in two and one-half hours at a Frontier single deck game, betting $25 to $1200. Teammates in early 1980 lost $156,000 at the casinos in Atlantic City before recovering. Two of our best players played eight hours a day for 61 days in France and Belgium, and they were down $30,000—probably the worst statistical aberration we've ever experienced (they eventually dug out and were up $35,000 after day 80).

There are two points to be made here. If the typical or Basic Strategy player has been winning heavily, chances are he is picking out a disproportionate number of white beans. He should not expect those results to continue indefinitely.

The second point: if you develop into a good card counter, you will not win all the time. In fact, there are times you will be ready to quit, thinking either that you must be playing wrong or that the gods are against you. The chapter on betting strategy (Chapter 9) will help to protect you against the inevitable "negative swings" that we all experience.

How to Use This Book

I've organized this book so it will be helpful and easy-to-use by players of different skill levels. The chapters are somewhat modular as follows:

Type Player

Suggested Approach

Below average player
You missed 7 or more questions on the quiz in Table 3-2.

or

The Social Player
You don't mind losing a little bit, and don't want to spend much time to learn, but you're willing to spend a few minutes to cut your losses somewhat.

Learn the seven simple rules at the beginning of Chapter 5. This isn't perfect Basic Strategy, but with 20 minutes of practice, you'll be able to avoid continuing to lose your shirt in the casino.

Basic Strategy Player
You don't want to have to keep track of the cards, but you're willing to spend a few hours in order to gain a good chance of breaking even in the long run or losing a small amount.

Study Chapter 5 and learn the Basic Strategy perfectly for the location and game you plan on playing. Cut out the flashcards and review them for 30 minutes or so before every trip.

Intermediate Player
You know Basic Strategy perfectly. In addition, you're willing to put in a few hours to keep track of a few cards so you can

Learn Basic Strategy perfectly by reading Chapter 5. Then take two hours to learn the ace-five count in Chapter 6.

have a slight edge over the house—not a big edge, not enough to bet high, but an edge nonetheless.

Advanced Player

You want to earn some money on weekends, but don't have the 50 or more hours necessary to learn an advanced count. You're not too comfortable with numbers. You're willing to spend 15 to 20 hours to learn to beat the game.

Learn Basic Strategy perfectly by reading Chapter 5. Then learn the Uston Simple Plus/Minus in Chapter 6.

Professional Player A

You're playing a low level count now (Simple Plus/Minus) and want to learn a professional-level system. You're considering becoming a full-time player.

Make sure you understand all the concepts in Chapters 5, 6 and 8. Consolidate your knowledge of the Uston Simple Plus/Minus and learn the Uston Advanced Plus/Minus by studying the last section of Chapter 6 and Chapter 8.

Professional Player B

You are now betting important money, are ahead of the game and are undoubtedly going to become a full-time player. You want to learn the *best system now available,* regardless of time or effort necessary.

Study and practice the Uston Advanced Point Count in Chapter 8. Then study Chapter 10 for single deck play or Chapter 11 for multiple deck play.

Chapter Four

Rules of the Game
and
How They Affect You

To be successful, it is essential for a blackjack player to have a complete and totally accurate knowledge of the rules of the game. This chapter, therefore, sets forth the rules most commonly used by the casinos in Atlantic City and Nevada. Variations in these rules are discussed together with the effect of each rule variation on the percentage advantage to the player or to the house.

Basic Rules

The Object Of The Game. The Player attempts to BEAT THE DEALER by obtaining a total of cards equal to or less than 21 so that his total is higher than the DEALER'S. Note that the emphasis is not on getting the closest one can to 21, without going over 21 (or busting), but on *beating the dealer*.

Number Of Players. The game generally has a dealer and from one to seven players. In Macao and other places, additional players are permitted to place bets on a player's hand.

Number Of Decks. In Atlantic City, six decks are generally used. In Las Vegas, casinos use single and double decks (dealt by hand) and four, five, six, and in rare cases, seven decks, dealt from a box-like apparatus called a "shoe." Most casinos in Reno and Lake Tahoe use one standard deck, dealt by hand; Loews' Monte Carlo and the Bahamas casinos employ four decks, as do the clubs in England and Korea. Six deck blackjack is prevalent throughout France.

35

Value Of Cards. Each card has the same value as its spots except for the ace and the picture cards. All 10's and picture cards are counted as 10. The ace can be valued as either 1 or 11, at the option of the player. A hand containing an ace that can be counted as 11 (i.e, by counting the ace as 11, the hand does not exceed 21) is called a "soft" hand. All other hands are referred to as "hard" hands.

Naturals Or "Blackjacks." If the first two cards dealt to a player are an ace and a ten-valued card (king, queen, jack or 10), the player has a natural or a "blackjack" and generally receives one and one-half times his original bet, which amounts to a win plus a 50% bonus. On the other hand, if the dealer has a blackjack and the player does not, the player loses the total of his original bet. If both the dealer and the player have blackjacks, the hand is considered a standoff or "push."

Hitting Or Standing. If the dealer draws a blackjack, the hand is settled immediately in Nevada. In all other cases, the Nevada player has the option of drawing additional cards, or "hitting." (In Atlantic City , the player plays his hand before the dealer checks to see if he has a blackjack.) If the player wants an additional card, typical practice is for him to scratch the surface of the felt with his cards (where cards are dealt face-down) or to scratch the surface with his finger(s) (where cards are dealt face-up and not touched by the players).

A player may draw as many cards as he wants, as long as his total does not exceed 21. When the player elects to stand, that is, to draw no additional cards, he tucks his first two cards under his bet in the spot before him (face-down games) or waves his hand in a lateral motion (in face-up games).

Busting. If the player's cards exceed a total of 21, he has "busted" and loses the hand regardless of the dealer's total. Typically, in face-down games, when the player busts he throws his cards in, face-up, and the dealer merely gathers in the cards and the player's bet. If the dealer busts, all players who have not busted win the hand from the house.

The Deal. Each player is dealt two cards in sequence, one at a time, either face-up or face down, depending on the rules of the house. The dealer also receives two cards, one face-down and one face-up. In some casinos, the dealer's face-down card may not be taken until all players are finished playing their hands. The dealer's card that is face-up is referred to as the "upcard," and the value of this card is the key piece of information in determining playing strategy. The dealer's face-down card is called the "hole card." Additional cards dealt to the player are dealt face-up, one at a time.

Ties. If the player and the dealer have the same total, and this same total is 21 or under, the hand is a tie, or a "push." No money settlement takes place and the dealer collects the player's cards. To indicate a tie to the player, the dealer typically taps the table several times with his knuckles or with the cards that he has picked up.

Dealer's Play. The dealer must draw cards until he has a total of 17 or above. In most casinos in Las Vegas and in Atlantic City, he must also stand if he has a soft 17 (for example, an ace and a 6). In most downtown Vegas clubs and in Northern Nevada, the dealer must hit soft 17, which provides the house with a slight additional advantage.

Doubling-Down. In most Vegas casinos and in Atlantic City, a player may double the amount of his bet after looking at his first two cards. The player turns the cards over (face-up) or announces "double-down" to the dealer and puts out an additional bet equal to his initial sum. He then receives one additional card only. The third card is dealt face-down in face-down games; face-up in other games. Most casinos in Northern Nevada allow doubling-down only on totals of 10 or 11, a restriction which is less favorable to both the Basic Strategy and skilled player.

Splitting Pairs. If the player's two cards are identical in value, the player may "split" them by betting an amount equal to his original bet on the second card. He then draws additional cards on each of the split pairs, playing each hand (from his right to his left) in turn. If the Nevada player receives an additional card of the same denomination, he may continue to split. In Atlantic City, pairs may be split only once. Most Nevada clubs permit splitting pairs three times, for a total of four hands played.*

If aces are split, a player is normally permitted to draw only one additional card on each ace, usually dealt face-down. (The Las Vegas Horseshoe provides an exception to this rule and permits re-splitting of aces.) In all other cases of pair-splitting, the player may continue to draw as many additional cards as he wants, assuming he doesn't exceed a total of 21. If the player busts on any of his split hands, the dealer picks up the busted hand and collects the bet. (In Atlantic City, hands split or doubled against a 10 or ace are left on the table until it is determined if the dealer has a blackjack; if he does, only the amount of the original wager is lost.)

Insurance. If the dealer's upcard is an ace, the player may make a side bet, referred to as "insurance." The amount of the side bet may be equal to as much as one-half of the player's original bet. If the dealer has a blackjack, the casino will pay the player 2-to-1 on his insurance bet. The bet is referred to as insurance since, if the dealer has a blackjack and the player does not, the insurance bet effectively has "saved" the player's original bet and there is no money settlement (the player has lost his original bet but has won an equal amount from his insurance bet).

---

*The Sands Hotel in Las Vegas allows splitting indefinitely. In some Nevada clubs and in France generally, the 10's must be identical; that is, two jacks may be split, but a jack and a queen may not. This combination of non-identical 10's is sometimes referred to as a "mixed marriage," a term commonly used in pinochle.

Some Northern Nevada casinos do not allow the insurance bet. English casinos allow insurance only when the player has a blackjack.

Burning A Card. It is traditional in most single deck, double deck or four and more deck games for the dealer to "burn" one card, the first card of the new deal (some casinos burn more than one card). The first card is placed in the discard rack, if there is one. If there is no discard rack (and often there is not for single deck games), the card is slid around the deck to the bottom of the deck, face up, so that it hides the face of the bottom card of the deck from the players at the table.

The experienced blackjack player should try to spot the value of this burn card and include it in his count. It is sometimes possible to see the bottom card as well. So, in a single deck game, if you can see both cards, you know the content of 1/26th of the deck before the deal has ever begun!

Betting Limits. In most major Las Vegas clubs, the betting limits are either $500, $1,000 or $2,000. All three of these maximums usually prevail at Resorts in Atlantic City. Minimum bets usually range from $1 up to $100, although $2 is generally the minimum in most clubs.

Players are allowed to bet up to $3,000 per hand at Caesars Palace and at the Riviera. In some of the smaller clubs in Nevada, the limit is below $500. The maximum limit can be circumvented quite easily, however, merely by placing more than one bet.

Shuffling. In single deck clubs, shuffling is often left to the option of the dealer. In many single deck clubs, the practice is to shuffle after approximately two-thirds of the deck has been depleted; that is generally the practice as Harrah's in Tahoe and Reno and at most Vegas single deck clubs. However, some clubs, despite the proliferation of card-counters, deal surprisingly far down in the deck, especially in Reno.

In two deck games, shuffling can either be at the option of the dealer, or can be indicated by the dealer placing a "joker" or plain-colored card somewhere in the deck. When this card is reached, the dealer will either continue the hand that is in progress and then shuffle the deck, or shuffle immediately and then complete the round (as at the Riviera).

In four, five and six deck games, the joker is generally placed from one-to-two decks from the bottom. In some clubs, when the bosses suspect counters, the joker will be moved up even further. Once, at Caesars, the bosses dealt me "one-round-and-shuffle" out of a six deck shoe. I stayed at the table, betting small, just to enjoy the ridiculousness of it all.

New Decks. Periodically, the house will replace the cards and bring in a new deck or decks. This practice has become more prevalent at several clubs which were "stung" heavily through the marking of cards. Pitbosses will generally collect the cards and sort them out to ensure that all the cards are there. In addition, they often inspect the deck to ensure that the player has not crimped or otherwise marked the cards for his own purposes.

Four decks of cards are replaced less frequently, since each card gets less use in a given time span. According to Nevada gaming regulations, the clubs are required to bring in four new decks to ensure that all the cards are included. However, I've noticed at some clubs that occasionally the cards have been replaced with other than brand new cards out of a fresh pack. This, of course, could be a questionable practice since the player has no way of knowing that four complete decks are being put into play. There is also the possibility that when new cards are brought into play, the house advantage can be increased through inadequate shuffling of the new deck, which results in the "clumping" of identical cards.

Rules Variations

The player who uses Basic Strategy, as described in the following chapter, is almost exactly even with the house, playing single deck under typical Vegas Strip rules, which are:

- Dealer must stand on soft 17.
- Player may double-down on any first two cards.
- Player may split any pair.

There are a surprising number of rules variations in Nevada (the rules are not specified by the Gaming Control Board), to say nothing of Atlantic City, the Bahamas and other countries. The primary ones are described below. The locations of places where these rules are available are subject to change without notice.

Player May Double-Down Only on Hard Totals Of 10 Or 11. This rule is nearly universal in Reno and in North and South Lake Tahoe (the MGM Reno is an exception). Computer analysis indicates that not allowing the player to double-down on a hard 9 costs the Basic Strategy player .14%, that not allowing the player to double-down on soft hands costs the player .14%, and that not allowing the player to double-down on other hard hands (8,7,6,5, etc.) costs the player virtually nothing. Thus, in total, the effect of this rule is to favor the house by approximately .28%, which is not insignificant.

Dealer Must Hit Soft 17. This rule, which favors the house by .2%, is also nearly universal in Northern Nevada and downtown Vegas. In Northern Nevada, therefore, the player can generally assume that he is playing at a .5% greater disadvantage than in the Vegas Strip casinos (.28% less because of restrictions on doubling-down and .2% less because of the dealer's hitting soft 17).

Player May Double-Down On Split Pairs. This rule is best demonstrated by an example. Assume that you have been dealt two

9's against the dealer's 5 and decide to split the 9's. On the first 9 you are dealt a 2, for a hard total of 11. Some clubs will allow you to double-down on this hand. This variation is referred to as "doubling-down-on-split-pairs." This practice is permitted currently in Atlantic City and in Nevada by Caesars Palace, 4 Queens, MGM, El Cortez and the Las Vegas Club.

Computer analysis reveals that this option is worth .13% to the Basic Strategy player and even more to the card-counter since the option is exercised more frequently in "plus" situations when the counter tends to have larger bets out.

Surrender. Another major rule variation is surrender. There are two variations, conventional and early surrender.

Conventional Surrender. This option, currently offered at Caesars Palace, Fremont, Riviera, Dunes, El Cortez and the Las Vegas Club, permits the player to throw in his hand and give up one-half of the amount that he has bet, retaining the other half. This may be done only on his first two cards and after it has been determined that the dealer does not have a blackjack.

The value of conventional surrender to the player depends to a large measure on whether the player is using the count to vary his surrender strategy and the size of his bets. For the non-counting Basic Strategy player, surrender is worth about .03%. Julian Braun has estimated that the surrender option benefits the card-counter by .25% if the player is using a 1-to-4 bet ratio and playing proper surrender strategy.

Surrender is an "ulcer-reducing" option because it tends to reduce fluctuations in the player's bankroll. There have been times when it seemed as if surrender has provided an unbelievable advantage to me. On one trip, I had lost $73,000 very rapidly at the Sands. It seemed as if I drew nothing but 14's, 15's and 16's. Had surrender been available, my loss would have been reduced by at least $15,000!

Early Surrender. A more advantageous surrender option is permitted in Atlantic City. The player is allowed to surrender his hand before the dealer checks to see if he has a blackjack. The value of this option to the card-counter is greater than it is to the Basic Strategy player (and the value to the casino is even greater due to its misuse by the typical player).

In Macao, the player is permitted early surrender if the dealer has a 10 up-card. Further, the player may surrender with any number of cards (such as a three-card 16) even after pair-splitting and doubling-down; Macao also offers four "bonus" rules not available in United States casinos.

Double Exposure (Zweikartenspiel)

This game, introduced by VegasWorld in Las Vegas, has become popular and has been adopted by other casinos in Las Vegas and Northern Nevada. The good news: the dealer exposes both his cards; the jack and ace of spades pays double; the player wins all blackjack ties and may double-down on any two cards. The bad news: the house wins all ties other than blackjack ties; blackjack pays even money; and the player may split pairs only once.

This game does offer an opportunity to win, but requires a unique Basic Strategy (included in Chapter 5) and a different approach in counting.

Bonus Options

Periodically, casinos introduce bonus-type options for the player in an attempt to attract business. They include:

Six-Card Automatic Winner. This option, offered at the Las Vegas Club in Las Vegas, gives the player an automatic win regardless of the outcome of the dealer's hand.

Double-Down On Any Number of Cards. Also offered at the Las Vegas Club, the player is permitted to double-down on any number of cards. For example, if the player held 3,2 and drew a 6 for a three card total of 11, he could double-down on the 11.

Two-For-One For Blackjack. This option is generally offered around Christmastime at Benny Binion's Horseshoe Casino in Las Vegas on bets of $5 or less. It increases by over 2% the expectation of the Basic Strategy player betting up to $5.

Joker's Wild. In this bonus, a joker is inserted into the deck and when it is dealt to the player, it may be used as a wild card. The Fremont offered this bonus several years ago. It lasted until two players extracted thousands from the casino. I haven't seen it since.

Numerous other bonus options periodically appear, such as insuring for any amount regardless of the original bet, the first player reaching "22" can tie if the dealer also has "22," and so on; they are usually quite temporary.

How the Rules Variations Affect You

The effect of the major rules variations on the Basic Strategy player's expectations is summarized in Table 4-1. As mentioned, the Basic Strategy player, facing typical Vegas Strip rules at a single deck game, is dead-even with the house. Thus, using Table 4-1, the reader can calculate from this base point the house or player edge for various sets of rules offered by most casinos around the world.

Expectation of the Basic Strategy Player

Table 4-2 summarizes the average expectation of the Basic Strategy player in Atlantic City, at Caesars Palace in Las Vegas, on the Las

41

Vegas Strip, in downtown Las Vegas, in Northern Nevada and in the Bahamas.

Caesars Palace in Las Vegas allows both double-on-split-pairs and conventional surrender. This combination of rules results in the Caesars single deck game (which has a $25 minimum) being the most favorable in the world; the Basic Strategy player enjoys a .15% edge over the house.

Table 4—1

Effect of Rules Variations
on the Basic Strategy Player

Rule Variation	Effect on Player's Advantage
Favorable To The Player:	
Early Surrender—first two cards	+.624%
Conventional Surrender —first two cards	
single deck	+.02
multiple deck	+.07
Double-Down On Split Pairs	+.13
Drawing To Split Aces	+.14
Re-splitting of Aces	+.03
Double-Down On Three Or More Cards	+.20
Unfavorable To The Player:	
No doubling on:	
Hard 11	−.89
Hard 10	−.56
Hard 9	−.14
Hard 8	0.00
Soft Hands	−.14
Dealer hits soft 17	−.20
Dealer takes no hole card (European rules)*	−.13
Two deck (vs. single deck)	−.35
Four deck (vs. single deck)	−.51
Six deck (vs. single deck)	−.60
No re-splitting of pairs	−.05

*The practice of not checking the hole card until after the players have played their hands, now prevalent in Atlantic City, does *not* cost the player anything. This is true because, if the player has doubled-down or split pairs against a 10 or ace, and the dealer has a blackjack, only the amount of the original bet is lost. In Europe, the *total* amount is lost.

Table 4—2

Average Expectation of the Basic Strategy Player
Six Casino Locations

RULE VARIATION	ATLANTIC CITY	CAESARS PALACE LAS VEGAS	LAS VEGAS STRIP	DOWNTOWN LAS VEGAS	NORTHERN NEVADA (RENO-TAHOE)	BAHAMAS
• Double-Down On:	Any 2 Cards + Split Pairs	Any 2 Cards + Split Pairs	Any 2 Cards	Any 2 Cards	10, 11	9, 10, 11
• When Dealer Has Soft 17, He Must	Stand	Stand	Stand	Hit	Hit	Stand
• Player May Split	Any Pair (once)	Any Pair	Any Pair	Any Pair	Any Pair	Any Pair
• Surrender—1st 2 Cards	Early Surrender	Conventional Surrender	No	No	No	No
PLAYER'S AVERAGE EXPECTATION						
• Single Deck	N.A.	+.15%	—.00%	—.20%	—.48%	N.A.
• Two Deck	N.A.	N.A.	—.35	—.55	—.83	N.A.
• Four Deck	+.20%	—.31	—.51	—.71	—.99	—.65%
• Six Deck	+.11	—.40	—.60	—.80	N.A.	N.A.

N.A.—Game not available

43

Chapter Five

Basic Strategy
Start by Playing Even

Objective Of This Chapter

This chapter is intended principally for two types of readers:

The Social Player: You just want to learn seven simple rules to help you improve your blackjack game. You'll be able to cut your disadvantage to 1-to-2%. Read pages 47 through 49.

The Basic Strategy Player: You're willing to spend five hours or so to learn how to break even with some games and lose only minor amounts at others, whether in Nevada, Atlantic City, the Bahamas, Europe or elsewhere. Study the entire chapter.

Obviously, the chapter should also be read and totally understood by readers interested in going beyond Basic Strategy into one of the counting techniques. Further, beginners to the game must learn to crawl before they walk or run. It is foolhardy for everyone to attempt a higher level strategy without a thorough knowledge of Basic Strategy. The Basic Strategy for the double exposure game is included at the end of this chapter.

Like 1 + 1 = 2

Although stated in Chapter 3, it bears repeating. All the rules in this chapter are based on extensive computer analysis of the game. It is *not* just the way Ken Uston recommends you play. It is *the* way to play based on exhaustive computer runs. All responsible blackjack books recommend an identical strategy.

Let me give you an example of how the strategies were derived. Take the case of a player's 12 versus a dealer's 3 upcard (actually a very close play). In the first case, hundreds of thousands of hands were run where the player hit the 12 versus a 3 upcard, pulling cards at random from the remaining deck (or decks). Then, a similar number of hands were run with the player standing on 12 versus a 3. The results were tabulated and compared. The strategy yielding the player the bigger win or the smaller loss then dictates the correct play. (In this case, Basic Strategy calls for the player to hit 12 versus a 3.) Similar exhaustive computer runs were made for *all* hands to determine the correct Basic Strategy.

Some of the plays may seem contrary to common sense. For example, hitting A,7 versus a dealer's 10 is the correct play. Yet, some of my students balk at this play. Once again, the computers have been run for hundreds of thousands of hands, both hitting and standing on this hand, and have reached the indisputable conclusion that this hand must be hit.

Remember also that these decisions are for the Basic Strategy or non-counting player. There are times, of course, when the content of the deck is such that variations from Basic Strategy should be made (such plays as splitting 10's versus a 4 upcard, doubling-down on A, 9 versus a 6, and so on). But, the Basic Strategy player must ignore these exotic plays and faithfully adhere to Basic Strategy. Every time the player deviates from Basic Strategy, it will cost him money in the long run.

On any given play, the player may deviate and get away with it. You may stand on 12 versus a 3, the dealer may have a 10 in the hole, hit with another 10 and bust. If you had hit, you would have lost the hand. This may happen over and over again. But, remember, IN THE LONG RUN, after many hours of play, such deviations will even out and the result will cost you money.

How much time should the aspiring counter (or indeed practicing counter) spend on Basic Strategy? As much time as is necessary to learn it perfectly. To this day, I run through the Basic Strategy flashcards before playing—and I've been playing nearly full time for five years. As we will see in subsequent chapters, a complete, automatic knowledge of Basic Strategy is needed by the advanced player because when he wants to deviate from Basic Strategy based on the count, he must know thoroughly what he is deviating from—or he'll become hopelessly confused.

There's an overwhelming tendency on the part of nearly all the students I've taught over the last three years to cut corners, to go on to the more complex systems, to play in a casino before being totally prepared. Try to avoid this pitfall. Even for the perfectly trained, the game is tough (remember the horrible losing sessions I described in Chapter 3). We in the business know how hard it is to win, even when playing nearly perfectly. Thus, we respect, even more, the importance of practice, study and training—and when you think you're good enough, train some more.

I'm not trying to scare you. Yes, money can be made from blackjack, but only by the totally prepared. I know dozens of sad stories where good players ended up "tapping out" because they didn't respect the possibility of losing, didn't exercise the proper self-discipline; they cut corners and became careless. I'll be repeating this message several times because no matter how hard I emphasize this essential point, people continually disregard it.

Seven Simple Rules For The Social Player . . . Or . . . How To Lose Less

This section describes a Simple Strategy that consists of only seven rules (eight for Atlantic City). It will help the social player lose less and is a good strategy to teach to non-blackjack-oriented friends, dates or spouses, so they can play blackjack with only a slight disadvantage to the house.

If the social player were playing $5 per hand, on average he would lose between $5 and $10 per hour playing this Simple Strategy. Many would view this as an acceptable charge for sitting at the table, enjoying the excitement of gambling and the casino environment, and receiving free alcoholic beverages or soft drinks.

The seven rules are:

1. *If the dealer's upcard is a 2 or 3, the player should hit until a total of 13 is reached.* So if the player had 12 and the dealer had either a 2 or 3 upcard, the player would hit. If the player had a total of 13 or greater (say 15 or 18), naturally he would stand.

2. *If the dealer's upcard is a 4, 5 or 6, the player should hit until a total of 12 is reached.* Thus, the player does *not* hit 12 versus a 4, 5 or 6. (For your information, with a 4, 5, or 6 upcard, the dealer has a 40%, 43% and 42% chance of busting by hitting his hand. Periodically, I will cite these common sense reasons for making various plays to make it easier for the reader to remember the rules. But, in each case, always remember the *real* reason is that the computer experts ran thousands of hands exercising various options, compared the results and told us what the optimum play is.)

3. *If the dealer's upcard is 7, 8, 9, 10 or ace, the player should hit until a total of 17 is reached.* Thus, if the player had a 16 versus a dealer's 8, he must hit. Yes, his chances of busting are high, but the computer tells us that we will lose less by hitting than by standing.

These three simple rules apply to the majority of hands the player will be faced with. Once again, to summarize:

47

If the dealer has:	Hit until you have:
2 or 3	13
4, 5, 6	12
7, 8, 9, 10, ace	17

This Simple Strategy has two rules for doubling-down:

4. *If the player has a total of 11, he should double-down if the dealer's upcard is 2 through 10.* In other words, the player automatically doubles-down on 11 in all cases except when the dealer has an ace upcard. (In certain situations the player should also double-down against the ace, but, in our Simple Strategy, we will ignore this refinement.)

5. *If the player has a total of 10, he should double-down if the dealer's upcard is 2 through 9.* A crutch for remembering these two rules is: you double if the dealer's upcard is less than the total of your hand—that is, double on *11* if the dealer has 2 through 10; and double on *10* if the dealer has 2 through 9.

6. One rule for splitting pairs: *always split aces and 8's.* Although the real reason for making these plays is because of exhaustive computer analysis, each of these plays can be better remembered if a "common sense" reason is cited:

    – With two aces, the player is converting a poor hand, which totals 12 (or 2, if both aces are valued as 1) into two possibly good hands starting off with the value of 11 each.

    – By splitting 8's, the player is converting a poor hand of 16 to two potentially good hands, starting with an 8 on each hand.

7. One final rule: *Never Take Insurance.* Insurance is a poor bet (even if you have a blackjack, as I'll explain later).

8. For Atlantic City players, there is one additional rule that is important to remember. *Surrender 12 through 17 versus a dealer's ace upcard.* This rule applies only to Atlantic City, where early surrender is available to the player (different from the surrender offered in several Nevada casinos). A pair of 8's, thus, should be surrendered against an ace upcard.

The beginning player can write these rules down on a cocktail napkin, card or envelope and hold them in front of him as he's playing. (See Table 5-1) Most casino bosses will happily accept this little cribbing device when it is used by a blackjack novice betting only a few dollars a hand.

Table 5—1

The Simple Strategy

	If The Dealer Has:	Hit Until:
1.	2, 3,	13
2.	4, 5, 6	12
3.	7 through ace	17

	Double-Down On:	If Dealer Has:
4.	11	2 through 10
5.	10	2 through 9

6. ALWAYS Split Aces and Eights.

7. NEVER Take Insurance.

8. Atlantic City only:

   If Dealer Has Ace,   Surrender 12 through 17.

Basic Strategy—Atlantic City

Unfortunately, there is no single Basic Strategy which applies to all blackjack games. That is because casino rules and the number of decks used vary from place to place, and both of these factors have an effect on the correct Basic Strategy. In New Jersey, where the rules are established by the Casino Control Commission, one Basic Strategy applies. However, in Nevada, where casinos have the prerogative of establishing individual rules, there are numerous basic strategy variations. In fact, the Basic Strategy for each of the following Las Vegas Clubs is slightly different: MGM, Caesars, Dunes, Sands, Riviera, Sahara (single deck), El Cortez, Golden Nugget and the Las Vegas Club. The player shouldn't get discouraged at this, however, since the strategy variations are relatively minor.

We will first discuss Basic Strategy for the Atlantic City casinos. With the exception of the Las Vegas Caesars Palace single deck game, the Atlantic City casinos offer the most favorable blackjack game in the world to the player. In Atlantic City: the player may double-down on any two cards; double-down after pairs have been split; and the dealer stands on soft 17. The player, however, may not re-split pairs. Although six decks are generally used, the early surrender option, which allows the player to surrender against a possible dealer blackjack, more than offsets this, such that the Basic Strategy player actually has a tiny edge over the house (about .1%). Following our discussion of Atlantic City Basic Strategy, we will discuss Basic Strategy for Las Vegas, Reno-Lake Tahoe and the Bahamas.

Hard Hitting And Standing. The three hitting and standing rules for hard hands are identical to those of the Simple Strategy. In fact, these three rules apply to *all* casinos in the world offering standard blackjack. Further, they are by far the most important rules in that they will be employed in the majority of hands. To repeat them.:

If the dealer has:	Hit until you have:
2 or 3	13
4, 5, 6	12
7, 8, 9, 10, ace	17

Soft Hitting And Standing. A "soft" hand is one in which the ace can be counted as "1" or "11." For example, soft hands include:

A,2	A,A	A,9	A,3,3,3
A,6	A,2,3	A,4,4	and so on.

The following hands are not soft hands since if the ace is counted as "11," the hand exceeds 21:

A,5,6	A,3,8
A,4,9	A,7,10

In all cases, you must hit soft hands until you have at least soft 18. Thus, you never stand on A,6; that hand should always be hit or doubled, as we will see later.

When the dealer has a 9,10 or ace upcard, hit until you have soft 19 (yes, you hit A,7 in those cases). If, for example, you hit A,7 with a 7, you then have a hard hand (hard 15 in this case) and you must revert to the hard-hitting rules in the previous section. Thus, you would hit your hard 15 until you attained a hard 17 or greater.

Insurance. The Basic Strategy (i.e., non-counting) player should never take insurance. One of the most common misconceptions in the game is that the player should always insure a blackjack. The argument goes, "You cannot lose the hand. If the dealer has a blackjack, you tie your regular bet and win 1 unit on the insurance bet. If the dealer doesn't have blackjack, you win your regular bet (1½ units), lose the ½ unit insurance bet, and thereby gain 1 unit." Thus, they argue, "You always win 1 unit."

However, if you do not insure your blackjack, you will win more than 1 unit per hand on average. The insurance bet is completely independent of your regular bet. It is merely a side bet, which pays you 2-to-1 if the dealer's hole card is a 10. Mathematically, it's a bad bet both in single deck and in multiple deck games. Let's look at the six deck possibilities. Assume your original bet is $2 and your insurance bet (at half your original bet) is $1. In a six deck game, there are 216 non-10's and 96 10's. Knowing the dealer has an ace up and you have an ace and 10 (whether this occurs at the beginning of the shoe or the middle is irrelevant, since you are not counting cards), there are among the unknown cards an average of 214 non-10's and 95 10's. In terms of money won or lost, insurance betting may be illustrated as follows:

	Frequency	Amount Bet at $1 per insurance	Amount won or lost
Dealer hole card is non-10	214 times	$214	−$214
Dealer hole card is 10	95 times	95	+ 190
	309 times	$309	−$24

You will lose your $1 insurance bet 214 times out of 309. You will win per $1 insurance bet 95 times out of 309 and be paid 2-to-1 for a total payout of $190. This yields a net loss of $24 for the $309 bet, which is a negative expectation of 7.8%! The odds against you here are worse than at roulette! (Similar mathematics apply to one (8.2%), two (7.9%) and four (7.8%) deck games.)

Yet, dealer after dealer and floorman after floorman will advise you (and they're usually well-intentioned) to "always insure a blackjack." It's bad advice.

You also hear, "Always insure a good hand." Since a good hand of 18, 19 or 20 is more likely to have at least one 10, it turns out that these are precisely the times you would be less inclined to take insurance, that is, betting money that the dealer's hole card is a 10.

In summary, *never take insurance*! (The exception to this is, if you're a card counter and know when the ratio of 10's to non-10's is likely to be greater than 1-to-2.)

Note on Atlantic City surrender options:
As we went to press, the surrender rule in New Jersey was eliminated. Until this rule is reinstated, disregard the Atlantic City surrender options referred to in this book. Instead of surrendering, hit your hand until you reach hard 17.

Table 5—2
Summary—Basic Strategy Atlantic City
HITTING

Hitting Hard Hands		Hitting Soft Hands	
Hit Until You Have:	If Dealer's Upcard is:	Hit Until You Have:	If Dealer's Upcard is:
Hard 13	2, 3	Soft 19	9, 10, Ace
Hard 12	4, 5, 6	Soft 18	All Else
Hard 17	7 through A		

SPLITTING PAIRS		DOUBLING-DOWN	
		Double-	If Dealer's
Split:	If Dealer's Upcard is:	Down on:	Upcard is:
AA	Any Card	11	2 through 10
8,8	2 through 9	10	2 through 9
9,9	2 through 9, but not 7	9	3 through 6
7,7	2 through 7	A7 + A6	3 through 6
6,6	2 through 6	A5 + A4	4 through 6
4,4	5 and 6	A3 + A2	5 and 6
3,3	2 through 7		
2, 2	2 through 7		

INSURANCE	SURRENDER	
Never take insurance		
	Versus:	Surrender:
	Ace	Hard 5, 6, 7
		and 12 through 17
	Ten	Hard 14, 15, 16
	Nine	10, 6 and 9, 7
		(Split 8,8)

Pair Splitting. The rules for pair splitting are simply learned and are capsulized in the Basic Strategy summary, Table 5-2. Remember that these rules apply only to Atlantic City (where doubling-down-on-split-pairs is permitted). The rules are:

—Always split aces.

—Split 8's against dealer 2 through 9 upcard (you would normally always split 8's also, but in Atlantic City, 8's are surrendered against a 10 or ace).

—Split 9's if the dealer has 2 through 9 showing, but not against a 7. (A crutch to remember the "7" exception is that you have 18 and the dealer is likely to have 17; thus you should not split.) The "real" reason here (as well as throughout) is that if you play a million hands and stand on 9,9 vs. 7, you will do better than if you play a million hands and split 9,9 vs. a 7.

—Split 7's if the dealer has 2 through 7.

—Split 6's if the dealer has 2 through 6.

—Split 4's if the dealer has 5 or 6.

—Split 3's and 2's if the dealer has 2 through 7.

Take a look at the flashcards on page 54a. The A,A card (reproduced below) should be interpreted as follows: "When do you split aces?" The answer, on the left side of the card, is "All," meaning "in all cases." The 9,9 card asks, "When do you split 9's?" The answer, "2-9, x 7" means, "when the dealer's upcard is a 2 through 9, but not if it's a 7."

Figure 5a

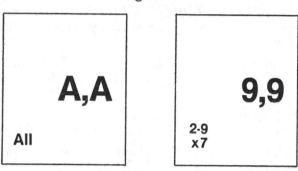

Doubling-Down. The rules for doubling-down, also summarized in Table 5-2, are as follows:

Double on 11 — If the dealer has a 2 through 10 showing (if he has a blackjack with his ten up, you will lose only your original bet).

Double on 10 — If the dealer has 2 through 9.

Double on 9 — If the dealer has 3 through 6.

Double on A, 7 and A, 6 — If the dealer has 3 through 6.

Double on A, 5 and A, 4 — If the dealer has 4 through 6.

Double on A,3 and A,2 — If the dealer has 5 or 6.

If you have split pairs and have an opportunity to double-down, obviously you do.

Surrender. With early surrender, you clearly will surrender more frequently than in conventional surrender against the ace and 10 upcard, since you are now permitted to lose only half your bet even when the dealer has a blackjack. The Atlantic City surrender basic strategy is as follows:

Versus an ace: Surrender all hard totals of 5, 6 and 7 and also 12 through 17 (yes, you toss in your 17's against a dealer ace).

Versus a 10: Surrender all hard totals of 14, 15 and 16 (this includes 7,7 and 8,8).

Versus a 9: Surrender 16 if you have 10+6 or 9+7. Split 8,8.

In Atlantic City, the surrendering player does not have to be concerned about getting "heat" or having the pitbosses suspect he's a winning player—many, many players surrender (often erroneously). This is not the case in Vegas, where the surrendering player can still raise eyebrows in the pit.

Basic Strategy Logic Flow. The flow chart below portrays the logic processes that the Basic player should go through while playing in Atlantic City.

If the dealer has an ace, 10 or 9 upcard, the player should determine whether he should surrender, in accordance with the rules given previously.

If the player does not surrender, and he has either A,A, 9,9, 8,8, 7,7, 6,6, 4,4, 3,3 or 2,2, he should determine if he should split pairs.

The player then determines if he should double-down, i.e. if he has one of the nine hands indicated to the left of the double-down box.

If not, he applies the hit-stand rules in the final box.

Figure 5b

Atlantic City
Basic Strategy Logic Flow

WHEN:			DECISION:		
Dealer: A, 10, 9			Surrender?	→ Yes →	Surrender
			↓ No		
Player					
AA	7, 7	3, 3	Split Pairs?	→ Yes →	Split
9, 9	6, 6	2, 2	↓ No		
8, 8	4, 4				
Player:					
11	A7	A4	Double-Down?	→ Yes →	Double-Down
10	A6	A3	↓ No		
9	A5	A2			

HIT vs STAND			
Dealer	Hit Until	Hit Until	Dealer
2, 3 :	13	Soft 19	9, 10, A
4, 5, 6:	12		
7 -A :	17	Soft 18	All Else

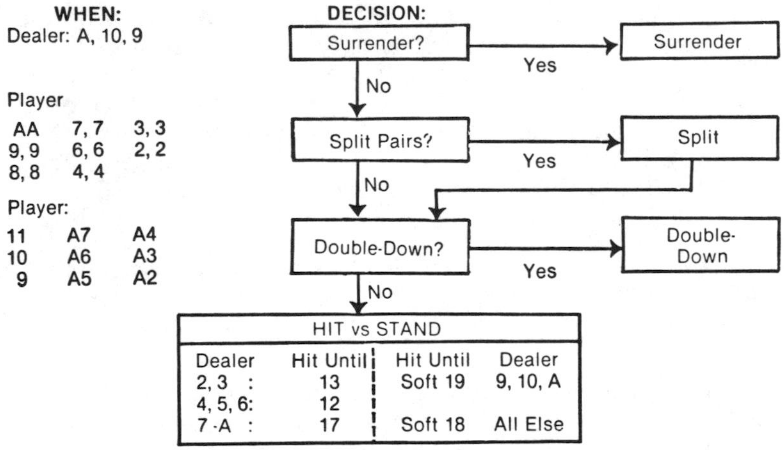

How To Practice Basic Strategy

The training and bet-to-bank advice in this section apply to all Basic Strategy players, whether studying the Atlantic City rules listed previously or the Nevada/Bahamas rules included below.

You should be able to learn the Basic Strategy rules in only a few hours of practice.

Flashcards. The first thing to do is to glue the flashcards (including the identification card) to any stiff paper that you'll be able

Basic Strategy Flashcards
Atlantic City

Basic Strategy Flashcards ATLANTIC CITY Objective: 3 times in 60 seconds	**11** 2-10	**10** 2-9
9 3-6	**AA** All	**9,9** 2-9 x7
8,8 2-9	**7,7** 2-7	**6,6** 2-6
4,4 5-6	**3,3** 2-7	**2,2** 2-7

A7 3-6	**A6** 3-6	**A5** 4-6
A4 4-6	**A3** 5-6	**A2** 5-6
ACE Hard 5,6,7 12-17 Surrender	**TEN** 14 15 16 Surrender	**NINE** 16 (not 8,8) Surrender

to handle. Then, cut them out. Put the ID card in front of the pack and, covering the "answer" with your left thumb, recite the proper Basic Strategy over and over again until you can do it perfectly, going through your flash cards 3 times in 60 seconds. The cards are designed for right-handed people; if you are left-handed and have difficulty, simply make a handwritten (or typewritten) set of your own with the answers on the right-hand side.

Dealing Hands. Then, take four decks of cards, shuffle and deal yourself hands. Do not bother to make any bets, and in fact, do not deal the dealer's hole card. Merely deal yourself two cards and a dealer upcard. Play the correct Basic Strategy and then immediately deal another hand. For a double-down, turn your draw card sideways. For surrender, just say "surrender," push the cards aside and deal the next hand.

At this point, you're not concerned with how the hands turn out or with the amount bet. You will be able to practice far more hands per hour than if you were placing bets or drawing to the dealer's upcard. Repeat the play of the hands until you find you can play Basic Strategy automatically—until it's second nature. At first, you'll probably have the most difficulty with soft doubling. To increase the frequency of these hands, you can remove the 8's 9's and 10's from the decks and deal yourself hands with the remaining cards. This is a rigorous but highly effective method of practicing soft doubling.

Alternate between the two training methods. Work with the flash cards for 10 minutes or so. Then, deal hands for 30 minutes. Return to the flash cards . . . and so on. Within several hours, you should be ready for casino play. Do not do this to the point of fatigue as it will be of little value. Always do your learning in a productive state of mind or you will need additional time.

When you're finally ready for an actual casino test, bet small until you feel entirely confident that you're playing perfect Basic Strategy under the new environment, and that you can cope with the dealers, pitbosses, other players and general distractions in the casino. If possible, learn Basic Strategy with a friend or spouse and verify each other's play. This will help avoid the possibility of recurring inadvertent errors in your play.

Bet-To-Bank Ratios. When you've mastered the simple steps outlined above, you will have a tiny edge over the Atlantic City casino(s). Remember that with such a tiny edge, large negative swings are still possible. Further, don't make the mistake of thinking that if, for example, you've lost $500, you're now more likely to win on your next play, since your results are supposed to average out to a small win and the "law of averages" is on your side. In this respect, the cards "have no memory" and you're just as likely to lose (or win) on your next play as on your last.

Never forget the following statistic: If you have $800 and play only $1 per hand, you have a better than a 1-out-of-20 chance of losing your entire bankroll with your tiny edge over the house. This applies to any comparable ratio, such as a bank of $8,000 and a $10 average bet or a bank of $20,000 and an average bet of $25. The fluctuations in blackjack are wide indeed and must be respected by the Basic Strategy player and the card-counter alike.

Remember, a 1-out-of-20 chance is not that unlikely. Every time, for example, that you see a dice shooter roll two 6's, a 1-out-of 36 shot has just come in! To look at the optimistic side, you also have about a 19-out-of-20 chance of doubling your bankroll.

Don't bet more than you can afford to lose. Most gambling texts include this truism, but for the Basic Strategy player (or card counter), the statement takes on more meaning. If you become overly concerned with your losses, the quality of your play may well be affected. You are likely to make errors, lose your edge over the house and continue to spiral down, losing even more.

How much to bet? There are strict mathematical rules my teams use when we're card counting. But, for the Basic Strategy player generally more interested in the sport of gambling, there's no specific answer. Bet enough to create for you the excitement of gambling, but not more than you can afford to lose. The commonly cited money management guidelines of betting more when you win (to increase the chances of a big win) and less when you lose (to avoid getting hurt - "steaming") are totally valid in this case.

Train carefully, play perfectly and have respect for the negative swings that are possible, maintaining a proper bet-to-bank ratio. You should have either a bank of at least 800 average bets or a strict stop-loss cut-off point.

Basic Strategy—Las Vegas

Las Vegas Strip—Single Deck. Contrary to popular opinion, a number of single deck games are still available on the Las Vegas Strip. The Basic Strategy player can break even with the house at these games and actually achieve a 0.15% edge at Caesars because of their special rules.

Why would one devote effort merely to breaking even? Many people enjoy playing blackjack. To be able to play "for free" hour after hour, and to enjoy the complimentary drinks and casino environment is appealing to many. Further, high-rollers can get "comped" in Vegas to rooms, shows and dinners, and in some cases, have their airline fares picked up by the casino. If the high roller plays even with the house, he can essentially enjoy an all-expenses paid vacation in Vegas. We will discuss this more fully in Chapter 20, "Living the American Fantasy Without Spending a Dime." For those interested in progressing to card-counting, a complete prior knowledge of the fundamentals of Basic Strategy is essential.

Las Vegas Strip single deck Basic Strategy is summarized in Table 5-3, and flashcards are included following page 58. The primary difference from Atlantic City Basic Strategy is the elimination of the surrender option and the tendency to split pairs somewhat less (2's, 3's, 4's and 6's) since double-on-splits is not generally offered.

Doubling-down occurs in several more cases because single deck requires more doubling than multiple deck(e.g. 11 vs. ace; 9 vs. 2; A,8 vs. 6; A,6 vs. 2; and A,3 and A,2 vs. 4). The hard standing and insurance rules are identical to Atlantic City (and in fact are identical for all games, whether in Northern Nevada, downtown Vegas, in the Bahamas or elsewhere).*

Note that you double-down on two types of "8's" (5,3 and 4,4) vs. a dealer's 5 or 6. For simplicity, I've omitted these on the flashcards because your edge is increased only slightly. Three other fine points, when you see no cards other than yours and the dealer's upcard, are these:

— Hit 10,2 versus the dealer's 4.

— Hit 10,3 vs. the dealer's 2.

— Stand on 16 vs. the dealer's 10 if you have 3 or more cards.

These fine points apply only to single deck. One blackjack expert advises against soft doubling for "cover" purposes. I disagree. More and more players are now soft doubling and the bosses are becoming more accustomed to this play than they were in the past.

Downtown Las Vegas—Single Deck.
Single deck games are offered at the Horseshoe, 4 Queens, El Cortez, Fremont and several small clubs downtown. At downtown clubs, the dealer hits soft 17. The Basic Strategy for these games is identical to that for the Strip (see Table 5-6) with just one exception; hit A,7 (or other soft 18's) versus a dealer's ace. The soft 17 rule costs the player .2%, so perfect Basic Strategy play results in an expectation of −.2% for the player.

Las Vegas Strip—Multiple Deck.
The next set of flashcards is to be used to practice Basic Strategy for Las Vegas multiple deck games. Table 5-4 lists the differences between single deck and multiple deck Basic Strategy. Notice that in multiple deck games, you tend to double-down and split less. For example, with a total of "9," you double-down if the dealer's upcard is 3 through 6, rather than 2 through 6. Remember that, unlike single deck, 7,7 versus a 10 should be hit. The practice objective for these flashcards is three times through the cards in 45 seconds. Then you'll be ready for casino play.

---

*There is one exception to this statement in single deck games: the player should stand on 7,7 versus a dealer 10 upcard.

Table 5—3
Basic Strategy Las Vegas Strip Single Deck

HITTING

Hitting Hard Hands		Hitting Soft Hands	
Hit Until You Have:	If Dealer's Upcard is:	Hit Until You Have:	If Dealer's Upcard is:
Hard 13	2, 3	Soft 19	9, 10
Hard 12	4, 5, 6	Soft 18	All Else
Hard 17	7 through A		

SPLITTING PAIRS

Split:	If Dealer's Upcard is:
AA	Any Card
8,8	Any Card
9,9	2 through 9, but not 7
7,7*	2 through 7
6,6	2 through 6
3,3	4 through 7
2,2	3 through 7

*Stand vs. a dealer's 10

DOUBLING-DOWN

Double-Down on:	If Dealer's Upcard is:
11	Any Card
10	2 through 9
9	2 through 6
5, 3 } 4, 4	5,6
A8	6
A7	3 through 6
A6	2 through 6
A5, A4 } A3, A2	4 through 6

INSURANCE

Never take insurance

Downtown Vegas—Multiple Deck. Basic Strategy is identical to the Strip, except that A,7 (and other soft 18's) versus ace is hit. Notice from Table 4-2 that the player has a negative expectation of .55% and .71% for two and four deck games downtown, respectively. These games are clearly not recommended.

Double-On-Splits and Conventional Surrender—In Nevada

At this writing, the double-on-split option allowed in Atlantic City is currently offered by about six clubs in Vegas, as is conventional surrender (i.e., surrendering after the dealer checks for blackjack). Table 5-5 below summarizes the Basic Strategy changes under these conditions, for both single and multiple deck games.

Basic Strategy Flashcards
Las Vegas Strip Single Deck

Basic Strategy Flashcards **LAS VEGAS SINGLE DECK** Objective: 3 times in 50 seconds.	**11** All	**10** 2-9
9 2-6	**AA** All	**9,9** 2-9 x7
8,8 All	**7,7** 2-7 (stand vs. 10)	**6,6** 2-6
3,3 4-7	**2,2** 3-7	**A8** 6

A7 3-6	**A6** 2-6	**A5** 4-6
A4 4-6	**A3** 4-6	**A2** 4-6

Basic Strategy Flashcards
Las Vegas Multiple Deck

Basic Strategy Flashcards LAS VEGAS MULTIPLE DECK Objective: 3 times in 45 seconds.	**11** 2-10	**10** 2-9
9 3-6	**AA** All	**9,9** 2-9 x7
8,8 All	**7,7** 2-7	**6,6** 3-6
3,3 4-7	**2,2** 4-7	**A8** Stand

A7 3-6	**A6** 3-6	**A5** 4-6
A4 4-6	**A3** 5-6	**A2** 5-6

Table 5—4

Differences in Basic Strategy Between Las Vegas Single Deck and Las Vegas Multiple Deck Games

	Dealer's Upcard:	
Player's Situation	Single Deck	Multiple Deck
Double on 11	All	2 through 10
Double on 9	2 through 6	3 through 6
Split 6,6	2 through 6	3 through 6
Split 2,2	3 through 7	4 through 7
Double-down on A8	6	Never
Double-down on A6	2 through 6	3 through 6
Double-down on A3	4 through 6	5 through 6
Double-down on A2	4 through 6	5 through 6
Soft 18	Ace—Stand	Ace—Hit
Double on 5,3; 4,4	5,6	Hit

Table 5—5

Basic Strategy Variations
Double-Down on Split Pairs and Conventional Surrender

DOUBLE-DOWN ON SPLIT PAIRS	If Dealer's Upcard is:	
	Single Deck	Multiple Deck
7,7	2 through 8	2 through 7
6,6	2 through 7	2 through 6
4,4	4 through 6	5 through 6
3,3	2 through 7	2 through 7
2,2	2 through 7	2 through 7

CONVENTIONAL SURRENDER ON:	If Dealer's Upcard is:	
10,6 and 9,7 (Split 8,8)	10 or Ace	9, 10 or Ace
Hard 15 (ex 8,7)	10	10
7,7	10	—

Fine point: in single deck, 9,7 vs. Ace should be hit; however, this is not critical.

What are the Best and Worst Games in Las Vegas? Be-
cause of the many rules variations among the casinos in Las Vegas, there is great variation in the house (or player) edge for the Basic Strategy player. The best (and worst) games in Vegas are listed below. Some casinos change rules frequently. Thus, this list may become out-of-date. However, it still serves to reveal the many varia-

tions in house edges in Las Vegas. The reader may use Table 4-1 to calculate the house edge for any given set of rules.

Table 5—6

The Best and Worst Games in Las Vegas

BEST GAMES	NO. DECKS	RULES	PLAYER EDGE
Caesars Palace	1	DS:Sur.*	+.15%
Circus Circus Sahara Castaways Stardust Silver Slipper	1	Standard Strip	.00
El Cortez	1	DS; Sur. Hit Soft 17	−.05
Fremont	1	Sur.; Hit Soft 17	−.18
Horseshoe; Mint	1	Hit Soft 17	−.20
Las Vegas Club**	6	Ds; Sur.; Hit Soft 17; Double on 3 + cards 6 cards auto. win	−.27
Riviera	2	Sur.	−.28
Caesars Palace	4	DS; Sur.	−.31
Flamingo Hilton	2	Standard Strip	−.35
MGM	4	DS	−.38
4 Queens	2	DS; Hit Soft 17	−.42
WORST GAMES			
Golden Nugget Union Plaza	5	Hit Soft 17	−.76
Mint	4	Hit Soft 17	−.71
Frontier	6	Standard Strip	−.60

*DS = Double-down on split pairs. Sur. = Conventional Surrender.
**Erroneously advertised as "The best blackjack rules in the world."

Basic Strategy—Reno-Lake Tahoe

Northern Nevada rules are unfavorable to the player. Doubling-down is generally permitted only on 10 and 11, and the dealer hits soft 17.

Basic Strategy Flashcards
Northern Nevada Single Deck

Basic Strategy
Flashcards

NORTHERN
NEVADA

Objective: 3 times in 30 seconds

11

All

10

2-9

AA

All

9,9

2-9
x7

8,8

All

7,7

2-7
(stand
vs.10)

6,6

2-6

3,3

4-7

2,2

3-7

Single Deck. Single deck Basic Strategy is identical to that for Las Vegas single deck games (Table 5-3) except that:

- A,7 (and other soft 18's) versus ace should be hit.
- Ignore the soft doubling and the "8" and "9" double-down rules.

Basic Strategy flashcards for Northern Nevada single deck games are on page 60a. The perfect Basic Strategy player gives up a .48% edge to the house.

Multiple Deck. Northern Nevada multiple deck games should be avoided, since even with perfect Basic Strategy play, the player is giving up nearly 1% to the house. The most notable exception to this is at the MGM Reno, where the player is essentially offered Vegas Strip rules, plus double-on-splits and surrender, with the dealer hitting soft 17. The MGM Reno Basic Strategy player gives up about ½% to the house, calculated as follows:

Four deck	− .51%
Hit soft 17	− .20
Double-on-splits	+ .13
Surrender	+ .07
Player's expectation	− .51

For the MGM Reno, the player may use the Atlantic City flash cards, altering the three surrender cards to reflect the conventional surrender rules on Table 5-5 and the splitting "8's" card to say "All." (For MGM Vegas, which has double-on-splits but not surrender, do the same but eliminate the surrender flashcards.)

Basic Strategy—The Bahamas

The rules offered at El Casino in Freeport and the Playboy and Resorts casinos on Paradise Island are also unique. The house offers four deck games, permits doubling-down on 9, 10 and 11, and the dealer stands on soft 17. Perfect Basic Strategy will yield the player a .65% negative expectation. The Bahamian Basic Strategy is listed in Table 5-7. Flashcards for use in the Bahamas are on page 62a.

The Basic Strategy player from the Northeast would be well advised to play in Atlantic City rather than in the Bahamas, unless he has an irresistible urge for palm trees and tropical beaches. The urge will cost him about .75% of the total amount bet on the blackjack tables, which is roughly equivalent to about one-half of his average bet, per hour of play. (For example, if your average bet is $50 and you plan to play 20 hours, it will cost you about $25 x 20, or $500 more, on average, to play in the Bahamas than in Atlantic City.)

61

Determining Basic Strategy For Other Locations

If you play in Europe, South America, the Orient or elsewhere, it is a simple matter to apply the Basic Strategy charts in this chaper once you have determined the local casinos' rules. The factors that will effect your correct play are: what is the number of decks; when may the player double, split, or surrender; and whether the dealer will hit soft 17.

Further, using Table 4-1 in Chapter 4, the player may be able to determine the house (or player) advantage for the Basic Strategy player. It is particularly important for the high-roller to take these steps, since many of the games offered abroad (such as in Puerto Rico where the house edge is over 1%) are poor for the player.

Table 5—7
Basic Strategy—The Bahamas

HITTING

Hitting Hard Hands		Hitting Soft Hands	
Hit Until You Have:	If Dealer's Upcard is:	Hit Until You Have:	If Dealer's Upcard is:
Hard 13	2, 3	Soft 19	9, 10, Ace
Hard 12	4, 5, 6	Soft 18	All Else
Hard 17	7 through A		

SPLITTING PAIRS

Split:	If Dealer's Upcard is:
AA	Any Card
8,8	Any Card
9,9	2 through 9, but not 7
7,7	2 through 7
6,6	3 through 6
3,3	4 through 7
2,2	4 through 7

DOUBLING-DOWN

Double-Down on:	If Dealer's Upcard is:
11	2 through 10
10	2 through 9
9	3 through 6

INSURANCE
Never take insurance.

Basic Strategy For
Double Exposure (Zweikartenspiel)

The Basic Strategy for the double exposure game, offered at VegasWorld, Silver City and other casinos in Las Vegas and Northern

Basic Strategy Flashcards
The Bahamas

Basic Strategy Flashcards **THE BAHAMAS** Objective: 3 times in 30 seconds.	**11** 2-10	**10** 2-9
9 3-6	**AA** All	**9,9** 2-9 x7
8,8 All	**7,7** 2-7	**6,6** 3-6
3,3	**2,2** 4-7	

Nevada, varies dramatically from other strategies primarily because tie hands (other than blackjacks) are won by the house.

In the five deck game currently offered by VegasWorld, the Basic Strategy player has a slight disadvantage (less than .5%) to the house. Against single deck double exposure, the player has an edge of about .25%.

The correct strategy was recently run off by a friend, Mark Estes. The player should be sure to employ this strategy (shown in Table 5-8), as several erroneous strategies have been printed (in two newsletters and in a text which assumed the double-on-split option was permitted).

Table 5—8

Basic Strategy for Five Deck Double Exposure 21*

Dealer's Hand 2-Card Total	Hit Until: Hard Hands	Hit Until: Soft Hands	Double-Down Hard	Double-Down Soft	Split Pairs
20	21	21			
19	20	20			
Hard 18	19	19			9
Hard 17	18	18			2,3,6,7,8
Hard 16	12	18 [*19*]	5-11	A2-A9	A-4,6-10
Hard 15	12	18	5-11	A2-A9	A-4,6-10
Hard 14	12	18	5-11	A2-A9	A-4,6-10
Hard 13	12	18	[*8*]7-11	A2-A9	A-4,6-10
Hard 12	12	18 [*19*]	8-11	A2-A8	A-4,6-9
Hard 11	14	19			
Hard 10	15	19			A
Hard 9	16	19	11		A
Hard 8	16	19	10,11		A,8,9
Hard 7	17 [*16*]	18	10,11		A,8
Hard 6	12	18 [*19*]	9,10,11	A3-A7 [*A2*]	A-3,6-9
Hard 5	12	18 [*19*]	9,10,11	A5-A7	A-3,6-9
Hard 4	12	18	10,11	A7	A,6-9 [*not 7-7*]
A7	19	19			
A6	18	18	11		A,8
A5	12	19	10,11	[*A7*]	A,8,9
A4	12	19	10,11		A,9
A3	12	19	10,11		A
A2	13	19	11		A
AA	13	19	[*11*]		A

Note: Assumes dealer hits "Soft 17."

* Courtesy of Mark Estes

63

Chapter
Six

Beyond Basic Strategy

Intermediate And Advanced Counting Systems
And
A One-Level Professional System

Levels Of Blackjack Play. The player interested in progressing beyond Basic Strategy has the choice of several levels of blackjack play. Five levels of blackjack skill were defined and published* by Stanley Roberts and D. Howard Mitchell, a researcher and author on blackjack. The five levels were: Basic, Intermediate, Advanced, Professional and Expert.

Their levels of play, their definitions and the corresponding components of this book are as follows:

Level of Skill	Definition	Refer To:
Basic	Perfect play of the hands, without card-counting.	Basic Strategy, Chapter 5.
Intermediate	Variation of bets in accordance with content of deck. No variation in play.	Ace-Five Count, this chapter.

Gambling Times Magazine, February, 1978.

Advanced	Variation of betting and playing of hands, in accordance with content of deck. No conversion of running count to true count.	The Uston Simple Plus/Minus, this chapter.
Professional	Bet and play variation in accordance with true count; side count of aces optional.	
One-level	—Card denominations are assigned values of plus or minus 1.	The Uston Advanced Plus/Minus, last section of this chapter.
Multi-level	—Card denominations are assigned values of greater than plus or minus 1.	The Uston Advanced Point Count, Chapter 8.

The "expert" strategies, as defined in the article, require keeping more than one count using up to four side counts of individual cards (multi-parameter counting), or even counting each card separately. These counts, in my opinion, are largely impractical and beyond the scope of human ability. Several of us, including Rob of Team 2, once attempted such a system, keeping a running count and four side counts, for single deck play. We abandoned the effort after a few weeks. For multiple deck play, such a system would result, I believe, in total confusion.

Contents Of This Chapter

The remainder of this chapter is organized as follows:

1. A comparison of the efficiency of professional level systems.

2. A discussion of the basic principle underlying all responsible card counting systems, so the reader will fully understand why card counting systems make it possible to gain an advantage over the house.

3. A detailed discussion of an intermediate counting system, the Ace-Five count, which is probably the simplest counting system possible.

4. Presentation of the Uston Simple Plus/Minus, an advanced system, with practice techniques and objectives so the reader will know when he is prepared to use this count in a casino.

5. An extension of the Uston Simple Plus/Minus to the Uston

Advanced Plus/Minus, a highly effective one-level professional system.

Professional Level Systems—
Which Ones Are The Best

Table 6-1a indicates the relative efficiency of the better professional level systems available. We evaluate the systems in terms of their betting efficiency, where 1.00 represents virtually perfect betting patterns and efficiency in playing the hands. A composite index, weighting both betting and playing, is used to provide an overall assessment of each system.

The multi-level systems listed, the Uston APC, Hi Opt II and the Revere APC, are, for all practical purposes, of comparable power. The minor (.01) difference would not be reflected in player profitability.

Table 6—1

Relative Efficiency of
Professional Level Blackjack Systems

| | EFFICIENCY | | |
SYSTEM	Playing	Betting	Composite
Multi-level:			
Uston Advanced Point Count	.69	.99	.87
Hi Opt II	.67	.99	.86
Revere APC (14 Count)	.66	.99	.86
One-level:			
Hi Opt I	.62	.95	.82
Uston Advanced Plus/Minus	.55	.95	.79
Braun Count *(Thorp Point Count)	.51	.97	.79
DHM Professional (Gordon)	.57	.92	.78

    * Same as Wong High-Low, but with several playing strategy errors corrected.

Notes: Based partially on formulas presented by Dr. Peter A. Griffin to the Second Conference on Gambling, Harrah's Lake Tahoe, June 15-18, 1975, and shown in his 1979 text (25).

The top four systems and the DHM system require a separate count of aces. Dr. Griffin's betting figures were modified to reflect the adjustment of betting in accordance with a side count of aces.

The Composite Index was developed by weighting the Betting Efficiency by 3 and the Playing Efficiency by 2, which is close to the actual impact each of these functions has on overall player profitability.

Among the one-level systems, Hi Opt I has the highest Composite Efficiency, largely because it requires a side count of aces. The Advanced Plus/Minus and the Braun Count are slightly less powerful than Hi Opt I, but are considerably easier to play since these systems do not require a side count of aces.

The dedicated player can win with any of these (and indeed selected other) systems. Long training, practice, self-discipline and a positive attitude are far more important to the player's bottom line than the mathematical difference in these systems. On the other hand, it has been our empirical experience that, in the hands of capable players, the more complex systems consistently win the most.

The Basic Principle behind Card Counting

As the cards are dealt in a game of blackjack, the odds continually change, swinging back and forth between the house and the player. Let's assume we're playing a single deck game with one other player, and on the first round dealt, the following cards are drawn:

Figure 6a

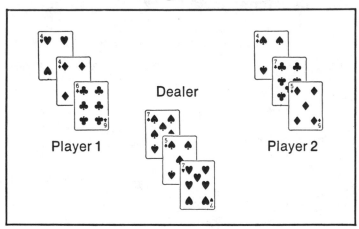

Player 1   Dealer   Player 2

On the next hand, the skillful player has an edge over the house of over 5%. Why? Because a disproportionate number of low cards has been played, and no 10's and aces have yet been seen. Thus, the remaining pack is rich in 10's and aces.

How does this benefit the player? In several ways:

Aces. When the deck is rich in aces, the player is more likely to receive a blackjack. Although the dealer is equally likely to receive a blackjack, the player with a blackjack is paid a bonus at the rate of 3-to-2, whereas the dealer's blackjack merely results in the player losing the amount of his bet, on a 1-to-1 basis. Thus, the greater the chance for a blackjack to occur, the greater the percent will swing toward the player. Further, with an ace-rich deck, the potential for splitting aces is greater and this factor benefits the player.

Tens. When the deck is rich in 10's, the dealer is more likely to bust since he *must* hit until he gets a hard total of 17. Thus, with "stiffs" of 12, 13, 14, 15 or 16, the dealer must draw and is more likely to bust. The player, on the other hand, can alter his play and not draw as frequently to stiff hands. Also, a blackjack is more likely since a 10 is one of the cards required.

Now let's take another example. Assume that on the first round, the following cards are dealt:

Figure 6b

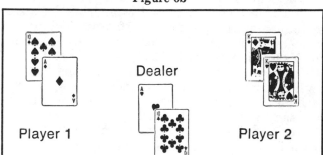

Player 1   Dealer   Player 2

On the next hand, the house has a significant edge over the player. This is because the remaining pack is deficient in 10's and aces, and rich in low cards, which, of course, works against the player.

The player who keeps track of the content of the deck can thus determine when the percentage has swung in his favor and make larger bets in those situations and smaller bets in poorer situations. He will tend to win a higher proportion of his larger bets and lose a higher proportion of his small bets, thereby enjoying a profit over the house. Needless to say, the more a player can vary the amount of his bet, the more profitable his play will be.

The casinos have become highly aware of this and extreme bet variation will raise the eyebrows of the dealers and the pitbosses; frequently, they will then begin observing the player to see if he is a card counter. If they suspect he is, they may shuffle up on him, ask him not to play blackjack or even to leave the casino. We will discuss how to minimize this problem in subsequent chapters.

The variation in the content of the deck has another effect upon the card counter. He not only can vary his bet, but he can also vary his play, i.e., when to hit, stand, double-down, split pairs, surrender or take insurance. In favorable situations (when the deck is 10's rich) the player will tend to stand more (since he does not want to hit stiff's and risk busting because of the 10's rich deck), double-down more (since the dealer is more likely to bust if he has a stiff and the player is more likely to draw a 10 on a good doubling hand such as an 11) and split pairs more (since the dealer is more likely to bust and since, with certain pairs, such as 10's, the player is more likely to draw additional 10's and get good hands).

In unfavorable situations, when the deck is rich in low cards, the reverse is true. The player will hit more (since there are proportionately more unplayed low cards), double-down less (since the dealer is less likely to bust and since the player is more likely to receive a low card, which will not improve most hard doubling-down hands) and split pairs less frequently (since the dealer is less likely to bust and the player is less likely to draw larger cards, giving him a total close to 21).

When this principle is understood, the concept of certain "odd" plays like splitting 10's becomes more understandable. It is sometimes to the player's advantage to split a pair of 10's, particularly if the dealer's upcard is 4, 5 or 6. In a 10's rich deck, the player's chance of drawing additional 10's for another total of 20 is good; in addition, if, for example, the dealer's upcard is a 6, it is more likely that he has a 10 in the hole and will hit himself with a 10, thereby busting. A very 10's rich deck can call for even more exotic plays, such as doubling-down on A,9 (which is already a good hand totalling 20), doubling-down on hard totals of 7, 6 or 5 against a dealer's upcard of 5 or 6, doubling-down on A,6 against a 7, and splitting 9's against an ace.

Summary. The content of the deck will affect the player's behavior in two ways—the amount bet and the way the hands are played. In favorable situations, the player will bet more and vary his play by standing more often, doubling-down, splitting pairs, surrendering more often and even taking insurance (in sufficient 10's rich situations, it is more likely that the dealer has a blackjack with an ace upcard, and insurance becomes a good bet). In unfavorable situations, the player will bet less and will vary his play by hitting more, by doubling-down, splitting pairs and surrendering less frequently.

The Ace-Five Count

We'll now discuss what is probably the simplest possible count system. It's included for those readers who are unwilling to put in hours of practice, but want to be able to achieve a small edge over the house. It's strictly meant for the recreational player who, we hope, is betting at low levels in the casino. We call the use of this count an intermediate level of play since the player, in addition to playing perfect Basic Strategy, will use a count to vary the size of his bet.

In Atlantic City and in Las Vegas single deck games, the ace-five count player has from .25% to .5% edge over the house. If your average bet is $10 per hand and you're averaging 100 hands per hour, your earnings will be only $2.50 to $5 per hour on average (with probably great fluctuations therein). Further, you will stand a 1-out-of-20 (or 5%) chance of losing 300 units, or $3,000. You will also have a 19-out-of-20 (or 95%) chance of winning $3,000 before you lose $3,000. (For other average size bets, you can make the appropriate arithmatical conversions.)

These earnings rates and financial risks are far from overwhelming. Unfortunately, the situation is worse for multiple deck games in Las Vegas, games in Reno and Lake Tahoe, and abroad. Even with the ace-five count, you are at a slight disadvantage to the house, as follows:

Game	House Edge Over Ace-Five Count Player
Vegas Strip—double deck	.05%
Vegas Strip—four deck.	.21
Reno & Tahoe—single deck	.30
Bahamas—four deck	.35

With these cautions, let's discuss the ace-five count. The five is the card of the greatest value to the house—primarily because the dealer must hit "stiffs" of 12 through 16, and a hit with a 5 gives the dealer "pat" hands of 17 through 21. Conversely, the ace is the card of the greatest value to the player, primarily because it constitutes the less frequent of the two cards (ace and 10) needed for blackjack. Assuming that the other cards are evenly distributed, it is to the players's advantage when the deck is unduly depleted of 5's. When the deck is unduly low in aces (or "ace-poor"), it's to the house's advantage. The ace-five count reflects these facts.

Counting (Column A in Table 6-2).

As the cards are dealt, keep a "running" count, starting at zero, and adding "1" to your count for each 5 seen and subtracting "1" from the count for each ace seen. When you reach the end of the deck in practice, your count will be restored to zero, if it is correct, since there is an identical number of 5's and aces, whether using one, four or more decks.

Whenever the deck is "plus," it will tend to be more to the player's advantage (more 5's than aces have been played). When the deck is "minus," the deck will tend to favor the house (more aces having been played than 5's). On average, the other cards will be evenly distributed and can be ignored in the count. In stronger counts, of course, other cards will be considered.

Betting (Column B).

Bet two units "off-the-top" of the deck (that is, immediately after the shuffle) and whenever the count is zero (i.e., when an equal number of aces and 5's have been played). Bet 3 units whenever you have a "plus" count (plus 1 or greater). Bet 1 whenever the count is minus.

71

Table 6—2
Ace — Five Count

A—Counting	B—Betting	C—Playing
For each 5 seen: Count +1	Bet 3 units with plus count	Play Basic Strategy
For each ace seen: Count −1	Bet 2 units with "0" count Bet 1 unit with minus count	Never take insurance

Playing (Column C). Play perfect Basic Strategy as outlined previously. Since the ace-five count adds about .3+% to your edge over the house:

- At Caesars Palace (single deck) you have about a .5% edge over the house, nearly equal to the house advantage in craps with double odds.
- In Atlantic City, you also have a .5% edge over the house.
- At other Vegas Strip single deck games, you have a .25% edge over the house.

You can increase your edge further by betting four, five or even more units with a plus count. However, higher ratios will increase your risk of being barred, or losing your bankroll. Having a percentage over the house does not guarantee you will win, any more than the house knows for sure that it will win every session at the craps table, even though it has the edge on *every bet.*

The Uston Simple Plus/Minus, An Advanced Count

In conducting seminars over the past several years, I've found that many students want a count system stronger than the ace-five count, but not as complex as the advanced systems such as the Uston Advanced Point Count, the 14 Count or Hi Opt II. I was finally motivated to design such a system in 1978, when a Hollywood producer asked me to put together a video-cassette presentation to teach the average player how to play blackjack.

The system, which I named "The Simple Plus/Minus," is unique among blackjack counting systems. It effectively "skims the cream off the top," by giving the player perhaps 60% of the advantage of the advanced systems, yet it requres only 20%-to-25% of the work, both in training and at the tables. The Simple Plus/Minus does not require a side count of aces nor a memorization of the fairly formidable numbers matrices which accompany all the advanced systems. It avoids the need to convert running counts to true counts (all these techniques and how they are used by the skillful player are discussed in Chapter 8).

The Simple Plus/Minus is a "one-level" count, that is, all the values of the card denominations are either +1 or −1. No special mathematical ability is required and the count can be learned by the average person in about 15 to 20 hours. I recommend this count to many of my students because it is *far better to play a simple count accurately than to use an advanced count and make errors*. The Simple Plus/Minus is a particularly effective count for the attractive Atlantic City game and can probably earn close to 1% if applied as described in this chapter.

For those players who wish to go on in blackjack, I have also developed a numbers matrix for the Simple Plus/Minus values, extending this system into what I call "The Advanced Plus/Minus." This count, on a par with Hi Opt I and the Braun (Wong High-Low) counts, can be learned by the student *after he has learned and played with The Simple Plus/Minus,* using the materials in the last section of this chapter and in Chapter 8.

For now, let's forget the more advanced counts and concentrate on learning The Simple Plus/Minus.

Card Values. We have seen that when small cards are played, the deck tends to be to the player's advantage, since the remaining deck is rich in 10's and aces. Thus, small cards are assigned "plus" values. In the Simple Plus/Minus, the player counts "plus 1" whenever a 3, 4, 5, 6 or 7 is played.

When 10's and aces are played, this tends to work to the disadvantage of the player since the remaining deck is richer in small cards. Thus, the Simple Plus/Minus assigns a value of "minus 1" to 10's and aces.

Notice that there is exactly the same number of plus cards (20 in a single deck) as there is of minus cards (the 10's, jacks, queens, kings and aces). The player keeps a "running count," that is, a cumulative count of the values of the cards played, as the game progresses.

COUNT "+1"   for 3's, 4's, 5's, 6's and 7's
COUNT "−1"   for ten-valued cards and aces
DO NOT COUNT   2's, 8's and 9's.

Step 1. The very first thing to do is to take a complete 52-card deck and go through it, card-by-card, reciting the values for each individual card. Go through the deck five or six times, until you're comfortable that you know the values "cold." After an amazingly short time, the values become completely automatic for you.

Step 2. Then, start counting the deck by reciting the cumulative value of the deck. For example, let's say the first card in the deck is a 10. You say, "minus 1." The next card is a king. You say, "minus 2," since the −1 you had before and the −1 from the king add to −2. The next card is a six. You say "minus 1," which is the cumulative total of the −2 you had, combined with the +1 value of the six. The table below illustrates this:

Table 6—3
Simple Plus/Minus Illustration

Card Seen	Card Value	Player Recites Cumulative Value:
10	− 1	− 1
king	− 1	− 2
6	+ 1	− 1
4	+ 1	0
3	+ 1	+ 1
8	0	+ 1
2	0	+ 1
10	− 1	0

etc.

When you have reached the end of the deck, you should have a count of "zero," since the total of all the plus cards equals the total of all the minus cards. If you have a final count of other than zero, you have made an error. Recount that *same* deck, without shuffling, until you have corrected your error. This will ensure that any biases in your counting are removed early and immediately. (Make sure, of course, that all 52 cards are in the deck; more than once, we've counted down decks getting other than zero at the end, only to find later that one or more cards were missing.)

Step 3. Look for combinations. Many blackjack hands consist of two cards, one a plus card and one a minus card. Obviously, these cards need not be counted since they net out to zero. The "zero-nettings" in the Simple Plus/Minus are:

Table 6—4
Simple Plus/Minus
Card Combinations Netting To Zero

10,3	A,3	2,2
10,4	A,4	2,8
10,5	A,5	2,9
10,6	A,6	8,8
10,7	A,7	8,9
		9,9

The first time you go through an entire 52-card deck, it will probably take you two minutes or more to state its cumulative value accurately. Your goal for casino play is 25 seconds. As you keep practicing, your speed will increase. The average player can learn to count a deck down using the Simple Plus/Minus in 8-10 hours.

Simple Count Strike Numbers. The purpose of keeping the count, of course, is to be able to bet more in favorable situations (less in unfavorable situations) and to vary the play of the hands based on the content of the deck.

Let's compare two situations. Assume we have a +10 count in a single deck game and there is one-half deck (26 cards) to be dealt. Assume a second situation in which we have a +10 count in a six deck game and there are 5½ decks (286 cards) left to be dealt. Clearly, there is a greater concentration of 10's and aces in the single deck example—the +10 count is spread out over only 26 cards, as opposed to 286 cards in the second example.

To reflect this, we have developed what we call"Strike Numbers." These are numbers which determine when bets should be increased or decreased and when the play of the hand should be varied. They are based on the total number of decks used in the game the Simple Plus/Minus player is playing and not on the number of decks remaining to be played.

In a single deck game, where only 52 cards are used, the strike number is ±2. That is, if the count is +2 or higher, the player should increase his bet and vary his play in accordance with a "plus" strategy that is provided with the Simple Plus/Minus. If the count is −2, or less (that is, a bigger minus number), the player should decrease his bet and vary his play in accordance with a "minus" strategy that is provided.

In double deck games, where 104 cards are used, the strike number is 3. For four decks, with 208 cards, we use 6; for six decks, we use 9. (If the player is playing a three, five, seven or eight-deck game, he should use 4, 8, 11, and 12, respectively.)

Table 6—5
The Simple Plus/Minus Strike Numbers

Number of Decks in Game	Strike Numbers	Use Plus Strategy and Bet 4 Units When Count is:	Use Minus Strategy and Bet 1 Unit When Count is:
1 Deck	2	+2	−2
2 Decks	3	+3	−3
4 Decks	6	+6	−6
6 Decks	9	+9	−9

Simple Plus/Minus Betting Strategy. The Simple Plus/Minus player must first determine the size of his betting unit, which in turn is dependent upon how much capital he is willing to risk in his blackjack endeavors. Table 6-6 lays out betting strategies for $1, $5, $25 and $100 units. Since many casinos now have $2 minimums, the $1 level may soon become academic.

Table 6—6
Simple Plus/Minus Betting Strategy

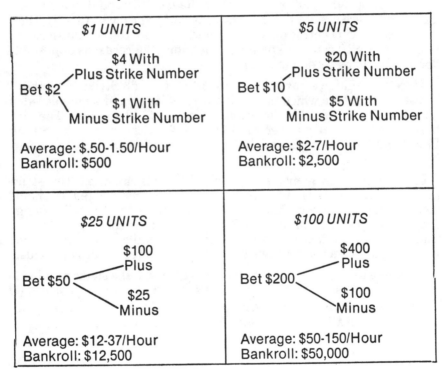

$1 UNITS	$5 UNITS
$4 With Plus Strike Number Bet $2 $1 With Minus Strike Number	$20 With Plus Strike Number Bet $10 $5 With Minus Strike Number
Average: $.50-1.50/Hour Bankroll: $500	Average: $2-7/Hour Bankroll: $2,500
$25 UNITS	$100 UNITS
$100 Plus Bet $50 $25 Minus	$400 Plus Bet $200 $100 Minus
Average: $12-37/Hour Bankroll: $12,500	Average: $50-150/Hour Bankroll: $50,000

In discussing betting, let's use the $5 unit as an example. The $5 bettor would make an opening bet of $10 (2 units) and remain at that level until the count reached the plus strike number or greater (betting $20, or 4 units), or the minus strike number or less (betting $5, or 1 unit). In Atlantic City and Vegas single deck games, the player should average about $7 per hour in earnings. In Vegas multiple deck games and Reno-Lake Tahoe games, the earnings expectation would fall toward the lower end of the range indicated in the table, around $2 per hour.

The "Bankroll: $2,500" entry means that the $5 bettor, playing perfectly and in *strict* adherence to the Simple Plus/Minus has a 1-out-of-20 chance of losing $2,500 and a 19-out-of-20 chance of doubling his $2,500 (what we call a "5% element-of-ruin," discussed in depth in Chapter 9).

The $25 unit player, betting from $25 to $100, should average $37 per hour in Atlantic City and Vegas single deck games. He has a 5% chance of losing $12,500 and a 95% chance of doubling $12,500. The $100 unit bettor, betting from $100 to $400, should average $150 per hour in the favorable locations, but must be willing to risk $50,000.

The Simple Plus/Minus Playing Strategy. As we have discussed, the player will be more inclined to stand in plus counts, to double-down, split and surrender, contrary to Basic Strategy. Plus strategy tables are included for both Atlantic City (Table 6-7) and Nevada (Table 6-9). Note, when using the Atlantic City Plus strategy table, the player now stands on 12 versus 9, and 16 versus 10. Further, he doubles-down more (e.g., double on 11 always, double on A,8 versus 5 and 6, etc.) and surrenders more (hard 4 versus a dealer ace). Similar plays are noted on the Nevada Plus strategy table.

In minus counts, the player will hit more, while doubling, splitting and surrendering less. This is reflected in the Minus strategy tables for Atlantic City (Table 6-8) and Nevada (Table 6-10). Note, on the Atlantic City Minus strategy table, the player hits 13 versus 2 and 3; hits 12 versus 4, 5 and 6; does not double on A,2; and surrenders only 12 through 17 versus a dealer's ace. Similar variations are noted in the Nevada Minus strategy table.

In order to facilitate learning the plus, basic and minus strategies, flashcards are provided for the Atlantic City and Nevada player. Note that the format of these flashcards is identical to the Basic Strategy flashcards in the previous chapter. The "answer column," however, now has three entries:

-The top entry lists the plus strategy.

-The middle entry lists the Basic Strategy.

-The lower entry lists the minus strategy.

> **See note on page 51 concerning Atlantic City surrender options.**

Table 6—7
Simple Plus/Minus
Plus Strategy Table—Atlantic City
Strategy When "Plus Number" is Reached

HITTING

Hitting Hard Hands		Hitting Soft Hands	
Hit Until You Have:	If Dealer's Upcard is:	Hit Until You Have:	If Dealer's Upcard is:
Hard 13	2	Soft 19	9, 10
Hard 12	3, 4, 5 or 6	Soft 18	All Else
Hard 16	10		
Hard 17	7, 8, 9, A		

*SPLITTING PAIRS**

Split:	If Dealer's Upcard is:
AA	Any Card
9,9	2 through 9, but not 7
8,8	2 through 9
7,7	2 through 7
6,6	2 through 6
4,4	5 and 6
3,3	2 through 7
2,2	2 through 7

DOUBLING-DOWN

Double-Down on:	If Dealer's Upcard is:
11	All
10	2 through 9
9	2 through 6
8	6
A8	5 and 6
A7, A6	2 through 6
A5, A4 }	4 through 6
A3, A2	

INSURANCE

Take insurance

*EARLY SURRENDER***

Versus:	Surrender:
Ace	Hard 4, 5, 6, 7, 12 through 17
Ten	Hard 14, 15, 16
Nine	10 + 6; 9 + 7, (Split 8,8)

* Different from Nevada because of double-down-on-split-pairs option.

**Surrender takes precedence over insurance.

See note on page 51 concerning Atlantic City surrender options.

Table 6—8
Simple Plus/Minus
Minus Strategy Table—Atlantic City
Strategy When "Minus Number" is Reached

HITTING

Hitting Hard Hands		Hitting Soft Hands	
Hit Until You Have:	If Dealer's Upcard is:	Hit Until You Have:	If Dealer's Upcard is:
Hard 14	2, 3	Soft 19	9, 10, A
Hard 13	4, 5, 6	Soft 18	All Else
Hard 17	7, 8, 9, 10, A		

SPLITTING PAIRS   *DOUBLING DOWN*

Split:	If Dealer's Upcard is:	Double-Down on:	If Dealer's Upcard is:
AA	Any Card	11	2 through 10
9,9	2 through 9, but not 7	10	2 through 8
8,8	2 through 9	9	5 and 6
7,7	2 through 7	8	No (Hit)
6,6	2 through 6	A8	No (Stand)
4,4	No (Hit)	A7, A6	4 through 6
3,3	2 through 7	A5, A4	5 and 6
2,2	2 through 7	A3	6
		A2	No (Hit)

INSURANCE   *EARLY SURRENDER*

Do Not Take insurance	Versus:	Surrender:
	Ace	12 through 17
	Ten	15 and 16
	Nine	No

* Different from Nevada because of double-down-on-split-pairs option.

Table 6—9

Simple Plus/Minus
Plus Strategy Table—Nevada
Strategy When "Plus Number" is Reached

HITTING

Hitting Hard Hands		Hitting Soft Hands*	
Hit Until You Have:	If Dealer's Upcard is:	Hit Until You Have:	If Dealer's Upcard is:
Hard 13	2	Soft 19	9, 10
Hard 12	3, 4, 5 or 6	Soft 18	All Else
Hard 16	10		
Hard 17	7, 8, 9, A		

*SPLITTING PAIRS***   *DOUBLING-DOWN*

Split:	If Dealer's Upcard is:	Double-Down on:	If Dealer's Upcard is:
AA	Any Card	11	All
9,9	2 through 9, but not 7	10	2 through 9
8,8	Any Card	9	2 through 6
7,7	2 through 7	8	5,6
6,6	2 through 6	A8	5 and 6
4,4	Do not Split (double)	A7, A6	2 through 6
3,3	4 through 7	A5, A4	4 through 6
2,2	3 through 7	A3, A2	4 through 6

INSURANCE   *SURRENDER*

Take insurance

Versus:	Surrender:
Ace	16
Ten	16 and 15
Nine	16

* Soft hitting rules apply to all Nevada (including Reno, Lake Tahoe and downtown Las Vegas).

** Substitute Atlantic City pair-splitting table if doubling-after-splitting is permitted.

Table 6—10

Simple Plus/Minus
Minus Strategy Table—Nevada

Strategy When "Minus Number" is Reached

HITTING

Hitting Hard Hands		Hitting Soft Hands	
Hit Until You Have:	If Dealer's Upcard is:	Hit Until You Have:	If Dealer's Upcard is:
Hard 14	2, 3	Soft 19	9, 10, A
Hard 13	4, 5, 6	Soft 18	All Else
Hard 17	7, 8, 9, 10, A		

SPLITTING PAIRS*		*DOUBLING-DOWN*	
Split:	If Dealer's Upcard is:	Double-Down on:	If Dealer's Upcard is:
AA	Any Card	11	2 through 10
8,8	Any Card	10	2 through 8
9,9	4, 5, 6 and 8, 9	9	5 and 6
7,7	2 through 7	8	No (Hit)
6,6	5 and 6	A8	No (Stand)
4,4	No (Hit)	A7, A6	4 through 6
3,3	5 through 7	A5, A4	5 and 6
2,2	4 through 7	A3	6
		A2	No (Hit)

INSURANCE	*SURRENDER*
Do Not Take insurance	Do Not Surrender

*Substitute Atlantic City pair-splitting table if doubling-after-splitting is permitted.

Summary—Steps In Learning The Simple Plus/Minus.

Step 1. Learn to count down a 52-card deck in 25 seconds perfectly. To facilitate speed, hold the cards in your hands and push them from one hand to the other. Do *not* waste time by flipping them down one-by-one on a table or other surface.

Step 2. Learn the plus, basic and minus strategies by using the flash cards provided.

Step 3. When you've learned the count and the strategies, deal hands. Use the same number of decks as in the game you plan to play—one deck, two, four or six. Vary your bet in accordance with the Simple Plus/Minus betting strategy and vary your play in accordance with the strategies, in both cases using the appropriate Strike Numbers.

When you reach the end of the deck(s), your count should be at "zero." If it's not, continue practicing until your count is accurate 19-out-of-20 times through the deck(s).

Step 4. When you've reached the above accuracy, *and not until then,* try a casino test of your ability, betting the smallest possible units. The intention here is not that you make money but that you become accustomed to playing amid the distractions of a casino, with the pit-bosses checking you out and the dealers dealing at varying speeds.

Step 5. When you're totally comfortable playing a casino and are convinced that you're making few errors, practice at home once again to ensure that you still have the 19-out-of-20 accuracy.

Step 6. Establish your blackjack investment ($500, $1,000 or whatever) and play in a casino in accordance with the betting levels in Table 6-6. If at any point you feel you're playing inaccurately, *stop* and return for a few more hours of practice at home. Initially, do not play sessions of more than two or three hours. You may not feel fatigued, but the chances are that after a few hours you will start to make a few errors. Remember, your edge over the house is tiny, only 1% at most, so only a few errors per hour can totally eliminate your advantage—then you're playing for nothing.

After you've played the Simple Plus/Minus successfully for several hundred hours, you should find you can play it almost automatically. If you begin to feel that the Simple Plus/Minus is not challenging (and if you've shown winnings at least equal to the expected value), consider progressing to a professional level of play (that is, either the Advanced Plus/Minus, or the Uston Advanced Point Count).

The Uston Advanced Plus/Minus

If you plan to play the Simple Plus/Minus as discussed above, disregard this section. However, *after* having mastered the Simple Plus/Minus, if you feel you would like to upgrade your play to that of a professional level system, it is possible to use the Simple Plus/Minus

Simple Plus/Minus Flashcards—Atlantic City

Simple Plus/Minus Flashcards ATLANTIC CITY ONLY	Top: Plus Strategy Middle: Basic Strategy Bottom: Minus Strategy	**11** All 2-10 2-10
10 2-9 2-9 2-8	**9** 2-6 3-6 5-6	**8** 6 Hit Hit
A8 5-6 Stand Stand	**A7** 2-6 3-6 4-6	**A6** 2-6 3-6 4-6
A5 4-6 4-6 5-6	**A4** 4-6 4-6 5-6	**A3** 4-6 5-6 6

A2	**AA**	**9,9**
4-6 5-6 Hit	All All All	2-9,x7 2-9,x7 2-9,x7

8,8	**7,7**	**6,6**
2-9 2-9 2-9	2-7 2-7 2-7	2-6 2-6 2-6

4,4	**3,3**	**2,2**
5-6 5-6 Hit	2-7 2-7 2-7	2-7 2-7 2-7

A	**10**	**9**
4-7;12-17 5-7;12-17 12-17 Surrender	14-16 14-16 15-16 Surrender	16 (not 8,8) 16 (not 8,8) No Surrender

Simple Plus/Minus Flashcards—Nevada Single Deck

Simple Plus/Minus Flashcards **NEVADA SINGLE DECK ONLY**	**Top: Plus Strategy** **Middle: Basic Strategy** **Bottom: Minus Strategy** * If playing multiple deck, substitute appropriate basic strategy.	**11** All All* 2-10
10 2-9 2-9 2-8	**9** 2-6 2-6* 5-6	**8** 5,6 5,6* Hit
A8 5-6 6* Stand	**A7** 2-6 3-6 4-6	**A6** 2-6 2-6* 4-6
A5 4-6 4-6 5-6	**A4** 4-6 4-6 5-6	**A3** 4-6 4-6* 6

A2	AA	9,9
4-6 4-6* Hit	All All All	2-9,x7 2-9,x7 2-9,x7

8,8	7,7	6,6
All All All	2-7 2-7 2-7	2-6 2-6* 5-6

4,4	3,3	2,2
5,6 5,6* Hit	4-7 4-7 5-7	3-7 3-7* 4-7

A		10		9	
16 16 No	Surrender	15-16 15-16 No	Surrender	16 (not 8,8) No No	Surrender

card values. Instead of using the simplified Plus and Minus Strategy Tables in this chapter, you may convert to a half-deck true count (as discussed in Chapter 8) and use "Matrix Numbers" for determining the play of the hands.

The student desiring to play the Advanced Plus/Minus should use the numbers contained in Table 6-11 to determine if a deviation from Basic Strategy is required. You will note that many more plays will be made with the Advanced Plus/Minus than with the Simple Plus/Minus. (For example, with sufficiently high plus counts, the player may stand on 15 or 16 versus a 7 or 8, the player may double-down on a hard total of 7, the player may split 10's, or double on A,9.)

The use of the matrix and the means to convert the "running" count to the "true" count is covered completely in Chapter 8. The student desiring to play the Advanced Plus/Minus should in fact study Chapter 8, which discusses how to learn to play a professional system. The student should concentrate on the sections relating to true count conversion and the use of the numbers matrix. Since no side count of aces is necessary for the Advanced Plus/Minus, the section on ace adjustment may be disregarded. After *thoroughly* understanding the Chapter 8 material, the student should then memorize the numbers contained in the Advanced Plus/Minus Numbers Matrix (Table 6-11).

You may generate your own flashcards for the Uston Advanced Plus/Minus System by following a procedure similar to the one used in Chapter 8 to generate flashcards for the Uston Advanced Point Count System. However, if you wish to obtain ready-made flashcards, on index cardboard stock, for all of the systems discussed in this book, please see pages 312-313 for details and ordering information.

To make this section self-contained, the use of the numbers matrix is briefly discussed here.

—The student should convert his running count to the true count by dividing the number of half-decks remaining to be played.

—If the true count which results *equals or exceeds the plus numbers* in Table 6-11, the student should stand, double-down, split pairs or surrender, contrary to Basic Strategy.

—If the true count that results *is equal to or is below* (a bigger minus) *the minus numbers* in Table 6-11, the student should hit; he should not double-down, not split pairs and not surrender, contrary to Basic Strategy.

The student playing the Advanced Plus/Minus is using a system with the efficiency of the counts at the lower end of the professional level range—roughly comparable to the Braun (Wong High-Low) and Hi Opt I strategies.

If the student desires to devote his time and energy to learn the very best of systems available, he should learn the Uston Advanced Point Count, using the steps outlined in Chapter 8. The additional efficiency of such a system does not come free, however, as the point values are more difficult and a side count of aces must be kept.

Table 6—11

Advanced Plus/Minus Numbers Matrix

Note: Deviate from Basic Strategy if the half-deck *true* count equals or exceeds the numbers in the matrix.

The numbers are composite numbers for both single and multiple deck games.

Where two numbers appear in the box, the top number is for single deck, and the lower number is for multiple deck.

INSURANCE: Insure with a True Count of:
+ 1 in single deck
+ 1½ in multiple decks.

HITTING OR STANDING
Dealer's Upcard

You Have:	2	3	4	5	6	7	8	9	10	A
17										− 4
16						+6	+5	+3	0	+4
15	− 3	− 4	− 4	− 5	− 5	+6	+6	+4	+2	+5
14	− 2	− 3	− 4	− 4	− 4	+8				+7
13	−½	− 1	− 2	− 3	− 3					
12	+2	+1	0	− 1	− 1					
7,7									−1**	
A7										−½ / +1

** With 7,7 versus 10, single deck ONLY, stand unless true count is − 1 or lower; then hit.

With A7 versus Ace, in single deck, hit if −½ or lower. In multiple deck, stand if +1 or higher.

HARD DOUBLING
Dealer's Upcard

You Have:	2	3	4	5	6	7	8	9	10	A
11	− 6	− 7	− 7	− 7	− 8	− 5	− 3	− 2	− 2	−½ / +½
10	− 5	− 5	− 6	− 6	− 7	− 3	− 2	− 1	+2	+2
9	+1	−½	− 1	− 3	− 3	+2	+4			
8	+8	+5	+3	+2	+1	+7				
7			+6	+5	+5					

Table 6—11 (Continued)

SOFT DOUBLING

You Have:	Dealer's Upcard					
	2	3	4	5	6	7
A9	+5	+5	+4	+3	+3	+7
A8	+5	+3	+2	+½	+½	+8
A7	+1	−2	−4	−5	−6	
A6	−½ / +½	−3	−4	−6	−7	
A5		+2	−2	−4	−7	
A4		+3	−½	−3	−5	
A3		+4	+½	−2	−3	
A2		+4	+2	−2 / 0	−2	

SPLITTING PAIRS

You Have:	Dealer's Upcard									
	2	3	4	5	6	7	8	9	10	A
AA	−8	−8	−8	−8	−8	−6	−5	−4	−5	−5/3
10,10	+6	+4	+3	+3	+3	+7				
9,9	0 / −1	−2	−3	−3	−3	+4	−5	−6		+3
8,8									④	*
7,7	−6	−7	−8	−9						
6,6	0 / +2	0	−2	−3	−4					
5,5										
4,4										
3,3	+4	+2	−2	−2	⑥					
2,2	+4	+1	−2	−3						

*Numbers in a circle ◯ designate the true count at which NOT to split (stand on 8,8 versus 10 and hit 3,3 versus 7).

Table 6—11 (Continued)

See note on page 51 concerning Atlantic City surrender options.

Atlantic City Modifications

Notes: Deviate from Basic Strategy if the half-deck *true* count equals or exceeds the numbers in the matrix.

All player hands on this page are hard hands, unless otherwise indicated.

EARLY SURRENDER

You Hold:	Dealer's Upcard			
	8	9	10	A
17		+6	+3	Su
16	+4	0	−3	Su
15	+4	+2	−2	Su
14	+6	+4	0	Su
13	+7	+5	+2	−7
12				−5
8,8		+4	−2	Su
7			+7	−5
6			+6	−3
5			+6	0
2,2			+7	+1

Su = Surrender regardless of count.

For simplicity, while not quite accurate, play 7,7 as a 14.

DOUBLE-DOWN AFTER PAIR-SPLITTING

You Hold:	Dealer's Upcard						
	2	3	4	5	6	7	A
9,9	−2	−3	−3	−4	−4	+2	+4
7,7							
6,6	−1	−2	−3	−4	−6		
4,4		+4	+2	$-\frac{2}{0}$	−½		
3,3	−1	−4	−6	−6	−8		
2,2	−2	−3	−4	−5	−7		

Replace the numbers in the Splitting Pairs Matrix in this table with the numbers above if double-after-splits is allowed.

Table 6—11 (Continued)

Other Modifications:

All player hands on this page are hard hands, unless otherwise indicated.

CONVENTIONAL SURRENDER

You Hold:	Dealer's Upcard			
	8	9	10	A
17		+6	+5	
16	+4	+1 / 0	-2	-1
15	+4	+2	0	+1
14	+6	+4	+2	+3
13	+7	+5	+3	+5
8,8		+4	+2	
7,7	+6	+1	0	+1

IF DEALER HITS SOFT 17
(E.G.: RENO, TAHOE,
DOWNTOWN VEGAS)

You Hold:	Dealer's Upcard	
	6	A
17		-3
16	-8	+2
15	-7	+3
14	-5	+5
13	-3	
12	-3	
A7	-7	Hit
A6	-8	
A5	-8	
9,9	-5	+3

Note: In some cases, particularly where the player should take action based on the specific card denominations of his hand, we have used a representative number applicable to all situations. Experience has shown, over and over again, that the minor gain from trying to remember minor refinements is offset many times over by player confusion and hence, error.

Chapter Seven

How We Won $4,000,000 Part 2 (Teams 3 and 4)

Team 3 And The Perfect Blackjack Player

In January 1977, a fellow I'll call Jerry H. phoned me at the Jockey Club in Las Vegas and said he'd developed a practical computer that could play perfect blackjack in a casino, far beyond the capability of the human mind—or for that matter, of a dozen human minds. Although I was skeptical, since most calls of this type never seem to pan out, I was impressed with Jerry's sincerity and intelligence, and I accepted his offer to meet with him for a demonstration.

The computer he brought with him was impressive. It needed some alterations to make it practical, but there was no question in my mind that Jerry had a viable money-making tool. I suggested some changes and told him that I would finance the effort. He returned home, made the changes, and in several weeks, returned with a revised version of the computer, which we both agreed, for security purposes, to refer to as "George."

George had been made possible by very recent technological advances in microelectronics. The input device consisted of four buttons which were programmed in a code called binary. The first button represented the value "1;" the second, "2;" the third, "4;" and the fourth, "8." Any number from 1 through 15 could be entered into the computer by pushing the correct combination of buttons. For example, the 1, 2 and 4 buttons pushed together represented the number "7" to the computer.

The computer itself (called the CPU for Central Processing Unit) was about as long and wide as a pack of cigarettes and half as thick. It consisted of a series of small electronic components of all shapes and colors. The components were epoxied to the unit so that if George were ever to fall into inquiring hands, the coating would have to be smashed, thus fragmenting the components and effectively destroying the system.

The output device was a small tapper which we fitted into an empty plastic rouge case. The tapper vibrated with dot-dash signals which designated numerical information. For example, a dot (a short vibration) represented 1; a dash (a longer vibration) represented 3. Thus, two dots and two dashes represented the value 8. We also had codes for the correct method of playing blackjack hands. One dot signalled that the optimum play was to hit; a dash designated stand; two dashes, double-down; three dashes, split pairs; and two dots, surrender. Finally, attached to the computer was a battery pack, two groups of four conventional batteries that powered the system for about four to six hours before they had to be replaced.

A First Unsuccessful Attempt. My Jockey Club condominium turned from a blackjack training headquarters with flashcards to an electronics workshop, replete with batteries, battery chargers, soldering guns, wires, proms and electronic components of all varieties.

I started practicing with Jerry. He would deal hands and I would try to enter into the computer accurately and rapidly enough to play in a casino. At the end of the deck, we would test my accuracy by asking George which card denominations were left in the deck. If we received the correct answer, we knew that my input fingerwork had been accurate. It was a long, arduous practice period; more than once did I become discouraged, convinced the project wouldn't work. Finally, more than two weeks later, both Jerry and I agreed that I was ready to give George a casino test.

On February 1, 1977, I took George into the Golden Gate casino in downtown Vegas. The system was attached to an ace bandage wound around my left thigh. I cut out my left pants pocket so my fingers could operate the keyboard. The output device was taped to a very sensitive part of my body so that I would feel the betting and playing signals accurately.

As I walked into the casino, I felt ill at ease and a little paranoid. I sat down at a $5 table (a high limit table for the tiny casino) and began playing the "nickel" ($5) level, betting from $5 to $20 at the single-deck game. I found that George responded accurately and my nervousness left. One of my cerebral blackjack teammates watched my game, employing a conventional count as I played George's count. He later stated that the differences in betting and playing strategy were substantial; George was far more accurate than the conventional counting system. After two hours of play, I won $190 and felt totally comfortable with my electronic companion.

I convened my team of blackjack players and outlined the plan (at the time, I was administering a team of eight card counters). The plan was to have the players pair off and work in teams. One player would stand by the table and operate the counting device while the other player would sit at the table and receive the computer's signals through the a tapper located on the instep of his shoe. The signal would tell the player at the table whether to hit, stand, surrender or double-down, and how much money to bet. By separating the counting and betting functions of the game, I hoped to minimize the risk of being noticed by the pitbosses, as the player at the table would be looking only at his own cards and not those of the other players.

It took about four weeks to train four counters to operate George proficiently. Jerry returned to his lab to produce more computers and accompanying transmitters and receivers. While the players were training, I would disguise myself and take the George that was functioning into the casinos. I was hoping to win enough money to make the operation self-supporting.

The next four weeks were hectic. I played two sessions each day and was dealt mostly single deck games at the Stardust, Hilton and Dunes. I began by playing quarters ($25 chips) and graduated to blacks ($100 chips). George and I were winning at a rate of over 2%, higher than any of our previous team winning rates. After several weeks, George and I had won $23,000 for the team.

Our training sessions were going more slowly than expected and many technical problems developed with the computers. We had to solder broken connections, replace old batteries, fix loose switches and solve a myriad of technological problems. When the players began casino play, they made serious errors. George still had some "bugs" (errors) and would occasionally tilt.

Team morale was low and arguments were frequent. My win had been eaten up by expenses, and the effort was now in the hole by $20,000. After working seven days per week for six weeks, I decided to take a two-week break for much needed R and R. I went to Europe for a few weeks where, using my brain for a change, I won about $5,000 in London and Loews' Monte Carlo.

A Second Try. After my return to Vegas, I called Jerry. While I was away, he had done a lot to keep our effort going. Three of the "counters" we had recruited became disillusioned and had left the team. I didn't have to wonder long how we would replace them. While I was in Europe, Jerry had trained two of his sons and his daughter to operate George. Our team now had six experienced counters: Jerry, me, one of the original counters and Jerry's three children.

My job was to recruit "big players" (BP's)—teammates who would wear electronic shoes with radio receivers. Potential big players, at first skeptical, would scratch their heads in amazement when they saw George and observed the "magic shoes" as we called them. After all, imagine having a custom-made pair of shoes that automatically signalled how much to bet on each hand and how to play each hand perfectly. To cite an example of the power of George, the computer went through over 200,000 processing steps in making a decision before transmitting the answer on whether to split pairs.

George would often signal us to make weird plays, which we would initially question. We were told to hit hard 17 and make such unbelievable plays as splitting 6's against a dealer's ace and doubling-down on hard 12 or 13. But we became convinced George was right; unlike the card counter, George knew the denomination of every card remaining to be played. We hoped these erratic plays would mislead the pitbosses into thinking our big players were fools and big losers.

After three more weeks of training, we were ready. We had eight Georges, six totally-trained counters and five trained big players. We decided to play graveyard shift (which runs from 4 a.m. to noon in the Vegas casinos) for several reasons. We knew that casinos assign their least-experienced pitbosses to the graveyard shift. Furthermore, the casinos would be less crowded, making it easier to select dealers who tended not to shuffle prematurely. We would play only single deck clubs initially, since single deck games are the most statistically favorable to the card counter.

We would send out four teams every night at 4 a.m. I would man the telephone in the condominium to receive calls from teammates who had problems. I would dispatch alternate counters with fresh batteries to relieve counters already out in the "field."

By the third night, we began to feel the power of George. In normal card counting, we expect on average to win about 60% of the sessions. With George, we were winning at the rate of 80%. The pitbosses seemed bamboozled, and after six days, we were up $59,000.

We distributed the win to the team members, giving each member his envelope and a pep talk, urging them to continue training for further accuracy. Most needed no urging. Jerry's youngest son, only 18 (but with false identification because it's necessary to be 21-years-old to play in a Nevada casino), was personally reimbursed $1,500 for less than a week's work. He kept shaking his head as he saw the team's bankroll grow. With our $50,000 starting bank and our first $59,000 win, we had over $100,000 in cash in the condominium.

After two more days of training, we began again. Some humorous things happened, though they seemed like crises at the time. Jerry's daughter, counting with George in the Stardust, felt George getting really warm.

She steadfastly stayed at the table, pushing the buttons of the computer for the big player, braving the heat which kept increasing in intensity. After a few minutes, she noticed smoke pouring out from under her skirt. She quickly ran to the women's room and found that the batteries were smoking. She disconnected them and taxied back to the team meeting room. Jerry prevented this problem from occurring again by putting fuses in the batteries and devising an asbestos casing for the batteries.

92

One counter dropped his transmitter in the Marina Casino. I phoned the security desk there and said, "Hi, I'm Dr. Smith from Phoenix. I think I lost my hearing aid in your casino. It's green and about 5 by 6 inches."

"Oh yes, doctor. We've found it."

I put on my disguise and retrieved the transmitter from the security guard, tipping him $5 for his trouble.

Our big players were getting comped all over town. One stayed in a suite at Caesars Palace, another was comped at the Marina, one at the Stardust and one at the Riviera. They would be given comps to the shows and dinners by the bosses who thought our people were losing suckers. The bosses hoped they would give their casinos the "action." Once we had four tables occupied at Palace Court, the expensive gourmet room at Caesars—all our teammates, courtesy of the house. While there, our people pretended not to know each other.

Our team continued to win, but we started to notice suspicious looking men following our teammates from casino to casino. At first, we thought they were thieves, looking for an opportune time to rip off our big players. But the same people kept reappearing in different casinos and the familiar face of one of the agents from the Griffin Detective Agency was spotted.

One of our big players was asked to leave the Hilton, our first computer barring. But we kept playing in other casinos and after just over a week, our total win with George amounted to $130,000. We again distributed the win to our players. Because of the "heat" in Vegas, we decided to move to Northern Nevada after a short break.

We packed up cartons and cartons of electronic gear, and the team split up temporarily. Jerry and his family returned to the San Francisco area. Other team members went to Los Angeles for the wedding of a former teammate. I stayed in Vegas and partied.

We were all convinced by now that we would win $2 or $3 million in the remaining seven months of 1977. Our "magic machine" was working beautifully; we had a finely-tuned organization of hard-working dedicated counters and big players, plenty of capital and lots of optimism. Our overconfidence would lead to serious problems when we introduced George to the casinos in Lake Tahoe.

Another Bust. Lake Tahoe is far more beautiful than Las Vegas. I rented a large house high up in the hills. The house looked out over the huge, deep blue lake and had a view of the mountains which were still snowcapped, even though it was May. I thought, "What a beautiful place to be making money."

We also rented several motel rooms, since our team had now grown to 15 members. Jerry drove up with his two sons and his daughter in a large van to accommodate the bulky electronic gear necessary for our computer blackjack endeavor. The rest of the team arrived from Los Angeles, Las Vegas and San Francisco.

I brought $70,000 in cash to finance our operation. On the first night, I scouted the three large casinos at Tahoe—Harrah's, Harvey's and the Sahara—while the counters practiced operating George. Jerry set up shop in the attic of the house, which was conveniently configured in one huge 30 x 30 foot room. A ping-pong table held the many pairs of electronic shoes and other components necessary for our operation. I made out a team schedule for the following day's play. We all retired early to get a good night's sleep prior to what we hoped would be a profitable and undetected assault upon the Tahoe casinos.

The following morning, I dispatched four teams to the casinos, each team consisting of one counter and one big player. Once again, I manned the phone that we had installed in order to reschedule and reassign the players if problems arose.

Our big players were betting from one hand of $100 to two hands of $1,000 (or up to three hands of $500 in the one $500 limit club). After several hours, the first team returned to the house. They had won $14,000—a good start. We fully expected to extract $100,000 or so from the Lake before travelling farther north to Reno. Then, we would return to Vegas and play the day shift there for a week or two.

Team optimism was high. We continued winning 80% of the sessions with George. It appeared that nothing could stop us from making well into seven figures over the next several months.

The second session of the day was also a winner, but not as profitable. When all four teams returned, we found we were up $20,000 for the morning session. We'd won another $6,000.

The following day at 1 p.m., I dispatched four teams once again and sat down by the phone. It didn't ring until 4 p.m., which I thought was a good sign. When the team was having trouble with equipment or finding a favorable table, the phone would ring frequently and I would have to redeploy the troops. When the team was "down," that is, playing and getting in lots of hands per hour, the phone rarely rang. As I picked up the phone, I wondered if perhaps we'd won $50,000 for the trip yet. At the levels we were betting, that kind of win would have been realistic.

It was Harry, a big player. "Ken, there's this guy across the pit who's taking my picture. Whenever I look at him, he ducks. When I turn away, he pulls out a camera."

I knew Harrah's was into photography (they had photographed some of my teammates on former trips). I felt Harry would probably get barred there soon, but decided that as long as he was "down," he might as well get as many hands in as necessary. We could use Harry later in other casinos. So I told him, "Hell, why not go back and play it? What have we got to lose? If they bar you, we'll just send you somewhere else."

The other teams hadn't checked in yet. I thought this was curious, but things seemed to be going well.

At 5 p.m., one counter, Rich, called. "Hi, Rich. What's happening?"

"I'm in jail," Rich said.

"Oh, no. What happened?"

Well, I was in Harrah's, playing with Harry. They pulled me into one back room. They searched me, found George and arrested me. I'm at the Zephyr Cove jail now. My bail is $2,000."

"Don't worry, Rich. Someone will be right down."

"Better bring some more bail money. There's a few more of us coming here, too."

Just then, Harry walked in the door. "I couldn't find Rich. He just disappeared. So I left the casino."

I was surprised that they hadn't arrested Harry too. Then the phone rang again. It was Jerry's oldest son. He, too, had been arrested, as had another one of our big players.

I dispatched one of our teammates to the jail with our people. They'd been charged with "bunco-steering," a Nevada gambling crime. The computers were confiscated and our teammates would not be arraigned until the district attorney could be reached to evaluate this rather unusual arrest.

Jerry was shaken. His underage son had been arrested. We decided that agents might be searching the area for the rest of the team. We quickly packed up the electronic gear, grabbed the team's bank (now $90,000 after paying the bail) and hid it in a cigarette carton box.

The team dispersed. Some drove back to Las Vegas, others to Los Angeles and San Francisco. I drove back to my San Francisco apartment with three teammates. The next day, I contacted lawyers. One lawyer wanted a retainer of $25,000 to handle the case. A second lawyer was interested in the civil rights aspect of the case and offered to do it on a time-and-expense basis. I chose the latter.

It turned out we had underestimated the exchange of intelligence among the Tahoe casinos. In Vegas, it's rare that one casino communicates information to others. But in Tahoe, $25 chip players are rare; $100 players stand out even more. For there to be four players simultaneously betting up to two hands of $1,000 was clearly unusual. Casino personnel apparently had exchanged information and for some reason they had decided to search Rich. To this day, we have no idea why we were picked up or how our computers came to be suspected. Some suggest that the casino had a radio-band scanning device. We'll probably never know for sure.

Jerry's wife had been applying pressure on him to get out of the blackjack business. The arrest of his son clinched it for her. I decided to "cool it" for a few months to see how the legal issue would be resolved. We put George on the shelf and I cancelled any blackjack play for the summer of 1977.

After a month, the Nevada Commission turned George over to the FBI to determine if George was a "cheating device" and thus, contrary to the Nevada statutes. The local FBI was baffled by George and sent it to Washington. It took the FBI five months before they reported back to the Commission that, in their opinion, George was not a cheating device but just a computer. The charges against our players were dismissed. The Commission refused to return the Georges to us. We considered instituting legal action for the Georges' return, but decided against it. If we ever decided to revitalize George, we reasoned, we had plenty of others.

It was ironic. We had baffled tougher Vegas bosses for weeks with George. On the second day in Tahoe, our team effort was dealt a mortal blow by what we considered to be far less experienced pit personnel.

I often look back on that little house on the lake with its electronics shop, the electronics genius Jerry, and the six highly-trained counters and five big players with their custom-designed "magic shoes." It was about as close to a real money machine as I've ever seen in my life.

After that experience, I left the world of electronic blackjack permanently for cerebral blackjack. I admit to often wondering just how much the team might have won with a more cautious approach. But, that's hindsight reasoning. Besides, we did make some money and it was an unforgettable experience.

Team 4 And The Gorilla BP's

After Team 3 broke up, the games in Las Vegas still offered an attractive opportunity for making money, but there was a serious problem. I was becoming more and more recognized by pitbosses in nearly every Vegas casino. Further, many of the good players with whom I'd worked in the past were getting heat in the casinos. In fact, one ex-pitboss, bitter at his former employer, provided me with pages of the Griffin Mug book in which were listed an appalling number of ex-teammates, with photographs.

I decided to take one of our ideas from Team 3. You'll recall that we had a "counter," who pushed the computer buttons, and a BP, who merely sat at the table with his "magic shoes" that told him how much to bet and how to play his hand. This type of BP, which we call a "gorilla BP," could drink, not look at any cards (theoretically he need not even look at his hand or the dealer's upcard), talk continually and act like the typical Vegas partying loser. The idea was to duplicate this configuration, but without the computer.

We'd have counters, either at the table or "on the rail" (standing behind the table watching the game) who would count and signal the BP how to bet and play the hands. The counters, we hoped, would get little heat since they were not playing, or if they were playing, would be betting only the table minimum. We felt that most of the players who had previously gotten heat could probably get away with this; I would wear disguises.

I went to Mike Westmore, the well-known Hollywood make-up man. He fitted me with false noses, teeth and wigs, and gave me a complete make-up kit. Pictures of many of the disguises, if you're interested, are shown in *One-Third of a Shoe* (7).

I got on the phone and "Sting"-style summoned some of the best counters in the world. They were in San Francisco, Vegas, Los Angeles and Texas. Eventually, we convened in Vegas and agreed to proceed with the plan.

BP's were recruited—people who didn't know how to count at blackjack, but who would be disciplined enough to understand that they must do exactly what the counters signal them to do—regardless of their hunches. They obviously had to be totally honest—we'd be giving them $10,000 to $20,000 and relying on them to report back their results accurately. While the counter would also be on the scene to provide some control, it's often difficult during the heat of battle for the counter to know, sometimes within three or four thousand dollars, how the BP did.

Our initial bankroll was $50,000. We planned to play until we doubled the bank, hoping that, as in the past, it would take about nine or ten days. We started by playing single deck clubs only, primarily the Stardust, Hilton, Sahara and Circus. We found it far more difficult to "get hours in" playing with our sub-teams of two, since the counter could not freely change from table to table when his game became unfavorable (usually due to premature shuffling) and since our little ploy would become obvious if the BP followed the counter all over the casino. When a game turned "bad," we were forced to call the session off.

Initially, our hours played were low and our results reflected this. After being ahead $15,000 in three days, we were back to even after two weeks of five counters and five BP's working full time (two sessions per day).

We played full tables so the counter could blend in with the crowd. While two rounds of a seven-player game was slow—65 to 75 hands per hour—it was a beatable game. We knew we were facing a slow grind, but at first we had no idea how slow the grind would be. Worse, our error rate was high, as the signalling between the counter and BP was slow, sloppy, or in some cases, just wrong.

After a month of playing full time, we were in the hole by $15,000. Some teammates were becoming discouraged. I tried to drum up as much enthusiasm as possible and we "kept on truckin'." A favorite expression of ours at the time was, "We have the advantage . . . but they have the money."

There were some interesting episodes. I appeared on the Frank Rosenthal TV show (Rosenthal was with the Stardust at the time) discussing card-counting. I wore a false beard so people wouldn't know I'd shaved my beard off. Also on the show were the casino managers of the Golden Nugget and the Hacienda. On the show, I counted down a deck and recited the value of the last card. All three casino people seemed impressed by this and concluded by saying, "We wouldn't let you play in *our* casinos."

The irony: on the very day of the show, we beat the Golden Nugget for $4,000. On the day after the show, we beat the Hacienda for $3,200.

The last play of that bank was one of the most unconventional we'd experienced and, at the time, it infuriated me—although I think it's funny now. A counter, call him Mike, and a BP, call him John, were playing at the Castaways. The pitbosses were giving Mike extreme heat, staring at him, remarking that he was giving signals and discussing him loudly so he could hear.

Mike signalled "end-of session" to John and quickly left the casino. John, who had been putting on his act, was half-drunk at that point. Mike came back to the Jockey Club. After a half-hour, there was no word from John. We dispatched a teammate to the Castaways to find him. He found John still sitting at the table, now totally drunk, betting $500 per hand. He had piles and piles of black chips in front of him. He got John out of the casino and back to the Jockey Club.

He responded, slurring, "I didn't want to make it obvious and leave the same time as Mike. So I stayed and played Basic Strategy." (John no more knew Basic Strategy than I knew how to speak Russian!)

He continued, "The cards were running good, so I kept betting $500 a hand. I won $6,000!"

John couldn't understand why the team, instead of praising him, berated him for irresponsibility. Ironically, though, John's win put us over the top—the bank was now doubled. The next day, we had a long, disciplinary talk with John—and taught all our BP's Basic Strategy.

It had taken 56 days to double the first bank. We decided to let Vegas cool off a bit and we moved to Northern Nevada. The "Gorilla BP" act totally hoodwinked the Tahoe and Reno bosses. We were getting far greater betting ratios because of this and our error rate dropped dramatically. The dealers, as is usually the case in Northern Nevada, were dealing much further into the deck. The result: we doubled three banks in 2½ weeks, winning over $200,000. Then, we returned to Vegas with a plan that we felt would totally outwit the Vegas bosses.

Our BP's had to pick up their cards so that the counter could see their hands. This seemed to be a weakness in our system, one that could draw heat from the bosses. We felt that if the counter obviously could *not* see the BP's hand, there was no way the bosses would snap to the fact that the BP was getting signals. We devised a set of signals so the BP could communicate the content of his hand to the counter by the placement of his hand on the table. Thus, the counter could sit at first base; the BP could sit at third base and, we hoped, there'd be no way the bosses would put the two together.

The signalling system was a complicated one because the counter had to know not only the total of the BP's hand, but whether the BP had a pair or a soft hand. We trained for two weeks before trying our new system. Our first play was in November 1977.

Our error rate was appalling and the results reflected this. We optimistically, and wrongly, assumed the error rate would drop and kept playing, instead of taking time off for training (there's a *real* lesson here). After a week, we were down $70,000. Everyone claimed the error rate was going down. The counters had a tough job. They had to keep the count and the number of aces, play their hands according to Basic Strategy, interpret the BP's signals, make the calculations and signal the BP what to do. The losses continued, but the counters insisted they were playing accurately. This led us to suspect BP dishonesty and we conducted some polygraphs. The BP's checked out, but our losses continued.

By Christmas, we were down $139,000. We suspended operations for some training and practice. The real reason for the losses became obvious. The practice sessions were appalling: the counters were misreading signals, dropping the count and sending erroneous signals. The BP's were sending the wrong signals and reading the counters' returning signals incorrectly.

We'd learned an expensive lesson. Merely playing a winning game of blackjack is tough enough. Playing and signalling to a BP is more difficult, but feasible. But playing, reading BP signals, counting and signalling back is virtually impossible for even an accomplished counter to do accurately. We dropped our little scheme, poorer but wiser. To this day, when we set up plays, we use the old army theory of "KISS"—*Keep It Simple, Stupid.*

Team 4 continued to play, without the elaborate signals. We slowly recovered, but it took us months to recoup the November-December loss. We played for most of 1978 and ended with a profitable year. But, the games in Vegas kept deteriorating. Eventually, whenever we put black chips into play, we'd draw heat. (In the "old days," black chips would take heat off, the bosses apparently thinking, "These guys are so rich they don't have to play blackjack to make money.")

Word was out that we were around—we'd been working in town for nearly a year. By fall of 1978, we found it virtually impossible to get a good game. We worked with some known high-rolling losers, which was successful for a while. They'd put up the money and we'd supply the counting ability—we'd split the win.

But the games kept deteriorating and eventually Team 4 broke up. Most of the team left Nevada for other pursuits. I decided to take an exploratory trip to Atlantic City, not suspecting that there'd be some exciting times in New Jersey in 1979.

The story is continued in Chapter 13.

Chapter Eight

The Uston Advanced Point Count

This chapter provides the material needed by the student interested in becoming a professional level player. The first portion of the chapter, describing the principles behind professional level systems and comparing the major systems, should be of general interest. The second portion of the chapter presents the Uston Advanced Point Count, discusses ways to practice and train, and includes tests our teammates use in determining whether the player is ready for casino play.

As we will see, professional level systems are based on the identical ingredients. Thus, this chapter can be used by the student of Uston APC, Hi Opt I or II, the Revere APC, or other counts as an assist in preparing for casino play.

Several of the one-level systems, notably the Uston Advanced Plus/Minus and the Braun Count, do not require a side count of aces (the aces are assigned a minus value for betting purposes). For students of these counts, the section pertaining to counting aces and adjusting for them can be disregarded.

Can You Play a Multi-Level Professional Count?

I know many players who use multi-level professional counts. There has been much reluctance among blackjack authors to recommend the use of multi-level counts. With the exception of the late Lawrence Revere, most well-known authors imply that it's not worth the effort to learn such a count. I believe the primary reason for this is that the authors don't use these counts themselves and thus, don't have a personal knowledge of the relative difference in learning and using multi-level counts versus one-level counts.

I know dozens of players, teammates and non-teammates alike, who play counts such as the Revere APC, Hi Opt II and the Uston APC. One player uses an even more complicated 17-count, and another, a 25-count!

The time necessary to thoroughly learn a multi-level count is equivalent to the time needed to become only an average chess, bridge or backgammon player. It takes no longer than the time some people spend in front of their TV sets in a month. Further, once you learn it thoroughly, it stays with you (although brush-up practice is required). Yet I continually hear, "It's too hard!" "It's not worth it!" or "You can't really use it in a casino."

The obvious answer to the challenge of learning so-called difficult material is to devise methods which facilitate quick learning. Our teams have developed some clever training aids, such as numbers flashcards, ace adjustment tests and true count conversion shortcuts, and have been using them for years. The inclusion of all such material in this and other chapters should help others to learn multi-level counts without difficulty.

I also hear, "You don't get that much more from the professional counts." Let me respond to that by citing just one experience:

During the winter of 1979-80, we had nine players in Atlantic City (the episode is described in detail in Chapter 13). All nine of us counted aces separately, adjusted to true counts and were given and passed the tests in this and subsequent chapters. There was another group of players, fully as dedicated and disciplined as we were, who played a one-level count with no side count of aces.

Coincidentally, both of our groups averaged close to 1,000 hours of play, a fairly healthy sample size. Our group averaged $350 per hour; their group averaged $150 per hour.

I'd do a lot of studying to be able to earn an additional $200 per hour.

Logic Flow of Professional Level Card Counting

Most professional level counting systems follow the logic depicted in Table 8-1.

Card Values. Values are assigned to specific card denominations, plus values for the small cards played and minus values for high cards (Box A). The total value of all plus cards equals the total value of all minus cards, so that the value of the completely counted deck(s) will total zero.

Running Count. The card values are kept cumulatively as play progresses through the deck(s)—the total of which is called the "running count" (Box B).

Table 8—1

Flow Chart of Principles Underlying
Professional Level Card Counting

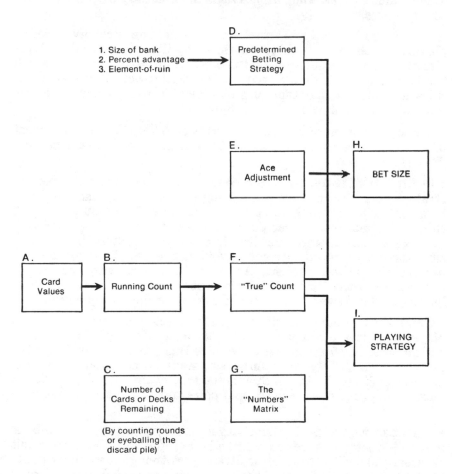

1. Size of bank
2. Percent advantage
3. Element-of-ruin

D. Predetermined Betting Strategy

E. Ace Adjustment

H. BET SIZE

A. Card Values

B. Running Count

F. "True" Count

I. PLAYING STRATEGY

C. Number of Cards or Decks Remaining

(By counting rounds or eyeballing the discard pile)

G. The "Numbers" Matrix

True Count. The impact of a given running count is affected by the number of cards or decks remaining to be played (Box C). As we have mentioned, with a running count of +10 in a typical system, the situation is more favorable or rich to the player with one-half deck remaining to be played, than it is with 5½ decks remaining to be played. Thus, the running count must be mathematically adjusted for the number of cards or decks remaining, giving what we call the "true count" (Box F). (It's not necessary to count the number of cards; there are shortcuts as we will see.)

Betting Strategy The stronger professional level systems assign a zero value to the ace, since the ace has a minor effect on *playing* strategy—it actually works slightly to the advantage of the dealer in playing situations. Thus, the player must keep a separate count of aces and adjust the true count for ace-richness or ace-poorness to calculate proper bet size. We call this "ace adjustment" (Box E). The simpler professional systems (The Advanced Plus/Minus, Braun) assign a minus value to aces, which thus avoids the necessity of keeping a side count of aces.)

All serious players must first devise a betting strategy, whether playing nickels or black chips. This strategy (Box D) is based on (1) the size of the player's bankroll, (2) the percentage advantage he has over the house, which is determined by the strength of his play and the rules, and (3) the risk of tapping out or losing the entire bank (the "element of ruin" with which he is willing to live).

The combination of the betting strategy (Box D), ace adjustment (Box E) and the true count (Box F) determines the player's bet size (Box H).

Playing Strategy. The true count affects not only the betting strategy, but also impacts the playing strategy. For example, Basic Strategy calls for hitting a 15 against a dealer's 10. Computer analysis shows that with a sufficiently high true count, it is to the player's advantage to stand, since the deck is disproportionately rich in high cards (the player is thus better off avoiding the risk of hitting and hoping for the dealer to bust). As we have shown with the Simple Plus/Minus, with a "plus" true count, the player will stand more readily, and double-down, split pairs and surrender more frequently.

Similarly, in minus situations, when the deck is rich in low cards, the player will often hit hands contrary to Basic Strategy. For example, with a total of 15 against a dealer's 2, Basic Strategy calls for the player to stand. However, in sufficiently negative count situations, the player would hit the 15. With a minus true count, the player will hit more readily, and double-down, split pairs and surrender less frequently.

All responsible professional level systems offer a "numbers' matrix"—that is, a series of numbers reflecting the true count necessary to deviate from Basic Strategy. Although it would be possible to express the data in other ways, such as verbal statements, a matrix is smaller in physical size and lends itself to memorization. For example, in the Uston Advanced Point Count, with a true count of +4 or higher, the player would stand on 15 versus a dealer's 10. With a true count of −7 or lower, the player would hit 15 versus a dealer's 2 upcard. There are approximately 150 numbers such as the two examples above that must be memorized by the serious player.

A comparison of the true count (Box F) with the appropriate "number" memorized from the numbers matrix (Box G) determines the player's correct playing strategy (Box I).

This chapter will discuss each of these functions and take the reader through the steps to learn each function perfectly. We will also include tests that the reader may administer to himself to determine if he is ready for casino play. The relative efficiency of professional level systems was discussed in Chapter Six and summarized in Table 6-1a. If you are not reading this text continuously, you might want to read that section again.

Comparison of Professional Level Blackjack Systems

Table 8-2 compares the major systems from several standpoints. The first ten lines (under Line A—Card Values) show the card values that each system assigns to each card denomination. The four one-level counts (to the right of the vertical line) are obviously the simplest—the cards have values of +1 or −1.

Hi Opt II constitutes what we call a two-level count—the card denominations are assigned values of ±1 and ±2. The Uston APC is a three-level count, with values of 1, 2 and 3. The Revere APC is a four level count, since the 5 is assigned a value of +4.

Griffin's (27) studies have indicated that once a system progresses beyond the third level, there are minor amounts to be gained in efficiency. He discovered that the optimum five-level count is actually less powerful than the optimum four-level count (which, interestingly, is not the Revere APC). The optimum four-level count is only minutely more powerful than the optimum three-level count (which is the Uston APC).

Five of the seven systems require that the ace be counted separately and for a calculation to be made prior to betting: the number of aces (rich or poor) times the "ace adjustment factor" must be added to or subtracted from the running count prior to calculation of the true count. The ace adjustment factors range from one through four, depending upon the system (indicated on Line B).

As shown on Line C, to derive the true count, the two Hi Opt counts and the Braun count adjust the running count by dividing the number of *full* decks remaining to be played. The Uston, Revere and Advanced Plus/Minus adjust to the nearest half-deck. While this factor is not critical, players seem to prefer a half-deck true count since, in multiple deck games, the running count is always divided by a whole number, an easier calculation. For example, when one half-deck has been played from a four deck shoe, we divide by 7 (7 half-decks remain in 3½ full decks). Hi Opt and DHM players must divide by 3½, which can foster inaccuracy.

Line D rates the five systems for ease of learning. The Advanced Plus/Minus and Braun Systems are the easiest to learn since they are one-level counts with no side count of aces. Next in difficulty are the Hi Opt I and DHM systems, one-level counts with a side count of aces. The Revere APC is the most difficult. The Uston Advanced Point count and Hi Opt II systems fall in between, in complexity.

Table 8—2

Table 8—2
Comparison of
Professional Level Blackjack Systems

CRITERION	USTON APC	HI OPT II	REVERE APC	HI OPT I	USTON ADVANCED PLUS/MINUS	BRAUN	DHM
A—Card Values:							
2	+ 1	+ 1	+ 2	0	0	+ 1	+ 1
3	+ 2	+ 1	+ 2	+ 1	+ 1	+ 1	+ 1
4	+ 2	+ 2	+ 3	+ 1	+ 1	+ 1	+ 1
5	+ 3	+ 2	+ 4	+ 1	+ 1	+ 1	+ 1
6	+ 2	+ 1	+ 2	+ 1	+ 1	+ 1	0
7	+ 2	+ 1	+ 1	0	+ 1	0	0
8	+ 1	0	0	0	0	0	0
9	− 1	0	− 2	0	0	0	0
10	− 3	− 2	− 3	− 1	− 1	− 1	− 1
Ace	0	0	0	0	− 1	− 1	0
B—Value of Ace in Betting	3	2	4	1	*	*	1
C—True Count Adjusted To:	½ DECK	1 DECK	½ DECK	1 DECK	½ DECK	1 DECK	1 DECK
D—Relative Ease of Learning	5	4	6	3	2	2	3
E—Availability	CHAPT. 8	LANCE HUMBLE. TORONTO	REVERE SCHOOL. LAS VEGAS	HUMBLE'S BOOK (9)	CHAPT. 6	BRAUN'S BOOK (8)	GAMBLING TIMES SYSTEMS SHOP

* The ace is assigned a negative count value and thus is automatically reflected in betting (obviating the need for a side count of aces).

Learning A Professional Level System

The remainder of this chapter will instruct the reader in how to learn a professional level blackjack system. Throughout, I will use the Uston Advanced Point Count as a reference, since this is the count I would recommend to the professional player today. However, if you are learning one of the other professional systems, the techniques herein equally apply.

Our teams have had players using a variety of professional counts.

Daryll, our team trainer par excellence, has in fact tested three or more teammates simultaneously, each using different systems. As long as they can recite the correct true counts for their system, state the reasons why they make various plays, and, of course, be able to predict the values of the last several cards at the end of the deck or shoe, we know they are playing accurately. My point: professional blackjack instruction is equally germane to all responsible professional systems. The concepts are the same; the only differences are the actual card values, the numbers in the matrices, and, in some cases, the divisor used to convert the running count to the true count.

Learning The Count. This section has only one objective—to get you to be able to count down a deck, with a side count of aces, in 25 seconds, the "loose" objective my teammates must adhere to in order to be rapid enough for casino play. (Actually, most of us take from 14 to 18 seconds!) Our goal for counting down four decks is 90 seconds; for six decks, 2 minutes and 20 seconds.

If you are practicing a one level count, it should take you about ten hours of practice to achieve this goal with complete accuracy. With the Uston count, 20 to 25 hours will be required.

Step 1. Take a 52-card deck and go through it, card-by-card, reciting the card values for each individual card. Do this several times until the values pop into your head automatically—this should take no more than ten times through the deck. The Uston APC card values are repeated below:

Card Denomination		Card Value
2		+1
3		+2
4		+2
5		+3
6		+2
7		+2
8		+1
9		−1
10		−3
Ace	(Counted separately)	0

Step 2. Count down a complete 52-card deck, reciting the *cumulative* value of the deck. When you have reached the end of the deck, you should have a count of "zero," since the total of the plus and minus cards are equal. Once again, if your final count is other than zero, recount that *same* deck without shuffling until you have corrected your error (be sure you have a complete deck).

Step 3. It is essential that you recognize combinations of cards that will allow the netting of plus and minus values to develop rapid counting ability. For example, a 5 (+3 value) and a 10 (−3

107

value) net to zero; so, whenever you see this combination, you can effectively ignore it in your count. The most common netting combination is a 10 (−3) and a 3, 4, 6 or 7 (each of which counts as +2)—these all net to −1.

There are five different values for cards (other than zero, which is assigned to aces and does not affect your running count). These values are:

−3	for 10's
−1	for 9's
+1	for 2's and 8's
+2	for 3's, 4's, 6's and 7's
+3	for 5's.

Thus, there are 5^2 (five squared), or 25, possible combinations. The most prevalent combinations by far are those involving 10's, since there are four times as many 10's in the deck as any other card. The combinations, which should be memorized, are:

Card Combination	Combined Value
10,5	0
10,3	
10,4	
10,6	−1
10,7	
10,2	
10,8	−2

Now, go through the deck, spotting combinations of 10's and other cards. After a few times through the deck, you will note that your cumulative counting time has dropped considerably, perhaps to a minute and a half or so.

Now, you're ready for some of the other combinations.

2 or 8	with a 9	nets to zero
3,4,6,7	with a 9	nets to +1
3,4,6,7	with 3,4,6,7	equals +4
10	with 10	equals −6
10	with 9	equals −4
3,4,6,7	with 2 or 8	equals +3
3,4,6,7	with a 5	equals +5
2 or 8	with a 5	equals +4

Learn these combinations and go through the deck 15 or 20 more times, using them when possible. Your counting time should be decreased even more; your time may now be down to a minute or so.

There are still more combinations to learn:

5 and 5	equals +6
5 and 9	" +2
9 and 9	" −2
2 and 2	" +2
8 and 8	" +2
2 and 8	" +2

Several three-card combinations that will increase your speed are:

10 with 3, 4, 6 or 7 and 2 or 8 equals 0 (quite a timesaver)
10 with two (3's, 4's, 6's or 7's) nets to +1

Step 4. Now, it's time to start counting aces separately. I strongly recommend that you count aces by using your feet, as do all my teammates. Some of you may say, "But if I play only single deck, why bother?" The response to this is that while there are numerous single deck games in Las Vegas, a good player will eventually be faced with multiple deck games. Further, in New Jersey and abroad, single deck games are not available (with rare exception).

There is quite a simple method of counting aces in single deck games. Each of the four fingers of the left hand (of a right-handed player) can be pressed against the left thumb, the rim of the table, a coffee cup or glass, or against the temple. Pressure with the index finger denotes one ace; middle finger, two aces; third finger, 3 aces; and pinkie, 4 aces. This method is no good while practicing counting, however, since both hands must be used to move the cards—another reason to start counting aces with your feet.

Our teammates have found the following to be about the easiest: the first eight aces are counted on the left foot, the second eight aces on the right foot and the final eight (in a six deck game) back on the left foot again.

The left foot, kept pointing straight forward, is rotated clockwise for the first four aces:

Left foot with toes on ground and rest of foot raised	1 ace
Left foot instep down	2 aces
Left foot heel down, toes raised	3 "
Left foot outstep down	4 "

For aces 5 through 8, the toe and heel are held up, as follows:

Heel down, toes up and pointing to left	5 aces
Heel down, toes up and pointing to right	6 "
Toes down, heel up and pointing left	7 "
Toes down, heel up and pointing right	8 "

Aces 9 through 16 are counted exactly the same way, but on the right foot. In six deck games, aces 17 through 24 (rarely are more than 20 aces actually encountered), can again be counted on the original left foot.

There are other methods, such as placing the left thumb on various positions on the four fingers (top of finger, aces 1 through 4; first joint, 5-8; second joint, 9-12, etc.). We've found foot counting to be by far the most practical.

These foot movements may seem awkward to you initially. However, after a few hours of practice, you will find that your feet will move automatically when an ace is seen. We all found that eventually the foot moves nearly subconsciously, not unlike steering a car, so that you won't even be aware of your foot position until it's necessary to recall into your consciousness the number of aces played. The student preparing for single deck play would be well-advised to begin using these foot movements; it will pay dividends subsequently.

> *Step 5.* Continue practicing with a 52-card deck, counting aces as well. If you get tired of counting, combine this practice with a review of the Basic Strategy flashcards and the numbers matrix cards discussed below.

We all turn the last card of the deck over so it cannot be seen. When we've counted the other 51 cards, we predict the value of the last card, turn it over and check our accuracy. For example, if you have a count of +3 and 4 aces after counting 51 cards, the last card must be valued at −3 to restore the count to zero (assuming you were accurate). Thus, the last card must be a 10. If you had a count of zero and 3 aces, your last card clearly must be an ace. If your count was −2 and 4 aces, the last card is either a 3, 4, 6 or 7. Practicing becomes almost "fun" to the student, as he "miraculously" predicts the value of the last card. (Sometimes you can amaze your friends by predicting 3 or more cards. For example, if you hid three cards from view and ended up with a count of +6, 3 aces, it's obvious the three hidden cards are two tens and an ace.)

It takes about 20 hours or so to be able to count down a deck in 25 seconds with this count. Accuracy is more important than speed, however. If your count is off, re-count the same deck, unshuffled, to correct your error. If you find your error rate continues high after counting many, many decks, you might consider converting to a simpler system, such as the Uston Simple Plus/Minus. To repeat yet again, it's far better to play a simple system accurately, than an advanced one inaccurately.

To assist in rapid counting, make up a "training deck" containing 8 aces and 4 extra 2's, 5's, 8's and 9's. This will give you more practice in counting some of the less-frequently encountered card values and will get your foot going through eight ace positions. This training deck is valued at +16, so when you've counted all but the last hidden card, the card should restore your count to +16, 8 aces.

Another tip: periodically count the training deck two cards at a time. This will force you to net in pairs, good practice since a player's cards are often turned up in pairs at the table.

Learning the Numbers. Table 8-3 displays the numbers matrix for the Uston Advanced Point Count (the numbers matrix for the Advanced Plus/Minus is contained in the last section of Chapter 6). Note that the numbers are organized into eight tables. They should be applied, as follows:

The Vegas Player: Use the hit and stand, hard and soft doubling and pair splitting tables.

If you play casinos which offer double-down-after-pair-splitting, use the double-after-split table, substituting those numbers for the corresponding ones in the pair splitting table.

If you play casinos which offer conventional surrender, use the conventional surrender table.

The Atlantic City Player: Use the hit and stand table, the hard and soft doubling tables and the pair splitting table modified by the entries in the double-after-split table. Also use the early surrender table (*not* the conventional surrender table).

See note on page 51 concerning Atlantic City surrender options.

The numbers in the tables represent the *true* (not running) count at which deviations from Basic Strategy should be made. This is why it is so important for the advanced player to have an almost subconscious knowledge of Basic Strategy.

Hit and Stand Tables. As you know, with a plus count, we will tend to stand more, contrary to Basic Strategy. Look at the "hit and stand" table. To the right of the heavy vertical line is a series of numbers, all plus (except the 16 versus 10, which is zero), for player's totals of 13 through 16. You will recall that Basic Strategy calls for the player to hit these stiff hands until reaching a total of 17 (the dealer upcards to the right of the vertical line are 7 through ace). The plus numbers in the right portion of this table designate the plus true count at which the player should stand on, rather than hit, these hands.

111

Table 8—3

Uston Advanced Point Count Numbers Matrix

Notes: Deviate from Basic Strategy if the half-deck *true* count equals or exceeds the numbers in the matrix.

The numbers are composite numbers for both single and multiple deck games.

Where two numbers appear in the box, the top number is for single deck, and the lower number is for multiple deck.

INSURANCE: Insure with a True Count of:

+2 in single deck
+2½ in multiple decks

HITTING OR STANDING

You Have:	2	3	4	5	6	7	8	9	10	A
17										−8
16	−11	−12	−15	−16	−14	+18	+20	+6	0	+10
15	−7	−8	−10	−13	−12	+20	+23	+11	+4	+12
14	−4	−5	−7	−8	−8	+18		+18	+9	+14
13	−1	−2	−4	−5	−5				+13	+17
12	+3	+2	0	−2	−1					
7,7									−2**	
A7										−1 / +2

* With A7 versus Ace, in single deck, hit if −1 or lower. In multiple deck, stand if +2 or higher.

** With 7,7 versus 10, single deck *only*, stand unless true count is −2 or lower; then hit.

HARD DOUBLING

You Have:	2	3	4	5	6	7	8	9	10	A
11	−13	−13	−14	−15	−16	−9	−7	−5	−5	+2
10	−11	−11	−13	−14	−15	−7	−5	−2	+5	+6
9	+2	−1	−3	−6	−7	+5	+11			
8	+14	+10	+7	+4	+3	+22				
7				+13	+12	+12				

Table 8—3 (Continued)

SOFT DOUBLING

You Have:	Dealer's Upcard					
	2	3	4	5	6	7
A9	+ 14	+ 11	+ 9	+ 7	+ 7	+ 23
A8	+ 11	+ 7	+ 4	+ 3	+ 3	+ 20
A7	+ 4	− 2	− 5	− 8	− 7	+ 22
A6	−1 +1	− 3	− 7	− 12	− 14	+ 13
A5		+ 4	− 5	− 9	− 14	
A4		+ 4	0	− 8	− 9	
A3		+ 6	+ 1	− 6	− 7	
A2		+ 6	+ 2	− 3	− 4	

SPLITTING PAIRS

You Have:	Dealer's Upcard									
	2	3	4	5	6	7	8	9	10	A
AA	− 14	− 14	− 14	− 15	− 16	− 12	− 10	− 10	− 10	−7 −5
10,10	+ 13	+ 10	+ 7	+ 5	+ 5	+ 19				
9,9	−1 0	− 3	− 5	− 7	− 6	+ 10				+ 8
8,8									+ 6 *	
7,7	− 10	− 13	− 15	− 18					− 2**	
6,6	+3 0	+ 1	− 3	− 7						
5,5										
4,4										
3,3	+ 11	+ 5	0	− 6	+ 10					
2,2	+ 10	+ 3	− 3	− 7						

* Numbers in a circle ◯ designate the true count at which *not* to split (stand on 8,8 versus 10, and hit 3,3 versus 7).

** With 7,7 versus 10, single deck *only,* stand unless true count is − 2 or lower; then hit.

113

Table 8—3 (Continued)

Atlantic City Modifications

Notes: Surrender if the half-deck true count equals or exceeds the plus number in the matrix.

Do not surrender if the half-deck true count equals or is less than the minus number in the matrix.

EARLY SURRENDER

You Have:	Dealer's Upcard 8	9	10	A
17		+13	+10	S
16	+10	+1	−7	S
15	+10	+2	−4	S
14	+13	+6	0	S
13	+16	+13	+4	−12
12				−8
8,8		+10	−2	S
7			+11	−8
6			+11	−2
5			+14	0
2,2			+11	+1

S = Surrender regardless of count.

For simplicity, while not quite accurate, play 7,7 as a 14.

DOUBLE-DOWN AFTER PAIR-SPLITTING

You Have:	Dealer's Upcard 2	3	4	5	6	7	A
9,9	−4	−7	−7	−8	−8	+3	+7
7,7							
6,6	−6	−7	−8				
4,4		+10	+6	−3/0	+1		
3,3	−3	−10					
2,2	−3	−5	−7	−9			

Replace the numbers in the Splitting Pairs Table on preceding page with the numbers above, if double-after-splits is allowed.

Table 8—3 (Continued)

Other Modifications

All player hands on this page are hard hands, unless otherwise indicated.

CONVENTIONAL SURRENDER				
You Have:	Dealer's Upcard			
	8	9	10	A
17		+13	+13	
16	+10	+1	−2	−1
15	+10	+2	−1	+2
14	+13	+6	+4	+6
13	+16	+13	+10	+13
8,8		+10	+3	
7,7	+13	+3	0	+2

IF DEALER HITS SOFT 17 (E.G.: RENO, TAHOE, DOWNTOWN VEGAS)		
You Have:	Dealer's Upcard	
	6	Ace
17		−9
16	−23	+7
15	−21	+9
14	−15	+14
13	−10	
12	−9	
A7	−20	Hit
A6	−25	
A5	−25	
9,9	−14	+5

Note: In some cases, particularly where the player should take action based on the specific card denominations of his hand, we have used a representative number applicable to all situations. Experience has shown, over and over again, that the minor gain from trying to remember minor refinements is offset many times over by player confusion and hence, error.

115

For example, Basic Strategy says a 16 should be hit against a 9. The table shows us that if the true count is +6 or greater, the player would stand on 16 against a 9. Another example: Basic Strategy says the player should hit 14 against a 10. The table indicates that with a true count of +9 or greater, the player should stand on 14 against a 10.

Notice the two plus numbers on the left side of the vertical line—for 12 against a 2 or 3 upcard. This is because Basic Strategy calls for us to hit these hands. But the table is telling us that, with a true count of +3 or +2, respectively, we should stand with 12 against a 2 and a 3. Here again, a plus true count leads us to stand, rather than to hit.

Notice that all the other numbers on the left side of the vertical line are minus numbers. This is because Basic Strategy tells us to stand on these hands (13 versus 3, 16 versus 4, and so on). The minus numbers in the table tell us to *hit* these hands if the true count has dropped to the number designated, or below. This, of course, makes sense, since with a negative true count, more high cards have been played, a disproportionate number of low cards are in the deck and the player is more likely to draw a low, non-busting card (a second reason to hit: the dealer is more likely to make a pat hand).

Hard doubling table. Notice, on the "hard doubling" table, the plus numbers next to the player's hand of 8. Basic Strategy would not call for the player to double on these hands. However, the table tells us that if the designated true count is reached, the player should double-down.

Notice the negative numbers on the table alongside the player's hand of 10, for dealer upcards of 2 through 9. Basic Strategy calls for doubling on these hands. But, the table tells us that if the minus number indicated is reached, we should *not* double. Again, with a richness of small cards in the deck, this makes sense.

The other tables. The same reasoning applies for the soft doubling, pair splitting and surrender tables. If the plus number is reached, the player should soft double, split or surrender, contrary to Basic Strategy. If the minus number is reached, the player should *not* soft double, split or surrender.

To make sure you understand the tables, follow along with them as I cite a few more examples:

— Basic Strategy says we should never split 10's. The "pair splitting" table tells us to split 10's against a 6 if the true count is +5 or higher.

— Basic Strategy says we shouldn't double on A,9. The "soft doubling" table tells us to double on A,9 against a 4, 5 or 6, if the true count exceeds +9, +7 and +7 respectively.

— Basic Strategy says stand on 13 versus a 2. The "hit and stand" table tells us to hit if a true count of −1 or less (that is, a bigger minus) is reached.

— Basic Strategy says to double on 11 against a 10. With a true count of —5 or less, we should hit, rather than double-down.

— Basic Strategy says to split 9's against a 3. With a true count of —1 or less, we should stand, rather than split.

— Basic Strategy says to double on A,6 against a 4. With a true count of –7 or less, we should hit rather than double-down.

As I said, for Atlantic City players and those playing double-on-split casinos in Vegas, the entries in the double-on-split table should be substituted for the entries in the pair splitting table. For example, the double-on-split table indicates that 7,7 should be split against 2 through 6, regardless of the count. Substitute this for the minus number entries (—10, —13, —15, —18) in the "pair splitting" table. Similarly, for 2,2 versus 2 through 5, substitute —3, —5, —7 and —9 from the double-on-split table for the +10, +3, —3 and —7 on the "pair-splitting" table.

I have found that it is far easier for students to learn the tables gradually. The plus numbers are obviously the more important, since they will be used more often when the player has large bets out. Further, the larger numbers are not nearly as important since the deck will infrequently reach these very low and very high true counts. In fact, it is not essential to learn the numbers below —10 or above +10 for the Atlantic City six deck game; they will rarely be used.

I find it easiest for students to learn the numbers by memorizing them in horizontal lines and by watching for patterns. For example, the numbers for hitting 13 versus 2 through 6 are —1, —2, —4, —5, —5, respectively. The line above it, for 14 versus 2 through 6, the numbers are —4, —5, —7, —8, —8.

Learn the plus numbers from 0 to +5 first. Then learn 0 through —5. Follow this with +6 to +10 and then —6 to —10. The higher numbers can be learned subsequently.

The Numbers Flashcards

On pages 124a through 124v flashcards are provided for the matrix numbers. Sample flashcards appear below. They should be interpreted as follows:

5
-2 12

— When we have a 12 against a dealer 5, we should hit if the true count is —2 or lower.

9
-2 10

— With a 10 versus a 9, we should *not* double, but hit, if the true count is —2 or lower.

5
+5 10,10

— With a pair of 10's versus a 5, we should split with a true count of +5 or greater.

117

Paste the page on stiff paper or cardboard, cut out the flashcards and arrange them in a pack. Flip through the cards one-by-one, reciting the true count number. If you're right-handed, the "answer" will be hidden under your left thumb, so you need not turn the card over to see if you were correct, promoting increased speed.

You should be able to average about 1½ seconds per card. Speed is important in this exercise because, while playing, you will want the number to pop into mind automatically. You'll be keeping the count, counting aces, and making other calculations; you won't have time to slowly reflect on the value of a given matrix number. Here, familiarity will come with practice. After you've played a while, you'll find that numbers are almost nearly automatic. For example, when dealt a 15 versus 10, you'll think "+4" almost instantaneously.

Summary To Date

The count and the numbers will take about 80% of the time necessary for you to learn the Uston APC. It's not difficult; it's only a matter of repetition. Take a +16 deck and the flashcards with you—they're quite small and easily fit into any pocket. Practice with them whenever you can: on airplanes; during TV commercials; at train stations; in taxicabs; etc. The more you practice, the sooner you'll be proficient—it's just a matter of time. If you get discouraged, just think of the potential rewards you'll enjoy from beating the casinos at their own game.

Converting Running Count To True Count

The two remaining steps to learn the Uston APC, while more complicated, take far less time to master. They are conversion to true count and ace adjustment. We'll discuss each in turn.

Six deck true count conversion. The running count cannot truly reflect the condition of the remaining deck(s) without being adjusted for the number of cards or decks to be played. The Uston APC (and the Uston Advanced Plus/Minus) adjusts the running count to the number of half-decks left to be played, to derive the true count. Some examples:

— With a running count of +20 and two decks left to be played, the true count is divided by 4 (there are four half-decks in two full decks), or +5.

— With a running count of −18 and three decks to be played, the true count is −18 divided by 6 (there are six half-decks in three full decks), or −3.

— With a running count of +7 and one half-deck left to be played, the true count is also +7 (7 divided by 1, since there is one half-deck to be played).

When playing a six deck shoe, such as in Atlantic City, the maximum conversion factor, thus, is 12 (since there are 12 half decks in the total shoe). A shortcut for knowing how many decks remain to be played is to use the discard pile, where the cards are stacked. When there is a half-deck in the discard pile, we know 5½ decks remain to be played. When there are 5½ decks left to be played, we know we must divide the running count by 11 since there are 11 half-decks in 5½ full decks. The following table results:

Table 8—4

Six Deck Conversion Factors

Number of Decks Seen in the Discard Pile:	Number of Decks Left to be Played	Conversion Factor (=#½-decks to be played)
½	5½	11
1	5	10
1½	4½	9
2	4	8
2½	3½	7
3	3	6
3½	2½	5
4	2	4

This, in turn, leads to another shortcut. When we look at the discard pile, the *only* thing we're concerned with is the conversion factor—while at the table, we couldn't care less about the number of decks or half-decks (we are also concerned with number of aces, but we'll discuss that later). So, we can calibrate our eyes to read the discard pile as sort of a meter, like the gasoline meter on a car, as follows:

Figure 8a

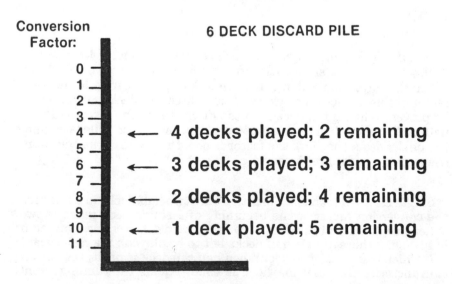

Conversion Factor:

6 DECK DISCARD PILE

0
1
2
3
4 ← 4 decks played; 2 remaining
5
6 ← 3 decks played; 3 remaining
7
8 ← 2 decks played; 4 remaining
9
10 ← 1 deck played; 5 remaining
11

Once you've trained your vision, a quick glance at the discard pile will determine the conversion factor (rounding to the nearest half-deck in multiple deck games yields sufficient accuracy). In Chapter 11, where we discuss multiple deck play, I'll include some practice techniques that will help the reader to train his vision.

Four Deck Conversion. When playing four deck, the maximum conversion factor is eight, since there are eight halfdecks in four full decks. When a half-deck has been played, there are 3½ decks remaining (seven half-decks), so, the conversion factor with a half-deck in the discard pile is seven. The player switching between four and six (and indeed five) deck games must be totally aware of this difference lest his conversion is off. The four deck "gasoline meter" looks like this:

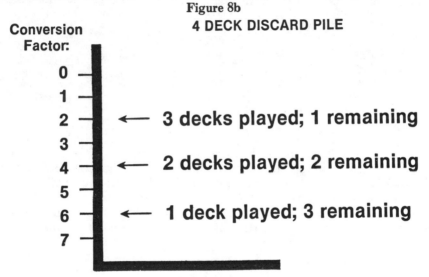

Figure 8b

4 DECK DISCARD PILE

Conversion Factor:

0
1
2 ← 3 decks played; 1 remaining
3
4 ← 2 decks played; 2 remaining
5
6 ← 1 deck played; 3 remaining
7

Double Deck Conversion. The initial conversion factor for a double deck game is four, since there are four half-decks in two full decks. When the player spots about one half-deck in the discard pile, he uses a factor of three, since there are 1½ decks (three half-decks) remaining to be played. When a full deck is in the discard pile, the factor is two (2 half-decks), and when there are 1½ decks in the discard pile (assuming the dealer deals that far), the factor is one, that is, the true count and the running count are the same.

Single Deck Conversion. Since there are two half-decks in a full deck, the conversion factor at the beginning of a single deck game is two. When one quarter of the deck is dealt (13 cards), the conversion factor is 1½ (since there are 1½ half-decks left to be played); the reciprocal is .67, which is far easier to use. When half the deck is dealt, the conversion factor is one, that is, the true count equals the running count.

When more than a half-deck is dealt (which is fairly rare these days), the conversion factor is actually less than one. The single deck conversion factors are as follows in Table 8—5.

Note that the theoretical conversion factors (Column C) are difficult numbers by which to divide. Thus, in Column D, we have developed the reciprocal of Column C, the numbers by which you can multiply and get exactly the same result. We've found it far easier to multiply these figures in single deck games.

Table 8—5

Single Deck Conversion Factors

A	B	C	D
		Theoretical	
# Cards Dealt	# Cards Remaining	Conversion Factor (= #½ − decks remaining)	Use: Reciprocal of Conversion Factor
0	52	2	.50
7	45	1¾ *	.60
13	39	1½	.67
19	33	1¼ *	.80
26	26	1	1.00
32	20	¾ *	1.30
39	13	½	2.00

* Rounded

Don't be concerned about having to keep track of the number of cards played. This is not necessary and later I'll show you several shortcuts to determine quickly and accurately the conversion factor. It is important here that you just understand the concept; shortcuts for both single deck and multiple deck play may be found in Chapters 10 and 11.

Ace Adjustment

Don't despair. There's only one more concept left to understand and then we're ready to put the whole thing together (students learning the Uston Advanced Plus/Minus can skim this section). You remember that we've been counting aces separately. Now it's time to use this information.

As you will recall, aces are valued at "zero" because we don't use them to influence our true count when determining how to play the hands, since the aces have little effect on the play of the hands. But aces are paramount cards in determining how to bet. Thus, prior to making a bet, we must determine whether the deck is unduly rich in aces (ace-rich), which is to our advantage, or low in aces (ace-poor), which is to our disadvantage.

For every ace it is rich, we add three (3) points to our running count *before* calculating our true count for betting purposes. For every ace it is poor, we deduct three points from our running count before calculating our true count for *betting* purposes (this calculation is *not* made when determining our true count for play-of-the-hand purposes).

Multiple Deck Games. Once again there are shortcuts in making ace adjustment, and the discard pile is the key. When a half-deck is in the discard pile, for aces to be "normal," two aces should have been played. This is because there is one ace for every 13 cards and, if 26 cards had been dealt (a half-deck) and aces came out in the normal 1-to-13 ratio, two would have been played. If in fact no aces were played during the first 26 cards, then the remaining pack is two aces-rich, that is, there are two extra aces in the cards remaining to be played. This is to the player's advantage, since he is now more likely to be dealt an ace.

Similarly, if after a half-deck had been played, five aces had been played, this is three (3) more than the normal 1-to-13 ratio of aces. Thus, the remaining pack is three aces-poor, which is clearly to the player's disadvantage.

Let's take another look at the discard pile, which can also be used as a "gasoline meter" to determine the normal number of aces that should have been played.

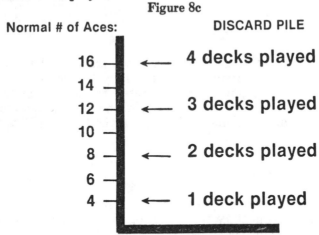

Figure 8c

Normal # of Aces: DISCARD PILE

16 — ← 4 decks played

14 —

12 — ← 3 decks played

10 —

8 — ← 2 decks played

6 —

4 — ← 1 deck played

Notice that the normal number of aces, happily, is the same, regardless of whether the discard pile is for two, four, five, or six deck games (as opposed to the conversion factor which varies, since it is dependent on the number of cards remaining in the shoe).

Now, we'll finally make use of those feet of yours that have been moving so mysteriously as you counted down deck-after-deck. Let's take an example: assume there is one full deck in the discard pile, according to your calibrated eyeballs, and your left foot is still on its toe, that is, in the one-ace-played position. Where are we, from the standpoint of aces? With one deck in the discard pile, four aces normally should have been played, but your foot indicates that only one ace has been played. Thus, we are three aces rich. We must multiply the three aces by the adjustment factor of three to adjust our running count before determing our bet size—more on this later.

Assume there are three decks in the discard pile and your right foot is in the toe-up-and-to-the-right position (14 aces played). Thus, 12 aces normally should have been played, but your foot indicates that 14 were played. We're two aces poor and must deduct six points (two aces poor times the factor of three) from our running count.

After a while, you will begin to relate positions of your foot with the discard pile. In other words, with your left foot on its outstep, you will automatically know that aces are normal if there is one deck in the discard pile, and so on. Your ace-rich, ace-poor factors will pop into your head much quicker.

Summary. Let me now summarize the steps that you, the Uston APC player, will take as you play:

You sit down at the table, and given your predetermined betting strategy (which we discuss in the next chapter), place your opening bet. As the cards are dealt, you count the values of the cards until it comes time to play your hand. If you have a hand that requires a "number" decision, you convert your running count to the true count (*not* using the ace adjustment factor since aces do not affect the play of the hand) and determine what the correct play is.

Then you sit and wait as the dealer deals the rest of the cards in the round and deals his own hand as you count those cards. As he is settling the bets with the players, you take your running count, adjust it for ace-rich or ace-poor, and once again calculate the betting true count (by using the conversion factor). You then place your bet and the process is repeated.

* * *

I know this sounds confusing at this point.

About this point, my students in my seminars begin shaking their heads wondering, "Can I learn all this?"

I usually respond, "You have been taught everything you need to know. It's all downhill from here, because we will now talk about how to simply consolidate this with a series of shortcuts. Also, remember that once you learn this and play it for hours and hours in the casinos, it will, believe it or not, come nearly automatically." (It was often frustrating to me that I was sharpest when a trip was over, after weeks of play. Then, after a long "vacation," the next trip was scheduled and it was time to sit down, shake out the cobwebs and go through the practice sessions again.)

Steps To Be Taken
To Learn the Uston APC

1. Use a regular 52-card deck (or the +16 training deck) and get your count down to 25 seconds (35 seconds with the +16 deck).

2. Use the number flashcards and learn the matrix numbers.

   —Atlantic City players need only learn the values up to +10 and down to −10, since rarely will numbers above that be used there, where the casinos normally deal down only to two decks remaining (thus running counts of over +40 would be required before these plays would be made.

   —Single deck players should learn all the numbers because high true counts occur far more frequently.

3. Read this chapter several times until you thoroughly understand the *concepts* therein. At this point, don't bother learning anything, since the learning steps will be presented in Chatpers 10 and 11.

4. Read the next chapter on betting strategy, so you have an idea what your betting strategy should be.

5. If you plan to play single deck, go to Chapter 10 and learn the remaining portions of the Uston Advanced Point Count.

6. If you plan to play in Atlantic City (or multiple deck games in Nevada), go to Chapter 11 and learn the remaining portion of the Uston Advanced Point Count.

Note: Do *not* try to learn both single and multiple deck at the same time. I always coach students to train only for a particular game; there are too many factors for the average student to learn in order to play all games simultaneously. Train for one particular type of game, master that game and, as necessary, train for other games. In Atlantic City, this happens as a matter of course since there is essentially only one game offered: six deck with identical rules. In Nevada, there are a variety of games with differing rules and numbers of decks. Home in on only one type initially (there are in fact players who play only four deck or single deck games—a wise specialization).

Flashcards For Uston Advanced Point Count

FLASHCARDS FOR USTON ADVANCED POINT COUNT **BEGINNING OF HIT OR STAND**	SD ONLY −2 **10** **7,7**	**A** −1 +2 **A7**
−8 **A** **17**	−11 **2** **16**	−12 **3** **16**
−15 **4** **16**	−16 **5** **16**	−14 **6** **16**
+18 **7** **16**	+20 **8** **16**	+6 **9** **16**

Flashcards For Uston Advanced Point Count
(continued)

10 **16** ₀	**A** **16** ₊₁₀	**2** **15** ₋₇
3 **15** ₋₈	**4** **15** ₋₁₀	**5** **15** ₋₁₃
6 **15** ₋₁₂	**7** **15** ₊₂₀	**8** **15** ₊₂₃
9 **15** ₊₁₁	**10** **15** ₊₄	**A** **15** ₊₁₂

Flashcards For Uston Advanced Point Count
(continued)

2 **14** −4	**3** **14** −5	**4** **14** −7
5 **14** −8	**6** **14** −8	**7** **14** +18
9 **14** +18	**10** **14** −9	**A** **14** +14
2 **13** −1	**3** **13** −2	**4** **13** −4

Flashcards For Uston Advanced Point Count
(continued)

5 − 5 **13**	**6** − 5 **13**	**A** + 17 **13**
2 + 3 **12**	**3** + 2 **12**	**4** 0 **12**
5 − 2 **12**	**6** − 1 **12**	END OF HIT OR STAND
BEGINNING OF HARD DOUBLING	**2** − 13 **11**	**3** − 13 **11**

Flashcards For Uston Advanced Point Count
(continued)

4 **11** – 14	**5** **11** – 15	**6** **11** – 16
7 **11** – 9	**8** **11** – 7	**9** **11** – 5
10 **11** – 5	**A** – 1 + 2 **11**	**2** **10** – 11
3 **10** – 11	**4** **10** – 13	**5** **10** – 14

Flashcards For Uston Advanced Point Count
(continued)

6 10 −15	7 10 −7	8 10 −5
9 10 −2	10 10 +5	A 10 +6
2 9 0 +2	3 9 −1	4 9 −3
5 9 −6	6 9 −7	7 9 +5

Flashcards For Uston Advanced Point Count
(continued)

8 9 + 11	2 8 + 14	3 8 + 10
4 8 + 7	5 8 + 4	6 8 + 3
7 8 + 22	4 7 + 13	5 7 + 12
6 7 + 12	END OF HARD DOUBLING	BEGINNING OF SOFT DOUBLING

Flashcards For Uston Advanced Point Count
(continued)

2 A9 +14	3 A9 +11	4 A9 +9
5 A9 +7	6 A9 +7	7 A9 +23
2 A8 +11	3 A8 +7	4 A8 +4
5 A8 +3	6 A8 +3	7 A8 +20

Flashcards For Uston Advanced Point Count
(continued)

2 +4 **A7**	**3** −2 **A7**	**4** −5 **A7**
5 −8 **A7**	**6** −7 **A7**	**7** +22 **A7**
2 −1 +1 **A6**	**3** −3 **A6**	**4** −7 **A6**
5 −12 **A6**	**6** −14 **A6**	**7** +13 **A6**

Flashcards For Uston Advanced Point Count
(continued)

3 **A5** +4	**4** **A5** −5	**5** **A5** −9
6 **A5** −14	**3** **A4** +4	**4** **A4** 0
5 **A4** −8	**6** **A4** −9	**3** **A3** +6
4 **A3** +1	**5** **A3** −6	**6** **A3** −7

3 **A2** +6	**4** **A2** +2	**5** **A2** −3
6 **A2** −4	**END OF SOFT DOUBLING**	**BEGINNING OF CONVENTIONAL SURRENDER OTHER MODIFICATIONS**
9 **17** +13	**10** **17** +13	**8** **16** +10
9 **16** +1	**10** **16** −2	**A** **16** −1

8 15 +10	9 15 +2	10 15 −1
A 15 +2	8 14 +13	9 14 +6
10 14 +4	A 14 +6	8 13 +16
9 13 +13	10 13 +10	A 13 +13

Flashcards For Uston Advanced Point Count
(continued)

+10 **9** **8,8**	+3 **10** **8,8**	+13 **8** **7,7**
+3 **9** **7,7**	0 **10** **7,7**	+2 **A** **7,7**
END OF CONVENTIONAL SURRENDER OTHER MODIFICATIONS	**BEGINNING OF PAIR SPLITTING**	−14 **2** **AA**
−14 **3** **AA**	−14 **4** **AA**	−15 **5** **AA**

Flashcards For Uston Advanced Point Count
(continued)

6 −16 **AA**	**7** −12 **AA**	**8** −10 **AA**
9 −10 **AA**	**10** −10 **AA**	**A** −7 −5 **AA**
2 +13 **10,10**	**3** +10 **10,10**	**4** +7 **10,10**
5 +5 **10,10**	**6** +5 **10,10**	**7** +19 **10,10**

2 0 −1 **9,9**	**3** −3 **9,9**	**4** −5 **9,9**
5 −7 **9,9**	**6** −6 **9,9**	**7** +10 **9,9**
A +8 **9,9**	**10** +6 <u>NO</u> **8,8**	**2** −10 **7,7**
3 −13 **7,7**	**4** −15 **7,7**	**5** −18 **7,7**

Flashcards For Uston Advanced Point Count
(continued)

10 SD ONLY **7,7** −2	**2** 0 +3 **6,6**	**3** +1 **6,6**
4 −3 **6,6**	**5** −7 **6,6**	**2** +11 **3,3**
3 +5 **3,3**	**4** 0 **3,3**	**5** −6 **3,3**
7 +10 <u>NO</u> **3,3**	**2** +10 **2,2**	**3** +3 **2,2**

Flashcards For Uston Advanced Point Count
(continued)

4 -3 **2,2**	**5** -7 **2,2**	BEGINNING OF EARLY SURRENDER ATLANTIC CITY MODIFICATIONS
9 +13 **17**	**10** +10 **17**	**A** S **17**
8 +10 **16**	**9** +1 **16**	**10** -7 **16**
A S **16**	**8** +10 **15**	**9** +2 **15**

10 **15** −4	**A** **15** S	**8** **14** +13
9 **14** +6	**10** **14** 0	**A** **14** S
8 **13** +16	**9** **13** +13	**10** **13** +4
A **13** −12	**A** **12** −8	**9** **8,8** +10

10 −2 **8,8**	**A** s **8,8**	**10** +11 **7**
A −8 **7**	**10** +11 **6**	**A** −2 **6**
10 +14 **5**	**A** 0 **5**	**10** +11 **2,2**
A +1 **2,2**	BEGINNING OF DOUBLE-DOWN AFTER PAIR-SPLITTING ATLANTIC CITY MODIFICATIONS	**2** −4 **9,9**

3 -7 **9,9**	**4** -7 **9,9**	**5** -8 **9,9**
6 -8 **9,9**	**7** +3 **9,9**	**A** +7 **9,9**
2 -6 **6,6**	**3** -7 **6,6**	**4** -8 **6,6**
3 +10 **4,4**	**4** +6 **4,4**	**5** -3 0 **4,4**

Flashcards For Uston Advanced Point Count
(continued)

6 +1 **4,4**	**2** −3 **3,3**	**3** −10 **3,3**
2 −3 **2,2**	**3** −5 **2,2**	**4** −7 **2,2**
5 −9 **2,2**	BEGINNING OF DEALER HITS SOFT 17—RENO, TAHOE, DOWNTOWN VEGAS, ETC. OTHER MODIFICATIONS	**A** −9 **17**
6 −23 **16**	**A** +7 **16**	**6** −21 **15**

+9 **A 15**	−15 **6 14**	+14 **A 14**
−10 **6 13**	−9 **6 12**	−20 **6 A7**
HIT **A A7**	−25 **6 A6**	−25 **6 A5**
−14 **6 9,9**	+5 **A 9,9**	

Chapter Nine

Determination of Betting Strategy

The Negative Swings

There are all too many counters who follow all the steps necessary to become good players and are still not successful. Why? Because they do not understand the statistics involved in determing proper bet size relative to the size of their bank. The statistical swings in blackjack are wide; losing periods can continue for far beyond what one would ordinarily think were reasonable intervals.

If you become a good blackjack player and begin playing for any length of time, it is virtually inevitable that you will experience periods when you will lose heavily, get discouraged and seriously consider leaving the business. It's happened to all of us. Let me cite a sobering statistic: if you were to play and enjoyed a 2% advantage on *every* hand (which is unrealistically optimistic), after 2,500 hands you would have nearly a 20% chance of losing. This statistic is continually borne out by our actual playing experiences; to cite some actual examples:

1. Several years ago, I played full time for 22 consecutive days in some of the most favorable games I've ever experienced. This interval included five days of playing only positive four deck shoes at the Fremont (team play), five days of a juicy single deck game at the Dunes and six days of playing only positive shoes at the Desert Inn. At the end of 22 days, I was down $35,000. On the 23rd day, I played a grueling five-hour session at the Marina, a favorable double deck game which was dealt down to 15-20 cards from the end, and lost again.

After the session, I disgustedly returned to the team meeting room and announced, "I've had it. You guys keep playing. I'm going back to San Francisco. If I see one more stiff, I'll tear the cards up."

One of the guys said, "You're just tired, Ken. Get a good night's sleep. You'll get 'em eventually."

My point: here I'd been playing nearly full time for over two years and should have been aware of the steepness of negative swings. Yet, I was almost ready to throw in the towel. (The cards did turn; the very next day, I beat the Trop for $12,000, the start of a $97,000 winning streak.)

2. A second example mentioned in Chapter 3: two of the best counters I know played in Europe for 61 days, full time, and were down $30,000. They, too, eventually recovered, by "hangin' in there."

3. The same two players dropped $156,000 in two weeks in Atlantic City in late 1979 in a highly favorable game (the rules had been restored after the "experiment" described in Chapter 13, to dealing two-thirds of the shoe, with no betting restrictions). Because they had an adequate bank behind them, they were able to recover.

Earnings Versus Risk

The determination of bet size requires a trade-off between potential earnings on the one hand and risk on the other. Let's take an example:

Players A and B both have a bankroll of $10,000. Player A decides to bet from $1 to $10. The likelihood of losing his $10,000 is very low, perhaps 1-out-of-2,000 or so. But he'll earn only $5 to $7 per hour.

Player B is more aggressive and decides to bet from $100 to $1,000. He should average perhaps $500 to $700 per hour, but his chances of tapping out are high—perhaps 4-out-of-10 (if we are winning players, the chances of tapping out are never more than 1-out-of-2).

In determining his bet size, the player must strike an acceptable balance between earnings rate and degree of risk.

Five Percent Element-Of-Ruin

Our teams nearly always use what we call a 5% element-of-ruin. Our bets are calibrated to yield us a 19-out-of-20 chance of doubling our bank and a 1-out-of-20 (5%) chance of tapping out. But we hedge. If we lost half the bank, we cut our betting in half, so we have restored a 5%

ruin factor with our depleted bank. With this strategy, we've got about a 1-out-of-300 chance of tapping out. (It's not 5% , or 1-out-of-400, since the likelihood of losing *half* of the first bank is higher than 5%.)

Over the past six years, we've had 125 to 150 winning banks and six losing banks. The ratio is less than 300-to-1 due in part to the fact that, in some instances, we didn't have nearly the edge we thought we had.

Element-Of-Ruin Curves. Take a look at Table 9-1. For any given player's percentage advantage, the table indicates the number of units of bank that is needed. Thus, to have a 5% element-of-ruin, with an edge of 1½% (read from 1½% up the dotted line to the 5% ruin curve and then read off the number of units to the left, on the vertical axis of the chart), the player must have 110 units of bank.

Table 9—1

Relationship of Number of Units Needed and Player's Percent Advantage at Three Element-of-Ruin Levels

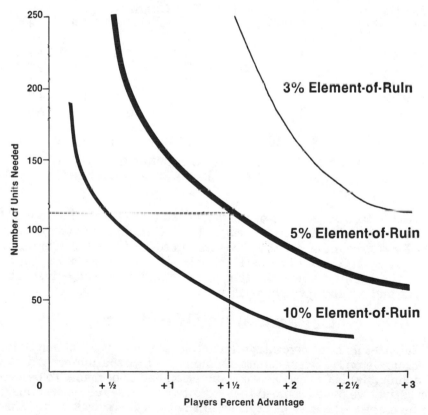

Thus, if a player wants an overall edge of 1½% over the house (the practical maximum that our teams have experienced in the long run), he should have 110 units of bankroll. (For those of you whose aversion to risk exceeds or falls below 5%, Table 9-1 also includes 3% and 10% element-of-ruin curves.)

But, we can be more precise than this. We can determine the size of *each* bet for a given element-of-ruin (henceforth, in our illustrations, we'll use a 5% element-of-ruin).

How To Know Your Edge On A Given Hand

On any given hand, the counter's percentage advantage is determined by two factors: (1) the true count and (2) the number of cards or decks which have not been dealt. Table 9-2 shows the player's edge for various Uston APC true counts and various numbers of decks remaining (assuming Las Vegas Strip rules).

Table 9—2

Player Edge at Various *True* Counts
Uston Advanced Point Count*

No. Decks Remaining	Uston True Count of:					
	0	+1	+2	+3	+4	+5
½ deck	+.8%	+1.1%	+1.4%	+1.7%	+2.1%	+2.5%
1 deck	0	+ .3	+ .7	+1.0	+1.4	+1.7
2 decks	−.4	0	+ .3	+ .7	+1.1	+1.4
3 decks	−.4	− .1	+ .2	+ .6	+1.0	+1.3
4 decks	−.5	− .2	+ .2	+ .5	+ .9	+1.3

* Assumes Las Vegas Strip rules

Note: Also assumes player is counting and making appropriate adjustments in the play of his hand.

With a true count of zero, the player is even with the house if one deck is remaining, and has an edge of .8% if a half-deck is remaining. With a true count of +4, the player has an edge of .9% with four decks remaining, 1.1% with two decks remaining. This information can be used to determine how much the player should bet for any given true count and for any given bank size.

Determination Of Bet Size

Table 9-3 lists the percentage advantage to the player (Column B) for various Uston APC true counts (Column A). Since the number of decks remaining is also a variable, an assumption had to be made. To be conservative, we have assumed that from two-to-three full decks remain to be played—the case most usual in the typical six deck game. This assumption makes our formula conservative for single, double and four deck games, which is fine. In determining bet size, it is always best to round on the side of conservatism, that is, toward the smaller bet size, to ensure that the 5% ruin factor is not exceeded. It's preferable to sacrifice some earnings in exchange for the assurance that we'll have a good chance of staying in business.

Table 9—3

Illustration of True Count and Bet Size
Using a $10,000 Bank

A	B	C	D	E
Uston True Count	Percent Advantage to Player	Number of Units Required for 5% Element-of-Ruin	Estimated Bet Size Amount	Number of Green Chips
+ 3	+ ½%	240	$ 40	2
+ 4	+ 1	150	60	2
+ 5	+ 1½	110	90	3
+ 6	+ 2	75	125	5
+ 7	+ 2½	65	160	6
+ 8	+ 3	55	190	7
+ 9	+ 3½	45	210	8
+ 10	+ 4	38	260	10
+ 11	+ 4½	35	300	12
+ 14	+ 5	32	325	13

NOTES: Same numbers are applicable to Revere APC.
Hi Opt II players should multiply Column A by 1.2
Hi Opt I players should multiply Column A by .6
Advanced Plus/Minus players should multiply Column A by .4

Reading from the 5% curve in Table 9-1, we can derive the number of units of bank (Column C in Table 9-3) that we should have for each percentage edge. Thus, with an edge of ½%, we need 240 units of bank, and so on.

Let's assume the player has a bank of $10,000 (these same calculations obviously can be made for any size bank). We divide the number of units of bank needed (Column C) into $10,000, and get the amount that may be bet for any given true count (Column D). In our illustration in Table 9-3, we may bet $40 with a true count of +3, $60 with a true count of +4, etc.

In casino play we obviously wouldn't adhere to these precise betting levels; so, in Column E, we round Column D to the nearest number of green ($25) chips, rounding down in most cases, to be conservative.

Compare Column E with Column A. You'll note an interesting pattern. The number of green chips the player may bet (Column E) is about one less than the true count (Column A) in nearly all cases. Thus, our betting strategy can be simply stated, "Bet the true count minus one, in green chips." This one statement effectively summarizes all of the calculations in Table 9-3 and makes the application of our betting strategy in the casino quite simple. All we must do is calculate the betting true count, subtract one (1), and bet that number of green chips. While playing, we need not even know the amount that we're betting— just the number of green chips!

Now we know how much to bet in "plus" situations. How about off-the-top (immediately after the shuffle) and in negative situations? The strategy depends on which game is being played.

In Vegas Strip single deck games and in Atlantic City, the player is essentially even with the house off-the-top and can safely bet more than elsewhere. Since our plus betting calls for betting from one-to-twelve or thirteen green chips, we can safely bet from one-to-three chips off-the-top (continually betting one chip off-the-top will tend to draw heat). Detailed betting tips for single deck games are included in the following chapter.

Off-the-top bets should be more conservative in Nevada multiple deck games (where we have a disadvantage of −.35%-or-more off-the-top) or in single deck Northern Nevada games (about −.5% off-the-top). We should try to come out, wherever possible, with minimum bets. This is not always possible. For example, if we've won a $200 double-down on the last hand of a four deck shoe, we should make a "cover bet" (i.e., a bet not in accordance with the count, designed to mislead the pitbosses) of perhaps $75 to $100, two hands of $50, three hands of $25, or something similar. Cover betting is discussed in Chapter 10 (for single deck games) and in Chapter 11 (for multiple deck games).

The house generally has the advantage when the true count is negative. The player should bet as little as he can get away with. Sometimes, particularly when the count is positive and drops suddenly, cover bets are required in negative counts. We can summarize our $10,000 bank betting strategy as follows:

—For Vegas Strip single deck and Atlantic City: Bet the true count minus one, in green chips. Bet $25 to $75 off-the-top and get down as low as possible with negative counts.

—For Northern Nevada and Vegas multiple deck: Bet the true count minus one, in green chips. Bet $25 off-the-top whenever possible and get down as low as possible with negative counts.

It is essential that the counter devise a betting strategy *in advance* and adhere strictly to it while playing. To do this, merely insert the size of your bank in the calculations in Table 9-3. Relate the results in Column E to Column A. A pattern nearly always emerges. Note that for a $2,000 bank, the number of chips in Column E is exactly the same as in the $10,000 illustration—except that the chips are now red ($5) rather than green. For a $40,000 bank, Column E is also the same—but with black ($100) chips. For other size banks, patterns will emerge—such as "the true count divided by two, in green chips," "the true count times two in green chips," and so on.

The ratios recommended herein are greater than those generally discussed in other blackjack texts. It *is* possible to achieve these kinds of ratios—we have for years. As you will see in the next chapter, the ratios depend, in large measure, upon the counter's "act" in a casino:

— The better the act, the higher the betting ratio.
— The higher the betting ratio, the higher the profit expectation.

Kelly Criterion

An alternative betting scheme is the Kelly Criterion. The Kelly Criterion basically states: determine the percentage advantage over the house and bet that percentage of the total bank.

Thus, if in a given hand the player has a 1% edge (assume a bank of $20,000) he may bet $200. If the player has a 3% edge, he may bet 3% of the bank, or $600.

If the player loses, his betting levels are reduced automatically. He theoretically has no chance of tapping out, that is, he has a zero percent element-of-ruin. If the bank is increased through winning, the player automatically bets higher.

The player using this technique to the extreme would re-calculate his betting after every swing of his bank, even while at the table. Thus, many calculations in addition to those normally required while playing may become necessary.

It is possible to modify the approach and adjust betting levels after every major change. However, this, too, may necessitate midsession changes in betting strategy if wide swings are taken.

The Kelly method is more adaptable to the individual player. With more than one player playing simultaneously, which usually means less than instantaneous and perfect communication between players, the mid-session betting adjustments are not feasible.

The Kelly method sensibly calls for more aggresive betting when the player or team is ahead and lower betting when losses are experienced. Effectively, the element-of-ruin approach discussed herein can be used to take swings into account as well as to consider instances of reduced betting should a predetermined percentage of the bank be lost (we generally use 50%), by increasing betting on the upside.

Earnings Expectations

Several of the responsible texts on blackjack mention earnings expectations of 3-to-4% or higher. We have found, through the actual playing of hundreds of thousands of hands, that a win rate of about

1½% in the long run is what the accomplished counter can expect to achieve if he is playing accurately at favorable games. The reasons for this disparity are several:

1. No player can play as accurately as a computer. All of us, even the most accomplished, make occasional errors. Because of the many calculations required in counting cards, counting aces, adjusting for aces, converting to true counts and so on, errors are inevitable. Because of heat from the pit, players will get nervous and distracted, further increasing the error rate.

   Our team members used to return to the meeting room saying, "I didn't make any errors," or "I played perfectly." We later found, through team testing, that these statements were absurd. A rough analogy might be made to tennis: players make errors, but the really good ones make very few.

2. Disregarding errors, it is still not possible to play a theoretically perfect game. Cover bets must be made; the more attention-getting plays (such as splitting 10's) must periodically be avoided.

3. Some dealer cheating does take place. While I don't believe cheating to be a major problem in the larger casinos (this is discussed in depth in Chapter 16), it is enough of a factor to lower the counter's earnings expectations somewhat.

So, if you're earning 1½% you're doing as well as can realistically be expected.

How To Calculate Expected Value

"Expected value" refers to the amount that the player (or team) may expect to win, assuming he has an "average streak of luck." As we said earlier, the worst player in the world may win in the short term and the best may lose in the short term. After a long period of time, the "true" percentages, or actual expectations, should prevail.

Look at the bell-shaped or "normal" curve in Table 9-4 which depicts a counter's expectations. The most frequent result will be a win of 1½%. In any given session, however, the counter may lose as much as 15% or more; or, if the cards are running in his favor, he may win 15% or more. Over many sessions, the player's results, if plotted, should approximate such a curve.

Table 9—4

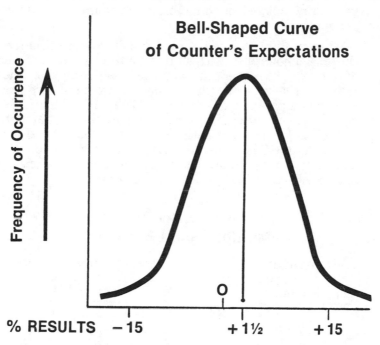

**Bell-Shaped Curve
of Counter's Expectations**

Frequency of Occurrence

% RESULTS   − 15   + 1½   + 15

To calculate expected value for a session, we take 1½% of the total amount bet. For example, assume we are playing to a $10,000 bank, betting from $25 to $250. If our average bet is $100 and we play 100 hands per hour, we have placed $10,000 of "action" into play each hour. With an earnings rate of 1½%, we would expect, on average, to earn $10,000 x 1½%, or $150 per hour.

This formula reveals several ways to increase expected value. Assuming that 1½% is the maximum achievable earnings rate, the ways to increase the total "action" per hour are limited, and therefore:

1. Increase the number of hands per hour.

    A. Head-on games are generally dealt at 150—200 hands per hour. A full table with seven players averages 65—75 hands per hour. Thus, the expected value of a head-on game is double or triple that of a full table game.

    B. Play as fast as you can, without sacrificing accuracy, at head-on games. I find that by playing fast, dealers tend to speed up with you. The accomplished player can actually play so fast as to not delay the dealer at all—that is, the dealer literally deals the hands as fast as he can, never delayed by the player placing bets or making playing decisions. It is possible in some face-up games in Europe, playing all seven spots, to average an incredible 700 hands per hour!!

2. Play multiple hands in positive situations, but *only* if in so doing you do not reduce the number of rounds dealt per deck or
per shoe.

When multiple hands are played, it is a statistical fact that
the total amount bet, with a given bank size and fixed element-
of-ruin, may be higher than when one hand is played. The player is not risking as much betting, for example, two hands of
$50 as compared to one hand of $100. His chance of losing
both $50 hands is less than that of losing the one hand of $100.
Occasionally, of course, both hands will be lost. But this occurs
proportionately less than the loss of a single hand. Because
of this, the player may bet a greater amount when playing
multiple hands with the same degree of risk.

Table 9-5
Multiple Hand Betting

Number of Hands Played Simultaneously	Allowable Increase in Total Amount Bet
2 hands	15%
3 "	22
4 "	26

Assume your betting strategy calls for a $200 bet. Table 9-5 in-
dicates that you may bet 15% more if playing two hands ($230, or two
hands of $115 *each*) and stay within the same element-of-ruin. You
have increased your action and thus, your earnings expectation, by
placing an additional 15% on the table. By the same token, by betting
four hands, you can increase the amount bet and thus, your earnings
expectation, by 26%. Playing multiple hands can be a useful way to increase earnings potential with the same size bank.

There is one key proviso, however. If, by playing multiple hands, you
reduce the number of rounds you would have been dealt in a given
positive deck or shoe, you haven't gained a thing—in fact, you may
have decreased expected value. For example, assume you're playing
head-on at a single deck game with three-fourths of a deck left and a
highly positive count. If you play one hand of $200, the dealer may
deal you four additional rounds. If the count stays positive, you have
bet four hands of $200, a total of $800 in action, before the shuffle.
But, if you spread two hands of $115 and the dealer gives you only two
more rounds, your total action has been reduced to $460. You then
would lose expected value.

On the other hand, assume you're playing at a table with three other
players and the dealer deals three rounds, whether you play an occa-

sional multiple hand or not. "Spreading" to two hands in positive situations will increase your total action and, thus, your expected value.

Multiple hands can also be used to good advantage toward the end of a shoe when the player knows the cut-card will come out on the next round. Not only is more money placed into action with no sacrifice in the number of rounds played (we will get only one more round at any rate), but the dealer is forced to deal further into the shoe, increasing the player's advantage. One time, in a highly positive four deck game at the Fremont, with a half-deck remaining in the shoe, I spread to seven hands of $500. The cut-card was the second card dealt. By the time the round was completed, there were only eight or nine unused cards in the shoe.

For the high-rolling counter, the playing of multiple hands provides a way to circumvent maximum house limits. If the betting strategy calls for a $2,000 bet and the club has a $500 limit, the player may bet four hands of $500 (actually five hands in this case, using Table 9-5).

Protection From The Long Run

The more hands played, the closer the player's results will be, on the average, to the expected percentage return (because of what the statistician's call "The Law Of Large Numbers"). This effect is shown in Table 9-6, which indicates the probability of winning (with a 1½% edge) for various hours of play.

Table 9-6

Probability Of Winning
At Various Hours of Play

Number Of Hours Of Play (at 100 hands per hour)	Probability Of Winning
1 Hour	56%
5 Hours	62
10 "	67
20 "	73
50 "	84
100 "	92
200 "	94
400 "	99.7

135

The table obviously does not refer to continuous hours played. It shows that the experienced player, playing a five-hour session, would expect to win 62% of the time and lose 38% of the time. If he were to play ten such sessions, totalling 50 hours of play, it is likely he would be ahead 84% of the time and behind 16% of the time. The more hours played, the greater the likelihood of the player being ahead (just as a losing roulette player will be more likely to lose the longer he plays, as the house "grinds" him out). A good counter, playing 40 hours per week for 10 weeks, or 400 hours, would have a 99.7% chance of winning.

This phenomenon explains why blackjack teams tend to fare so much better than individual players. A team with several players will get into the "long run" faster than an individual player. In late 1979, our Team 6 had nine players, each averaging ten hours per day, playing in Atlantic City. Each day, we put in a total of nearly 100 hours, smoothing out fluctuations and considerably reducing the "ulcer factor." In Chapter 12, we will discuss how you can capitalize on this factor by playing with others.

This same phenomenon explains why the huge Atlantic City casinos, with 70—100 blackjack tables, are much more likely to show a profit day in and day out than are the smaller Nevada casinos with only three-to-five tables. The larger casinos are close to being in the "long run" each day.

The figures in Table 9-6 should clear up several misconceptions about card-counting. Counters have over-confidently said to me, "Well, I think I'll go down to the Stardust and make a few hundred." I wish it were that easy.

Just as erroneous are the statements of the pitbosses when they say a counter has only to sit at a table and play a few hours to leave several thousand dollars richer. These are the bosses who, if they suspect a counter, will rush to shuffle-up or bar him before thousands of dollars of casino money can be lost. These bosses don't understand that counting is a long, hard grind. They would be better advised to allow the suspected counter to play for an hour or so, taking their time to size the player up. If the player turns out to be a good counter, the house may have sacrificed a few hours of expected value, perhaps a few hundred dollars. If he's not, the house may gain hours of play from a losing player. Despite this fact, hundreds of non-counters have been barred in Nevada and Atlantic City.

The figures in Table 9-6 also expose another fallacy to which counters fall prey. This is best described by relating one of our experiences. It was December 15 and we'd just doubled a bank. Four of us had no obligations for about a week so we agreed to stay in Vegas for a few days "to make some more money for Christmas." The result: by December 23, we were stuck $40,000 and had to break the bank because all four of us had other commitments.

The moral of the story: don't play unless you have the time to "get into the long run." You might get lucky and double your bank in a few days, but what happens if you get stuck and don't have the time to "dig out?" The part-time player can get into the long run by continuing trips over a period of time, say 20 hours per weekend over several months.

Planning a short, finite trip (without the opportunity to return) is a gamble. And the last thing a counter wants to do is gamble.

Chapter Ten

The Art
of
Playing Single Deck

This chapter discusses the techniques we've developed through the years in learning, practicing and playing single deck. Many of the concepts, particularly at the end of this chapter, have never been published—indeed, some of them remain unknown except to a handful of professional players.

The first portion of this chapter, pages 139-146, instructs the reader interested in using the Uston (or other) Advanced Point Count in playing single deck. I recommend that all serious students of the game read this chapter, but the Advanced Point Count student should not study the chapter in depth until he has mastered the "count" and "numbers" material in Chapter 8.

Learning To Become A Professional Level Single Deck Player

Unless you're reading this chapter for general background, you are now ready to "put it all together." You have studied Chapter 8 and can count down a deck in 25 seconds and recite the number flashcard values nearly automatically. You understand the other concepts in Chapter 8 as well. You've read Chapter 9 and have determined what your betting strategy will be when you're ready to play for real. This section trains you to become ready to play single deck in a casino—and gives you guidelines so you know for sure if you're ready.

I refer to the "art" of single deck, because single deck is far more of an intuitive-type game than multiple deck. Multiple deck calculations, using, for example, the nearest half-deck in the discard pile, are made in a fairly mechanical way. Two excellent players using the same system, will often make exactly the same bets and play the hands the same. Single deck involves more "rounding," more interpolation, more of a "feel" for the game.

True Count Conversion. We've developed shortcuts that simplify playing single deck which are based largely on the fact that, on average, 2.7 cards are played per hand (this figure is slightly lower in Altantic City because of early surrender, but is of no import here, since there are currently no single deck games in Atlantic City).

Assume you're playing head-on with the dealer. During every round, 5.4 cards on average are used (2.7 times one hand for you and one for the dealer). After five rounds, 27 cards are used (5.4 times 5 rounds), almost exactly a half-deck (26 cards). This permits an interesting extrapolation, shown in Table 10-1.

Table 10—1

True Count Conversion—Head-on Games

# Rounds Played	# Cards Played	Conversion Factor*	Conversion Factor (CF) Rounded
1	5.4	.56	.6
2	10.8	.63	.7
3	16.2	.73	.8
4	21.6	.86	.9
5	27.0	1.00	1.0
6	32.4	1.30	1⅓
7	38.8	1.97	2.0
8	44.2	3.33	3.0

$$*CF = \frac{26}{52\text{-}n} \text{ where } n = \#\text{cards played}$$

Using the rounded conversion factors (CF), the head-on single deck player need only to start with a factor of .6 during the first round and progress through .7, .8, .9 and finally 1.0 during the fifth round. During the sixth round, a CF of 1⅓ is used, indicating that the true count actually exceeds the running count by one-third. Today, rarely are single deck games dealt beyond the sixth round. While the CF's have been rounded so that accuracy is not to the nearest card played, they are sufficiently close for winning play. The shortcut precludes the player from being concerned with counting the number of cards played.

During minus decks, fewer cards will tend to be used (more high cards tend to be dealt and thus fewer cards per hand are required). During plus decks, more cards will tend to be used (more small cards are in play). However, this factor is not significant, and over the long run, will average out.

Ace Adjustment. Note that after five rounds, when an average of 27 cards have been played, two aces should have been played for aces to be "normal." The player can visualize a meter, relating the number of "normal" aces to rounds played, as follows:

Table 10—2

Number of Rounds Played

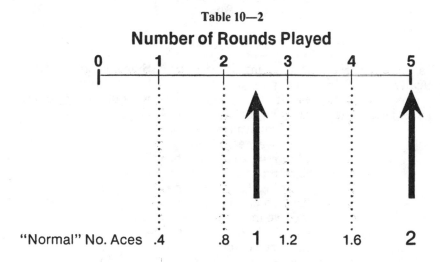

Playing head-on, two aces should have been played after five rounds and one ace should have been played after 2½ rounds. In other words, we would expect .4 aces to be played on each round for aces to be normal.

Thus, after the first round, if no aces had been seen, we would be .4 aces-rich. Since we multiply the number of aces-rich or poor by the ace adjustment factor of three, we would get a product of 1.2 (or rounding, one) to add to our running count before deriving our true count.

To take another example, assume we played two rounds and two aces were played. We would expect .8 aces to be played—so, we are 1.2 aces-poor, times the ace adjustment factor of three, giving 3.6. Thus, we would deduct three or four points from our running count before determining the true count. (The running count, after it is modified for aces, is called the "adjusted running count.")

Illustrative Hands. To clarify the above, let's assume we're playing head-on. We've learned the count and the numbers. Our betting strategy (as determined in Chapter 9) is: "Bet the true count in green when the deck is plus; come off-the-top with one-to-three greens and get down as low as possible in negative situations."

The Deal:	Our Thought Processes:	Our Action:

First hand:
We are dealt 4,6.

The dealer's upcard is 7. Our running count is +6. Basic Strategy is to double since the count is positive.

We double-down, putting out 2 more green chips.

We're dealt a three. the dealer has a 9 in the hole and hits with a 3, beating us.

Our count is +9, no aces played. We are about .4 aces-rich. Multiplying times the ace adjustment factor of 3, we get 1.2, or 1, which we add to the running count of 9, totalling 10. Since the first round is completed, we multiply by the CF of .6, giving a betting true count of 6 (10 running x .6 CF).

Forget all the numbers except the original running count of +9.

Since we're betting the "true in green," we put out 6 green chips.

Second Hand:
We're dealt A,8, versus a dealer's 5.

Our running count is now +13. From the numbers matrix we have memorized, we need a true count of +3 to make this play (that is, to double-down). Our CF is now .7 (second round), so our true count is (ignoring aces now since we're not betting) 13 x .7, or about +9. This is way in excess of the needed +3.

We double-down, putting out 6 more chips.

We're dealt a 10. The dealer has a 10 in the hole and hits with a 10. We win the hand.

Our running count is now +4 and 1 ace played. We are just about even in aces (actually .8 aces should have been played, so we're .2 aces–poor; that's small enough to disregard). Two rounds have been played so we use a CF of .7 times our running count of +4, giving +3 (rounded).

We bet 3 green chips.

Third hand:
We're dealt 10,2 versus a dealer's 4.

Our running count is still +4. Our matrix number for 12 versus 4 is zero (i.e., stand if the true count is greater than zero).

We stand.

The dealer has a 10 in the hole and hits with an ace, another ace, and finally an 8, busting. We win the hand.

Our running count is now +2, 3 aces have been played. We've finished the third round and 1.2 aces should have been played. Thus we're nearly 2 aces-poor, times the ace factor of 3, equals 6 points to deduct from our running count of +2. Thus our adjusted running count is negative, a −4 (+2−6). Whenever the adjusted running count is negative, the true count is also negative. Thus, there's no need to convert.

We bet the minimum, 1 green chip.

Your first reaction may leave you overwhelmed. But, notice there are several simplifying factors. First, whenever the adjusted running count (the running count adjusted for ace-richness or ace-poorness) is negative, so is the true count. Since, while betting, we usually don't

143

care how negative the deck is, there is no need to use the CF's during the time the adjusted running count becomes negative (fully one-third of the time in this case).

Further, the only time we must calculate the true count for playing purposes is when we have a close play. Whenever we are dealt a hard 17, 18, 19 or a blackjack, no calculations are necessary. Additionally, in plus decks on hands where we would double, split or surrender according to Basic Strategy (such as the 10 versus 7 in the first hand above), no calculations need be made. Calculations for play of the hand are needed in only about 15% of the hands.

Go through the above example a few times until it becomes totally clear. It shouldn't take long. Remember, if it were easy to play a professional level count against the house, thousands would be doing it and the opportunity to beat the house wouldn't exist. Further, *it is far easier* to become an expert at blackjack than it is at chess or bridge, and the potential financial rewards are much greater.

The Single Deck Final Test. Assuming that you've mastered the count and the numbers, you're now ready for the final test to determine when you'll be ready to play single deck in a casino.

Take a single deck of cards, deal yourself two cards up and give the dealer two cards, one up and one down. Bet and play exactly as you would in a casino, using the count, the numbers and your predetermined betting strategy (get some $1 or $5 chips to practice with). Play through to approximately two-thirds of the deck (there's no sense practicing conversions at levels that will rarely be dealt to you in a casino). After you've completed two-thirds of the deck, take one card, unseen, and lay it on the table. Continue your running count and number of aces until you've counted all the cards in the deck except the one card on the table. Then, predict the value of the last card as you did when practicing the count:

 —As an example, if your count is +3, 4 aces, after counting all the cards but the last one, the hidden card should be a —3 card or 10.

 —If your count was zero, 3 aces, the last card should be an ace.

 —If your count was —1, 4 aces, the last card should be a +1 card, either a 2 or 8. And so on.

If you can predict the last card 19-out-of-20 times without fail, after having made the bets, made the plays, counted aces, converted running to true counts and recalled the matrix numbers, you are probably ready for casino play.

It will probably take you 15-20 hours of work with the final test before you achieve that level of accuracy. It's also important that, as you practice, you feel confident that you're making the bets and the playing decisions correctly. Most good players, I find, spend far *more* time than is really necessary in practicing before playing. Practice becomes fun once you become competent. It's like a mathematical puzzle, making the calculations, placing the bets, dealing the cards and predicting the value of the last card. You'll experience a great deal of personal satisfaction along the way as you begin to recognize your own competence. Try to turn your study into a game—a continual test of self-improvement.

If the count seems to come a bit slow, take the +16 training deck and count it down for a half hour or so. If the numbers come slow, take the numbers flash cards and go through them eight or ten times.

Please, please don't attempt to play in a casino until you've met these requirements. Practicing in a casino will be expensive. Resist the urge to play in a casino because you have "gambling fever." If you do, you are not ready by definition. You should only go when you feel competent and are ready to test your skill—like a new pilot who feels he is ready to solo.

Summary For The Single Deck Player. To make sure that you've assimilated the material in Chapters 8, 9 and 10, I'll summarize the steps that should be taken by the potential professional level single deck player.

1. You must know single deck Basic Strategy perfectly. Even though you're a professional level player, you should continually run through the single deck flashcards with total accuracy—three times in 50 seconds.

2. Count down a standard 52-card deck in 25 seconds and a +16 practice deck in 35 seconds with near perfect accuracy. If you make more than one mistake per 50 times through the deck, you're not good enough.

3. Go through the numbers flashcards at a rate of one card per 1½ seconds. Use only those flashcards needed for single deck play; initially, disregard the surrender and double-on-split numbers. Rarely will you find these options in a single deck club.

4. Totally understand running count conversion and ace adjustment, as described in Chapters 8 and 10.

5. Read the betting strategy material in Chapter 9 and set aside your blackjack bankroll. Determine your ultimate betting strategy.

6. Take the Final Test, dealing deck after deck until you're totally comfortable with all phases of the game. You should be able to predict the count value of the last card in 19-out-of-20 trials.

7. Take a trip to a casino, betting SMALL amounts—perhaps the true count in silver (if you can find a $1 club) or the true count in $2. Play just as you would if you were at your ultimate betting level. You're getting live practice, but not risking important money. Play until you feel totally comfortable and have *no* doubt that your accuracy is high.

8. Advance gradually to your betting strategy (for example, if you decide to devote the bankroll to bet the true count in green, bet the true in red for a few days until you feel comfortable). If you find, when you advance to higher betting, that you're nervous and thus possibly inaccurate with large bets out, back off to lower levels for more experience, which, in turn, will breed confidence.

Some of our players, at first, were extremely nervous betting black chips. We now insist that all players begin by betting red chips, then green chips. We don't move them up until we know they can handle the "black action" with total confidence.

True Count Conversion And Ace Adjustment When Not Playing Head-Up.

Knowing that 2.7 cards on average are played per hand, we can develop guidelines for true count conversion and ace adjustment for other than head-up games. With two players at the table, 8.1 cards are used per round on average (2.7 x 3—2 players and the dealer). After three rounds, an average of 24.3 cards are played, roughly half the deck.

Table 10—3

True Count Conversion Factors—Two Players

# Rounds Played	# Cards Played	Conversion Factor*	Conversion Factor (CF) Rounded
1	8.1	.59	.6
2	16.2	.73	.7
3	24.3	.94	1.0
4	32.4	1.33	1⅓
5	40.5	2.26	2¼

$$* \ CF = \frac{26}{52\text{-}n} \quad \text{where n} = \text{\# cards played}$$

As in head-on play, the player need not count the number of cards played, merely the number of rounds. Notice that after three rounds are dealt (roughly a half-deck) we would expect two aces to be played. Thus, on average, ⅔ of an ace should be played on each round.

Table 10-4 summarizes the CF's that should be used with two players at the table. During the play of the hand in the first round, a CF of .6 is used. After the round is completed, the betting true count is determined using a CF of .6, adjusting for aces (⅔ of an ace should have been played for aces to be "normal"). If one ace were played, the deck would be ⅓ ace-poor, times the ace adjustment factor of 3, meaning that the player must deduct one point from his running count before calculating the betting true count.

During the second round of play, the player uses a CF of .7 while playing his hand. After the round is completed, he determines his betting true count using a CF of .7, adjusting for aces (1⅓ aces are normal); if one ace is played, we are ⅓ ace-rich and add 1 point to the running count; if no aces are played, we are 1⅓ aces-rich and add 4 points to the running count. If 2 aces are played, we are ⅔ aces-poor and deduct 2 points from the running count.

During the third round of play, the true count equals the running count—for both play-of-the hand and betting purposes, since the CF is 1.0. During the fourth round, the player need only increase the running count by ⅓ to get the true count.

Table 10—4

CF and Ace Adjustment—Two Players

Cards dealt by dealer	Player plays hand using CF of:	Hand is settled	Player makes bet using CF of:	"Normal" # aces played
1st round dealt:	.6		.6	⅔
2nd round dealt:	.7	↓	.7	1⅓
3rd round dealt:	1.0		1.0	2
4th round dealt:	1⅓		1⅓	2½
5th round dealt:	2¼		2¼	3

While it is best for the single deck player to play head-on or with only one other player (for reasons described below), CF factors are presented for various numbers of players at the table (Table 10-5).

Table 10—5

CF for Various Numbers of Players—Single Deck

# Rounds	3 Players	4 Players	5 Players	6 Players	7 Players
1	.6	.7	.7	.8	.9*
2	.9	1.0	1⅓	2.0	3.0
3	1⅓	2+	—	—	—

* OK to use 1.0

After many hours of play, the experienced single deck player will be able to "sense" where the dealer is in the deck—another reason why playing single deck is more of an "art," as opposed to multiple deck play. This skill is particularly helpful when players jump in and out of games, varying the number of hands played. This annoyance can be minimized by playing during lull periods in the casino.

Fine Points Of Single Deck

Assuming that the player plays accurately (and that the game is honest), player profitability depends on two factors: the number of cards seen and the betting ratio.

Number Of Cards Seen. This factor is too often neglected by players, and in my opinion, is the main reason why some competent players lose in the long run. To cite an example, two perfect "dining room table" players from Team 2 seemed to lose continually.

We tested them; they tested out perfectly. We observed their casino play; everything seemed fine. But they kept on losing—and losing—and losing—until the two of them were down $80,000 of our money. Their results defied every statistical dispersion test we applied. We finally pulled them out of play.

We now understand a key reason why they lost; they simply weren't playing good single deck games; that is, they didn't see enough cards (the other factors, we now believe, were inadequate betting ratios and something called "preferential shuffling," which is discussed later).

Subsequently, to tighten our quality control, we developed standards as to what constitutes a good single deck game. These standards are based on the knowledge, once again, that 2.7 cards are dealt per hand on average. Thus, if the head-on player is dealt 7 rounds, he will see, on average 7 times 2.7 times 2 (one hand for the player, one for the dealer), or 37.8 cards out of 52 cards, just under 3/4 of the deck. If he's dealt 6 rounds, he sees 32.4 cards, an acceptable amount, about one round more than half-a-deck. With five rounds, he sees only 27 cards and is making his last bet well before half-a-deck is played.

Experience has shown us that, with an acceptable betting ratio, 7 rounds of head-up play constitutes a highly beatable game, yielding the good player more than our overall goal of 1½% over the house. Six rounds is acceptable. Five is unacceptable.

We've developed standards for an acceptable number of rounds played, depending upon the number of players at the table, shown in Table 10-6. All our teammates have this table memorized.

Table 10—6

What Constitutes a Good Single Deck Game?

Number of Players at the Table	Number Of Rounds Dealt		
	Unacceptable	Fair	Good
1	5	6	7 (38 cards seen)
2	4	—	5 (40 + cards seen)
3	3	—	4 (43 cards seen)
4	2	—	3 (43 cards seen)
5	2	—	—
6	1	2 (38 cards)	—
7	1	—	2 (43 cards seen)

The best games are 7 rounds of head-on play, 5 rounds with another player at the table, 4 rounds with 3 players, 3 rounds with 4 players, or 2 rounds of 7 players. Note there are no good games with 5 players, since there are usually not enough cards to be dealt 3 rounds (it does happen on occasion, particularly in Northern Nevada). Six players at the table also do not constitute a good game, since even with 2 rounds, only 38 cards are dealt and the player's second bet is made at only 19 cards played.

Of the good games, clearly the best is 7 rounds of head-on play. The player receives the most hands per hour, up to 200 hands or more with a fast dealer. The worst of the good games is at a full table where 65 to 75 hands are dealt per hour. In effect, one hour at a head-on game is the equivalent of playing three hours at a full table. Further, the player's count is totally up-to-date as he makes each bet and each play. In addition, this game is less fatiguing because there are no interruptions from the other players, which tend to break one's concentration.

Too often, the counter remains in a marginal game, optimistically hoping that conditions will improve, that the dealer will take a break, etc. I've seen player after player fall prey to this wishful thinking and then win at below an acceptable rate, or worse, record long-term losses.

Back in 1977, we could rigidly enforce our standards for number of rounds dealt. By 1978, Vegas was counter-conscious and many single deck (and two and four deck) games were unacceptable. But the pendulum has begun to swing back in the other direction as of this writing. I suspect that this has happened for the following reasons:

1. There are fewer good counters playing in Vegas.

2. The casinos realize that many high-rollers prefer fewer decks. Caesars has retained its single deck game, and in fact, has raised its limit to $3,000. The Frontier and Aladdin (before it was closed temporarily) introduced single deck in 1980.

149

Insist on playing favorable games. Absolutely refuse to play marginal ones, even if the pitbosses "love you," you feel like playing or you can think of the many other alibis I've been given. Basically, you're wasting your time.

Creating A Good Game. There are creative ways to try to create a good game. Let's say you're playing a 6-round head-on game and suddenly someone joins the table. The dealer now deals out only 4 rounds. Try playing two hands and see if he'll deal a 4-round/3-hand game. If so, you've restored a good game. Or, say you're at a good 4-player game and someone joins. making it a 5-player game. Spread to two hands and get a "fair" 6-player/2-round game until a player leaves. Then, cut back to one hand, getting the original 4-player game once again. There are many other possibilities, which careful study of Table 10-6 will reveal.

Preferential Shuffling. Preferential shuffling occurs when the dealer shuffles away good decks and deals down in bad decks. The natural fall of the cards tends to promote an automatic preferential shuffle. When the deck goes favorable, more lower-valued cards have been played and thus, more cards tend to be played. When the count goes negative, the reverse is true, as fewer of the higher-valued cards will tend to be played. If the dealer always deals down to the same level in the deck, he will tend to deal fewer rounds when the count goes positive and more rounds when the count goes negative. Fortunately, in single deck games, this effect is usually not strong enough to significantly affect the number of rounds dealt.

But some dealers, while not counting, utilize the knowledge that when many little cards are played, they should shuffle more—and when many 10's and aces are played, they should continue to deal. In fact, many of Caesars' single deck dealers practice this, which is why, despite the fact that this game offers the best rules of any game in the world, it should generally be avoided. I've observed dealers at Reno's Riverside, and at the Stardust, the Sahara, the Castaways and the Silver Slipper in Las Vegas who practice this as well.

There is no counting system in the world that will beat continual preferential shuffling. Yet, I observe many nervous players who concentrate on the count, worry about their losses, savor their wins and attempt to outfox the pit. They will totally ignore dealer shuffling patterns—and work real hard, but with a disadvantage to the house.

In summary, make sure you're seeing enough cards—and watch continually for preferential shuffling.

Betting Ratios. The second factor affecting the player's win rate is his betting ratio. Our teammates are supplied rules-of-thumb as to what constitutes acceptable ratios. We shoot for a 6-to-1 ratio at single deck, 10-to-1 at double deck and 18-to-1 at four or more decks. A 6-to-1 ratio is acceptable in Atlantic City because of the favorable rules (this should earn 2 units per hour on average). While the Nevada ratios may seem high, we have found that a "good act" often can yield higher ratios. Many times, our players have enjoyed betting increases from $25 to three hands of $500 in Nevada games—occasionally, we've gone from two hands of $25 to two hands of $1,000, with total endorsement from the pit. The ratio often depends upon the player's comportment in a casino—the act—the little body language movements and expressions that should be used to convince the pit that the counter is a losing player.

Some blackjack texts recommend a steady betting pattern of, for example, 2 units off-the-top (right after the shuffle), increasing to 4 units if the count goes up and the player wins, decreasing to 1 unit if the count goes down and the player loses, and so on. We've found that not only does this earn less because of the lower ratios, but it often actually draws *more* heat from the pit because it's an obviously detectable betting method repeated over and over again.

Let me describe what we call the "steaming approach," which is best explained using an actual example. A player, call him Tim, walked into the Hilton and cashed in three $100 bills for $25 chips. So as not to draw too much attention early in the game, Tim bet $75 off-the-top. His betting strategy was "the true count in black." The deck stayed negative and Tim stayed with green chips, betting as little as $25 per hand.

Finally, a deck went positive and Tim had lost all his green chips. Then, his act began: a flush came over his face as Tim "nervously" reached into his pocket and pulled out a wad of $100 bills. Tim said to himself (but loudly enough so the bosses watching could hear), "Sonuvabitch—I gotta get that money back," and threw down three $100 bills on the betting square, shaking his head and sighing, as if to communicate, "Goddam it, here I go again—losing control and steaming."

He lost the hand. The count went up further. Tim's face got redder. He swore more and his hands shook more noticeably. He pulled out more bills and threw them recklessly on the square, sighing again and saying, "Bet the sonuvabitch." At this point, it is unlikely that the dealer would shuffle. The dealer and bosses have seen "steamers" time after time—they lose control, they chase their money, they lose their heads. If the dealer were to shuffle, the 45-second delay might allow this "steamer" to come to his senses.

Tim lost that hand, too, and the count stayed up. There was only a quarter of a deck left. Tim hesitated—the dealer made no move to shuffle. Tim swore again, reached into his pocket, pulled out a huge sheaf of $100 bills (about $5,000) and said, "How much can I bet?" (He knew, of course, that the Hilton had a $1,000 limit.)

The boss told him. Tim threw out a stack of bills (about 14 or 15) and said, "Go ahead—if I lose, take 10." He looked down, flushed, disgusted and depressed, as if he'd lost a month's pay.

Tim won the $1,000. He pulled the bills and chips back, breathed a sigh of relief, and, as the dealer shuffled, "regained control," and bet $100 off-the-top.

When the cards seem to run against you as the count increases, this approach can be used with great effectiveness. When the player is losing consecutive hands, he can order drinks loudly and happily, "parlay" his money by doubling his bet, doubling it again and perhaps even again. There are many, many ruses similar to this one—it's difficult to teach them since most occur as the player is at the table and depend upon the specific situation. Improvisation is the key to putting on a good act.

Mixing Colors. Mixing colored chips is often successful in disguising from the bosses and dealers the fact that your betting is moving with the count. Let's assume you're betting strategy is predicated on a bank of $12,500 and that you're betting the true count in $25 to the extent that you can get away with it.

When betting off-the-top, vary your bets, so you show no pattern. Bet 2 green chips one time. The next time off-the-top, bet one green and 3 red chips. Or bet 1 green chip, or 2 red and 2 green chips.

Say you've got out 2 red and 1 green off-the-top and the count goes up. If you win the hand, leave the 2 green chips out, slide another green chip underneath and put a red chip or two on top. Now you've gone from a $35 bet to an $80 or $85 bet. Then, let's say the count goes down. Leave out 5 chips, all red. It looks like a tall stack, but it's all red and you're betting only $25. Had the count gone up, perhaps you'd bet 4 green and 1 red—also five chips—but now you've got $105 out.

If you have four greens and a red, and win a double-down, chances are that the dealer may slip you two black chips. If the count goes up, slide one of the black chips under several green and a red. If the count goes down, change your blacks, as if saving them as your "reserve."

It's impossible for me to describe all the variations we've used. There are literally hundreds of them. But as you play more and more, they should occur to you. Remember, your goal is to look like an erratic bettor, varying strangely, perhaps according to superstition or some losing "system." Many counters get paranoid about spreading bets and putting out a good ratio. Watch some non-counting players. They often spread far more widely than most counters would dream possible. Try to emulate them—except of course your wide variation will be dependent upon the count.

Mixing chip colors not only confuses the bosses as to the amount you're betting by making it difficult for them to total your bet, but it takes the heat off big bets, since the bet is capped with a red chip. Further, your stack always looks about the same height (contrast this with the player who tries to bet from 1 green chip to 8 green chips—very obvious and something I'd never try for long). Another reason to mix colors—it makes the payoffs on insurance and surrender difficult. This is beneficial to you because the dealers and the bosses are concentrating on ensuring that the payoffs are correct—a preoccupation that tends to take their minds off whether you're counting or not.

Card Eating. A highly effective, and heretofore unpublished, method of increasing betting ratios is by what we call "card-eating." Many counters (and bosses) feel that a common way to increase the ratio is by spreading to two (or more) hands in positive decks. Unless you're a high bettor bumping up against the house limit, this is not true (unless, as I said earlier, you can do it without reducing the number of rounds dealt).

For example, assume you're betting $25 to $300, or the true-in-green. Let's say the deck is positive; you bet $125 and win the hand. The deck now goes negative; yet, you have $250 out there and feel sheepish (justifiably) about cutting back to a $25 or $50 bet. A good technique now is to bet two or three hands of $25 each.

Why? First, your bet is actually cut from $125 to $50 or $75. Secondly, your risk (from an element-of-ruin standpoint) is cut because, as we have seen, with three bets of $25 you are risking less than with one bet of $75. Most bosses will not suspect that you're cutting back your bet—spreading is generally considered a "bullish" move by the pit. Further, by periodically spreading in negative decks, you will move the game toward the shuffle faster; in our example, each of your three hands will eat up cards. Spreading in negative decks sometimes even *causes* the dealer to shuffle; there may not be enough cards to complete the next card-consuming round.

Take another example: you've just bet 4 greens and 2 reds and won the hand. The count has dropped. Spread to two hands of 2 red each—or even 3 hands. You've cut your bet way down and you're eating up cards in this negative situation. Again, the dealer is pushed more rapidly toward the shuffle and you will tend to be dealt fewer negative hands.

When the deck is positive, you want to "spread vertically," as we call it. Put your chips on one square and play the hand. You're using up less cards and are likely to get dealt more rounds from the favorable deck.

We've done studies which show the power of card-eating. If you vary from one black chip to 4 black chips, your ratio is 4-to-1. If you vary from three hands of $25, $50 and $25 (which also totals $100) on the down side, to one hand of $400, your effective bet ratio, and thus expected value, has increased significantly to about 6-to-1. This is because you are using up three times as many cards in the negative situations as you are in the positive ones (actually even more, because more cards per round tend to be dealt when the deck is negative since there are more smaller cards in the deck.)

Summary. Playing single deck is a skill that can be achieved by using shortcuts in true count conversion and ace adjustment. The player must watch for favorable games. There are creative ways that he may create a good game for himself.

The skillful single deck player can utilize such tricks as mixing colors and card-eating to ensure that (1) he sees a sufficient number of cards and (2) he gets winning bet ratios. These two critical factors depend in large measure on the player's "act," his ability to convince the pit that he's just another losing player. The act is discussed in detail in Chapter 17, "Getting Barred."

Chapter Eleven

Multiple Deck Play

This chapter discusses the techniques we've developed in learning, training for and playing multiple deck games. The first portion of this chapter, pages 155-162, instructs the reader interested in using the Uston (or other) Advanced Point Count in playing multiple deck. I advise all serious students of the game to read this chapter; but the Advanced Point Count student should not study the chapter in depth until he has mastered the "count" and "numbers" material in Chapter 8.

Learning To Become A Professional Level Multiple Deck Player

Since a good portion of the multiple deck players come from the East and plan on playing in Atlantic City, I will gear the first portion of this chapter to the Atlantic City player. Later, we will discuss the adjustments and refinements applicable to the multiple deck player in Nevada and elsewhere.

Once again, unless you're reading this chapter for general background information, you are now ready to "put it all together." You have studied Chapter 8 and can count down a deck in 25 seconds and recite the number flashcard values automatically. You understand the other concepts in Chapter 8, you've read Chapter 9 and have determined what your betting strategy will be when you're ready to play. This section will train you to play in Atlantic City and will give you guidelines so you'll know for sure when you're ready.

True Count Conversions—Ace Adjustment Tests. The following practice techniques were developed over the past three years and have proven invaluable in preparing players for playing multiple deck games accurately.

Secure 19 decks of cards, the standard "Bee-type" cards used by most casinos; they should be new or infrequently used. Arrange the cards into eight separate packs, consisting of:

1.	26 cards	(½ deck)
2.	52 "	(1 ")
3.	78 "	(1½ decks)
4.	104 "	(2 ")
5.	130 "	(2½ ")
6.	156 "	(3 ")
7.	182 "	(3½ ")
8.	208 "	(4 ")

All packs should have the same colored card on top (either blue or red back). Put rubber bands around each pack and arrange them on a flat surface as follows:

Figure 11a

Number of Decks	½	1	1½	2	2½	3	3½	4
# Normal Aces	2	4	6	8	10	12	14	16
Conversion Factor	11	10	9	8	7	6	5	4

As you've probably guessed, these packs represent various numbers of decks in the discard pile (we don't go beyond four full decks since most Atlantic City dealers don't deal beyond four decks—although if you find one that does, definitely play him, because that game is more favorable to the player).

Assuming each of the above packs was in the discard pile, how many aces should be played for aces to be normal? Clearly, under the half-deck pack, the answer is 2 aces, since there are 2 aces per 26 cards on average. Under the one deck pack, 4 aces. Then 6 aces, 8, 10, 12, 14 and finally, 16 aces under the four deck pack.

Now, we're going to play a little learning game. Take another 52-card deck of cards and shuffle it. This deck will represent the number of aces actually played in our hypothetical game—an ace means one ace played; a deuce, 2 aces played, 3, 3 aces, ... 10, 10 aces. Let the jack represent 11 aces played, the queen 12 aces played and the king 13 aces played.

Now, take the deck and put the top card face up, in front of the half-deck pack lying on the table. Assume the value of the card is a 5. This means that, in our hypothetical game, there is a half-deck in the discard pile and 5 aces have been played. What does this mean to us in terms of ace-rich or ace-poor? Since 5 aces have been played, and were aces normal (meaning 2 aces would have been played), we are 3 aces-poor. Recite "minus (for poor) 3."

Then, take the next card off the deck and place it up in front of the one deck pack. Let's say this card is a 3. Now, we have one deck in the discard pile, meaning that 4 aces normally would have been played, but 3 aces have been played. Thus, we are 1 ace-rich. Recite "plus 1."

To ensure you understand this test, let's assume that the first eight cards you place in front of each of the packs are a 5, 3, 10, 8, jack, 10, king and 9. You would recite the answers as indicated below:

Figure 11b

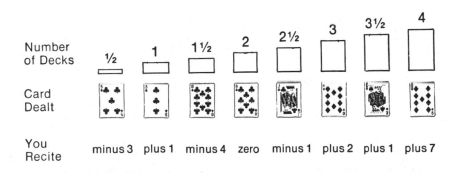

Number of Decks	½	1	1½	2	2½	3	3½	4
Card Dealt	5♣	3♣	10♣	8♣	J	10♦	K	7♦
You Recite	minus 3	plus 1	minus 4	zero	minus 1	plus 2	plus 1	plus 7

— In the third case, a 10 is placed under 1½ decks: 10 aces played, 6 should be played. We are 4 poor. Recite "minus 4."

— In the fourth case, 8 aces are played, and the 8 should be played. Recite "zero."

— In the fifth case, a jack is under the pack, representing 11 aces played. Ten aces should have been played. Recite "minus 1." And so on.

Keep dealing cards in front of each of the packs until you've exhausted the deck. Then, shuffle the deck and begin again. After a while, you will become used to the fact that the number of "normal" aces keeps going up by two as you go from pack to pack, since the packs are arranged in ascending order.

At this point, rearrange the packs randomly and begin the test again. Now, determine "normal" aces by eyeballing the packs. This is precisely what we want to accomplish; to get you to be able to look at the discard rack and determine within a half-deck how many aces should have been played. Repeat the test over and over again, until you get used to the new sequence. Then, once again, rearrange the packs randomly.

At first, you will find this test goes agonizingly slow. After only one or two hours, however, you will start to recite the values rapidly. When you feel totally comfortable with this test, it's time to go on to the next test.

Ace-Rich Or Ace-Poor Times Ace Adjustment Factor Of

"3." Repeat the test as before, except this time, instead of reciting plus 1 for every ace-rich and minus 1 for every ace-poor, multiply times the ace adjustment factor of 3 and recite the answer.

Taking the same eight examples as on page 156, you would now recite:

> minus 9
>
> plus 3
>
> minus 12
>
> zero
>
> minus 3
>
> plus 6
>
> plus 3
>
> plus 21

The purpose of this test is to get you to automatically multiply the aces-rich or poor by the factor of 3 to get the number which must be added or subtracted from the running count before deriving the betting true count. Once again, after working with this for an hour or so, your speed will pick up dramatically.

Ace Adjustment And Betting True Count Test.

After you handle the previous test, you're ready for the ultimate test—the one which will thoroughly prepare you to quickly and accurately determine your betting levels.

Instead of dealing one card in front of each pack, now deal two cards; the first card, as before, represents the number of aces played. The second represents your hypothetical *plus* running count at that time (remember that negative counts do not need to be adjusted for betting purposes unless aces are extremely rich).

Your mission? To adjust the running count for the aces-rich or poor and then to calculate the betting true count. Let's assume once again that the packs are arranged as they were originally and let's take some examples:

Figure 11c

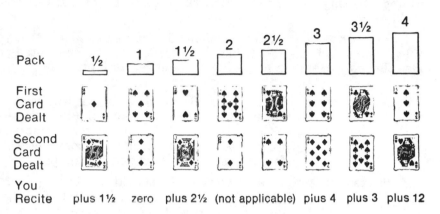

Pack	½	1	1½	2	2½	3	3½	4
First Card Dealt								
Second Card Dealt								
You Recite	plus 1½	zero	plus 2½	(not applicable)		plus 4	plus 3	plus 12

Take a closer look at the eight packs above. What do they really mean to the blackjack player? The first pack on the left, the half-deck, really means only two things to the Atlantic City six deck player:

1. Two aces should be played.
2. We must divide by 11 to convert the running count to the true count (there being 5½ decks, or 11 half-decks, left to play).

Our objective is to get you to look at each pack and know instantaneously (1) how many aces should be played and (2) what the conversion factor is.

Now, let's take the first example. The first card dealt in our little test is an ace, meaning that 1 ace has been played. The second card dealt is a king, meaning that our plus count is +13. What is our betting true count?

We are one ace-rich and, thus, must add 3 points to our running count of +13 to get +16. Our conversion factor is 11, so we divide 16 by 11 and get about 1½, which is our betting true count. We recite "1½." If this were a four deck game, you would divide by 7, since 3½ decks or seven half-decks remain to be played. Your answer would then be "2" (16÷7=2+).

Second example: The first card dealt, a 5, indicates that 5 aces have been played. The second card means our running count is plus 3. What's our betting true count? Five aces are played; 4 should have been played. We're one ace-poor, so we deduct 3 points from our running count of +3, giving zero. No need to divide by the CF (which is 10 in this case) so we recite, "zero." Four decks would also yield zero.

Third example: Two aces have been played, 6 aces should have been

159

played. We're 4 aces-rich, so we add 12 to the running count of +11 (indicated by the jack), giving 23. Divide by the conversion factor of 9, giving a betting true count of 2½. We recite "2½." Four decks would yield 4½.

I will step you through the remaining 5 examples to ensure that you fully understand this test (which is about the most complicated and also the most useful) in preparing for multiple deck play.

Fourth example: 9 aces played, 8 should be played. One ace-poor. Deduct 3 from running count of +2, giving −1. No need to convert with a negative count (since we'll be betting the minimum, if possible). Ditto four decks. Go on to the next example.

Fifth example: 13 aces played. 10 should be played., 3 aces-poor. Deduct 9 from running count of +4, giving −5. No need to convert a negative count. Ditto four decks. Go on to the next example.

Sixth example: 6 aces played. 12 should be played. 6 aces-rich. Add 18 to running count of 8, which equals +26. Divide by conversion factor of 6 equalling betting true count of "4" (round to nearest whole number). Four decks = +13.

Seventh example: 12 aces played (queen). 14 aces should be played. 2 aces-rich. Add 6 to running count of 10, which equals +16. Divide by conversion factor of 5, equalling betting true count of "+3." If by some chance the four deck shoe was not shuffled, the true count = +16.

Last example: 3 aces played. 12 should be played. 9 rich. Add 27 to running count of +12, equalling +39. Divide by conversion factor of 4, which equals betting true count of "+10." A four deck pack would be shuffled.

Up until the publication of this book, there weren't more than a handful of blackjack players in the world who used these tests and some of the others in Chapters 8 and 9. I think this is one of the reasons why so many people assumed professional level counts were so difficult to learn. The answer to learning is repetition. It doesn't take a mathematical wizard to learn this material; all it takes is time and dedicated effort.

The Multiple Deck Final Test. Assuming that you've mastered the count and the numbers, and are comfortable with the above tests, you're now ready for the final test to determine when you'll be ready to play multiple deck in Atlantic City or elsewhere (throughout this example, I'll assume Atlantic City).

Take six decks of cards and put about 20 low cards in front of the pack so they'll be dealt first. We want the count to rise to give you practice in calculating your bet size.

A distressingly high proportion of six deck shoes doesn't progress into sufficiently positive situations to make betting calculations necessary. When the shoe is minus, we don't care how minus from a bet standpoint. We'll be putting out our minimum bet in any case, unless the shoe becomes outrageously minus, in which case we might consider leaving for another table.

Deal yourself two cards face up, and give the dealer two cards, one face up and one face down. Bet and play exactly as you would in a casino, using the count, the numbers and your predetermined betting strategy—secure some low denomination chips for practice.

Play through to two-thirds of the shoe—that is, until about two full decks remain. After you've completed two-thirds of the shoe, take one card and lay it face down on the table. Continue your running count and number of aces as you go through the remainder of the undealt cards, until you've counted all the cards in the shoe except the one card on the table.

Predict the value of the last card, as described in the single deck final test, page 144.

If you can predict the last card, after counting through 311 cards, after having made the bets, made the plays, counted aces, converted running to true count and recalled the matrix numbers, you know you've accomplished something. If you are accurate 9-out-of-10 times (and not too far off, say by 2 or 3 points, on the tenth time), you're ready to try a casino test, at low betting levels.

Summary For The Multiple Deck Player. To ensure that you've assimilated the information in Chapters 8, 9 and 11, I will summarize the steps that should be followed by the potential *Advanced Point Count* multiple deck player.

1. You must know the appropriate (Atlantic City or Nevada) multiple deck strategy perfectly. Even advanced and professional level players must run through the multiple deck Basic Strategy flashcards with total accuracy.

2. Count down four decks in 90 seconds—or six decks in 140 seconds. You should be accurate 19-out-of-20 times.

3. Go through the numbers flashcards at the rate of one card per 1½ seconds. Atlantic City players must remember to substitute the double-on-split flashcards for the standard pair-splitting cards and use the early (not conventional) surrender flashcards.

4. Work with the ace adjustment and betting true count tests until you are totally comfortable with the calculation of the

betting true count.

5. Using Chapter 9, determine your ultimate betting strategy, given the size of your blackjack investment.

6. Take the "final test," dealing four (or six) decks over and over until you're totally comfortable with all phases of the game. You should be accurate to the last point, 9-out-of-10 times.

7. Take a trip to a casino, betting small amounts. Play just as you would if you were at your ultimate betting level. Continue until you are completely confident that your accuracy is high.

8. Gradually advance your betting levels until you are able to bet at your ultimate betting levels with complete accuracy and minimal nervousness.

Betting Ratios And Number of Cards Seen

Assuming that the player is accurate and that the game is honest, profitability in multiple deck games depends upon two factors: the number of cards seen and the betting ratio. The rules-of-thumb that we use are strict, but the player is advised to be discriminating. With sufficient scouting (sometimes it will take as much time to find a good game as to play a session), the following standards can be met:

Double deck (Strip rules):	game dealt down to 26 cards remaining, 8-to-1 ratio.
Four deck (Strip rules):	game dealt down to ¾ deck; 12-to-1 ratio.
Six deck (Strip rules):	game dealt down to ¾ deck; 15-to-1 ratio.
Six deck (Atlantic City):	game dealt down to 2 decks; 6-to-1 ratio.

Games will be found to meet the above guidelines. Multiple deck games in downtown Vegas and in Reno are more unfavorable and should be avoided. The player should be able to play many months before running out of games as favorable as those listed above.

Tips On Double Deck Games

The player's off-the-top bet should be as low as possible since the player is at a disadvantage of .35% after the shuffle. At the very beginning of the deal, with slightly less than two decks remaining, the player obtains the edge when the running count (adjusted for aces) reaches +5. Thus, if you were to see a 5 and a +2-valued card (3, 4, 6 or 7) as the burn and bottom card, you would have a slight edge off-the-top.

Pitbosses watching double deck games do not generally become as alarmed over bet variation as those watching single deck games. But the player can still draw heat by being detected betting small at the front of the deck and moving up to much larger bets toward the end. Occasionally cover bets, such as spreading to two hands off-the-top (to spread the risk, as we discussed) should be effective in avoiding heat.

Card-eating is an effective tool in double deck games. If, for example, you're playing green chips and the count drops way down, spread to three hands, betting perhaps $10, $25 and $10. You've got only $45 on the table and will "eat up" many cards, pushing the dealer to the shuffle point sooner. If you have a spouse, date or friend, you can signal that person to play $2 per hand on these occasions.

In some double deck clubs, the dealer stops dealing when he reaches the cut-card and immediately shuffles, while the partial hands lay on the table. When this practice is used, the counter must be aware of the placement of the cut-card to avoid placing a big bet toward the end of the pack, only to have the dealer shuffle after dealing a few cards. (This practice originated in England. An enterprising club owner observed that his patrons tended to leave the game while the shoe was being shuffled. He initiated this practice to keep the players at the table between shuffles. He was lauded by the other club-owners, who soon adopted this practice.)

The most favorable double deck game currently being dealt is at the Riviera in Vegas, where the surrender option is offered (but not advertised). Be careful though; when the player surrenders there, the dealer usually announces it to the pit—it's a red flag used in searching out counters.

Tips On Four Deck Games

The enterprising player can achieve surprising bet variation in four deck games. One counter, willing to spend much time travelling from club to club, would bet $5 off-the-top of a shoe. When a shoe became favorable (about 12% or one-eighth of four deck shoes reach a true count of +3 or higher), he would appear to "steam."

If he was losing, he would triple and quadruple his bets. If he was winning, he would double-parlay, by doubling his bet and then capping it with yet another bet of equal size. By the end of the shoe, he would often be betting $500 or higher. When the shoe ran out, he'd leave the club, win or lose, as the pitbosses watched yet another steamer heading out the door. A good approach to avoid heat—but a slow way to make money, since only one hot shoe is played in each club.

High bet ratios can be attained by mixing colors, as discussed in Chapter 10. To a distracted pitboss, betting one green chip and four red ones on one hand, and four green chips and one red on the next, doesn't seem to be an untoward bet variation. Indeed, an occasional black chip can be slipped under the stack, especially in the larger clubs such as the MGM and Caesars, where black chip action isn't that unusual.

163

The MGM is so large that there are three different pits to play in on crowded evenings; it's essentially like playing three different clubs, since the bosses are all different.

If you have a friend (or teammate) who can also keep the count, he can be of considerable help to you in a four deck club. Using a variation of team play, have your friend count a shoe down by "back counting," that is, standing behind the chairs and watching the game, (he need not even play the shoe) while you're playing at another table. When the running count gets to a predetermined level (say +20 or so), he signals you. Assuming you're not playing a "hot shoe," leave your table and receive the count from your friend (either through signals or a whisper) and come in with a big bet at the second table. That shouldn't raise any eyebrows since Vegas hasn't seen concentrated team play in several years.

Tips For Atlantic City

Atlantic City currently is a "candy store" for anyone willing to settle for a few hundred dollars per day. With current rules and the current practice of dealing to one-third of the shoe, the player betting 1-to-6 quarters should average $50 per hour if playing accurately. Since the player has a small edge off-the-top, it's possible to make off-the-top bets of 2, 3 or even 4 quarters, without undue risk (colors can also be mixed, as discussed, to confuse the bosses). A bankroll of $10,000 will more than sustain a 1-to-6 quarter level of betting at a 5% element-of-ruin. The risk here is that the player will get greedy and increase betting levels. If they're still barring in Atlantic City—watch out!

There is a way to increase earnings rates in Atlantic City without going beyond six green chips as the top bet. As the player's bank grows beyond $10,000, he may bet his top bet of six chips faster, that is, at lower true counts, and stay within a 5% element-of-ruin. The data in Chapter 9 were used to derive the information shown in Table 11-1.

Thus, with a playing bank of $11,250, the player may put out his maximum bet at a true count of +6, instead of at +7, in accordance with the $10,000 betting schedule. At a bank of $16,500, he may put out his maximum bet at a true count of +5. As the bank increases, the maximum bet may be placed at lower and lower true counts until at $90,000, only a true count of +1 is needed.

With a bank of $135,000, the player could bet six quarters off-the-top (900 units of bank are needed with a .1% edge) and remain at six quarters with any zero or plus *running* count. Not only does this increase earnings, but it makes the game far simpler: the player need not convert the running count to the true count, since he's placing his maximum bet in any zero or plus situation.

Such a strategy would earn about $125 per hour. While this doesn't

Table 11-1
Betting 1-to-6 Green ($25) Chips
in Atlantic City
When the Player May Place
Max. Bet of 6 Green Chips ($150)

Size Bank	Uston APC True Count of:	Advanced Plus/Minus True Count of:
$ 10,000	7 or higher	3 or higher
11,250	6 ″ ″	2½ ″
16,500	5 ″ ″	2 ″
22,500	4 ″ ″	1½ ″
36,000	3 ″ ″	1 ″
65,000	2 ″ ″	1 ″
90,000	1 ″ ″	½ ″
135,000	0 ″ ″	0 ″

Notes: —assumes 5% element-of-ruin; based on data In Chapter 9.

—maximum bet is always $150.

appear overwhelming in light of the huge bank required, consider that the player would average $5,000 per week, a 4% *weekly* return on investment (over 200% per year).

The use of modified team play (see Chapter 12) is particularly effective in Atlantic City, since the casinos currently are often crowded. The signalling "counter" has a good chance of being lost in the crowd. Nevertheless, avoid open communication with teammates because the Atlantic City casinos have the most advanced "skies" in the world. Their cameras can follow you and several confederates simultaneously anywhere within the casino, complete with close-ups and photographic prints.

If you live in the Northeast, you have excellent opportunities to make money at blackjack on a part-time basis. With a $10,000 bank, the skilled player should be able to average $1,000 per weekend.

In Nevada, favorable single deck games currently exist. Also, there are numerous multiple deck opportunities available for players who become "burned out" at single deck clubs.

Realistically, I don't believe that fortunes can be made at blackjack today; black chip action draws considerable heat. But the well-financed, disciplined green chip player has attractive financial opportunities, in both Atlantic City and Las Vegas. I believe that the capable full-time player can earn up to $100,000 per year, and maybe more.

Chapter Twelve

Blackjack Team Methods

Several years ago, before I started playing blackjack professionally, an associate of mine and I would practice the Thorp point count. This was more of a diversion than anything else. We would take an occasional trip to Lake Tahoe, happy to win $40 or $50. Once, while driving back to San Francisco, we wondered if somehow the two of us, both with a knowledge of counting, could somehow synergistically combine our expertise, that is, in some way capitalize on the fact that we both knew how to count. We thought and thought, but didn't come up with anything.

It turns out that there are phenomenally profitable options available for a group of two or more players with skill at blackjack. This chapter discusses ways in which players may combine their individual skills so that the combined effort produces far, far more than would the sum of the individual efforts. The techniques include (1) team play, (2) joint bank, (3) gorilla BP's and (4) insurance counters.

Team Play—The Big Player And The Little Counters

How It Works. As narrated in Chapter 2, our first two teams combined individual skills in an ingenious way which allowed us to enjoy betting ratios far in excess of those that could be employed by an individual player. The method, "team play," requires careful training, coordination and synchronized signalling among several players.

Several "counters" are stationed at four or five different tables in a multiple deck club. The counters make minimum bets and play Basic Strategy. They count down the shoe, using a common counting system. When the deck becomes sufficiently "hot" (that is, the count goes up), the counter calls in the "big player," employing a furtive signal. The big player (BP) then places a big bet at the counter's table, as he receives the count and the number of aces played from the counter through another set of signals. The BP continues to play at the table until the shoe either runs out or is no longer favorable to the player. Then the BP leaves the table and waits to receive similiar signals from the other counters in the casino.

The net result of this approach is that the BP *never* plays in negative situations. He has an edge over the house on every bet. The counters, of course, are playing at a disadvantage to the house, approximately —.5%, but their small losses are offset many times over by the BP's wins.

We played for about a year, our BP's betting up to many thousands of dollars. Even at those levels, it took the bosses a long time to snap to what was going on. Normally, the BP is accepted as an erratic high-roller who just likes to jump around from table-to-table. He obviously isn't counting, the bosses feel, because he starts playing in the middle of the shoe. Even if he was counting, the bosses reasoned, there'd be no way he could count down five or six tables at the same time.

Could the team approach be used today? I believe so, although not in quite as concentrated a way as our Team 1 used it.

Since 1977, team play has been used only on a limited basis in Vegas. A modified team approach would probably mislead a good many of the bosses; many of the newer bosses in Nevada, and Atlantic City and abroad, have never observed team play. Several variations are probably employable today:

— The BP plays primarily single deck. Periodically, he's called into a hot shoe. This is possible in clubs which have both single and multiple deck games, such as the Sahara, Stardust, Frontier and Caesars Palace.

— The BP plays double deck on his own. He's periodically called into other games by counters, but perhaps 50 or 75% of the time, he's playing individually.

— The BP plays four deck or six deck on his own. He has one or two counters counting down other shoes and calling him in. Thus, the BP will be able to play all hot shoes at two or three tables rather than just one. This is usable in Vegas four deck clubs, such as the MGM and Sands, in Atlantic City, in the Bahamas and in Europe.

If the BP "bops," as we call it, too much from table-to-table, he will probably draw heat; the bosses may suspect him of team play. But, many players change tables as they try to avoid "hot" dealers, so an occasional "bop" would not appear out-of-line. The high bets that the BP makes coming to the table in the middle of shoes may take heat off him and permit him to play more effectively and with greater bet ratios than if he's playing individually.

The team concept sounds simple—and it is. However, the recruiting, training and scheduling problems involved in the team approach can be formidable. One must first train counters to count down multiple deck shoes accurately and rapidly. They must be taught to convert the running count to the true count, adjusting both for the number of aces played and for the number of decks remaining in the shoe (although we'll discuss shortcuts to this later). After learning how to count, the counter must be trained in the proper ways to smoothly and subtly convey signals.

On the bright side, the counter need not know the numbers matrix; he plays only Basic Strategy and he's not concerned with calculating the size of his own bets, which would usually be the table minimum. In fact, training to be a counter is an excellent way for someone to learn part of the game and experience some actual casino play before going on to the more advanced aspects of the game. It took most of our Team 1 counters from five to six weeks of training to be ready for a trip with the team (they played a multi level professional count).

The BP must know all aspects of the game (as discussed in Chapters 8 through 11). He must be thoroughly trained in ace adjustment and true count conversion, must know all the numbers in his system's matrix and, of course, be capable of adhering to the team's predetermined betting strategy.

Our Team 1 BP's actually needed to know only the "plus" numbers; they never played in minus decks. BP's also playing individually must know all the numbers.

Establishing Modified Team Play.
In this section, we discuss a modified team approach, modified because the BP will play individually on his own as well as play for the team when called into hot shoes. In Atlantic City, with its favorable rules, the Simple Plus/Minus or the Advanced Plus/Minus would be strong enough to attain a healthy edge over the house. In Nevada, either the Advanced Plus/Minus or Uston APC would be effective.

Assuming you plan to be a BP, your first step is to recruit some counters. You should seek out people who basically are *not* gamblers. Rather than superstitious craps-shooters or hunch-players, you want people who can fathom the concept of having to adhere to a predetermined set of rules in order to gain an edge over the house. We found, as would be expected, that computer programmers, systems analysts, accountants and mathematicians generally make good counters. Yet, properly trained non-technical people can be as good. Our Team 1 included a housewife, a used car salesman, a nurse and a waitress. If the Simple Plus/Minus or Advanced Plus/Minus is used, training of average people is particularly feasible.

You'll find that many people, fascinated with the prospect of being able to earn money in a casino, will express interest in your idea. Many, however, will not be willing to devote the time and effort to become good counters. Be selective and train only those who appear to be sincerely interested; in the long run, you'll save yourself much time and effort.

We've developed a shortcut which precludes the necessity for counters having to convert the running count to the true count. We've established what we call "call-in" numbers. Call-in numbers reflect the running count required to call in the BP at various levels in the shoe. For the BP to have about a 1% edge, the call-in numbers are as follows:

Table 12—1

Call-in Numbers

| | Simple +/- or Advanced +/- Running Count | | Uston APC Running Count Adjusted For Aces | |
| (A) | (B) | (C) | (D) | (E) |
Number Of Decks In Discard Pile	Atlantic City Six Deck	Las Vegas Four Deck	Atlantic City Six Deck	Las Vegas Four Deck
½	+ 13	+ 11	+ 33	+ 28
1	+ 12	+ 10	+ 30	+ 24
1½	+ 11	+ 8	+ 27	+ 20
2	+ 10	+ 6	+ 24	+ 16
2½	+ 8	+ 5	+ 21	+ 12
3	+ 7	+ 4	+ 18	+ 8
3½	+ 6	—	+ 15	—
4	+ 5	—	+ 12	—

Notes: For Las Vegas four deck, Uston APC true count of +4 used; for Atlantic City, true count of +3 used, since A.C. game is roughly ½% better than Las Vegas game.

If the team is using the Simple Plus/Minus or Advanced Plus/Minus, the running count should equal the number in Columns B (Atlantic City) and C (Vegas four deck) before the counters call in the BP. If the team is using the Uston APC, the comparable figures are shown in Columns D and E. Note that in the latter case, the counter must first adjust his running count for ace-richness or ace-poorness (adding three points for every ace rich to the running count and deducting three points for every ace poor). This, of course, is not necessary with the Simple Plus/Minus or Advanced Plus/Minus, since aces are automatically reflected in the count.

Team Signals. In order to communicate information without being detected, it's necessary for the team to develop a set of signals, or "offices," as they're sometimes called. In team play, signals are needed to communicate the running count and, if an advanced system with a side count of aces is used, the number of aces played. There are numerous alternatives for establishing signals. The publication of our signals might make it necessary for the reader to develop other signals, although I really doubt it; our teams, to this day, use the signals revealed in *The Big Player,* which was published in 1977. I'll describe our signals. The reader may want to use them—or, they may stimulate other ideas in those who intend to use signalling in casinos.

Count Signals. The primary set of signals we use to transmit the count from the counter to the BP (we call them the "arm signals") are as follows:

1. Positions On The Left Arm (tens position value of running count):

> The counter's left arm rests on the table and is used to indicate the tens position value of the running count. The placement of the right hand on the appropriate part of the left arm indicates which tens position applies.

Figure 12a

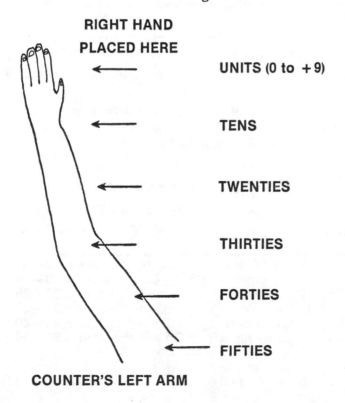

**RIGHT HAND
PLACED HERE**

UNITS (0 to +9)

TENS

TWENTIES

THIRTIES

FORTIES

FIFTIES

COUNTER'S LEFT ARM

For example, the positioning of the right hand on the left fingers indicates a count from 0 to +9. Positioning the right hand on the back of the left wrist indicates a count of +10 to +19; on the forearm, a count of +20 to +29; on the elbow, a count of +30 to +39; on the bicep, a count of +40 to +49; on the shoulder, a count of +50 to +59 (rarely needed).

2. Movement Of Right Hand (units position value of running count):

The movement of the right hand signals the units value of the running count:

— Rubbing the right wrist back and forth horizontally on the appropriate part of the left arm (that is, perpendicular to the left arm) indicates a unit value of zero.

— Rubbing the wrist up and down vertically (that is, toward and away from the body, or parallel to the left arm) indicates 1.

— Rubbing the fingers of the right hand against the appropriate part of the left arm horizontally indicates 2; up and down, indicates 3.

— Four fingers placed on the left arm indicates a unit count of 4.

— Five fingers placed on the left arm indicates a unit count of 5 (the 4 and 5 signals are always the easiest to learn).

— Rubbing the right-hand knuckles horizontally indicates 6; vertically, 7.

— Rubbing the ends of the fingers in a scratching motion horizontally indicates 8; vertically, 9.

These signals are shown in chart form in Table 12-2.

Table 12—2

Arm Signals for the Count

UNITS (Given by right hand on left arm)		TENS (Location on left arm where right hand gives signal)
Wrist:	Side-to-side = 0	On left fingers = 0—9
Wrist:	Up-and-down = 1	On left wrist = 10—19
Palm:	Side-to-side = 2	On left forearm = 20—29
Palm:	Up-and-down = 3	On left elbow = 30—39
4 Fingers:	Stationary = 4	On left biceps = 40—49
5 Fingers:	Stationary = 5	On left shoulder = 50—59
Knuckles:	Side-to-side = 6	
Knuckles:	Up-and-down = 7	
Fingertips:	Side-to-side = 8	
Fingertips:	Up-and-down = 9	

It's easiest to learn the tens position, that is, on what part of the left arm to give the signal. As an aid in learning the unit signals, note that the side-to-side, horizontal movement (perpendicular to the left arm) indicates even numbers; an up-and-down vertical movement (parallel to the left arm) designates odd numbers.

All this signalling might seem strange and complicated to you. Rest assured, the signals become almost automatic after a few hours of practice. We used a training aid, similar to that shown in Table 12-3, to practice these signals. For each designated running count (and number of aces if the Uston APC is used), give the appropriate signal. We'd take this test in front of a large mirror to ensure that our movements were subtle and natural. When two or more of us practiced, the first would give the signal; the second would recite his interpretation of the signal.

Table 12—3

Practice Exercise for Signalling the Running Count and Number of Aces Played

Give the correct signal for the following situations:

SITUATION		SITUATION		SITUATION	
Running Count	Number of Aces Played	Running Count	Number of Aces Played	Running Count	Number of Aces Played
+ 9	14	+22	3	+39	11
17	12	38	11	8	2
24	7	16	9	28	4
29	4	27	7	6	6
4	3	2	13	30	1
11	8	19	5	12	10
21	14	32	2	15	2
7	1	36	10	23	5
31	4	5	9	3	8
14	7	37	1	18	3
1	12	13	4	25	6
26	2	20	7	33	11
35	8	40	6	10	9
51	5	34	10	45	13

If using the Simple Plus/Minus or Advanced Plus/Minus, signal the running count only.
If using the Uston APC, signal running count and number of aces played.

While the arm signals were largely undetectable by the bosses, we developed an alternate set of chip signals to further confound them. The chip signals are much easier to learn and transmit, but since they are given on the table, we used them sparingly since they could be seen and photographed from the "sky." The arm signals were given just off the edge of the table and more likely to be out of the range of the sky camera and thus, less likely to be detected.

In using the chip signals, the value of a stack of chips placed on the far left designated the running count; the value of the chips in a stack to the immediate right of the first stack indicated the number of aces played. The rest of the counter's chips were placed elsewhere on the table. For example, four "nickel" chips and two $1 chips, placed on the far left stack, indicated a count of +22.

Figure 12b

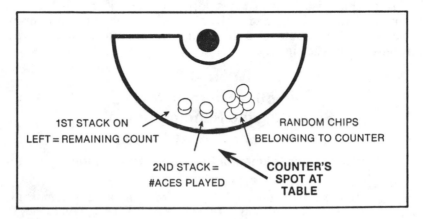

Signals For The Number Of Aces Played. The primary set of signals we employ to designate aces, also called "arm signals," are depicted in Table 12-4. These are always given with the right hand:

Table 12—4

Arm Signals for Number of Aces Played

Number Of Aces Played	Place The Right Hand As Follows:
0	On the left side of the abdomen
1	On the belt buckle
2	In the middle of the stomach
3	On the neck (where the tie knot is)
4	Fingers across the neck
5	Pinching under the chin
6	Pinching the end of the chin
7	Rubbing just under the mouth
8	Finger in mouth
9	Rubbing just above the mouth
10	Touching end of nose
11	Just above the nose
12	Touching forehead
13	At hair line
14	Scratching top of head

174

These signals are easy to learn. Notice that the greater the number of aces played, the higher the right hand touches on the body.

The chip signals for aces, as I said, were done on the table. The chip denominations in the stack to the immediate right of the stack designating the count indicated the number of aces played. For example, a $5 chip with three $1 chips indicates eight aces played.

It is essential that a standard sequence be developed for giving the signals. We signalled the count first, since that number is of greater importance to the BP. This is because the BP has probably already placed his first bet on the strength of the counter's "hot" signal. His first decision at the table requiring a calculation will be the play of the first hand. For this, the count, and not the number of aces, is necessary.

Back-counting. The counter can often back-count, that is, not play but stand behind the players at the table as he counts down the shoe. When back-counting, the counter must obviously use arm, not chip, signals. The subtleness of back-counting is revealed in the following scenario, which has occurred hundreds of times:

> Jim is standing in back of the players, counting down a shoe, totally unobserved by the pit. The deck gets hot. Jim signals to Bill, the BP, casually putting his hand on his cheek. Just as the round is completed, Bill approaches the table. Jim starts to walk away. As they pass, Jim signals the count and aces played with arm signals. As Bill sits down and begins to play, Jim is nowhere near the table.

General Signals. Whenever two or more players work together in a casino, another set of signals is useful to convey general information. The signals described below, many of which were also published years ago, are being used by our people up to this very day. Given casually and naturally, they defy detection.

Message	**Signal**
The shoe is very hot	Hand placed on chin

Given by the counter to tell the BP that the "call-in" number has been exceeded by six-to-eight points.

The shoe is hot	Hand placed on cheek

Given by the counter to tell the BP that the "call-in" number has been reached. This signal comprises a common pose for blackjack players. The next time you're in a casino, look around; you'll notice about one-fifth of the players seemingly giving the "hot signal."

The shoe is warm	Hand on back of neck

Used by the counter to tell the BP that the shoe is getting close to "hot." It tells the BP to "stick around." We use it if the running count is within six to eight points of the call-in number.

As we played through the years, new situations arose leading to the development of other signals that we found helpful in coordinating the activities of the team:

Change tables	Rubbing or pinching the nose

Used by the BP to instruct the counter to change to a different table. The BP, who often is standing and better able to survey the casino, might have spotted an empty table where the shoe is about to be shuffled; or perhaps he wants to move the counter away from a section of the pit because of "heat" from a particular boss.

End of session	Hand on chest

Given by the BP to the counter(s) to indicate that the session is over. Counters should continue to play for 15 minutes or so before leaving the casino. In addition to good cover, they can glean valuable information from the pit if they overhear the bosses discussing the play of the BP.

Leave the casino immediately	Tapping chest with fist

Given by any teammate if he feels the bosses have "snapped" to a play. Used by all six teams to indicate a possible emergency developing.

Meet me in the men's room	Hand on crotch

A rather inelegant signal to indicate that a message must be communicated verbally, or that money must be transferred.

I understand	Rubbing forehead with thumb and forefinger

We use this signal frequently. It indicates, "That's a big 10—4," to use CB radio parlance; in other words, one teammate has understood the signal just transmitted by another. The BP would use this to let the counter know he understood the counter's signals. Or, if the BP has flashed "end-of-session," the counter might respond with "I understand;" then, the BP knows his signal was received.

Taking a break	Hands together, cracking the knuckles with palms out

Given by a teammate who needs to take a short break, most usually a stop in the rest room.

Summary—Team Play. Modified team play will probably always be a viable approach to increasing earnings at blackjack. It looks perfectly normal since nearly all players periodically change tables—small players and high-rollers alike. Occasional "bops" will probably always be tolerated. Too much bopping, of course, may draw heat. The disadvantage here is the time, effort and expense of training and using players. One must ensure that this is warranted, by increasing profits over individual play.

Joint Bank

Probably the most dramatic situation where blackjack counters can benefit by combining efforts is in the formation of what we call a "joint bank." Let's assume that you, a capable player, have a bankroll of $5,000. This bankroll should permit you to safely bet from $10 to $100 and earn around $25 per hour, or $200 per eight-hour day.

Now let's say that you have an honest friend who knows how to count as well as you do. He, too, has $5,000, and playing alone could average $200 per day. If the two of you combined funds, you could each play to a $10,000 bank, betting $20 to $200. *Each* of you would then average $50 per hour, or $400 per eight-hour day.

Further, assume that you both know three other capable players, each with $5,000. Forming a team of five, you could each bet to a €25,000 bank and each average $1,000 per day. Total team earnings are 25 times that of each person's earning's capacity, playing alone. Each player personally will average five times as much in earnings. Mathematically, in a joint bank, team earnings increase by the number of members on the team, squared—in our example, 5 squared equals 25. The mathematical formula is $T=p(n^2)$, where T=team earnings, p=each player's earning if playing individually, and n=the number of players on the team.

Joint bank is even more advantageous than the above figures demonstrate. If each of you plays eight hours per day, the team in total gets 40 hours of play under its belt every day. Table 9-6 showed how the probability of winning increases as the number of hours played goes up. A joint bank team effort smoothes out the swings on individual players. The team, overall, gets into the long run faster and has a far greater chance of winning over a given period of time than any individual member.

To take an analogy from the other side of the table: compare the likely financial results of a casino with only one blackjack game to that of an operation like Resorts with about 100 games open. The smaller casino would probably lose one-quarter to one-third of the days it was open. Resorts, on the other hand, rarely has a losing day at blackjack.

There are other benefits, too, from joint bank. In addition to combining bankroll, a team provides an opportunity for exchanging expertise, new ideas and intelligence on good conditions in various casinos, on liberal shifts, on which dealers give favorable games, and so on.

Another major benefit of joint bank is a psychological one. I recall a time early in my career when I played at Caesars losing $6,000. Then, I went to the Marina and lost about $2,000 and I was barred. I was $8,000 poorer and barred from a good club to boot. When I went to the team meeting, I found the other players were up $15,000. My spirits immediately soared—not only were we in the black for the day, but there were five other players who could go back into the Marina and play. Thus, joint banks can overcome the problem of being barred from good clubs. If a player is barred, the team can send other players into that same club. As we say, "We can train 'em as fast as they can bar 'em."

There are problems in joint bank operations. Honesty is obviously one of them. One fellow ripped off our first team for $60,000 or so, and I suspect someone may have stolen $10,000 from us about a year ago. We now use polygraphs and have a standing rule that "anyone may call a polygraph on anyone else at any time." I myself have been polygraphed several times.

While the polygraphs are not perfect, they seem to have worked in our case. There have been four instances where a teammate flunked the test because he had a minor expense on his mind—in one case the player used team money to toke the maitre d' for a ringside table in a show. In all four cases, we re-tested the teammate, rephrasing the question (e.g., "did you steal more than $100 from the team?") and our man came out clean. The new voice test—psychological stress analysis—is more accurate than a polygraph. There are also machines that combine polygraph with voice tests.

To outsiders, it's difficult to explain why honesty is not more of a problem than it is. It is true that a teammate could steal many thousands of dollars without fear of going to jail and probably without fear of physical reprisal—I say probably because we've had an occasional teammate who, I believe, would have the capacity for violent reprisal should a thief be identified.

Generally, teammates understand there's more money to be made playing blackjack with us, so it's better to be honest than to steal and risk getting kicked off the team. Also, having a common "enemy," the casinos, is a unifying factor. We experience huge financial ups and downs together; it seems we are all so dedicated to getting that bank doubled, that our personal goals often get subordinated to team objectives. There have been many times when other teammates and I, in doubt about whether a cabfare, for example, came from personal money or team money, would give the benefit of the doubt to the team.

The last thing I am is moralistic, but it really gives one a good feeling to know you're totally honest and to be absolutely confident that the guys you're dealing with are too.

There are additional problems, too, in playing with others. No two counters have exactly the same ability. Sometimes the better ones feel they're carrying weaker players. The weaker players may get overanxious to demonstrate their contribution to the team and want to win so badly that it can affect the quality of their play. You don't have the freedom you would if playing alone. You're often forced into playing full time for weeks on end, when you'd like to kick back for a while.

The advantages of joint bank, I believe, far outweigh the disadvantages. Others are beginning to realize this, too, which is why blackjack teams have proliferated over the last few years.

Gorilla BP's

The "Gorilla BP" concept requires two players at a blackjack game. A counter, who either bets small at the table or back-counts, does the counting. A BP, called a "gorilla" because he need not, and generally does not, know how to count, is at the table, "betting the money." The counter calculates all the BP's betting and playing decisions and signals these to the BP. As narrated in Chapter 7, Team 4 used this approach with success. We're still using it today.

The benefit of this approach, of course, is that the BP need not look at the cards. He can talk with the dealer, the bosses or the other players, act totally distracted from the game and in fact drink heavily, as long as he doesn't get so drunk that he can't decipher the counter's signals. Such behavior usually totally baffles the bosses, often to the extent that laughable betting ratios can be obtained. We've enjoyed 100- and 200-to-1 bet ratios on many occasions with this approach with the BP's who "could really lay it down."

This approach may not make too much sense to the average counter. If the player has a good "act," he probably has a long blackjack life ahead of him, both in Nevada and Atlantic City. Why would he take the trouble to train a BP, run the risk of misread signals and have to share the profits with the BP?

However, consider this possibility. You and a friend both count. You feel you're getting minor heat on one of the shifts in a club with a favorable game. You'd hate to lose the opportunity to play there by getting barred.

What if *you* played the gorilla BP and your friend called plays for you for a while? You could play in that casino, make a point of not looking at the cards, get half-drunk and yet play with accuracy as your friend signalled you how to bet and play the hands. When you subsequently returned to count for yourself, the bosses might well conclude, "He doesn't count; he was in here yesterday, half-drunk, talking all the time, ignoring the cards." Or they may think, "He counts sometimes, but he's a drinker and a gambler; sometimes he gets drunk and loses control." In either event, you've set yourself up for future play in that club.

Some of the funniest sessions I've played were with teammates who called plays for me, as I drank heavily and carried on with the dealers, the pitbosses, the cocktail waitresses and the other players. Once, after eight vodka grapefruits, I varied from one hand of $5 to three hands of $500 as the Casino Manager of the Sahara Tahoe, Paul Syphus, stood next to me, joking with me and offering every service his hotel could provide—complimentary, of course.

There are some outrageous things the creative BP can do. He should improvise as he goes along. In the Sahara session, when the counter signalled a small bet, I'd walk a few yards away from the table, as if I could care less about the game, looking for a cocktail waitress, following a good-looking girl, or to banter with someone at the next table.

I'd pick up my hand so the counter could see it and I couldn't. I'd drunkenly slur, "I don't know what it is, but I'll stand." The bosses salivated at these seemingly lunatic plays (the counter, of course had seen the hand and signalled).

It's possible to have two counters, calling plays at two contiguous tables, flashing the "hot" signal when the deck or shoe gets good. Then, the player jumps back and forth, playing favorable situations at two tables, further increasing the edge. To this day, the gorilla BP play has been pulled up on only a handful of occasions.

As recently as two weeks before writing this, we put this play down at the Frontier, where I was playing their $2,000 single deck game. I was undisguised, and the shift manager told me, "Some of my people think you're Kenny Uston."

I replied, "I wish to hell I was. Lemme havva double vodka grapefruit."

Insurance Counters

Most counting systems assume correctly that as the count increases by a certain amount, the player should take insurance. This is a generalization, however, since the insurance bet is determined solely by the ratio of non-tens to tens. In order to increase our profitability, we sometimes have a teammate "count insurance" for another counter. The insurance counter usually stands "on-the-rail," that is, behind the table, to avoid increasing the number of players at the table.

The insurance counter uses a different count, one that is totally accurate for insurance. Tens are counted as −2; all other cards, including aces, are counted as +1.

In a single deck game, the starting count (after the shuffle) is −4. This is because four non-tens must be seen before the non-tens to tens ratio can become exactly 2-to-1 (32 non-tens to 16 tens), the exact insurance pay-off. When the count is at zero, insurance is a dead-even bet and can be taken at the player's option (with a zero insurance count, we usually take insurance if the player has a blackjack or good hand—it looks like he's "protecting" his hand, a good move for cover purposes). With any plus count, insurance is a favorable bet; with any negative count, insurance should not be taken.

In double deck games, the starting count is −8, since eight non-tens must be seen before the ratio can be restored to 2-to-1. In four deck, start at −16. In six deck, start at −24.

The insurance counter signals, of course, only when the dealer shows an ace upcard. In our case, he touches his ear to indicate "insure," keeps his hands low to indicate "don't insure," and turns away from the table if he has dropped the count (in the last case, the player uses his own count to make the insurance decision).

Chapter Thirteen

How We Won $4,000,000 Part 3 (Teams 5 and 6)

Team 5 — We Play Openly For The First Time

Things were looking bad in Las Vegas toward the end of 1978. We'd been playing continually for almost a year and the heat was starting to come down. As one boss confided, "Every time somebody plays black chips, we figure it's one of you guys."

The single deck games, for the most part, were unplayable; most Strip clubs were dealing half-a-deck or less if a player bet black chips. The multiple deck games were becoming unbeatable as well, due to unfavorable cut-card placement. These conditions were eroding our earnings and finally we got the message. Team 4 broke up. It appeared as if we'd be out of the blackjack business for a while.

In January 1979, Ty, a counter friend, called me from Atlantic City. He related the hard-to-believe good news that, as of January 7, 1979, the New Jersey Casino Control Commission would require Resorts International, the only casino open in Atlantic City, to cut off a maximum of one-third of the cards in the playing shoe. At the time, they were dealing a four deck game and had thwarted counters by moving the cut-card up to half the shoe, or even further, from the rear.

It was then generally assumed that casinos were not allowed to bar counters in New Jersey. With the favorable Atlantic City rules, due primarily to early surrender, this new ruling could lead to an unusual earnings opportunity. In effect, the counter had an edge off-the-top of the shoe, could vary his bet by 40-to-1 or even more, and have no fear of being barred. The opportunity was too good to pass up.

I made arrangements to form a $25,000 bank and recruited several players: Rob and Mike, who had played on Team 2; Jack, one of the stronger Team 4 counters; and Ty, the fellow who informed me about the opportunity. On January 16, we converged on the Philadelphia airport, flying in from Los Angeles, San Francisco, and Vegas. Ty drove us to Atlantic City, where we checked into the Barclay Motel, a small, $24-per-night spot about a block from Resorts. Our plan: to bet $25 to $200 initially, moving up to higher betting levels, if, and as, we won.

We were playing to a relatively small bank for several reasons. Team 4's last bank, $30,000, was totally lost because we had been playing marginal games, we had had a marginal counter or two, and, I think, someone stole $10,000 from the team. Rob and Mike had been experimenting with their own blackjack computer and had invested about $50,000 in its development. But the project wasn't successful and neither of them had any money to invest in a bank. In my case, I had become heavily invested in real estate, and to protect myself from my huge monthly "nut," I was unwilling to dip very far into my cash buffer to play in an unknown environment.

On the first morning in Atlantic City, not really believing I'd be allowed to play unaccosted in a casino if known, I put on a disguise and went to Resorts. The casino was more crowded than any I'd ever seen; hundreds of patrons were lined up for the 10:00 a.m. opening. As I started to play, it was obvious most of the dealers were inexperienced and the game was dealt at an excruciating slow 45 hands per hour. At our small betting levels, it was going to be a long, slow grind.

The disguise didn't work. Within a few hours, a number of people, both inside and outside the pit, having recognized me, watched me play. The Resorts Shift Manager, Rick Howe, came over and said, "Hi, Kenny. Could I talk to you for a minute?"

I thought, "I knew it was too good to be true. Here it comes."

I was wrong. Rick handed me his business card and said in a friendly way, "It's an honor to meet you. There's a Casino Control Commission employee who's into counting who would like to meet you. Would you be willing to talk to him?"

Relieved, indeed flabbergasted, I said, "Of course."

We exchanged small talk for a while and I returned to the table, shaking my head with incredulity over the openness of the situation. It seemed so pleasantly unreal—like a dream. I wondered if blackjack could ever be like this universally—where skill would be respected, instead of feared; where a competent player wouldn't feel like a quasi-criminal.

Despite the mellow playing environment, our group couldn't make an inroad. After three days of playing full time, our play was even; we were actually in the hole by the $2,000 in expenses.

As we analyzed the situation at a team meeting, we calculated that our expected value was about $50 per hour. That, times 4½ players (Ty had a job in Philadelphia and was playing part time), times eight hours per day, yielded $1,600 per day, or $11,000 per week, for the five of us. This was a depressingly low earnings rate and I began to consider the alternatives.

Another counter, a multiple deck specialist named Peter, was in town playing to a $25,000 bank. While I'd never worked with him, I'd heard from reliable sources that he was a winning player. After a series of meetings, we agreed to combine efforts, form a $60,000 bank and increase our betting levels accordingly, to $25-to-$500. With the six of us playing, we estimated we could average $10,000 per day (an example of the "power" of joint bank, as discussed in the previous chapter).

On the first day of the new bank, we had a minor loss of about $1,000. But we were more confident than ever that we would win in the long run, assuming we were allowed to play long enough to get into the long run, because many of the factors that lead to losses in Nevada were not present in Atlantic City:

— Occasional cheating occurs in Nevada; we were convinced that the game was totally clean in Atlantic City.

— We didn't have to make the cover bets so necessary in Nevada to avoid detection.

— In team play or gorilla BP play, we ran the risk of making errors in sending and reading signals; since we were all playing individually, there was no need for signalling.

— In Nevada, we were continually faced with detecting and avoiding poor quality games (due to insufficient betting ratios and/or numbers of cards seen). In Atlantic City, we could employ whatever betting ratio we chose; and, we were assured that two-thirds of the shoe would always be dealt.

The team's luck changed on the following day. (Peter and I, coincidentally, each won $8,800 and, overall, the team was up $25,000.) We recalculated our betting strategies for the new bank of $85,000; our max bet was now $600.

Things looked fine, but there were clouds on the horizon. Dozens of counters, some good, some average and some bad, were at Resorts. It looked like a "counter convention," with a counter at nearly every one of Resorts' 70 tables. Some of the more aggressive counters began ruthlessly exploiting the situation. They back-counted shoes, refused to play anything but positive shoes and jumped in with big bets when the count turned positive. They acted smug and superior and were annoying non-counting players. In fact, they were irritating counters as well, since, in effect, they were creating a reverse "card-eating" situation (described in Chapter 10). By their jumping in, more cards per round, and thus, fewer rounds, tended to be dealt in positive shoes. It didn't seem realistic that this "circus" could continue for long.

I called a brief meeting with some of the high-rolling counters. To make the opportunity last longer, we agreed to take one step to try to maintain an important measure of casino profitability, the "hold." The hold is the relationship between the house "win," divided by the "drop," which is the cash converted at the table by players, plus markers drawn by players. If we kept coming into the games with cash, at our high betting levels, we would increase Resorts' drop in addition to decreasing the win, thereby reducing the hold even more. We agreed to keep enough chips so we would not have to come in with cash at the tables.

Despite this measure, I still doubted that the situation could last more than several weeks, at most. Other counters felt differently.

One told me, "They can't change anything here. Resorts' temporary license expires February 26 (six weeks away). They won't do anything to rock the boat until then."

I didn't dare hope that the situation would last that long. If it did, our team had a good chance of earning a half-million or more!

We won $12,000 on the following day. The team was now up $37,000. On the next day, we received a rude surprise. Resorts had taken their second counter-measure (their first, restricting play to only one hand of $1,000, had been taken about a week earlier, when we first got into town). Up until then, Resorts had established more than 80% of their tables at $25-to-$1,000, knowing there was a casino full of losers. Now, there were only four $1,000 maximum tables in the entire casino; all the rest had $200 or $500 maximums.

A Resorts official confided that the hold had dropped 6%. I had no sympathy. Over the past several months, Resorts had set a series of new casino win records; on several days, they won an unprecedented $1,000,000! They were by far the most profitable casino in the world. They were virtually manfacturing cash; yet, the amount siphoned off by the counters seemed to be a bone in their throat.

Resorts had no competition. They charged fancy prices for their rooms, their meals and their drinks. They offered virtually no "comps." They were enjoying a situation that every casino manager dreams of: they had "the only game in town," and they were capitalizing on it to the hilt.

The next several days were winning ones for us—we were up $51,000, then $59,000. Now, Resorts was counter-attacking by lowering the maximum limit as we played at the table. We'd get a seat at a $1,000 table, play a few hands and then watch a boss unexpectedly change the limit sign to $5-to-$300. The battle of wits continued.

We had planned on breaking the bank when we won $60,000. This would give Rob and Mike an opportunity to invest in the second bank and thus earn more money. Our formula for distributing the win was the one we'd used for years:

Half of the win went to the investors, based on the proportions invested; the other half of the win went to the players, allocated in accordance with (1) the number of hours played and (2) the amount won, in equal proportions. This was to provide an incentive to "get hours in," bringing the team into the longer run as soon as possible, and to reward the players who won more since, in the long run, the stronger players would win the most.

Because we had several players playing simultaneously and they didn't know each other's results, we broke through the $60,000 barrier without knowing it and ended up with a playing win of $79,000 before breaking the bank. We had played about 200 hours; our average hourly win rate was just under $400.

The breaking of the bank is usually quite a ceremony. The team-mates gather all their cash and chips and throw them on a bed or table. It usually takes us an hour or more just to figure out how much we have. Then, we try to balance our cash with the playing records of each team member. We never seem to balance; in the heat of battle, we forget how much "we went in for" at the table, how much we had when finishing play, or we forget to keep our records up-to-date.

We calculate the number of hours played and the wins (or losses) of each player. Each player puts in his expenses, airfares, motel rooms, taxi fares, or rental cars. We run through a voluminous series of calculations on a hand calculator. Then, we calculate how much each player has coming from the bank and separate the cash into piles for each player. Here, again, we usually don't balance the first time. Breaking the bank generally takes us four or five hours. But throughout, as you can imagine, there's a festive, joyous air in the room.

By this time, we'd all moved into Resorts. We had been keeping up to $60,000 in the poorly-protected Barclay Hotel rooms and were often walking the deserted streets of Atlantic City at 4 or 5 a.m. with 15-to-30 thousand dollars in our pockets. It soon became obvious that relocating to Resorts—even though the rooms were $60 per night—was the thing to do. We wouldn't have to leave the hotel and we all could get safety deposit boxes in the hotel.

We formed a new bank totalling $116,000. Again, we calculated how much each of us could bet, yet stay within a 5% element-of-ruin. This was no mean task since we were using four different counting systems. We spent a lot of time on that trip calculating betting strategies; we redid them every time we fluctuated by $25,000 or so. Each time we did, we went through the calculations in Table 9-3, four times. With our $116,000, most of the team was betting the true-count-times-two in black chips, topping out at the house max of $1,000.

Jack, who hadn't played yet that day and was rested, went out to make the first play on the new bank, while the rest of us napped. He returned later with good news and bad news. The good news: he'd won $8,500. The bad news: Resorts had taken another countermeasure.

They'd installed six deck games at the $25 games.

On the following day, through casual conversation, I tried to lead the Resorts bosses into thinking that the six deck games were favorable to us. Overheard by pitbosses and shift managers, I'd remark to some other at my table, "Man, these six decks are far out. If the count goes up and we get some luck, we could win 20 or 30 grand in just one shoe!"

This argument was smokescreen, since obviously, the fewer the decks dealt, the better for the counter, both in terms of the overall statistical edge, as well as the percentage of favorable situations that could develop. It seemed, though, that some bosses may have been convinced, as they overheard our "confidential" discussions.

We won another $25,000 over the next two days. Then, the Resorts people did something that baffled us; they inexplicably put in double deck games dealt from a shoe at two tables and restored the maximum at those tables to $1,000. Some of us thought that they'd bought our six deck argument. As I played the double deck game, I'd try to perpetuate the fallacy saying, "You guys finally figured it out. With this double deck, when the shoe gets hot, the dealer ends up shuffling in a round or two. Good move."

There was only one trouble. The counters swarmed around the double deck games like bees around honey. The Resorts people couldn't be fooled for long: if six decks was so good for us and the double deck so bad, why was it that most counters tried to get a seat at the double deck game?

Some expressed the belief that the double deck games were intended to draw the counters into a consolidated spot, to make surveillance and filming easier. Yet, they had pictures of all of us at that point. Perhaps, we felt, they did it to purposely lose more at one or two tables so they could approach the commission with convincing statistics that the counters were winning inordinate amounts. We didn't know the reason, but we kept playing the game as long as it was available.

I kept playing, but noticed groups of counters gathering in the aisles. Things were looking strange. There were virtually no floormen in the pits; fully 90% of the games were unsupervised by floor personnel. I spotted the swing-shift-manager; he looked too happy and self-assured. I was now convinced that something was up. We signalled all our teammates to leave the casino and we adjourned to the team meeting room upstairs.

Rob said, "Looks like it's over. The rumor about the barring is circulating everywhere."

We sent the teammates to the safe deposit boxes to get our funds. We threw the cash and chips on one of the beds and totalled it up. There was $181,600, almost one-fifth of a million dollars, on the bed. Our win for the second bank was $66,000. The total win for both banks for the 14 days of play was $145,000.

Commission Chairman Lordi Lowers The Boom

We had a series of winning days and by Monday, January 29, we were up $56,000 for the second bank, which now totalled a healthy $172,000. Our win for both banks was now $135,000. The following day—Tuesday, January 30, 1979—was destined to become historic in the annals of Atlantic City gambling.

As I was playing that day, a counter came over to my table and said, "The commission's lowered the boom. They're going to bar all the counters tonight."

The news was startling, but I didn't pay it much heed. This was the same person who had started a number of false rumors; indeed, he was the one who assured me earlier that Resorts' hands were tied until February 26.

The rumor was now circulating that the barring was scheduled for 10 p.m. It was 9:45, so I decided to try to cash in our chips (about $40,000 worth) before the heat came down. I seemed to be the logical person to convert the chips—I was known so it didn't matter if I was barred. The others might be able to play again, albeit in disguise.

I threw the huge piles of chips into a plastic hotel laundry bag and went down to the cashier's cage, took the chips out of the bag, and stacked them on the ledge.

There was a commotion in back of me. I turned and saw an entourage heading toward me, led by an older man in a business suit. He was followed by three plainclothes security guards and two uniformed security guards. No one looked friendly.

The older man asked my name, address and social security number. I responded. He wrote the information down. Then, he took out a little 3" by 5" card and read from it:

> "I represent the landlord of the premises. I am informing you that you are considered to be a professional card counter, and you are not allowed to gamble at any blackjack table in this casino. If you attempt to gamble at a blackjack table, you will be considered to be a disorderly person and will be evicted from the casino. If you are evicted from the casino and return, I will have you arrested for trespassing. If you refrain from gambling at a blackjack table, you are welcome to participate in any other game offered by the casino."

As he was reading, I became relieved. It didn't appear that the chips would be confiscated or that I'd go to jail. The Resorts people were being quite cautious in their method of barring.

After he finished, I said, "Yessir," and the entourage dispersed. I turned to the cage, and the teller began the formidable job of rearranging my chips by denomination and counting them down. The cage manager instructed the cashier to stack the chips neatly on the ledge. Then I realized what was happening. They were planning to photograph the event from one of the many bubble-domes mounted on the ceiling.

After the modeling session was over, the cashier gave me a pile of $100 bills in $5,000 stacks, which I stuffed into my pockets. Pockets bulging ridiculously, I walked out of the casino, with a train of security guards following me.

Back in our room, members of the team had gotten word that several other barrings had taken place. None of our people, other than me, was barred.

Overall, our effort had been successful. Jack earned $20,000. Mike, on this win alone, doubled his net worth and would have cash to pursue another interest he had—a computer analysis of the game of pan.

The next day, January 31, we had a final team get-together. As we said goodbyes, we expressed hope that we'd play again somewhere, somehow, although I don't think any of us really felt that we would. Then, Jack, Rob and Mike left for the West Coast. I stayed behind to file a lawsuit against Resorts for the barring.

Little did we know that we'd be together before the end of the year.

The Battle Moves From The Casino To The Courts

We later found that the barrings were allowed because Resorts' attorney Joel Sterns wrote a letter to the commission, stating that Resorts' earnings and the future of Atlantic City gaming were being jeopardized by the card counters. On the same day, with a hand delivered letter, Commission Chairman Lordi unilaterally, without consulting the commission, gave Resorts permission to bar. This action would be the first of several to raise eyebrows in the future.

After what came to be known as Black Tuesday, the day of the barrings, we had several good players who had not been seen playing in Atlantic City. We dispatched them to Resorts during the spring and summer, where they were successful, winning nearly as much as our group had in January, but over a six-month period of time. They spent some time in France and Belgium as well.

In the meantime, Morris Goldings, the lawyer *extraordinaire* from Boston, and I pursued the legal issue of whether Resorts, according to New Jersey law, had the right to exclude players they thought were skilled. Resorts claimed their interest was in having the option of excluding "professional card counters." Indeed, the signs they displayed in several places attested to this motive by stating:

> "Professional card counters are prohibited from play at
> our blackjack tables."

But, their subsequent barrings of many other counters and non-counters alike made it clear that they were more interested in the privilege of excluding *any* skilled players—or as one reporter phrased it, "To allow only the losers to play." The legal issue of barring is discussed more fully in Chapter 17.

On October 24, 1979, the commission finally reached a conclusion on the barring issue, nine months after my complaint was filed. They ruled that, in their opinion, New Jersey casinos had the legal right to exclude counters, based on common law. But as a matter of policy, the commission felt it undesirable that skillful players be excluded. They concluded that the rules should be made more difficult for suspected counters, but that all players, skilled or non-skilled, should be allowed to play.

The commission agreed to proceed with an "experiment," whereby the rules of blackjack would be made tougher and all players would be allowed to play. The rules changes would be:

— The cut-card could be moved to half-way from the back of the shoe.

— The house could shuffle the cards if the players tripled their previous bet at $25 tables (and increased it five times at lower limit tables).

— The house could shuffle if a player joined a $25 game with a bet of $200 or more in the middle of a shoe ($100 at lower limit games).

To give the two casinos (Caesars Boardwalk Regency had opened during the summer) enough time to prepare for the experiment, and to allow for a meaningful comparison of month-end data, the start of the experiment was set for December 1, 1979.

During the last ten days of November, several teams converged on Atlantic City and played under cover. We used several of the players from Team 5 and several played in disguise; others used "gorilla BP's." The ruse worked—neither Resorts' nor Caesars' bosses knew what was going on.

Team 6 And The Great Blackjack Experiment

On the first day of the experiment, counters again came to Atlantic City from all over the country. But there were not nearly as many as in January. Resorts' management accepted the counters and took the experiment in stride, largely because its management had already been acclimated in January to an "open environment" where counters were allowed, by law, to play.

Caesars' management, however, reacted differently. Suspected counters were not served drinks or coffee at the table. Floor personnel reflected the negative attitudes of upper management and many acted impolite or hostile to counters.

Caesars offered many $1,000 maximum games, all six deck shoes, and the player could play two hands. Resorts had $25-to-$500 games and $100-to-$1,000 six deck games, and a few four deck games at the low limit tables.

We had nine players on our team, Team 6, including myself, Jack, Rob and Mike. Also on the team were three players from Nevada and two from New Jersey whom we had trained over the previous months. We were playing to a $100,000 bank.

On the very first day, the casinos' inventory of outstanding black ($100) and purple ($500) chips increased by about one-quarter of a million dollars. The commission later erroneously concluded that this figure indicated that untoward profits were made by counters. Actually, we were again holding the chips to avoid increasing the drop and thus, decreasing the hold. In fact, we were doing only what most high-rollers do—cashing in for chips at the beginning of a trip and holding the chips until the end. Had all counters cashed in their chips each day and bought in for cash on each subsequent day, the casino drop would have been inflated by several hundred thousand dollars per day, making their profitability, as measured by the hold, look far worse than it really was.

The casinos actually showed an increase in profits on the first day of the experiment, but their profits dropped dramatically on the second day. I tried to convince the commission not to be swayed by daily results, arguing that these kinds of swings must be expected. Similar fluctuations would be felt if 40 high-rollers suddenly began betting two hands of $1,000 at the baccarat tables.

Casino managment reported to the commission that 120-150 counters were threatening their tables. On hearing this, I walked from table-to-table with Mike Santaniello, a staff member of the commission, on the evening of the third day of the experiment. I spotted six counters I knew and one I didn't know but suspected after watching him for several minutes. Mike then asked the Caesars people to give him an estimate of the number of counters currently in the casino. They returned later and responded that 24 were playing. This was absurd. I may have missed one or two counters, but certainly no more than that. It was obvious that the casinos were seeing "counter skeletons" in every closet.

The five teams other than our own weren't winning. After four days, one team, which started with a $40,000 bank (and had several marginal players), went broke. The other teams were either in the red or at break-even. Yet total casino profits were down significantly and I doubted that these figures were doctored. I attributed the decrease to two factors:

1. The cut-card was now at half of the shoe, rather than at the previous position of one-third. We clocked the average number of rounds dealt, which decreased from 55 to 48 rounds per hour, a drop in volume of nearly 13%. Thus, on capacity nights (most week-end nights and Sundays operate at capacity), blackjack profits would be expected to drop by 13%, or perhaps $50,000 per day, without the counters making a nickel.

2. Our team was exceptionally lucky and won far more than expected value in the first four days. (One player said it was due to "karma," since we alone had payed the legal fees in the long fight to gain readmittance.) The chances were about 1-out-of-1,000 that we would have won so much. We, of course, enjoyed the win, but were concerned about its "unnatural" effect on casino profitability.

From the start, the commission was supplied inaccurate data from the casinos on the amounts that were won by counters. A task force at Caesars tried to keep track of counter wins.

As one of the members of that group told me, "Kenny, it's a joke. We have no idea how much you guys are winning. You change tables. You come in and out of your pockets with chips. It's laughable, but we're instructed to keep figures. If anyone wins a batch of black chips, we put him down as a counter. That takes the heat off the top guys and the heat off of us."

On Day 4, Caesars restricted customers to playing only one hand; we could no longer play two hands of $1,000. We were surprised they hadn't thought of this far earlier.

On Day 5, the commission met to discuss the experiment. Mike Santaniello reported lower profits for Days 2-through-4. He recommended that, if profits continued as low, the allowable ratios be dropped to 2-to-1, instead of 3-to-1, at the $25 games. He suggested Day 8 for the start of this rule.

At this point, it seemed to me that the counters should coordinate efforts to ensure that the experiment would continue. The leaders of the major teams met that night at 4:40 a.m. in the Resorts mezzanine. Of the major teams, two were in the red, one was tapped out, another, which had lost vast amounts, was making a slow, tedious comeback, and we were ahead way beyond expected value. It appeared that the game was beatable by highly skilled players. But, it wasn't easy and the number of counters in town was decreasing.

We discussed the casinos' falsification of counter wins; several of us had heard from casino personnel that this was taking place. It was also noted that, for the first time, pit personnel at one casino were suspiciously recording the table-tray count in pencil, instead of pen, upon instructions from above (but the authorizing signatures were still made in ink).

191

We concluded that these actions showed the casinos were not taking the experiment in good faith and that even if we treaded softly, they would push for the barring of counters. We decided not to restrict our play, feeling that unless we all won far above the expected value, casino profits would not be noticeably eroded. We were concerned with the effect of the cut-card on profits and I promised to make the commission aware of this factor once again.

On Day 6, I brought this information to the attention of the commission. We found that Caesars had now lowered its limit to $500. Several of our group flocked to Resorts. Earl Yanase, their affable shift manager, asked, "How come all you guys are here?"

He soon found out and, two hours later, the Resorts limits, too, were lowered to $500.

On Day 8, the commission implemented the 2-to-1 ratio. The new ratio made it tougher. Our group, playing with a $350,000 bank, came off-the-top with $250 so we could get to the $500 limit on the second round if the shoe went favorable. We found we'd get trapped if we dropped to $75 or $50 in negative counts, since, if the shoe reverted to being favorable, we could bet only $150 or $100 on the following round. Thus, we adjusted by playing higher amounts in negative shoes, clearly a dilution of expected value. I felt confident that the new restrictions would be closer to the equilibrium that we and the commission were searching for (the only "equilibrium" the casinos wanted was to get us out of there).

Despite the 2-to-1 ratio, our group won big on Day 8, around $51,000. At this point, an interesting phenomenon occurred within our group. Several of the guys had been in town, playing full time for over three weeks. Despite our unprecedented wins, apathy developed on the team. The guys made comments like:

"Man, I'm burned out. I want to go to California and just lie on the beach."

"Let's blow this place and come back after Christmas."

"It's no challenge playing this game. All the calculations are easy now. Any edge and we bet $500." (He didn't mean the game was too easy to beat. He was referring to the fact that although several calculations were usually made to determine bet size, because of our huge bank and the lower $500 limit, no such calculations were necessary; we merely bet $500 with any plus running count.)

I, too, was tired and didn't view the opportunity in the proper perspective. I'd been playing in Germany the week before December 1 and was ready for a rest as well. We decided to play for a few more days, distribute the win and form a new bank for the players who wanted to stay on. We agreed that I wouldn't play for a while, since my playing seemed to attract a lot of attention. My "cooling it" and staying out of sight might help to lengthen the experiment.

On Days 9-through-11, we lost heavily and were now in the red since "phase 2" of the experiment had begun. It looked like the new ratios were striking a fair balance. After discussion with the team, we agreed to supply these figures to the commission to show them how tough the game really was.

One teammate said, "We know the casinos are lying. So we should report our losses higher than they are." The rest of us didn't agree. We decided to furnish totally accurate figures. Unaltered, they proved our point. They showed that the nine of us. playing 213 hours and placing $3.4 million into action, earned a total of $1,211, or $6 per hour (less than the dealers), for an earnings rate of .03%.

That night, I toured the casinos to see how many counters were still playing. I spotted six in Resorts and eight in Caesars. Now I *knew* the game was tough. In January, counters were everywhere and their number grew as news of the "candy store" spread. Now, the number of counters was decreasing, obviously because they weren't making money and were leaving town.

On Day 12, the commission announced further tightening of the rules. To eliminate back-counting, the casinos were given the right to shuffle on any player who joined the game after the cut-card had been inserted into the shoe. I was elated. I felt impressed with the wisdom of the commission staff because I now felt that this one Solomonic rule could effect the equilibrium we were all looking for, for the following reason:

> Since so few counters were still playing, fully 90% of the tables could now be restored to cutting off only one-third of the shoe. The casino profits would be largely restored to pre-December 1 levels. If a counter was suspected, the cut-card could be placed at half the shoe. The 20 or so counters still in town could grind away with the 2-to-1 ratio and the half-a-shoe. If they could grind out their $100 per hour or so, so be it. They'd have a relatively minor impact on casino bottom lines.

I again walked through both casinos and saw only a handful of counters. But the cut-card was still at half the shoe at *all* the tables! I urged the Caesars and Resorts managers to move the cut-card back at the vast majority of the tables where no counters were playing. If they did, it seemed that the solution would be reached! I was elated.

My optimism was short-lived. The rude awakening came the very next morning, when Frank Fee, another staff member of the commission, called me. He told me that our old buddy, Chairman Joe Lordi, had decided to conclude the experiment (once again without consulting the rest of the commission). I urged Frank to hold off the decision until I had a chance to meet with him and explain why I thought an equilibrium had been reached. But, he sounded as if the decision was a *fait accompli*.

That afternoon, I met with Frank Fee. He told me the casinos were still reporting seriously-reduced blackjack profits, even for the previous day. I again tried to point out that much of the reduction was due to the cut-card placement, that few counters were playing and that the casinos had instructed their employees to exaggerate counter wins (a second casino official the previous night reiterated that employees had been instructed to over-report counter win figures). I also told Frank about the fill slips being written in pencil.

But, Frank said that Lordi was irrevocably committed to conclude the experiment that very night.

I was puzzled by the magnitude of the lower profit figures and wondered whether the casinos would alter their figures, with the attendant risks, merely to rid themselves of the counters. Frank and I reviewed their cash and counting-room procedures in detail. They appeared totally foolproof, although it was suggested by someone else at our meeting that the casinos had been in the business for years and that for every control, an imaginative, experienced casino person could probably find a way to circumvent it. It was, he went on, an ideal opportunity for the casinos to "skim," blaming the losses on the counters. I personally doubted that the casinos would risk their $600,000 in daily earnings; Frank agreed.

We had a team meeting. We agreed to play as long and as hard as we could on our last day. At this point, we had only six teammates; three had left town. I had hoped we'd win big on our last day, particularly at Caesars, which had been so hostile to counters. As a result, that night I played in a far more aggressive way, leaving tables whenever the deck was negative, table-hopping frenetically, forcing "open games" to be broken with $500 off-the-top bets and playing head-on as much as possible to maximize the number of hands played.

Previously, we'd all played far more conservatively. We didn't want to give the appearance of disrupting casino operations in any way. But now, we had only one day left, due possibly to the duplicity of the casinos. Frank Fee came into Caesars to watch. I felt sheepish playing so aggressively and was disappointed that Frank was observing this mode of play, which was so contrary to our low-key approach during the first 12 days.

I won $8,000 on that last day, but overall our team broke even. At the end of the experiment, the teams exchanged results. During the 13 days, the counters won slightly over $600,000; the casinos reported $1,400,000. Four teams were profitable; one team went broke. Other individual counters both won and lost.

I stayed in town for the commission meeting several days hence. On the very next day after the conclusion of the experiment, both casinos restored the cut-card to one-third from the end. It was a Friday. Both casinos were mobbed. I felt their profits would soar and Lordi's decision would be seen as justified. Sure enough, the casinos reported a $510,000 blackjack win on December 14 (versus $259,000 on the day before), the largest daily win in December (but also larger than any day in November except one, a month when the experiment was not being run).

Yes, I was bitter. I felt an equilibrium had been achieved, but the "tap-dancing" of the casino people successfully prevented it from being implemented. I vowed to redouble our legal efforts to effect a no-barring policy in New Jersey. We left town.

The Experiment Succeeds But No One Knows It

Permit me to hypothesize for a moment. If the experiment had continued for one more week, I believe only a handful of counters would have remained in town. The casinos might have been moved to replace the cut-card to one-third from the end of the shoe at most tables and the casino win rates would have been largely restored. Most of the "professionals," including some of our group, had already left town for more favorable opportunities in Nevada and elsewhere in the world.

What would the casinos have lost in the long run? If 20 counters had remained, playing 40 hours per week and averaging $100 per hour, they would have averaged $80,000 per week (with *wide* fluctuations), or less than $6,000 per day for each of the two casinos then in Atlantic City. I would think this would be a small price to pay for the State of New Jersey to offer an open environment in blackjack.

These players, too, would have filtered out and been replaced by others, perhaps keeping the figures at these levels. As more players learned to count, the casinos would lose somewhat more. But for every player who became a winning player, the knowledge that the game could be beaten with skill would generate many players who would try unsuccessfully to win, thereby generating even more profits for the casinos. I believe the experiment was concluded by Lordi far too early.

To this day, the Atlantic City casinos reserve the right to bar counters and non-counters alike. In January 1980, two brothers were barred by Caesars; one betting $5 chips, was ahead $40. He was a reporter for the Atlantic City Press and the story made page one of that paper. Morris Goldings has filed an appeal with the New Jersey Appellate Court, the details of which are discussed in Chapter 17.

The permitting of barring effectively grants casino personnel the privilege of excluding just about anyone they want, under the guise of being "professionals." Photographing, surveillance and harassment of persons suspected of being skillful is the result. A general atmosphere of suspicion, unfriendliness and resentment between casino personnel and players is fostered, as floormen monitor players' behavior to determine their playing ability and casino security guards are called upon to eject players.

It would appear that a more sensible solution to this problem lies in exactly what the commission attempted. That is, establishing blackjack conditions that do not work to the disadvantage of the general public, but which still eliminate a significant portion of the skilled player's statistical advantage over the house.

This, combined with a no-barring policy, will create an "open environment," where the skilled blackjack player and the pitboss will not be placed in adversarial positions. A positive, healthful atmosphere will be created, in which, just as with chess, backgammon and bridge, skill at blackjack will be viewed with respect.

Chapter Fourteen

Front-Loading

This chapter and the following chapter describe hole card play. No knowledgeable information has been written about these techniques to date* and yet, hole card teams have been operating in Nevada for years.

I have personally steered away from hole card play. However, I can't say that it's necessarily because of a sense of morality since I feel front-loading is legal. But on the few occasions I've tried front-loading, I've felt uncomfortable. My "act" in the casino is predicated upon being the bon vivant, the big-time, free-spending, heavy-drinking gambler who banters and jokes with the pit and the people at the table. When I play a front loader, I feel I have something to hide. My act is destroyed; I look suspicious, I'm sure, to the bosses with "street sense;" I get nervous; I probably make errors.

A former teammate, call him Val, formed his own team several years ago and won over $750,000 playing holecards, mostly in Northern Nevada. I traveled with Val's team for several weeks. I even put down a few minor front-loading plays with them. They were a hard-working group, fully as disciplined as the best of my "on-the-square" counting teams. They developed new techniques heretofore unpublished. Since they are now out of the business, and because what transpired is definitely part of blackjack lore and the knowledge of the game, I have decided to publish these two chapters (with Val's blessing).

Hole card play is currently impossible in Atlantic City because of

---

*Front-loading and spooking have been written about in only one text, but they're treated superficially and don't display an in-depth knowledge of these techniques.

the dealing practices there:

— Hand-held decks are forbidden by law, which precludes front-loading.

— The hole card is not looked at by the dealer until after the players have played their hands, making spooking and "playing with the help" impossible.

— In addition, all cards are dealt face-up and not touched by the players, which precludes forms of player cheating, such as card-mucking, marking and daubing discussed in Chapter 16.

I believe the solution to part of the hole card problem in Nevada is to take steps similar to those taken in New Jersey. However, it may not be practical to do away with hand-held decks, since single deck games are so prevalent, especially in Northern Nevada. But, not allowing the dealer to look at his hole card before the players play the hands precludes others from looking at it, too. It also prevents the dealer from helping players by revealing his knowledge of the hole card. This countermeasure will not do away with front-loading, but it does prevent "spooking" and "playing with the help" (described in the next chapter), which are somewhat "gamier" techniques..

What Is Front-Loading

A front-loader or "loader" is a dealer who exposes his hole card to the player as he pulls it out of the deck, or, prior to or during the process of sliding it under his upcard. Front-loaders who hand-hold the deck offer the potential of seeing every hole card and are money in the bank to the player. A front-loading play is the most lucrative legal situation that exists in blackjack for the player.

Dealers are usually carefully trained not to expose their hole cards while dealing. Despite this training, it's inevitable that some dealers will develop sloppy dealing habits that allow the player to read the hole card. This is particularly the case during the crowded summer periods in Northern Nevada, where dozens of inexperienced dealers are needed to handle peak tourist loads.

In front-loading, the card is visible to one or more players at the table, usually from third base (first base with left-handed dealers) or the middle of the table. There are not many front-loaders in Nevada, perhaps 1-out-of-200 dealers, so tedious preliminary scouting is often required.

The front-loading player has the opportunity to read *every* hole card. This gives the player a tremendous advantage. For example, if the dealer has a "stiff," that is, a bustable hand of 12 through 16, it is almost always to the player's advantage not to hit his own hand if he, too, has a stiff. Thus, the dealer takes the risk of busting. An even more dramatic example: if the dealer has an ace upcard and the player knows the hole card, the player *always* will be correct on the insurance bet. The player could gain greater than a 2% edge just by playing even with the house on his other play and winning all insurance bets!

Thorp (1) estimates that a player with knowledge of the dealer's hole card is playing at a 9.9% advantage if he uses perfect hole card Basic Strategy (Table 14-1). We have found, however, that the player, with typical Las Vegas rules, is actually at a 5-6% advantage, for the following reasons:

— Many Basic Strategy hole card plays cannot be made. If the player were to hit 19 against a dealer's 20, the men in the sky would probably fall through their one-way mirrors. Many such plays cannot be made for cover purposes.

— The player can rarely spot every single hole card. A good front-loader is "readable" 80-to-90% of the time; others may expose their hole card only 25-to-35% of the time, or less.

— Reading errors occur. I once split 4's against a dealer 20, a horrible play, with a $500 bet out. Somehow, the 10 of clubs in the hole looked like a six.

On the other hand, there are two offsetting factors which work to the player's advantage:

1. The player always wins the insurance bet (at a 2-to-1 payoff) if the hole card is seen. On average, the dealer will have an ace up 7.7% of the time (1-out-of-13); in 31% of those times (4-out-of-13) the dealer will have a blackjack. Thus, 31% times 7.7%, or 2.4%, of the dealer's hands will be an ace-up blackjack. If the player were to flat bet and play even with the house, and win 2-to-1 on every insurance half-bet, he'd have a 2.4% edge. So, insurance adds a 2.4% edge in favor of the player facing a 100% front-loader.

2. Thorp's 9.9% edge is predicated upon playing hole card Basic Strategy. There are times when the counting player can use matrix numbers in varying his play:

— For example, if the dealer has a hard total of 7, counting both his hole card and his upcard, perhaps a 5 and a 2, the player can play as if the dealer had a 7 upcard and he had not yet drawn a hole card. The matrix numbers for these plays (16 vs. 7, 15 vs. 7, etc.) can be applied, giving the player a greater edge.

— Special hole card numbers have been developed. For example, while Basic Strategy calls for standing on 12 versus a 12, when the deck is sufficiently minus, this hand should be hit. Hole card numbers for the more common plays for the Advanced Plus/Minus and the Uston APC are included in Table 14-2.

199

For element-of-ruin purposes, we assume a 5% advantage with a 100% front-loader, a 4% advantage with an 80% dealer, 3% with a 60% dealer and 2% with anything less.

The Ethics Of Front-Loading

According to the letter of the law, front-loading appears to be totally legal. Nevada has made specific laws on what actions constitute cheating. We've studied these laws in detail and front-loading appears to violate none of them.

The only applicable section of the Nevada Statutes (as of this writing) is NR 465.070, which states:

> "Every person who, by color, or aid of any trick or sleight-of-hand performance, or by any fraud or fraudulent scheme, cards, dice or device, shall win for himself, or for another, any money ... shall be punished by imprisonment ...."

The other cheating statute, Section NR 465.080, refers solely to the use of bogus chips, marked cards, dice, cheating devices and unlawful coin, the use of tools, drills and wires or coins attached to strings, or wires or electronic or magnetic devices when playing slot machines.

So the question is — does glancing at the dealer's hole card, as the dealer is dealing the hand, constitute "fraud or a fraudulent scheme?" The player is making use of information made available to him by an unskillful dealer. If a card counter spots a burn and/or hole card, it would appear to be within his province to use that information to advantage if he has the capability to do so.

The casinos, of their own volition, offer the game of blackjack to the public. The Nevada casinos make the rules and the playing conditions exactly as they see fit. If they choose not to offer insurance, they don't. If they choose to hit soft 17, they do. If they choose to deal down to the last card (as they often do at the Nevada Club in Reno), they do. In fact, in the game of "zweikartenspiel" or double exposure," both of the dealer's cards are shown (although the rules are changed so that the game is unfavorable).

Thus, the player accepts the game as offered to him and plays it to the best of his ability. If that ability includes the occasional spotting of a hole card, one might argue that he should be able to use that information as he can.

A player reading a hole card was arrested in 1978 at Circus-Circus, as was the dealer. The bosses thought the two were working in concert. After it was determined that the player and the dealer didn't know each other, the Vegas judge threw the case out, saying, "If they show the card, why shouldn't he (the player) look at it?"

Let's test the law a little further. In order to fool the bosses and perpetuate play, Val's team introduced the use of a "relay." The relay plays at the same table, betting the minimum, reads the hole card and signals its value to the Big Player so the BP can make the appropriate play. The BP, for cover purposes, sits in a spot where he obviously cannot read the hole card. Is this legal, moral or ethical?

At games of roulette and baccarat, the bosses are happy to let two or more players jot down the sequence of results and work together on fallacious mathematical progressions, as one player works the pencil and the other makes the bets. The bosses love this "collusion." Does the use of a relay in front-loading constitute "fraud" because the collusion is surreptitious? I leave the answer to your conscience and to the courts.

Front-Loaders We Have Known

If the moral question of front-loading doesn't bother you, you should be observant enough to know when you're facing a front-loader. To give the interested reader an idea of what types of "moves" to look for, I'll describe some of the loaders who have been spotted. Many of these dealers are no longer with the clubs mentioned, but who knows? You may even run into one or two of them some day.

Jeanne. Blonde, friendly, 30-ish, Jeanne dealt at the Sahara Tahoe on graveyard shift (4 a.m. to noon). Her nametag read, "Jeanne, Medford, Oregon."

She was right-handed, usually dealt rapidly and kept the deck low to the table. However, as she pulled the hole card out of the deck, she would flick it out to the right with a sudden twisting motion of her wrist, exposing the upper right-hand corner of the card to the player. Since the "index" number of the card is printed on this corner, it made her hole card easy to read accurately. (The player often doesn't see the index and has to rely on determining the value of the card by reading the "pips" on the card—an essential skill to the hole card player that will be described in the next chapter.)

Jeanne could be read best from just to the left of the center of the table. The hole card was visible whether she was dealing head-on or to a crowded table. When she dealt either very rapidly or very slowly, the card couldn't be seen. But, in her affable manner, she would often ask, "Am I dealing too fast (or too slow)?"

It was more than occasionally suggested that she speed up or slow down, as necessary, for the hole card once again to become visible.

Ann. A dark-haired lady of about 50 who dealt at the Ponderosa in Reno (at this writing she is a pitboss there). Ann could be read from the center of the table, regardless of the number of players at the table (the configuration of the players at the table often dictates whether a dealer is "readable.") She flashed the card best when head-on; the card was readable about 75% of the time, The faster she dealt, the higher the card went.

201

Front loading at the Ponderosa is frustrating because the insurance bet is not offered. The player will know the dealer has the blackjack before the dealer knows it, since the 10 is visible as it is slid under the ace upcard. Since there is no insurance, the player just sits there helplessly as the dealer turns over her blackjack and collects the bets.

A second front-loader, Nita, dealt at the Ponderosa. She was oriental, with freckles, and could be read about 50% of the time from the middle of the table.

Barbara.(#1) Young, frazzy hair, brunette, at the Sahara Tahoe. Worked swing-shift and "flashed" best when there was someone at third base. Her dealing motion could best be described as "up, up and away." As she dealt to a full table, from left to right, her left hand, the one holding the deck, went higher and higher. By the time she dealt all the way around to third base, it was impossible for her to recover and she flashed her hole card as she pulled it out of the deck, which was nearly level with her ears at that point.

On several occasions, Barbara's left bra strap was loose and would fall off her shoulder. She'd hold her left shoulder higher, to keep the strap from falling more. During these times, it was impossible to spot the card. But a few minutes later, she'd adjust the strap and the hole card appeared once again. (She'd be far more profitable if she were braless.)

Barbara tended to tighten up when big bettors were at the table, a tendency of some front-loaders. One player, betting quarters, could see her hole card with no difficulty. When he graduated to $100 chips, the card disappeared, as Barbara held her hand down and became more careful in dealing.

Once, Val stationed someone at third base, to keep her "up, up and awaying." He put a relay in the middle of the table and he played at first base. The theory was that she'd concentrate on keeping her hole card away from the high-roller at first base, making it even more obvious to the relay in the center of the table. It worked.

Sylvia. Sylvia was about the most lucrative front-loader in the business. As of 1979, she'd worked at Harrah's for 24 years. About 55, she is blonde, pleasant and friendly. Many players knew her and made a point of playing her table because of her pleasant manner. She was in tight with the bosses; they viewed her as an "old-timer," a pro they didn't have to worry about. Thus, they didn't watch her games closely. She had some friends "upstairs," too; she once told me of a trip she took to Seattle in one of Bill Harrah's jets.

Sylvia often dealt at the $5 tables, where the upper limit was $1,000 (versus $200 maximums at other tables). She's dropped over $50,000 to players reading her hole card.

Under the right conditions, she could be read 100% of the time. She was best when someone played the sixth spot, but not the seventh, and with a crowded table. She was also readable head-on. When a boss stood nearby, she unconsciously held her card down, and it was no longer readable. But, in 80% of the situations, her card came across clearly. It was best seen when sitting in the third or fourth spot. Just as she pulled the card up from the deck, she flashed it. Sylvia, alas, is now dealing roulette.

Eleanor (or "El"). From Garden Grove, California, she dealt at Harold's Club in Reno. Short, blonde hair. Best read from sixth or seventh spot, just as she tucked her card under. She had a habit of bending back the upper right-hand edge of the card as it went under, exposing the index. Val caught her 75% of the time when someone sat at first or second base.

Barbara. (#2) Dark-hair, outdoors-looking, huge bust, about 35. Deals day shift at Harold's Club in Reno. Readable from the third and fourth spot. I socialized with her briefly. She was an invaluable source of information on dealers shooting the house and on the Griffin agents (she called them "a bunch of jerks.")

Killer. Yes, that's the name on her tag. Also works at Harold's. Blonde, 35-ish, sometimes a bit testy unless she's being tipped. Readable about 50% of the time.

Patty. On day shift at Harold's Club. Cute, frosted blonde hair, about 25, nice figure. Readable only 25-to-35% of the time, but a joy to look at.

Sundowner Dealer. About 30, dark hair, Italian, buxom and usually pleasant. Can be read from the middle of the table. Absolutely no problem playing "nickels" with her. With bigger action, she tightened up.

Her motion is unusual. She tilts the deck when dealing, the top of the deck to the player's right; the bottom to the left. If the player tilts his head a bit to the right as she's pulling the hole card from the deck, it becomes totally visible.

Lois. Swing Shift at Harrah's Reno. Val beat her for $14,000 in five hours of play, but his "act" must have been convincing to the bosses since he returned the following month and won about the same. Lois was 100% readable from the fifth spot. The table had to be full, though. Val had both his girlfriend and his relay play two hands each.

Jean. At the Riverside. A cute lady from Edinburgh, Scotland. About 55, with white hair and a friendly smile. Best read from second base, with a player at the sixth or seventh spot. Val would station the BP at first base and put a relay in the middle of the table. Readable about 50% of the time, depending upon the table configuration.

The Mint Duo. Two dealers, both on days at the Mint, flashed hole cards. One was "Nick, Illinois" according to his name tag. Tall, ruddy complexion, friendly, Nick could be read if there was someone at third base. He pulled his hole card from the deck with a funny wobbling motion. The card hovered in mid-air for a brief instant and could be read during that time. Then he lowered it and slid it under his upcard. He dealt at the Sahara Vegas for years, but the bosses felt he was "unlucky" and fired him. He could be read about 40% of the time, but he often ran the roulette game and obviously was of no help there.

The other dealer on the same shift at the Mint was Murphy. Short, capable-looking, fast dealer. Val filled up the table, put a relay in the center, the high-roller at first and "took off" his 5%. Murphy is now gone from the Mint, but maybe someone will find him somewhere else.

Suzie. Harrah's, Lake Tahoe. Pretty gal, dark hair. Val beat her for $10,000 before the bosses pulled her. Another one of his team won $3,200 in two 40-minute sessions. She pulled herself off the table; she told the boss she was sick. The boss dealt the game for 15 minutes (unreadable).

Suzie disappeared from the scene for a few months, returned for several months and was played heavily, and once again quit the business.

Suzanne Powers. Another pretty brunette at Harrah's at the Lake. Val and a player named Steve played her and won about $3,000. Steve split 10's against a 16 and won $1,600 on the hand. But it was a very expensive play for him, too, because he was barred—for counting. Val stayed and played her the following day, but lost. Yes, you can lose to front-loaders.

How To Play Front-Loaders

If you happen to encounter a front-loader, the first thing to do is to "clock" him, that is, determine the percentage of the time that the hole card can be read accurately. Don't risk getting any heat while clocking—just flat bet small amounts and play Basic Strategy. Watch the dealer as he deals to different table configurations to determine when he "shows" it. Perhaps the card will be readable with a full table, with the seventh spot open, head-on, etc. Loaders differ widely in this. Determine if the dealer returns to the same table after his break or whether he's "rubber-banded," that is, the dealer is assigned to various tables after the break (so-called because a rubber band is often placed around a clip-board under the name of the last dealer assigned). After you've gotten the necessary intelligence, adjourn to your hotel room or home and plan your strategy.

Playing Strategy. Study Table 14-1, which gives the Basic Strategy for hole card play. If you want, you can make up flashcards, as follows:

Figure 13a

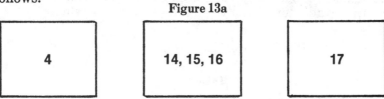

The flashcard illustrations list the value of the dealer's total for both his cards. Recite your playing strategy for each:

— For the first card, you'd say, "Hit 'til hard 14, soft 18, double 10, 11, A6, A7 and split aces, 7's and 8's."

— For the second card, recite, "Hit to hard 12, soft 18, double everything from 5 up, split all pairs but 5's."

— For the third card, recite, "Hit to hard 17, soft 18, split 2, 3, 6, 7, 8."

Keep going through the flashcards until you can recite the playing strategy automatically.

Betting Strategy. You've clocked the dealer and determined the percentage of time he's readable. Establish your betting strategy as follows:

%Readable	%Edge	Portion of your bank that you can bet (from Table 9-1).
100%	5%	1/32
80	4	1/38
60	3	1/55
40 or less	2	1/75

Using only the hole card Basic Strategy, the player may enjoy up to a 5% edge. The degree to which this is highly lucrative is shown in the following example:

With a 5% edge (a 100% front-loader), the player can safely bet up to 3% of his bank on each hand, since only 32 units are required to stay within a 5% element-of-ruin. With a $10,000 bank, the player may bet $300 per hand. Assuming 100 hands per hour, the player will place $30,000 into action per hour. With an average expectation of 5%, he will earn $1,500 per hour, on average, which is one-seventh of the total bank, per hour of play!

These numbers explain why Val's team put so many shifts in the red in Northern Nevada during the years the team was playing.

Table 14—1

Optimum Front-Loading Basic Strategy

Dealer's Hand	Hit Until: Hard Hands	Hit Until: Soft Hands	Double-Down On:	Pair Splitting
Hard 20	20	20	—	—
Hard 19	19	19	—	9
Hard 18	18	19	—	2,3,7,8,9*
Hard 17	17	18	—	2,3,6,7,8
Hard 14,15,16	12	18	5,6,7,8,9,10,11 A2,A3,A4,A5,A6 A7,A8,A9	All pairs except 5's
Hard 13	12	18	7,8,9,10,11 A2 through A9	All pairs except 5's
Hard 12	12	18	8,9,10,11 A2 through A9*	All pairs except 5's
Hard 11	15*	18	—	A
Hard 10	16*	19	11	A*
Hard 9	17*	19	10,11	A,8,9
Hard 8	17	18	10,11	A,7,8,9*
Hard 7	17	18	10,11	A,2,3,7,8
Hard 6	12	18	9,10,11*	A,2,3,6,7,8,9*
Hard 5	13	18	10,11,A2 through A8	A,2,3,6,7,8,9
Hard 4	14	18	10,11,A6,A7	A,7,8
Soft Hands				
A,9	20	20	—	—
A,8	19	19	—	9
A,7	18	19	—	2,3,7,8,9
A,6	17	18	—	A,2,3,6,7,8
A,5	13	18	9,10,11,A6,A7	A,2,3,6,7,8,9
A,4	13	18	10,11	A,2,6,7,8,9
A,3	14	18	10,11	A,7,8
A,2	15	18	10,11	A,7,8
A A	16	18	11	A,8

* There are minor variations depending upon the specific card values of the dealer's hand which can, for all practical purposes, be ignored.

Table 14—2
Hole Card Numbers Matrices for
Uston Advanced Point Count
and
Uston Advanced Plus/Minus

Notes: Deviate from hole card basic strategy (Table 14-1) if the true count (half deck) reaches the numbers in the matrix.

Numbers apply to single deck, but are close enough to be used for multiple deck play.

Hole Card Numbers Matrix—Uston Advanced Point Count

HIT & STAND

DEALER'S TOTAL

Your Hand:	10	11	12	13	14	15	16	17	18	19	20
16	0	−3	−18	S	S	S	S	H	H	H	H
15	6	0	−16	−17	S	S	S	H	H	H	H
14	15	6	−13	−15	−18	S	S	H	H	H	H
13	H	13	−10	−12	−15	−18	S	H	H	H	H
12	H	H	−8	−10	−13	−16	S	H	H	H	H

DEALER'S TOTAL

Your Hand:	A A	A 2	A 3	A 4	A 5	A 6	A 7	A 8	A 9
16	0	−2	−6	−7	−11	H	H	H	H
15	1	1	−3	−5	−8	H	H	H	H
14	3	4	0	−2	−5	H	H	H	H
13	7	6	2	1	−2	H	H	H	H
12	13	11	6	5	2	H	H	H	H

Table 14—2 (continued)

Hole Card Numbers Matrix—Uston Advanced Point Count

HARD DOUBLE

DEALER'S TOTAL

Your Hand:	10	11	12	13	14	15	16	17	18	19	20
11	0	H	D	D	D	D	D	8	13	19	H
10	H	H	D	D	D	D	D	7	12	20	H
9	H	H	−13	−15	−19	D	D	19	26	H	H
8	H	H	−4	−7	−11	−16	D	H	H	H	H
7	H	H	5	−1	−5	−10	−18	H	H	H	H
6	H	H	10	3	−1	−6	−13	H	H	H	H
5	H	H	12	5	0	−4	−11	H	H	H	H

DEALER'S TOTAL

Your Hand:	A A	A 2	A 3	A 4	A 5	A 6	A 7	A 8	A 9
11	−4	−5	−9	−10	−11	7	12	18	27
10	3	−1	−3	−5	−8	8	13	20	H
9	22	12	6	5	2	18	27	H	H
8	H	23	16	14	12	H	H	H	H
7	H	H	21	20	18	H	H	H	H
6	H	H	26	23	23	H	H	H	H
5	H	H	26	24	23	H	H	H	H

Table 14—2 (continued)

Hole Card Numbers Matrix—Uston Advanced Point Count

SOFT DOUBLE

DEALER'S TOTAL

Your Hand:	10	11	12	13	14	15	16	17	18	19	20
A9	0	0	0	1	3	−7	−12	S	S	S	S
A8	S	S	−5	−8	−10	−15	D	S	S	S	H
A7	H	H	−18	D	D	D	D	S	S	H	H
A6	H	H	D	D	D	D	D	H	H	H	H
A5	H	H	D	D	D	D	D	H	H	H	H
A4	H	H	−17	D	D	D	D	H	H	H	H
A3	H	H	−14	−17	D	D	D	H	H	H	H
A2	H	H	−11	−18	−17	D	D	H	H	H	H

DEALER'S TOTAL

Your Hand:	A A	A 2	A 3	A 4	A 5	A 6	A 7	A 8	A 9
A9	28	21	17	14	12	S	S	S	S
A8	26	19	14	11	8	S	S	S	H
A7	24	14	8	5	−3	S	H	H	H
A6	H	18	10	6	0	H	H	H	H
A5	H	26	15	12	3	H	H	H	H
A4	H	25	14	9	3	H	H	H	H
A3	H	25	14	9	4	H	H	H	H
A2	H	22	15	9	5	H	H	H	H

Table 14—2 (continued)

Hole Card Numbers Matrix—Uston Advanced Point Count

PAIR SPLIT

DEALER'S TOTAL

Your Hand:	10	11	12	13	14	15	16	17	18	19	20
AA	−12	−6	P	P	P	P	P	0	2	4	5
10,10	S	S	7	−1	−5	−8	−12	8	S	S	S
9,9	S		P	−17	P	P	P	18	P	P	H
8,8	0	H	P	P	P	P	P	P	P	H	H
7,7	15	H	P	P	P	P	P	P	H	H	H
6,6	H	H	P	P	P	P	P	H	H	H	H
5,5											
4,4	H	H	P	P	P	P	P	(−11)	(−20)*	H	H
3,3	H	H	P	P	P	P	P	P	P	H	H
2,2	H	H	P	P	P	P	P	P	14	H	H

DEALER'S TOTAL

Your Hand:	A A	A 2	A 3	A 4	A 5	A 6	A 7	A 8	A 9
AA	−9	−10	−12	−13	−15	−2	1	5	18
10,10	S	20	15	13	12	9	S	S	S
9,9	5	7	1	1	−4	18	P	P	H
8,8	−17	−19	−11	−17	−18	P	P	H	H
7,7	4	−1	−4	−3	−7	P	H	H	H
6,6	19	8	3	0	−1	(17)	(−8)	H	H
5,5									
4,4	H	22	15	12	6	(−12)	H	H	H
3,3	22	14	6	3	−2	P	27	H	H
2,2	23	11	8	4	−1	P	16	H	H

* Numbers in circle ⬭ mean split if equal to or *less* than the number.

Table 14—2 (continued)

Hole Card Numbers Matrix—Uston Advanced Point Count

Notes: Deviate from hole card basic strategy (Table 14-1) if the true count (half deck) reaches the numbers in the matrix

Dealer 17, 18, 19 and 20 include soft hands.

Su = Surrender regardless of count.

CONVENTIONAL SURRENDER

Your Hand:	Dealer's Total 10	11	17	18	19	20		Your Hand:	Dealer's Total 10	11	17	18	19	20
16	−7	−10	18	4	−14	Su		A9						
15	−3	−7	19	8	−10	Su		A8						Su
14	0	−4	22	12	−8	Su		A7					7	Su
13	5	0		22	−4	Su		A6		25		25	12	−15
12	16	6			−4	Su		A5	23	18			18	−6
								A4	27	21			23	1
11						H		A3		24				5
10						H		A2						11
9						Su								
8					−16	Su		AA						
7	22	19		13	−11	Su		10,10						
6	17	14		26	8	Su		9,9						Su
5	19	15			11	Su		8,8	−6	−9			−11	Su
								7,7	−5	−8		8	−15	Su
								6,6	14	6			20	Su
								5,5						
								4,4					−14	Su
								3,3	16	12			8	Su
								2,2	23	17			22	Su

Table 14—2 (continued)

Hole Card Numbers Matrix—Uston Advanced Plus/Minus

Notes: Deviate from hole card basic strategy (Table 14-1) if the true count (half deck) reaches the numbers in the matrix.

Numbers apply to single deck, but are close enough to be used for multiple deck play.

HIT & STAND

DEALER'S TOTAL

Your Hand:	10	11	12	13	14	15	16	17	18	19	20
16	0	−1	−7	S	S	S	S	H	H	H	H
15	2	0	−7	−7	S	S	S	H	H	H	H
14	6	2	−5	−6	−7	S	S	H	H	H	H
13	H	5	−4	−5	−6	−7	S	H	H	H	H
12	H	H	−3	−4	−5	−7	S	H	H	H	H

DEALER'S TOTAL

Your Hand:	A A	A 2	A 3	A 4	A 5	A 6	A 7	A 8	A 9
16	0	−1	−2	−3	−4	H	H	H	H
15	½	½	−1	−2	−3	H	H	H	H
14	1	2	0	−½	−2	H	H	H	H
13	3	2	0	0	−½	H	H	H	H
12	5	4	2	2	½	H	H	H	H

Table 14—2 (continued)

Hole Card Numbers Matrix—Uston Advanced Plus/Minus

HARD DOUBLE

DEALER'S TOTAL

Your Hand:	10	11	12	13	14	15	16	17	18	19	20
11	0	H	D	D	D	D	D	3	5	8	H
10	H	H	D	D	D	D	D	3	5	8	H
9	11	11	0	0	0	D	D	8	11	H	H
8	H	H	−2	−3	−4	−7	D	H	H	H	H
7	H	H	2	−½	−2	−4	−7	H	H	H	H
6	H	H	4	1	−½	−2	−5	H	H	H	H
5	H	H	5	2	0	−2	−4	H	H	H	H

DEALER'S TOTAL

Your Hand:	A A	A 2	A 3	A 4	A 5	A 6	A 7	A 8	A 9
11	−2	−2	−4	−4	−4	3	5	7	12
10	1	−½	−1	−2	−3	3	5	8	H
9	10	5	2	2	½	7	11	H	H
8	H	9	7	5	5	H	H	H	H
7	H	H	9	8	7	H	H	H	H
6	H	H	10	9	9	H	H	H	H
5	H	H	11	9	9	H	H	H	H

213

Table 14—2 (continued)

Hole Card Numbers Matrix—Uston Advanced Plus/Minus

SOFT DOUBLE

DEALER'S TOTAL

Your Hand:	10	11	12	13	14	15	16	17	18	19	20
A9	S	S	½	−½	−1	−3	−5	S	S	S	S
A8	S	S	−2	−3	−4	−6	D	S	S	S	H
A7	H	H	−7	D	D	D	D	S	S	H	H
A6	H	H	D	D	D	D	D	H	H	H	H
A5	H	H	D	D	D	D	D	H	H	H	H
A4	H	H	−7	D	D	D	D	H	H	H	H
A3	H	H	−5	−7	D	D	D	H	H	H	H
A2	H	H	−4	−7	−7	D	D	H	H	H	H

DEALER'S TOTAL

Your Hand:	A A	A 2	A 3	A 4	A 5	A 6	A 7	A 8	A 9
A9	11	9	7	5	5	S	S	S	S
A8	11	8	5	4	3	S	S	S	H
A7	10	5	3	2	−1	S	H	H	H
A6	H	7	4	2	0	H	H	H	H
A5	H	11	6	5	1	H	H	H	H
A4	H	11	5	4	2	H	H	H	H
A3	H	11	5	4	2	H	H	H	H
A2	H	10	6	4	2	H	H	H	H

Table 14—2 (continued)

Hole Card Numbers Matrix—Uston Advanced Plus/Minus

PAIR SPLIT

DEALER'S TOTAL

Your Hand:	10	11	12	13	14	15	16	17	18	19	20
AA	−5	−2	P	P	P	P	P	0	1	2	2
10,10	S	S	3	−½	−2	−3	−5	3	S	S	S
9,9	S	S	P	−7	P	P	P	7	P	P	H
8,8	0	H	P	P	P	P	P	P	P	H	H
7,7	6	H	P	P	P	P	P	P	H	H	H
6,6	11	11	P	P	P	P	P	P	H	H	H
5,5											
4,4	H	H	P	P	P	P	(−4)	(−8)		H	H
3,3	H	H	P	P	P	P	P	P	P	H	H
2,2	H	H	P	P	P	P	P	P	8	H	H

(* above the −8 for row 4,4)

DEALER'S TOTAL

Your Hand:	A/A	A/2	A/3	A/4	A/5	A/6	A/7	A/8	A/9
AA	−4	−4	−5	−5	−6	−1	1	2	7
10,10	S	8	6	5	5	4	S	S	S
9,9	2	3	½	½	−2	7	P	P	H
8,8	−7	−8	−4	−7	−7	P	P	H	H
7,7	2	−½	−2	−1	−3	P	H	H	H
6,6	8	3	1	0	−½	(7)	(−3)	H	H
5,5									
4,4	H	9	6	5	2	(−5)	H	H	H
3,3	9	5	2	1	−½	P	P	H	H
2,2	9	4	3	2	−½	P	P	H	H

* Numbers in circle ⬭ mean split if equal to or *less* than the number.

Table 14—2 (continued)

Hole Card Numbers Matrix—Uston Advanced Plus/Minus

Notes: Deviate from hole card basic strategy (Table 14-1) if the true count (half deck) reaches the numbers in the matrix

Dealer 17, 18, 19 and 20 include soft hands.

Su = Surrender regardless of count.

CONVENTIONAL SURRENDER

Your Hand	10	11	17	18	19	20	Your Hand	10	11	17	18	19	20
16	− 3	− 4	7	2	− 5	Su	A9						
15	− 1	− 3	8	3	− 4	Su	A8						Su
14	0	− 2	9	5	− 3	Su	A7					3	Su
13	2	0		9	− 2	Su	A6		10		10	5	− 6
12	7	2			− 2	Su	A5	9	7			7	− 2
							A4	11	9			9	½
11						H	A3		9				2
10						H	A2						4
9						Su							
8					− 7	Su	AA						
7	9	8		5	− 4	Su	10.10						
6	7	5		11	3	Su	9.9						Su
5	8	• 6			4	Su	8.8	− 2	− 4			− 4	Su
							7.7	− 2	− 3		3	− 6	Su
							6.6	5	2			+ 8	Su
							5.5						
							4.4					− 5	Su
							3.3	7	5			3	Su
							2.2	9	7			9	Su

Should You Count When Front-Loading?

If the front-loading player does not count, he still enjoys a healthy edge over the house. However, the edge can be increased even more by counting. Favorable and unfavorable situations apply equally in front-loading and can be reflected in betting levels. When the count is high, the player's edge is even higher than for on-the-square play; when the count drops, the player often still has the edge. The player has a healthy edge off-the-top and the player can come off-the-top with his big bet, which usually eliminates heat for counting.

If you are able to count comfortably while front-loading, you should. You can vary your bets, perhaps 2-to-1 or even 3-to-1, depending upon the count. But don't vary much more than that—the last thing you want to do while front-loading is get thrown out for counting.!

When front-loading, it is possible to include the value of the hole card in the count before making your play—probably a first in compiling and using available information in the game of blackjack. But there's a risk here—be sure not to include the value of the hole card in your count twice, once when it's dealt and again as the dealer turns it over.

If you feel capable of more advanced play, you may count and also vary the play of the hands in accordance with the count. If the dealer has a two-card total which equals 4 through 11, you may play from the numbers matrix just as if the dealer upcard was equal to the sum of the two cards. In our earlier example, with a dealer 5 and 2, you can play just as if the dealer had a 7 upcard.

To increase your edge even more, learn some of the numbers in Table 14-2, which indicates, for the Uston Advanced Plus/Minus and the Uston APC, how to vary the play of the hand in front-loading (and indeed other hole card play). To my knowledge, this is the first time such numbers have ever been published.

If counting and varying the play of the hands confuses you, don't do it. You have a healthy edge without it; don't jeopardize it, by getting confused and making errors. You've got plenty of other things to be concerned with, including reading the cards accurately, playing the hole card Basic Strategy and watching for heat from the pit or the dealer.

You'll find that front-loading play takes the heat off counting play, and vice-versa. This is because, in front-loading, you can flat bet, drop the count periodically and bet high off-the-top. If you subsequently put on a counting play in front of the same boss, they probably will have totally discounted you as a counter, which may give you more freedom in your bet spread and result in dealers going further into the deck.

Casino Comportment

I'm sure anyone with common sense will know how to approach a front-loader in a casino. Just to make sure, I'll comment briefly on the subject.

Obviously, we don't walk into a casino the moment a front-loader goes on duty, sit at his table, play continuously until his break, leave his table, come back when he does, and change tables when and if he changes tables.

217

It's preferable to play with a few dealers on-the-square before you play the loader. You can count and be playing at an advantage over the house. Then, casually move to the loader's table. When he goes on break, stay with the relief dealer. If the dealers "return" (that is, are assigned a given table for the entire shift), you can remain at that same table, playing the loader and the relief. But don't make obvious variations in your betting patterns; avoid flat betting with the loader and bet spreading with the other dealers.

If the club rubber-bands, don't follow the loader around the casino. The bosses may catch on. Or worse yet, they may think you're "playing with the help," that is, playing in concert with the dealer to bilk the house, which is a felony in Nevada (more on that in the next chapter).

Many clubs have closed circuit TV and video equipment in their skies. Even if you don't spot any bosses watching you, always act as if you were being watched continually (especially at Harrah's and the Hilton, where players with the worst heat often appear to be watched the least from the pit).

Using A Relay

The use of another player, we call him the relay, can be of great benefit in front-loading play. The relay's job is simply to read the value of the dealer's hole card and signal its value (or, more frequently, the type of hand the dealer has) to the BP. The relay makes sense for several reasons:

— The BP, who is getting most of the attention by betting the bigger money, can sit at first base, or at some other position, from which the hole card obviously can't be seen. He can sit high in his chair and look around casually while the loader is dealing.

— The relay, unobtrusively betting the minimum, is more free than would be the BP to sit lower in his chair (which is often the great benefit in reading loaders). He can concentrate on getting the card and not have to worry about the count or the play of the hand. It's helpful for the relay to wear a golf hat or some other natural-looking hat with a visor, to conceal his eyes from the pit.

— The loader may be more apt to show the card in the relay's direction; loaders sometimes subconsciously keep the card away from the "money" on the table.

Val's team simplified the playing strategy so that the relay was required to send only one of four signals and yet there was only a minor loss in playing efficiency. This made the BP's job far easier, in fact, one of the easiest of all assignments in blackjack, because he had only four ways to play his hand. The strategy is as follows:

Table 14—3

Simplified Front-Loading Strategy

Dealer's Total	*Playing Strategy*
"Big Pat"	
Hard totals of 17, 18, 19, 20, 11, A6, A7, A8, A9	Hit until you have a total of 17. Double-down and split *nothing.* Soft hands—hit until 18 (19 with 9 and 10 upcard).
"Little Pat"	
Hard totals of 7, 8, 9, 10, AA, A2	Hit until 17. Split AA and 8,8. Double down on 10, 11. (Not precisely right for hard total of 10, where you shouldn't double on a 10, but better to do this than to make the 10 a "Big Pat," and not get the 11 double-down and the AA and 8,8 splits.)
"Big Stiff"	
Hard totals of 12, 13, 14, 15, 16	Hit until 12. Split and double *everything* you can get away with (obviously double 5,5; don't split).
"Little Stiff"	
Hard totals of 4, 5, 6 Soft hands of A3, A4, A5	Play as if the dealer had a "5" upcard.

Some comments on the simplified front-loading strategy follow.

Big Pat. Obviously, the player would never hit 17, no matter what the dealer's total. The bosses would flip—and then throw you out. Val often relates how he violated this rule on the very first front-loading play of his career. Against Sahara's Jeanne, betting $500, he hit a hard 17 against an 18. He hooked a deuce, beating her with 19. Jeanne laughed and remarked to the pitboss how "humorous" the play was, as Val cringed.

Basic Strategy calls for the player to split a few pairs against 17,18 and 19; but these plays are dropped in the interest of simplicity.

Little Pat. Again, we generalize the rules for simplicity. The player always hits to 17. Basic Strategy calls for standing on 16 versus A,A, and on 15 versus A 2. (We should also stand on 16 against certain card

219

combinations when the dealer totals 9 or 10, but these may be disregarded.) But, the little pat rule gets us close enough.

Big Stiff. This situation leads to the most dramatic plays. In generalizing for simplicity, we stand on 12 (which is Basic Strategy), and double and split anything we can get away with, particularly in casinos where double-after-splits is allowed. For cover purposes, the player is advised to hard double only on totals of 8, 9, 10 and 11. Doubling on 7 versus a 10 would draw laughter from the bosses at first, until they became aware that the dealer always had a stiff when the player did this. Then the jig would be up.

During one of my few front-loading sessions, I was reluctant to exploit the potential of the Big Stiff. I decided against splitting 7's versus a 10; on another hand, I avoided splitting 2's against a 10 upcard. I later realized that many poor players make these weird plays with regularity. I recently saw a player stand on A A versus a dealer's 5 upcard (he didn't want to take the dealer's bust card). Some of the weird front-loading plays may not draw the attention one would think.

Imagine playing a loader at Caesars, where doubling-on-splits is allowed. If we knew the dealer had a 10-up 16, and we had a pair of deuces, we'd split. If we hooked a 3 on the first 2, we'd double-down. If we hooked another 2, we'd re-split. If we were dealt a 4 on the second 2 and a 5 on the third 2, we should double-down on both. All this, against a 10. I'd guess this type of play would pass for madness for about 15 minutes. Then, either the dealer would be corrected or the player would be ejected, or both. Unfortunately, the probability of encountering a loader at Caesars is slim (though this has happened; one Caesars' loader is now a floorman in Atlantic City); Caesars' single deck dealers are highly trained.

Little Stiff. In this instance, it's possible to improve on the hole card Basic Strategy. With Little Stiff, the dealer has a (hard or soft) total of 4, 5 or 6. Since the matrix numbers for playing against a 4, 5 or 6 are close to each other, the player can take the middle ground and play his hand as if the dealer had a 5 upcard. He can thus apply the numbers, reflecting the count in his decision. For example, playing the Uston APC, he would normally stand on 12 against a Little Stiff. But if the true count were −2 or less, he would hit the 12; if the count were −5 or lower, he would hit 13 against a Little Stiff, and so on.

It can be difficult, after many hours of conventional play, to imagine that the dealer has a 5 up, when the upcard is actually a 2, ace or something else. The player becomes so accustomed to using the upcard in determining his play that it's virtually impossible to look at a 2 and play as if it were a 5. One solution: when the dealer has a Little Stiff, include the upcard in the count, look away, ignore the upcard, visualize a 5 in your mind and make the appropriate play.

How To Use The Relay

The relay job is quite easy. He need not be able to count cards. He need not know Basic Strategy, although if he plays too poorly, the losses on his play may become significant. The relay has merely to read the dealer's hole card and give one of four signals: Big Pat, Little Pat, Big Stiff or Little Stiff. Here is one set of signals that can be used:

Big Or Little Pat: Hold chips (preferably metal dollar chips) in hand. Big Pat: hand is up over the table, palm up or to the side, fingering the chips. Little Pat: palm is down, hand over the chips, riffling the chips and making a clanking noise with the silver. This is an effective signal, because the BP can hear "Little Pat" and need not even look over at the relay.

Big Or Little Stiff: No chips in hand. Big Stiff: palm up or to the side. Little Stiff: palm down, flat on the table.

Simple? It's one of the easiest blackjack assignments ever.

It's also necessary to signal the BP whether to take insurance. One possibility: if the dealer has a blackjack, the relay says "no" when the dealer asks, "Insurance?" The BP immediately insures when he hears the "no", another audible signal. If the dealer doesn't have blackjack (the hole card is not a 10), the relay takes insurance. The BP spots this, preferably with peripheral vision, and ignores the dealer's question about insurance.

How To Train The Relay

Because of the simplicity of the relay job, it should be easy to recruit and train a relay.

Give the relay some chips. Take a deck of cards and toss out two cards at a time, face up. These represent the dealer's hand. The relay then gives the appropriate signal with his hand, with or without the chips, as outlined previously. It's so simple that after about three times through the deck, the relay will give the signals almost automatically. The hardest combinations to get used to are AA and A2 (Little Pat) and 11 (Big Pat.) But, even these are learned quickly.

How To Train The BP And Coordinate The Effort

It's then necessary to practice with both the relay and the BP, to ensure (1) that the signals are being given correctly, (2) that the BP is reading the signals correctly and (3) that the BP is making the correct plays. Have the relay deal two cards to the BP and two to himself (one upcard and one hole card). The latter two cards represent the dealer's hand. Both cards are seen by the relay, but only one is seen by the player. The relay gives the appropriate signal and the BP makes the appropriate play. This will accustom the relay and BP to working with each other. This training is more effective if a knowledgeable third party audits the training session. After about 45 minutes of this practice, the signalling and playing will become quite smooth.

Signalling The Exact Value Of The Hole Card. It is possible to increase the edge even further by playing perfect hole card Basic Strategy with a relay. However, more training and practice are required and the risk of error is greater.

The BP must learn the hole card Basic Strategy, as shown in Table 14-1. The relay signals to the BP the *exact* value of the dealer's hole card (instead of Big or Little Pat or Stiff). The BP then makes the Basic Strategy play.

One way to signal the exact card is by the placement of the relay's cards *on* the table in front of him. Imagine a 3 by 3 table, giving 9 positions, signalling ace through nine (see the diagram below). The relay signals a dealer's 10 holecard by holding his cards *above* the table.

Figure 14a

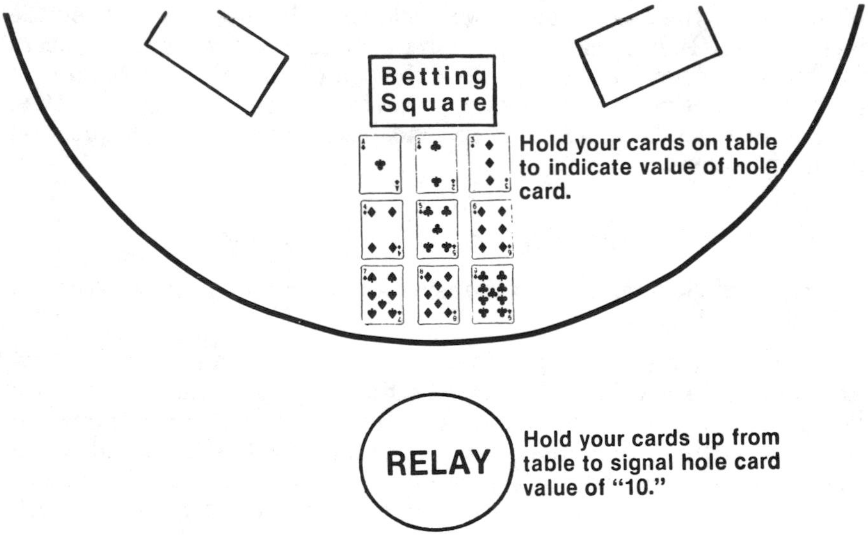

Betting Square

Hold your cards on table to indicate value of hole card.

RELAY

Hold your cards up from table to signal hole card value of "10."

Summary

As long as there are hand-held decks, there will be front-loaders. I doubt that there will be enough loaders around for someone to make a living solely from this source. But, for the skillful player, front-loading can periodically enhance on-the-square earnings dramatically. Best of all, training a non-counter (spouse or friend) to be a relay takes almost no time at all and makes the play far smoother. In front-loading, as in other phases of blackjack play, planning and preparation get the money.

Chapter Fifteen

Spooking
and
Other Hole Card Play

Spooking

Spooking is a technique where the dealer's hole card is read from the rear as he is checking to see if he has a blackjack. The value of the card, or of the dealer's hand, is signalled to an agent playing at the dealer's table. More than one player is needed to set up a spooking play.

I believe spooking to be unethical, even though, according to the letter of the law in Nevada, it does not appear to be illegal. I regard spooking at blackjack as similar to stationing an agent behind an opponent at poker to find out what cards are in the hole.

Val's team spooked as well as front-loaded while I was observing them and did it quite profitably. The team tended to duck the moral issue, but on the rare occasions when I brought it up, the most common response was, "They're doin' everything they can to take money from us; why can't we do everything we can to take money from them?" Their argument, I believe, doesn't hold water, since it could be extended to include player cheating (such as card-marking, card-mucking, etc., as discussed in the next chapter)...and two wrongs don't make a right.

I am including this chapter on spooking and, in fact, will discuss "playing with the help" (a felony in Nevada) because these acts fall within the realm of blackjack lore and knowledge, and because neither subject has ever been covered knowledgeably.

Although I will discuss some of the diversionary measures and fine points of spooking play, I am in *no way* encouraging the reader to make these plays. However, a personal perusal of this chapter may add to the player's general knowledge of the game; and, it makes interesting background reading.

Although I'm not enthralled about the idea of helping the casinos—I've always been on "our" side of the table and have never consulted with or advised casino management—some pitbosses may be able to perform their jobs better by knowing how spooking teams have pulled the wool over their eyes in the past. I suppose that's okay, because, as I said, I consider spooking to be unethical. Today, in nearly every club in Nevada, it's all too easy to put down a well-disguised spooking play.

How Spooking Works. A "spook" is a person who spots the dealer's hole card from the rear when the dealer checks to see if he has a blackjack, which, of course, is only when the dealer has a 10 or ace upcard. The spook determines the value or category of the hole card (or the dealer's total hand), signals it to a player at the dealer's table and then, the player uses this information in deciding how to play his hand.

It's easy to see why spooking isn't as profitable as front-loading. In front-loading, the player potentially can read every hole card and adjust his play accordingly. In spooking, the player knows the value of the hole card only when the dealer has a 10 or ace upcard—5-out-of-13 situations on average, or 38% of the time. Nevertheless, this added information, combined with card counting and bet variation, can yield the player an impressive advantage over the house. The player gains an additional advantage primarily in two situations:

— When the dealer has a "stiff," although he has a 10 or ace up. In most cases, the player would have hit his own stiff hand, taking the first risk of busting. If the player knows the dealer is stiff, he can stand on his stiff and let the dealer risk busting. Additionally, with knowledge of a dealer's stiff hand, the player can exploit double-down and pair-splitting opportunities that would ordinarily be missed.

— When the dealer is "pat." In this case, the player would hit his stiff. There are times, particularly with positive true counts, when the player would ordinarily stand on a stiff (for example, with 16 against a 10). Knowing the dealer is pat, the player obviously will hit his stiff, since he has nothing to lose; he knows he will lose the hand if he doesn't hit. He also avoids making double-downs and pair-splits that might otherwise have been made.

The clubs are not unaware of spooking. As part of the Sahara Tahoe dealer orientation, for example, dealers are instructed that the most prevalent forms of player cheating are looking at hole cards and marking cards. Bosses often watch for spooking. To the experienced boss, it's not difficult to spot and pull up a spooking play which can have a serious effect on the casino's take. If he sees one player betting high and making strange plays—such as splitting 7's against a 10—and he spots another fellow, call him player 2, at a table to the rear of the dealer, evidencing unusual interest in the first game, the chances are good that a spooking team is operating.

The boss should watch player 2; if the player's eyes wander to the first table whenever the first dealer happens to have a 10 or ace up, the evidence points strongly to a spooking operation. If the player at the first table has a line-of-sight to player 2, that generally clinches it.

But, you will ask, "How can a spooking play be set up?" The answer to that, as in front-loading, is through the use of a relay. For some reason, pitbosses often overlook the possibility that a relay is being used, perhaps thinking that most people wouldn't take the trouble of coordinating three people in a single play. In fact, I know of only a few bosses who "snapped" to a relay spooking operation and busted it up.

The player "taking the money off," or "take-off" man (let's call him the BP once again), sits at an angle where he can't possibly see the spook—say at first or third base—and *never* looks across the pit. The relay sits at the same table in a spot where he can see the spook. He receives the spooks signal (or "office" as it's called) and passes it on to the player with an "office" of his own. The operation is particularly hard to detect if the office is an audible one, such as the relay clanking his metal gaming tokens. Then, the BP need not look for a signal and can stare at his own cards and the dealer's upcard.

The Edge In Spooking. It's difficult to quantify the precise value of spooking in terms of percent advantage to the player because of the many variables, such as percent accuracy in reading the hole card and the amount lost on the play of the relay and the spook (the latter must sometimes be forced into making ghastly plays because at the precise moment he is called to make a playing decision, he may have to look across the pit—spooks usually neglect pair splits and double-downs—and on more than one occasion, have hit 19's and 20's). Another variable is the degree to which the BP uses counting in varying bets and deviates from hole card Basic Strategy.

We do know that the edge is not nearly that which is gained in front-loading. In addition to knowing the card only 38% of the time at most, the BP usually isn't given the exact total of the dealer's hand. This is because the spook generally reads the pips and can only tell if the hole card is a 7 or more, or a 6 or less. Further, as we shall see, there is a built-in automatic error rate when the spook uses the pips.

We estimate that, in Northern Nevada, assuming 100% reading accuracy, spooking adds about 1% to the player's edge. In Las Vegas, it's value is probably 1½-2%, since the player has more doubling options. In clubs where surrender (particularly) and doubling-on-splits is available, the value of spooking is even greater. I'd estimate that the spooking team, with a card counting BP, making plays based on the count and employing a 3- or 4-to-1 spread, is playing at about a 3% edge in Las Vegas and a 2% edge in Northern Nevada.

A Spooking Team Is Formed.
While playing with Team 2 in Vegas, I ran into several fellows from Texas who had spooked in the past. One of them, call him Doug, had spooked extensively in Vegas and was known to virtually all the clubs there and to the Griffin Agency. Doug's fellow Texan, Eddie, had also done extensive spooking in Nevada.

They had both been members of a team, organized in the late 1960's by a Mr. D. from Texas. Mr. D., a highly disciplined task-master, organized the team and trained them in counting and spooking. He commissioned a computer expert to develop the numbers for a multi-level count, which was to be the forerunner of the Revere APC. In the late 60's, the team pulled $300,000 to $400,000 out of Vegas before they were caught. They were detected by a suspicious Tropicana pit-boss who followed them out of the casino into the parking lot and noticed that the team, which had pretended not to know each other in the casino, got into three different cars—all with Texas license plates. He took down the license numbers, called Griffin, and the team soon got pulled up wherever they played.

Mr. D. returned to Texas, but Doug and Ed remained in Vegas for years, trying to eke out a living. They didn't have the discipline of Mr. D. and they were dead broke when they met me ten years later. They had an idea: they had the ability to spook and were still clean in Northern Nevada, but needed BP's and a bank; I had the BP's and the bank. They offered to meet me in Lake Tahoe and give me a demonstration.

As Doug said, "Once you've seen it, you'll like it. Man, it's smooth."

I introduced them to Val, who was fascinated with the idea. Val, Doug and Ed tried a few plays at the Sahara Tahoe. It worked perfectly, as Doug had predicted, and Val's team was formed. It was a perfect match. Doug and Ed had the hole card expertise; Val had the discipline and the bank.

The team began by playing the Sahara Tahoe extensively and successfully. Then, they pulled $11,000 out of the tiny Nugget in Carson City; the bosses had no idea what hit them. (The group returned to the "CC Nugget" a few months later for an encore. The result: spooking cost that club $30,000 from the two visits.)

Then, the team made the Reno circuit, concentrating on many "leaks" at Harrah's. The Harrah's bosses, an intelligent well-trained group by and large, were skeptical, but couldn't figure it out.

As Val told me, "The heat was sizzling. They didn't like it, but they didn't know why. As long as they rode it, we kept on showin' it to 'em."

The team would take over $100,000 from Harrah's Reno. Then, they moved on to the Riverside . . . to the Mapes . . . the Ponderosa. The bosses scratched their heads as they watched the money marching out the door. The team moved to Harrah's at the Lake and played there for weeks.

Val and I were like a couple of mafia bosses; we had the state of Nevada carved up. Val would work the north, while I worked the south with my counting team (Team 2). When we went north, Val would come to Vegas. They spooked the Aladdin, the Riviera, the Stardust and Caesars. One time, both teams were in Vegas at the same time. We had the Griffin agents working overtime.

Val's team gradually grew in size. Over the next year or so, his team would win about $750,000.

How To Spook. The first prerequisite is to find dealers who expose their hole card when checking for blackjack. If you've ever noticed a dealer checking his hole card, flipping it up quickly with his right hand, carefully shielding it with both hands and the deck, you'd conclude that this is virtually impossible.

But if you're curious, try an experiment. Stand across the pit, behind and slightly to the left of a right-handed dealer. When he checks for blackjack, you'll see the face of the hole card a surprisingly high proportion of the time. I'd guess about 10% of the dealers can be read from behind the back by the average person. By a skilled spook, such as Doug, 15% (or more) of dealers are readable.

Doug's skill involves positioning himself to establish a "window," a channel of sight between the left side of the dealer's body and his left arm. The effective spook must also have good eyesight and a complete knowledge of the configuration of the pips on each card, as well as a good sense of timing to know when to look across the pit. Another essential ingredient is "casino savvy," an intuitive ability to "do the right thing" to avoid drawing heat.

Dealer training varies greatly from casino to casino. Val was able to beat the CC Nugget so soundly because the dealers were trained so carelessly. On one play, the Nugget's bosses joked derisively as they discussed among themselves the outrageous plays that Val made. They were confident that, in the long run, the house would bury him. But, just to be safe, they kept changing dealers and assigned seven dealers to Val's table during an 8-hour play. Doug could read every one of them!

Today, dealers at most casinos in Reno and Lake Tahoe are "spookable," except for Harrah's (they finally figured it out and tightened up their dealer training to be the most stringent in the state). Most Vegas clubs have spookable dealers, both at single and multiple deck games.

As in front-loading, exhaustive preliminary scouting is a prerequisite to a lucrative spook play. A dossier of all readable dealers should be made, with comments on "how clear they show it;" if possible, clubs where the dealers return should be played, rather than those that rubber-band.

When the play is to be made, the spook enters the club and tries to spot a table where both the regular dealer and the relief dealer are readable; if not, he selects a table where the regular dealer is readable. Then, the spook "sets up" by getting a seat at a table to the rear of the dealer, from which he has a "window." It's sometimes possible to spook from the rail, that is, by sitting at a roulette table or standing by a slot machine, depending upon the angles in the casino.

When the spook is set up, he gives an office telling the relay that "we have a good situation." The relay then "sets up," finding a seat at the readable dealer's table from which he has a line-of-sight to the spook, as direct a line as possible so he doesn't have to look to one side to get the spook's office. When the relay is set up, he signals the BP, who takes a seat (when it's available) at the readable dealer's table, facing away from the spook so he can't see across the pit. Then play begins.

Figure 15a

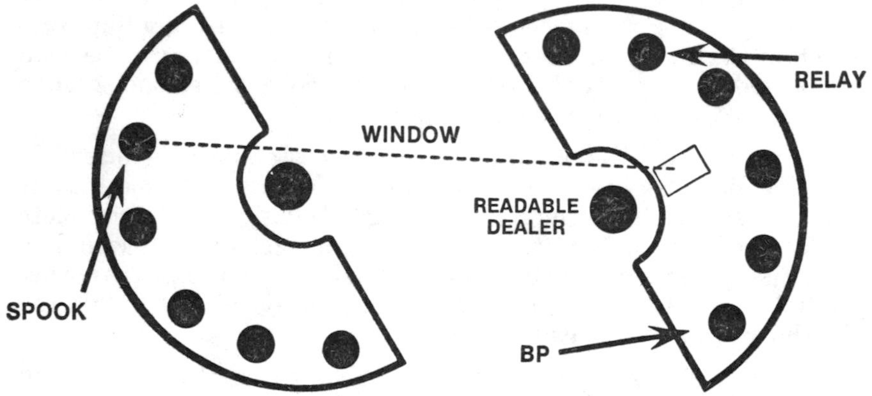

When the dealer checks for blackjack, the spook sends the office to the relay, who sends it to the player. Here is one set of signals that can be used; variations on these are limited only by the player's creativity:

> *Pat.* To signal hard totals of 17, 18, 19 or 20, and AA, A2, A6, A7, A8 or A9, the spook puts his hand somewhere on his face. The relay then picks up his chips and rattles them. The player can "hear the pat."

> *Stiff.* For all other hands (hard totals of 12 through 16 and A,3, A,4 or A,5) the spook keeps his hands away from his face. The relay puts his hand on the table without chips in it.

> *"I didn't get it."* The spook moves back from the table, hands in

lap. The relay takes his hands off the table. The player plays "normally," i.e., according to the count.

Making the correct play is fairly simple. If the dealer is pat, hit until 17; double and split nothing (the Big Pat strategy shown in Table 14-3). If the dealer is stiff, hit until 12; double and split anything (the Big Stiff strategy in Table 14-3) without blowing cover with the bosses. When there's no signal, make the plays according to the count.

Unlike front-loading, it's essential that the BP count since spooking without counting is a marginal game at best. The BP should spread his bets in accordance with the count, perhaps 2- or 3-to-1; he can bet big off-the-top, about 1/75th of the bank, since he has a healthy edge.

Sometimes it's hard for the BP not to laugh. I observed Val splitting 4's against a 10, which on the surface appears to be a dumb play. He put out a second $500, the dealer turned over his six in the hole and predictably busted. Sometimes it almost seems too easy. But, it's not—spooking often seems to "backfire." In losing sessions, Val could get hand-after-hand where he had, for example, a 12; the dealer, with a 10 up, would be stiff. Val would stand. The dealer would have, for example a 2 in the hole and draw an 8, winning. In many such cases, regular Basic Strategy would have called for Val to hit and he would have won the hand. But, the hole card Basic Strategy was used and caused the loss of the hand. That's the way it is in games that are subject to statistical variation.

Learning To Read The Pips.

The effective spook must have the layout of the pips on the cards completely memorized, since the index of the card is often not visible. Pull out the 2 through 10 of hearts and lay the nine cards side-by-side. The 2 through 10 denominations are shown in the diagram below. With a 10 up, the dealer is pat if has a 7, 8, 9 or 10, or "paint" in the hole. He's stiff if he has a 2, 3, 4, 5 or 6 in the hole.

Figure 15b

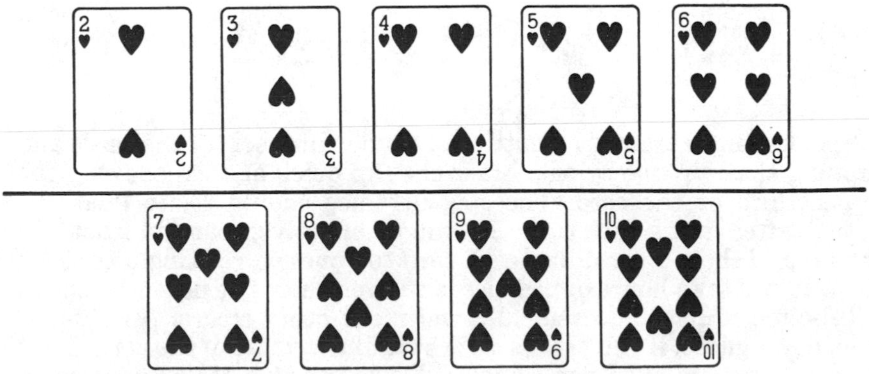

Notice any difference in the two sets of cards? Notice that all the pat cards (7 through 10) have a pip in the middle of the card (crossways). Notice also that the center pip is above the center of the card (lengthwise) for all pat cards, except 9, where the middle pip is in the exact center of the card. So, if you see a high center pip, you know the dealer is pat.

A difficult card is the 9. Its center pip is exactly in the middle of the card, similar to the 5. If only the top third of the card is seen, the spook won't see a center pip. But, notice how closely the four side pips are arranged on the side of the 9. Thus, the spook, in addition to watching for the center pip, must also observe the density of the side pips.

Now, for the spook's nightmare. Take another look at the 7. The card is not symmetrical. One end has a center pip—the other doesn't. In fact, the end without the center pip is identical to the 6 and is impossible to distinguish from the 6.

When the 7 underneath the dealer's upcard is facing so that the part without the pip is closest to the dealer, the spook will read it as a 6 (unless he happens to spot the index). This is referred to as the "upside-down 7."

There's nothing the spook can do about this—it's his concession to the house. He must read the card as a 6 and signal accordingly; the BP must play the hand as a stiff, with a 10 upcard. On average, however, the upside-down 7 is encountered only one out of 26 times and is not critical when the dealer's upcard is an ace (since both A,6 and A,7 are pat hands). This calculates to about a 3% error rate, so the player's advantage is not seriously affected. Further, this does not affect all the hands since some player hands do not require a variable decision such as hard 17, 18 or 19.

Figure 15c

TOP THIRD OF CARD

Spooks can be trained by cutting the index number off the cards and flipping them up one-by-one. Make the flip quick and expose only the upper third of the card. The spook-trainee should recite "pat" or "stiff" after seeing each card. Even more effective, stand in front of a mirror and show one-third of each card to yourself, reciting after each card. It will take hours of practice, and even then, the potential spook will be fooled by an occasional 9 and make other errors. An obvious rule; don't guess; if you are not 98% sure of the value of the card, don't send it over; signal "I don't know." Do so because, if you are wrong, and the BP starts standing against pat hands and hitting against stiff hands, he'll give up far more to the house than he would have gained from the correct plays.

Cover. Extensive cover measures were taken by Val's team. Spooks, relays and BP's act as if they don't know each other. They enter and leave the casino at different times. While playing, they rarely, if ever, look at each other.

The spook looks across the pit only on two occasions:

— During each round, when the dealer first turns over his upcard, to determine if the upcard is a 10 or ace.

— A second time, during the roughly 38% of the rounds when the dealer has a 10 or ace up, to read the hole card.

The spook draws less heat if he uses a quick passing glance rather than a direct bead on the table. He should never look at the BP's table unnecessarily, to see how well the BP is doing or for any other reason.

The relay also never looks across the pit needlessly. He avoids looking directly at the spook by reading the spook's office with peripheral vision. Assuming 100 hands per hour, the relay, on average, needs to shoot a two-second passing glance across the pit 38 times per hour. This is in an hour's play, the elapsed time during which his eyes are directed across the pit is around 80 seconds. Both the spook and the relay should give casual, natural-looking signals and avoid quick, jerky motions while signalling. Neither, of course, should react if the BP wins or loses a big bet; that should be totally irrelevant to them.

The BP never looks across the pit. He tries to hear the relay's audible signals; when receiving the office visually, he uses peripheral vision. As the dealer is turning over his hole card after the players have played their hands, the BP should show an interest in the value of the card and act surprised, happy, sad, etc., as he "discovers" the value of the card as it's exposed by the dealer to the players at the table. This tends to conceal his prior knowledge.

As his team grew in size, Val rotated his spooks and relays from one session to the next when playing the same pitbosses. In a given session, it generally wasn't necessary to rotate players, since it's quite common for blackjack "addicts" to play for hours and hours. When the BP returned for a subsequent session, however, different personnel were employed to prevent the bosses from putting the team together.

The BP counted and employed bet variation. Not only does this increase the edge, but it tends to take heat off the spook; for a while, the bosses are distracted as they try to figure out if the BP is putting on a counting play. (After a few "weird" plays, such as splitting 6's against a 10, this suspicion is allayed and wider bet variation often becomes possible.)

Val's group undertook painstaking reconnoitering of a casino prior to playing. They would log all spookable dealers and front-loaders. Faces, name tags, physical descriptions and "readability" were recorded. Then, the team would be assigned responsibilities and finally be dispatched to the casino. Multiple plays were often put down to confound the bosses. Consider the following example:

Doug, a spook, enters a casino, aware of 5 dealers that can be read—four from the back and one from the front. When the one who is readable from the front checks for blackjack, her hole card can be seen when standing by her left shoulder at the table. There's also a front-loader on duty. Doug cases the dealers for a half-hour, spanning one dealer relief period, to see which dealers are assigned tables and will deal for 40 minutes and which dealers are on relief and will deal for 20 minutes at each of two tables. He happily notes that both the primary and relief dealer at one table can be spooked. He finds a spot at a table behind the dealer's position, with a good angle on the dealer's game. He goes to the phone.

Ten minutes later, Val, who is the BP, comes into the casino. He sits down at a head-on game with a non-readable dealer and plays on-the-square, counting and varying his bet 4-to-1, for 15 minutes. When the bosses watch him, he lowers his bet when there's a lot of little cards on the table and raises it when there's a lot of paint on the table. The bosses shrug, unconcerned.

A relay enters the casino. He spots a signal from Doug and sits down at the table where the spookable dealer is dealing. After a few minutes, Val loses three bets in a row. He says, "You're too rough for me," throws the dealer a $5 toke, picks up his chips and looks, ostensibly, for a luckier dealer. He spots a signal from Doug and suddenly he knows where his lucky dealer is.

Val casually wanders over to the third base of the table where the relay is playing; Doug is completely hidden from his view by the dealer. Val gradually increases his bets until he's betting $500 per hand. This begins to draw the attention of the bosses. But, Val is spotted betting $500 off-the-top and he's seen standing on 12 versus a 10. The bosses relax again.

After 30 minutes of play, the dealer takes a break and the relief dealer (also readable) comes in. Val plays her too, still betting $500 off-the-top. After 20 minutes, the original dealer returns. He continues to play. He starts winning heavily now, up about $5,000, and the bosses pull the dealer even though it's not time for her to take a break.

A non-spookable relief dealer is put in. Val continues to play, this time, on-the-square, with a 4-to-1 bet variation; he gradually lowers his off-the-top bet to $100.

After 10 minutes, Val gets up and goes to another table. The dealer here can be read from the front, and in fact, a second spook is playing at that table, standing up and reading the hole card from his elevated vantage point. He signals it to Val. Val plays here until the dealer takes a break. He plays the relief (unreadable) for 10 minutes, now putting down a 5-to-1 bet spread.

Val goes to the restroom and returns to a new table at which a front-loader is dealing. For 30 minutes, Val reads the dealer himself in a head-on game which averages 200 hands per hour. He wins another $3,000, flat betting $500. The dealer breaks and the next dealer, unreadable, comes in. The game is still head on; Val remains, gradually varying his bet, this time up to 8-to-1. The bosses, while watching Val's results closely, are used to his action and his erratic and seemingly harmless betting and playing patterns. He's been all over the casino now and played with seven dealers.

The front-loader returns to the table. Then, the relay joins Val at the table and Val moves over to first base where he can't possibly see the front-loader's hole card as she deals. The relay reads the card, however, and signals it to Val. The process continues until the loader's shift ends. As Val stays with the relief dealer, the relay leaves the club. Ten minutes later, so does Doug. Val plays head-on (on-the-square) for 15 minutes. Then he quits—a $14,000 winner.

On the way to the cage, the pitboss comes up to Val and says, "Here's my card. Let me know if there's anything you want."

Sound far-fetched?

I personally observed this play at the Mapes Hotel in Reno.

Spooking The Bahamas.

Before we leave the subject, I'll describe what was probably the most lucrative spooking opportunity ever available. Several years ago, the El Casino in Freeport, Bahamas, converted from plastic to cardboard cards. The casino managers, to avoid creasing the new bendable cards, instructed the dealers to pull up the hole card without bending it or the upcard when checking for blackjack. Some dealers practically stood the hole card on end, so that 98% of the card, including all pips and both indexes, was visible to the observant spook.

Val somehow got wind of this and took his team down. He found that fully 50% of the dealers were spookable. Many dealers lifted their cards so high that Val's spooks didn't need to sit at the table behind the dealer. The cards were visible from just about anywhere behind the dealer and Val assigned many of his spooks on-the-rail, that is, standing around ostensibly watching play at various tables as they spooked the BP's table. The cards were not visible to the "inspectors," who sat in chairs between each pair of tables. On more than one occasion, crowds would gather to watch Val play—he was playing three hands of $300—and Val would conceal his relay in the crowd. The team extracted nearly $30,000 in about 10 days' play.

El Casino finally tightened up this practice, but to this day, the angles between the tables there are favorable for the spook. I would especially caution against spooking there. I have no idea how they would react if you were caught, but why risk spending time in some Bahamian dungeon?

Summary. The spooking team enjoys about 2-3% edge over the house if the BP also counts. Spooking without counting is a marginal game at best. The highly skilled spooking team, using a relay, is difficult to detect, especially if cover measures are strictly enforced.

If the spook avoids looking needlessly at the BP's table, he will find it necessary to stare across the pit 2% of the time. Similarly, the well-trained relay rarely needs to look across the pit at the spook, perhaps 80 seconds per hour of play. With proper use of peripheral vision and a good act by the BP, the average pitboss is totally baffled.

Please understand that I am *not* encouraging the reader to try to put this kind of play down. On the contrary, I believe there's far too much opportunity in Nevada, New Jersey and elsewhere to get involved in this type of operation.

Playing The Warps

There are rare occasions when the player can attain knowledge of the likely value of the hole cards in decks that have remained in play for long periods of time. When the dealer checks for blackjack, a 10 or ace is always the upcard. Thus, 10's or aces tend to get bent in one direction; all other cards (2 through 9) tend to get bent in another direction since, whenever the dealer checks for blackjack, these cards may be in the hole, face down.

The face of the 10 or ace tends to be concave, as it is bent upward by the dealer. Thus, when the 10 or ace is the hole card, it will appear to be arched, or raised in the middle. When a 2 through 9 is the hole card, it will appear to be raised on the ends. The astute player can attempt to notice the bend of the hole card and vary his play accordingly.

Playing the warps is dangerous. Its accuracy is *far* below that of spooking and, of course, front-loading. The effect of just a few mistakes per hour can be devastating. As I said earlier, the player who stands with a stiff against a pat, in error, is giving his money away—he's 100% sure of losing the bet. It's obviously costly to hit a stiff against a stiff in error, as well. In most cases, the warp player ends up outsmarting himself and loses more (with errors) than he gains (with correct warp-reading).

On rare occasions, a warp play works. The most dramatic play took place two years ago in the Seoul and Inchon casinos in Korea. In a single deck game with surrender and double-down-on-split pairs, the cards were left in play for hours. The warps could be read with a high degree of (though not total) accuracy; almost all 10's and aces were raised in the middle when dealt as the hole card. The players took $51,000 out of the two casinos; in both places, the bosses eventually "snapped" to the play and started changing the cards more frequently.

I don't recommend spending much effort in playing the warps. If you try to do it, look for clubs that don't change cards often, usually smaller ones. The Las Vegas Club tends to have bent cards because their shuffle of the six decks is so inadequate; this can be helpful, especially in light of its liberal rules, which allow conventional surrender, doubling on more than two cards, and the resplitting of aces. Other possibilities include the Sands (where used cards are sometimes brought into play) and the clubs in North Las Vegas and Sparks. Start betting low at first and clock the accuracy. The chances are that the error rate will be unacceptable—more than one error out of 4 or 5 cards.

If you do find an acceptable warp play, nearly three-fourths of your edge will be in taking insurance when there's a suspected 10 or ace in the hole. Obviously, you will tend to hit and surrender more if the dealer is pat, and stand, double-down or split more if the dealer is stiff, as shown in Table 14-1.

Playing With The Help

This activity is totally illegal and, in fact, constitutes a felony in Nevada. Don't do it! If you get caught, you can go to jail!

"Playing with the help" refers to an outside player (the bosses call him an "agent") working in concert with a casino employee, usually a dealer, to extract money from the house. The most common form of this occurs when the dealer, after checking for blackjack, signals the player-agent whether he is pat or stiff. The player plays his hand accordingly. In effect, the dealer is the spook.

The practice is so sufficiently widespread that standard percentage splits have been developed. Normally, the dealer gets one-third of the win, but does not suffer any portion of the loss. The dealer usually agrees to "make up" any loss to the player by playing with him subsequently. But, these obligations often become similar to financial bad debts—the dealer owing time instead of money. They are often not honored for one simple reason: the dealer chooses not to risk arrest and loss of job since he will not share in profits until the win (if there is one) more than offsets previous losses.

The one-third fee is a high price for the player to pay. Even with the additional advantage (as in spooking, it adds about 1% to the player's edge in Northern Nevada, and 1½-2% in Vegas), the swings can be wide and the player has to eat the loss all by himself. If dealers welch on their time debt, the player finds himself taking 100% of the loss and only 67% of the win—far from a good deal in the long run.

Today, there are dealers in Reno, Lake Tahoe and Vegas who will play with an agent, and the technique can be utilized at either single deck or multiple deck games. I've never played with the help—and never will. My experience with counters indicates that most competent players don't feel that they need to cheat, and those who do unethical acts are generally incompetent or former casino employees with bad records.

Val tried it briefly. It worked smoothly (although he lost $3,000). He concluded that this type of operation was too risky. However, it can be hard to detect, especially with smooth, subtle signals. One that normally cannot be detected by the sky is for the dealer to open his mouth slightly for "pat" and close it for "stiff" (or vice versa). Dealers may also lean against the table for stiff and move back slightly from the table for pat.

Another possibility that's been used: dealer blinks for pat; does not blink for stiff. Signals can be made even more subtle to defy detection by the sky, the cameras or closed circuit TV. For example, signals can be given one way when the dealer's upcard is red and reversed when the dealer's upcard is black. It would take an awfully smart boss to pick up on that one.

Statistically, the edge obtained in playing with the help is greater than that derived from spooking because the accuracy is 100%. The player need not worry about mistakes, upside-down 7's and 9's, or cocktail waitresses or pitbosses blocking the "window" as they walk through the pit. A refinement in playing with the help involves establishing a set of signals for the counting player to send to the dealer to instruct him to shuffle away negative decks and deal the positive decks down further (size of bet is one of the easiest and most sensible).

Dealers, of course, can help players in other ways as well by paying pushes, paying losing hands, pushing on losing hands or over-paying (we'll discuss this in greater depth in the following chapter). Pitbosses, and even higher officials, sometimes get involved in these scams. *Very* recently, a shift manager at one of the Strip's fanciest hotel-casinos lost his job because he was caught "ripping off the house" in a blackjack marker scam. The player-agent would sign $500 markers and be paid $5,000. The sky was supposed to look the other way—he didn't. It was sad. The manager lost a $75,000-a-year job for a piece of what turned out to be a $15,000 scam. And, he'll probably never be able to work in the industry again.

Crime sometimes doesn't pay.

Chapter
Sixteen

Cheating

When professional blackjack players get together, the subject of cheating in Nevada and abroad is often discussed. Our teams have had numerous meetings about cheating and we've dwelled on the subject for dozens of hours, particularly after having suffered losses that were statistically unlikely. Others share our concern. At the Second Conference on Gambling, held at Lake Tahoe a few years back, many of the participants felt that the most interesting session was the one that covered cheating.

Views on the extent of cheating vary widely. In his 1966 book, Ed Thorp estimated that the player would run into cheating 5-to-10% of the time (1). Lance Humble, in three books, avers that cheating is widespread in Nevada (9, 28, 29).

The fellow that brought me into blackjack, Al, played extensively in Nevada during the mid-1960's and believed that cheating was so widespread that he took countermeasures. The following story is ironic and completely true:

> Al and his brother, call him Dan, were counting in the Riviera. As Dan played, Al's job was to watch the dealers with whom Dan was playing to detect cheating. (The good cheat is usually completely undetectable—especially to the player who is preoccupied with the many duties of card counting.) Al thought that by standing at various angles and concentrating solely on watching the dealer's moves, he'd have a better chance of spotting cheating.

> Al and Dan both wore a simple battery-operated signalling device, hidden from view. The plan: if Al detected cheating, he would signal Dan with the device. Dan would change dealers

immediately. Al and Dan pretended that they didn't know each other.

Dan was ahead $1,500 when they were both accosted by security guards and led into the security office. They were frisked and threatened with arrest. Their winnings were confiscated.

One boss accused Al and Dan of spooking; they thought Al was signalling the value of the hole card to Dan—not an unreasonable suspicion since spooking teams do use devices of this sort for that purpose. Al and Dan were eventually released, but to this day, they are listed in the Griffin Mug Book as cheaters.

Cheating, in the 1960's, was probably widespread. However, our thousands of hours of observation in Nevada casinos, and our statistical results, indicate that cheating is far, far less prevalent today in Nevada and virtually non-existent in New Jersey. Why is this so? There are probably a number of factors, including:

1. The improved (but still inadequate) enforcement techniques of the Nevada Gaming Commission.

2. The stringent controls introduced by the New Jersey Casino Control Commission.

3. Technological advances in casino surveillance equipment and improvements in surveillance procedures.

4. The apparently dwindling control over the casinos by organized crime (in 1979, the Nevada Commission ruled that both the Aladdin and Argent Corp. should be sold because of hidden ownership).

5. The influx of the Hilton, Holiday Inn and Ramada corporations and other apparently legitimate owners.

Continually increasing casino revenues in Nevada and unprecedented earnings in New Jersey make the financial risk of being closed down for cheating far greater than in the past. Moreover, if the house itself were to cheat, this fact would have to be known by at least some employees, which destroys the basic integrity of the house and tends to make it more vulnerable to inside employee cheating, a phenomenon that has caused the closing of casinos.

Dealers In Business For Themselves

Some cheating of the player does take place in Nevada. But, its underlying cause is not house-motivated, as one would assume. Dealers can steal for themselves by working with agents at their tables. In order for their results not to be out-of-line, they must then cheat other players at their tables.

There are hundreds of dealers in Nevada, and, as in other walks of life, there will be a certain percentage who are dishonest. Dealers are particularly tempted because of the huge amounts of cash and negotiable chips that they handle day in and day out.

Dealers earn a salary of $20-to-40 per shift. Stealing only one green chip per day will nearly double that salary. (Dealers, of course, receive tips as well, which range from $15-to-20 per day or less in small clubs to $75-to-100 per day in major Strip casinos.)

Nevada tends to attract a large proportion of drifters and "crossroaders." It's inevitable that some of them will end up with jobs in the casinos, the largest employers in the state. Some even rise to key positions. There are dishonest employees in the casinos. Let me cite three actual examples:

1. A girl I knew at Lake Tahoe, a cocktail waitress at a big Tahoe hotel-casino, complained because the bartenders' formula, in dividing up the amount stolen from the hotel by not ringing up drinks, gave the girls only $50 per day, only half the bartenders' portion. Not only was stealing going on, it was so prevalent that a standard financial arrangement was negotiated between the bartenders and the waitresses.

1. Bob B. worked as a dealer for several casinos in Reno. He freely admitted to me, "Man, I'm a thief" (not a derogatory term in his jargon; just an objective description of his occupation). "I've taken it off from the inside many times." I asked him if there was much of it going on. His answer was "Sure. Hell, the King's Castle (now the Hyatt Lake Tahoe Resort Hotel & Casino at Incline Village) went under because it was taken off from the inside by everyone—dealers, bosses, bartenders, even security guards. When I was workin' there, some security guards got caught. They'd take the cash boxes from the tables on an elevator to the counting room. They had duplicate keys to the boxes and they'd grab some cash in the elevator. The assholes got caught 'cause they took out a fill slip one day." The manager had independent records of fill slip activity, knew a fill slip was missing and realized that the guards had their hands in the till."

3. A Strip casino manager, over a few drinks, confided, "I had a hard time finding clean floormen for my joint because over the years, I'd stolen with most of those guys myself."

Stealing does take place in Nevada casinos, every day, just as it does in other areas of human endeavor. For every dishonest dealer, there are many, many more honest ones. Most dealers simply view their jobs as a legitimate way to support themselves and their families, just like bank clerks, secretaries, or anyone else.

The job is a fairly good paying one. The fringe benefits, particularly in the larger clubs, are similar to those enjoyed by employees of any large corporation, with health and dental insurance, retirement plans and the like. There is, however, no job security since they can be fired on the whim of a pitboss, even after many years on the job. The dealer who cheats the house or the player has a lot to lose if he's caught. He may be prosecuted, will undoubtedly be blacklisted and will find it difficult to work again in the industry (the days of broken knuckles in the Las Vegas desert are over).

How Dealers Steal

There are numerous ways for the dealer to steal money for himself (indeed, informed sources reveal that far more is taken off "from the inside" than counters will ever win in casinos). This is one of the reasons the casinos go to the trouble and expense of installing catwalks, one-way mirrors, video-taping cameras, television monitors and other expensive surveillance equipment. Another reason is that the gaming commissions, both in Nevada and New Jersey, require it. I'll discuss a few of the more prevalent forms of cheating. All of them lower the dealer's "p.c." and thus create the motivation for the dealer to cheat the player to make up the difference.

— Bob B's favorite technique was to use what's known as a "sub," a pouch sewn into a jacket, pair of pants, or just about anything; its purpose is to house the chips palmed by the dealer. Bob was never caught.

— Another dealer stashed, a green chip in his mouth as he covered his mouth when coughing. One night he involuntarily sneezed; a wet, green chip came flying out of his mouth and he was fired on-the-spot.

— I saw a dealer at Circus Circus take a $100 bill cashed by a player, roll it up skillfully, pretend to put it in the drop box while sliding it surreptitiously under his belt. Just a few of these a week and his after tax earnings are increased substantially (the pitbosses caught him).

— A Harold's Club dealer, whom I dated, told me, "Some of the girls are ripping off the house. They stick chips in their hair—a quarter chip a day can add up. But it got a lot tighter when Hughes took over the club. The bosses and Griffin Agents watch us pretty close." She added, "I went out with a Griffin guy once. They don't know anything; they're a bunch of jerks."

— "Pitching" is when the dealer (usually craps, not blackjack) gives extra chips to an agent at the table. With training, chips can be palmed and transferred inconspicuously from hand-to-hand with amazing agility, undetectable from the sky. This is why most houses now require the craps dealer to place chips on the table, rather than hand them to the player. Usually reliable sources report that "pitching" cost the Riviera $250,000 not too long ago.

— A form of cheating involves the dealer "dumping off" money to an agent. He can pay pushes, pay losing hands or overpay by hiding large denomination chips in a stack of smaller chips. He can also peek at the top card and deal a second to help the agent.

— The dealer may send subtle signals indicating whether his ten-up or ace-up hand is pat or stiff (as discussed in the last chapter). There are dealers today in Reno, Lake Tahoe and in Vegas who have offered to do this for me. One small-stakes variation of this approach occurs every day of the week. Male dealers have an irrestible urge to help young attractive girls at the table by dealing past them when the dealer is stiff and by hestitating, urging them to hit, when pat. Dozens of girls have mentioned this to me, including my sister, who claims she can find a dealer to help her in this way virtually at will. Indeed, a sharp female can induce this behavior.

How Much Cheating Is There?

The dealer who steals consistently can be motivated to cheat players so that his results are not continually out-of-line with other dealers. Most casinos keep records by table; in many clubs, a regular dealer is assigned to each table (usually dealing in 40-minute intervals) and spelled by a relief dealer (who deals for 20 minutes at each of two tables). If, over a long period of time, one table shows consistently lower than normal results, the regular dealer would be subject to question.

Barbara, the Harold's Club front-loader referred to earlier, once told me, "Sure, they can measure what I do for the house. Even though I have a relief dealer, they know what my table's done. They don't really give you any heat, though recently, a boss has been sort of kidding me about my not winning as much. But, there's a little seriousness behind the kidding, I think."

Based on years of playing, I believe that the chances of encountering a cheating dealer today in large Nevada casinos are small. If pressed to give a figure, I'd say ½% at most. Certainly, cheating is not so rampant that a skilled player cannot make money in Nevada.

Paranoia persists, however. One blackjack author, notorious for seeing cheating dealers in every closet, recently told me, "Last time I was in Vegas, I played six times for about an hour each, betting $5-to-40. I lost every time. There's got to be a lot of cheating going on."

My guess is the real reason for the losses was a short-term bad run—the sample size was very small.

If the player exercises normal caution (such as avoiding dealers with whom past losses were statistically unlikely and adhering to practices discussed later in this chapter), he will probably lose far less from cheating than he would from inaccurate play.

Cheating in England, Germany, Macao and the Bahamas is probably minimal, based on our experiences there. There is occasional, but rare, cheating in France and in Belgium; in both countries we encountered "short shoes" (shoes from which 10's or aces were removed, or perhaps a 5 or so added). I advise against playing in Yugoslavia; stories about short shoes in that country are numerous. The games in the Caribbean appear clean, although the Aruba and Curacao casinos have the annoying habit of changing house rules arbitrarily and without warning.

Methods Of Cheating The Player

Peek And Second Deal. The most common form of cheating involves the peek and second deal. This is possible only with a hand-held deck (although cheating shoes do exist, as discussed later). The dealer peeks at his top card, a move easily accomplished merely by bending the card slightly and looking at the index. If the card benefits the player (or hurts the dealer), he will deal a second by sliding the card back with his thumb and removing the next card by grasping its upper right-hand edge, as shown in the photograph below. Although the dealer is not sure of the value of the second card, the avoidance of the first card statistically gives him an insurmountable edge over the player.

The photos below are furnished courtesy of the Stanley Roberts School of Winning Blackjack. Use of cards from the Sahara Hotel, for the purposes of these illustrations, does not imply improper conduct at that establishment.

Note: Several of the photographs below have been deliberately blurred to show the speed with which dealers perform their cheating techniques.

THE MECHANIC'S GRIP

THE FRONT PEEK

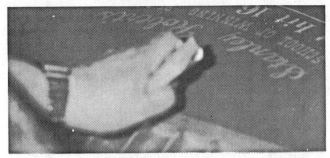

THE BACK PEEK

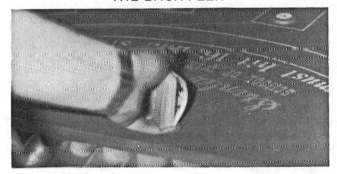

SLIDING THE TOP CARD BACK

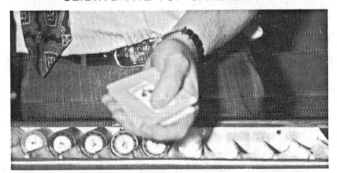

DEALING THE SECOND

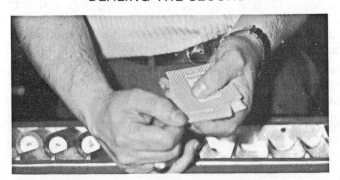

The good "mechanic" (cheating dealer) can deal a second indiscernibly, no matter how intently you stare at his hands or how good your eyesight is. In the old days, mechanics devoted many hours to practicing their trade and became unbelievably dexterous. (I recently saw a 12-year old boy deal seconds indistinguishably—and he'd been practicing only for a few weeks.) Some mechanics are able to deal the third card, or bottom or other cards as well.

Most second-dealers, also called "deuce dealers," use what is called the "mechanic's grip," a way of holding the cards with the index finger hooked around the upper end of the deck and three fingers on the side of the deck, with the thumb touching the upper right-hand corner. Serious blackjack players should learn to detect this grip and avoid playing with these dealers.

Stacked Decks. There are numerous ways to arrange the cards within the deck to the detriment of the player. While I believe these techniques to be generally unused today, I'll discuss some of them:

— Keeping a clump or "slug" of highers cards together, most often such that they are never played. In single deck games, the clump would be at the bottom of the deck and never put into play since the dealer would shuffle the deck prior to using these cards. This requires the dealer to preserve the clump during the shuffle and to induce the player to cut so that the clump remains at the bottom of the deck (or neutralizing the player cut through sleight-of-hand).

— "High-lowing" the deck, by picking up discards such that high and low cards are interspersed to the players' detriment.

— Prearranging a clump of cards to be used in play, such as the so-called "Kentucky Step-up," which is useful against one-to-four players. The standard Kentucky step-up is 8, 9, 10, 10, 10, 10, 10, ace.

I do not expect that the player will experience these forms of cheating. They went out with high button shoes.

Selective Dealing. As a guide to avoiding *possible* cheating, Lance Humble has conducted a survey among members of the International Blackjack Club. According to the survey, age and sex influence the possibility and frequency of cheating dealers. Humble concludes that young female dealers are preferable while old male dealers should be avoided.

One effective and subtle way of cheating was actually first brought to my attention by a casino owner. At the end of the deck, the dealer merely peeks at the top card, prior to dealing. If the card is a small card, such as a 4, 5 or 6, the round is dealt and the small card is given to the player. If the card is a 10 or an ace, the deck is shuffled. It would be virtually impossible to catch and prosecute a dealer using this approach; there's no evidence and no proof.

Cheating Dealers We've Known (Or Suspected)

Over the years, we've encountered questionable dealing practices in a number of casinos. However, statements (which I hear continually) like, "They really cheat at (name of club)," or "You should really be careful at (name of club)," make absolutely no sense. Cheating dealers, for the most part, are in business for themselves and may be working anywhere.

I'll relate some of our experiences so the reader will have an idea of what kinds of "moves" to look for. I will "tell it like it is," identifying the club at which each incident happened. This is not to imply that the club encourages or permits its dealers to cheat in any way.

The Disappearing Burn Card—Rusty At The Dunes. A teammate, Rusty, was playing against a single deck dealer at the Dunes who accidentally exposed his burn card as he rolled it over to the bottom of the deck, not an uncommon phenomenon. Rusty, of course, noted the card each time and included it in his count. When the dealer broke the deck to shuffle, he separated the used portion of the deck, exposing the first card facing upward, which should have been the burn card. On several consecutive deals, Rusty noticed that this card was different from the burn card.

What happened to the burn card? Did the dealer use it sometime during the play of the first round by dealing bottoms? Did he roll (reverse) the deck? We have no idea, but suspect the dealer was doing something inimical to the players' interests.

The Selective Upcard—Rick At The Stardust. Let me put it in Rick's words: "I was playing four deck with a tall male dealer, with exceptionally large hands, who handled the cards like a magician. He'd deal the first round of cards, leaving his own card face down. Then he'd deal the second round of cards, dealing himself his card last, naturally. Sometimes, he'd turn his first card up as his upcard and sometimes, he'd turn up his second card. I couldn't get over the proportion of the time that his upcard was a 10."

It's possible that the dealer was reading his cards as they came out of the shoe (it's highly unlikely that the deck was marked). The dealer could then turn up the card that was a 10, which would lead most of the players to hit their stiff hands, risking busting.

To illustrate this, assume the dealer's two cards are a 10 and a 6. By peeking, he makes the 10 his upcard. The players would, against a dealer's stiff hand of 16, tend to hit their stiff hands, taking the first risk of busting. Further, if the upcard had been a 6, the players would have been able to capitalize on doubling-down and pair-splitting opportunities, which they would not do with a dealer's 10 upcard.

The Crinkled Five—Ron At Caesars Palace. Ron was playing a particular hot four deck shoe at Caesars and placed a $2,000 bet. He drew a pair of 9's against a 6. Ron split the 9's with another $2,000 bet. He drew a 2, doubled-down, getting a 7. Then, he drew another 9 and split again, drawing two 10's. He had $8,000 on the table and held an 18 and two 19's against the dealer's 6. Things were looking good. The player to Ron's left had a 5 and 7, and hit, busting out. The dealer turned over his hole card, a 10. He hit with a 5, winning Ron's $8,000.

Ron noticed that the dealer's 5 was strangely crinkled, far more than any other card. Could the 5 have been palmed by the dealer as he collected the hand of the busting player? Could the dealer, knowing that he had a 6 upcard, have played the odds and palmed the 5 in his large right hand, turned over his hole card, reached over to the shoe with his right hand (the normal dealing motion) and pretended to pull a card out of the shoe, crinkling the card in the process? Had the dealer busted, Ron would have won $8,000; thus, the 5 ended up benefiting the house's bottom line by $16,000. Would the dealer risk a two-second palming for $16,000, or was the 5 a legitimate draw?

The Incomplete Shuffle At The MGM Vegas. Several years ago, I was playing at a $25-minimum table, head-on, when the boss brought in four brand new decks. I observed incredulously as the dealer shuffled them. He took the first fresh deck and shuffled it into the second fresh deck, shuffling only three times. Then, he did the same with the third and fourth decks, put all four decks together and extended the cutcard to me for the cut. Since all new decks are arranged identically (ace through king for two suits, then king through ace for the other two suits), this method of shuffle in effect clumps similarly valued cards.

(Later at home, I duplicated the dealer's shuffle, giving four new decks three perfect shuffles. The results were revealing: of the 80 10's and aces, 20 were clumped together in the middle of the deck and 10 were clumped at each end, thus joined together into another mass of 20 when the shoe was cut, The remaining 40 10's were in groups of 10, interspersed with 2's, 3's, 4's and 5's, all stiff hands.)

As we began to play, I couldn't believe how the cards were coming out. Seven of the first ten cards were 4's. Then, a batch of 3's came out, followed by a group of 6's; then, a clumping of 10's and aces. I kept track of the count, which soared astronomically, as more little cards came out. Staying at $25 minimum bets, I lost hand after hand.

Would casino managers encourage this type of shuffling to win more from the players? I tended to doubt it, but consider this. Many casinos are huge businesses, generating in some cases over $200 million per year in casino winnings. Most large companies utilize computers, sophisticated mathematical techniques and advanced scientific methods to maximize profits. Would casinos be any different? With the billions of dollars in "action" gambled each year, a technique that could increase the house advantage by a mere .01% would have a huge dollar effect on their bottom lines. Would casinos be motivated to hire computer experts to identify ways to find additional fractions of .01 percentage points here and there, which translate into hundreds of thousands, or perhaps millions, of dollars in annual revenues?

Both the Vegas and Reno MGM casinos now use the proper method of shuffling each deck *individually* and then mixing them together. But, as of this writing, although I've brought it to the attention of the Casino Control Commission, Caesars Boardwalk Regency in Atlantic City uses an inadequate shuffling method, resulting in card clumping.

Used Cards At The Sands. When the bosses change cards at the Sands, rather than opening four fresh decks, they occasionally give the dealers cards that have already been used and are already mixed together. Thus, it is impossible for the player or dealer to know if all the cards are present. We called the Nevada Gaming Commission to complain about this practice. Their response: "Well, they shouldn't be doing it, but I guess maybe some casinos do." The Sands has been doing this for five years now.

The best way to protect against playing against a shoe that may have too many 5's, or not enough 10's or aces, is to be in the casino when the new decks are brought in at the beginning of a shift and to inspect the cards. But, if you join a game in progress, there are warning signals. If the count goes way up, shoe after shoe, and never seems to restore to zero toward the end of the shoe, chances are the decks are wrong. If you suspect an irregular deck, play the minimum (or better yet, back count) and count the number of 5's, 4's or both. If you total more than 24 of them in a six deck game, something's wrong. If you constantly count 22 or 23 of them, and there's a deck or so left to be played at the shuffle, why take chances—avoid the game.

Dealer's Choice In France. Kathy was betting heavily in a casino in France. A small bettor was playing with her, at first base. Kathy noticed that the dealer sometimes dealt the player and sometimes passed the player by—the player was slow in placing his bet in the spot. Kathy also noticed that the dealer would look at the value of the first card as he turned it over to lay it face up on the table. If it was a 10, he'd give it to the small bettor on Kathy's right; if it was a poor card, he'd deal it to Kathy. Very effective.

Hitting 17 In France. KP had five hands, all totalling 19 or above, and close to $1,000 on the table. The dealer had a 6 up and drew to his hand. He turned over a 5; then drew another 5; then he drew an ace. Then he drew again, getting a 4, for 21.

"*Vingt et un,*" he said, as he reached to collect KP's bets.

Did the dealer hit his hard 17 because he knew his hand would lose to KP's hands, all exposed face up on the table, or was it an honest error? Al was watching the play, raised hell and KP was paid.

The Slug At The Nugget. Al related a strange episode that occurred at John Ascquaga's Nugget in Sparks, Nevada: "There was this dealer who didn't look old enough to deal the game. She'd go down to 13 cards or so and then actually look at the unused cards. They were always high cards. Then she'd shuffle in a way to preserve the clump of high cards and try to get the player to cut so they were always on the bottom.

"After each deal, she'd check and make sure those cards were down at the end. I could see her sort of smile, like she was proud of herself to be able to do it right. Then, somebody cut the deck differently and the clump was broken up. She checked the last cards after the deal, and they were small cards. I could actually tell she was mad that she screwed up and lost her clump."

Special Shoes. Players feel they're protected from second-dealing when the club uses a shoe. This is not necessarily true. An ex-pitboss at the Dunes, who subsequently went to work in a Yugoslavian casino, had a second-dealing shoe on the market for $1,500. Cheating shoes were also displayed at the Second Gambling Conference. One shoe exposed to the dealer the value of the first card; another revealed it to the player at first base. Both shoes used an elaborate configuration of lights and mirrors.

A casino off the coast of Nicaragua employed such a peeking shoe. A friend of mine was given the shoe to examine. It looked perfectly normal to him until he spotted a square area in the wood that was not quite as sun-bleached as the rest of the surface. This was because the mirror that was usually placed there, about an inch square, had been removed prior to the inspection.

Use of an illegal shoe is risky. The shoe constitutes *prima facie* evidence against the casino. I doubt if you'll find one in a major casino in the U.S. But, I do know they're manufactured—and I doubt that they're all just souvenirs.

That, by the way, is one reason I rarely play in private games—especially in Texas.

How To Protect Yourself Against Cheating

There are several habits that the card counter (or other player) should form in order to protect against cheating. Initially, these practices require additional effort and self-discipline. But, if followed continually, they'll eventually become second nature. I urge you to take the time and trouble early in your blackjack career to adopt these practices. If you're being cheated, even for small proportions of your total playing time, it can seriously erode your long run profits from the game.

The player in Nevada and abroad should follow all of these practices. The Atlantic City player, because of the controlled conditions there, need only be concerned, as of this writing, with steps 1, 2, 3, and 4.

1. *The Shuffle.* Watch the shuffle. Make sure it's a complete one that intersperses all the cards from both portions of the deck. Look for a clump of cards that never seems to get separated. If you detect such a clump and feel it's likely to be due to honest, inadequate shuffling, cut right in the middle of

it when you're given the cut.

2. *The Hands.* Always add up the value of your hand and the dealer's; don't rely on the dealer to settle the hand correctly. Watch especially those confusing 4 or 5-card hands, with one or more aces. Your edge is small so that one dealer error per hour in favor of the house can seriously affect your win rate.

3. *The Pay-Out.* Always watch the pay-outs, especially the more complicated ones that take place after surrendering, taking insurance or getting a blackjack. I've caught thousands of dollars in dealer pay-out errors.

4. *Cash And Chips.* Watch all cash and chip transactions at the table and at the cashier's cage. Here again, I've caught errors favoring the house totalling thousands of dollars.

5. *Single Deck Top Card.* Notice how the dealer holds the cards. If the grip resembles the mechanic's grip, particularly if the back of the deck is resting against the dealer's palm, be on guard. Watch the dealer as he pulls cards from the deck. The single most effective protection against hand-held cheating is to *watch the top card coming off the deck.* You'll be able to follow it as it's drawn off by watching the logo on the back of the card, follow that logo from the deck to the table, as the card is pulled off. Be particularly observant in the few clubs that use the Bee No. 67 cards with no logo on the back; it's difficult to watch the top card coming off. If you suspect second-dealing, watch the dealer's eyes to see if he glances down at the deck; if you spot a dealer with an unusual visual fascination with his deck, leave the table.

6. *Cutting the Single Deck.* Aces and 10's tend to get bent during play, as the dealer checks for blackjack when they're the upcard. If the player cuts the deck in accordance with the natural folds that develop in the deck, he will tend to cut just below a 10 or ace, cutting such a card to the bottom of the deck and out-of-play for the next deal. This, of course, results in a natural (and potentially serious) bias against the player.

To avoid this, as a matter of habit, I *always* squeeze the deck tightly prior to cutting and riffle past a few cards before selecting the cut location.

7. *Big Losses.* If you lose heavily to one dealer over a long period of time, there is a minor possibility of cheating. If there are other similarly good games that can be readily played in the same casino, you have nothing to lose by leaving the table.

Don't over-do this, however. The counter must play strictly according to the statistical probabilities of the game. We, of course, would never leave a so-called "hot" dealer because he is on some mystical "streak." If you're getting a good game, can see that the dealer is not cheating and are getting good bet variation and little heat from the pit, it makes sense to stay at the same table despite a long series of losing hands.

8. *Small Clubs.* Avoid playing big money in the small clubs without a good reason (such as the favorable rules at the El Cortez in Las Vegas, the dealing of all 52 cards at the Nevada Club in Reno or occasional bonus options that may be offered). While it's unlikely you'll be cheated, why take chances—there are many large clubs around.

9. *Hole Card Sequence.* Make sure the dealer's hole card is always dealt in the same sequence, that is, that the hole card is always the dealer's first card dealt or always the second card dealt. If you spot variation (i.e., sometimes the hole card is the first card, sometimes it's the second), don't play with that dealer.

10. *Used Card Sequence.* Make sure the dealer picks up the used cards in the same sequence after each hand is played—the interspersing of high and low cards, called "high-lowing," can work to the detriment of the player. Any variation should be suspect. Rarely, if ever, would you spot such a practice in major casinos; but, be on guard in Henderson, North Las Vegas and in other small towns.

Cheating By The Players

There's an understandable temptation for many of the cross-roaders and drifters who find their way to Nevada to try to rip off casinos. Where else can someone, for the price of a $2 bet, have access to a trayful of chips, worth from a few thousand dollars to $100,000 and more? Many of the scams are in violation of Nevada statutes, but there are always those who are greedy—or desperate—enough to take the chance. You might be interested in some of the more prevalent ways of "taking off a casino from the outside."

Marking Cards. This is a popular and potentially lucrative scam. Marking the cards can give the player the knowledge of the dealer's hole card or of the next card to be dealt. The advantage of knowing the hole card is obvious and was discussed in detail in Chapters 14 and 15. Knowledge of the next card can be used to hit or avoid a hit, make or not make a double-down, etc. At the beginning of a round, if the player will get the first card dealt, he can up his bet if he knows a 10 will be his first card . . . (he has a 13% edge with that knowledge) or, better yet, that he'll get an ace (58% advantage). Knowledge of both the hole card and the next card can be used in combination to influence the total that the dealer will draw, to the player's advantage.

Players mark cards in various ways, from nicking the edges of the cards with fingernails (one player was caught with tiny razor blades attached to the ends of his fingernails for nicking—the sky had a telescope trained on him) to "daubing" the cards (daub, a coloring device, can be purchased at any gambling supply house or magic shop) to just crimping certain cards. Cheats have used "shannon-glow," an invisible paint that can be detected only with special glasses; some houses employ ultraviolet lights from their skies to detect this.

An elaborate inside-outside marked card scheme was detected at Harrah's. A pitboss, high up in the management echelon, arranged to have Harrah's cards marked and wrapped in brand new packages. He would authorize the use of the decks and his agents would "take the money off." When they caught him, they had no idea how long the scheme had been going on—it was detected only because of anomalies in their computer analyses of profits by shift. As one of their floormen told me, "He was doing it for years—we have no idea how long. He must have pulled out unbelievable amounts. We're prosecuting him to set an example. In fact, I have to go testify next week."

For smaller violations, the houses are more relaxed about card markers. Barbara, the Harold's Club dealer, told me, "We had a guy that would bend the 5's and 6's. The bosses just put in another deck on him. They wouldn't make a scene or prosecute the guy. He was only playing silver and it's too hard to prove, so why stir up a scene? If he kept doing it, though, they'd ask him not to play here any more."

Cold Decks.
A "cold deck" (or "cooler") is one in which the cards are prearranged so that the player will win a large proportion (or all) of the hands. A team was caught and prosecuted by the Frontier for substituting a deck of cards through sleight-of-hand as one of the cheats was offered the cut.

A more blatant scheme took place when a team substituted an entire four deck shoe at Caesars Palace. The feat took highly developed *legerdemain* and a compliant dealer and pitboss. The team was caught. The group took a great risk, but, if they had been able to net 20 winning hands in the shoe, at $500 per hand, they would have won $10,000. People rob banks for less.

Mucking.
"Card-mucking" or "holding-out" is a highly effective way of securing an edge over the house of 20% or greater. It requires great skill and a larcenous heart. The player, after hitting a hand several times, through *legerdemain*, will retain one of the cards. He will substitute that card, as necessary, to improve subsequent hands. To demonstrate how powerful this technique is, let me give you an example:

A player has a two-card total of 7 and hits his hand with 3 or 4 more cards, purposely busting. As he throws in his hand, he keeps a 5. His next hand is 10,6. He hits, draws a 10 and substitutes the 5 for the 10 in his hand, giving him a total of 21. His next hand is an A,4. He substitutes the 10 for the 4 and turns over his blackjack. The process goes on and on. The player, flat betting $500 or $1,000, can make a quick score of thousands of dollars (with virtually *no* element-of-ruin) and be out of the front door before the pit personnel know what hit them.

Clubs which deal multiple deck games face-down are particularly subject to the ravages of card-muckers because it is impractical to change decks frequently and to ascertain quickly if all the cards are in the shoe. This is why most multiple deck games are dealt face up, with the players not touching the cards. It is also why, in the single deck clubs, the decks are often changed abruptly and without warning; the boss then immediately checks the deck to ensure that it is a complete one.

Joe B. related this mucking experience to me: "I was working for a guy who 'held out' in Harrah's just last week. My job was to sit at third base to distract the dealer. We had the whole table covered (i.e., the group filled every seat at the table). But, a boss changed decks suddenly and caught the 'take-off' man, who still had a card palmed. He and his buddies hit the door as fast as they could. They got away. I stayed and played. The boss asked me if I knew them. I said I didn't and kept playing for an hour or so."

I have never been involved in any such operation—nor will I ever be. However, I have observed muckers in action. There are revealing moves that can be spotted by the experienced observer, which tend to give the mucker away. Yet, the competent mucker, like the experienced mechanic, is so smooth and his movements so quick and subtle, that it's difficult to detect him. As in any other profession, legal or otherwise, extensive training and prior preparation are necessary to increase the likelihood of success. Some muckers employ mechanical devices, called "hold-outs," usually hidden under the right sleeve, which can exchange cards. These devices often work quietly, quickly and subtly. They are risky since they constitute prima facie evidence of cheating.

Capping. "Capping" or "pressing" is when the player increases his bet *after* he has been dealt a good hand (or decreasing it after he's been dealt a poor hand). While there are frequent attempts by amateurs to cap bets, the highly-trained, professional "capper" is difficult to spot, either from the pit or from the sky. A capper will often vary his bet size to confuse the dealer; often, he uses his cards to block the line-of-sight between the dealer and his bet.

A Harrah's dealer described one who played at Harrah's Reno: "This guy was so good he played for hours before the skyman discovered what he was doing. He was smooth—like a magician. You'd never have caught him changing his bet size. He was so good, they filmed him for a long time before arresting him. They use the film in pitboss training to show them what to look for."

Cappers can work in teams. When they do, the confederates usually sit on opposite ends of the table. For example, the take-off man at third base might have a $200 bet out. Just as he's dealt a blackjack, the player at first base, betting $5, spills his drink. The dealer is distracted and reaches out to protect the cards on the table from the drink. By the time she looks back at third base, the player with the blackjack has a $400 bet out. The dealer, though instructed to try to remember what each player has bet, in all the commotion isn't sure of the size of the original bet. Our third baseman just made a $300 profit. He can make a nice living doing this just once a day.

Capping is particularly frowned upon in Atlantic City. In late January 1979, one of the counters (not on my team) had a $500 bet out at Resorts International, in the form of one purple chip. He'd been playing for ten hours and was fatigued. He won the hand, and, concentrating on calculating the size of his next bet, inadvertently drew back his $500 bet and placed $1,000 (two purple chips) on the betting circle. The dealer, unaware of the change, paid the player $1,000 for the winning hand. The player, sensing an opportunity for a quick $500 profit, withdrew all four chips. Alas, both the cameras in the sky and the bosses in the pit picked up this action. The player was arrested, taken to jail and relieved of his bankroll of about $5,000. He was released ten hours later on $5,000 bail and is awaiting trial. I am informed that the State's Attorney General is shooting for a jail sentence. While I doubt that he'll be successful, the point is that the New Jersey authorities are out to make examples of casino cheats to let the public know that cheating will not be tolerated in Atlantic City.

Let the cheater beware!

There are many more ways to rip off the house, both at blackjack and at other games. In fact, casinos lose more from slot machine scams than from any other single method. As one old-time boss told me, "The most money goes out of here to people with drills and pliers," which is one reason some casinos are quite wary over the huge ($300,000 and higher) progressive jackpots that are offered.

The most blatant cheating attempt I saw was in the Union Plaza in downtown Las Vegas. A fellow came into the casino and, in full view of players, bosses and dealers, grabbed a handful of chips from the dealer's tray. He dashed for the front door, but the bosses signalled "security" fast enough for the automatic doors to be locked.

The thief, frantic, ran right through the glass front door, leaving streaks of blood on the scattered glass shards. Although he did get away, I would guess he had to use the booty to pay for his stitches—definitely not a recommended way to make money in the casinos.

Chapter Seventeen

Getting Barred

As in other professions, the blackjack player can be "fired" by a boss; although, in his case, this translates to being barred or prevented from playing blackjack by a pitboss or other casino representative. Today, most casinos in Nevada, England, and France, and all of them in Atlantic City (although this latter case may be quite temporary), assume the right to bar players.

The serious blackjack player must understand what steps to take to avoid getting barred. First, so the player will know what he might encounter, we'll discuss actual cases when casinos have barred players. They vary dramatically in approach, as you will see. Then, we'll present steps you can take to decrease the likelihood of being barred. Finally, we'll discuss how to act if you get barred, to minimize its negative impact on your blackjack career.

How It Happens

Casinos justifiably have the right to throw out or detain players who are cheating at the tables. These cheats include practitioners of some of the techniques discussed in the preceding chapter, including card-marking, mucking and capping. Casinos, I feel unjustifiably, also assume the right to throw out or prevent from playing, skillful players, ones they consider to be sufficiently skillful to turn the odds in their favor.

Once the bosses have determined that a player is skilled, they will resort to various techniques which are described below. I'll also cite actual examples of barrings that we've encountered.

Atlantic City. In Atlantic City, one or more casino representatives, usually with a security employee (who wears a badge designated "U"), approaches the player, asks him to stand away from the table and secures the player's name and address, which is written down. Then, a statement is read to him, such as:

> "You are considered to be a professional card counter. You are not allowed to gamble at a blackjack table in this casino. If you attempt to do so, you will be considered a disorderly person and be evicted from this casino. If you subsequently return to the casino, you will be subject to arrest for trespassing. You may participate in games other than blackjack offered by the casino."

Resorts International, Caesars Boardwalk Regency and Bally's Park Place have barred players, counters and non-counters alike, on numerous occasions, as have the other Atlantic City casinos.

Nevada. Barring in Nevada is far less standard. In some cases, the Atlantic City approach is used, where the player may remain in the casino if he doesn't play blackjack. The pitboss may approach the table and say, "You've just made your last bet," pushing the player's chips back from the betting square. Or, the boss may ignore the player and say to the dealer, "Deal him out," without a word to the player.

Sometimes the bosses will flatter the player: "You're just too tough for us. Feel free to play baccarat or anything else but blackjack."

On occasion, the barring can be quite mellow. Once a teammate was told, "Listen, Steve, please don't play on my shift. What you do on the other shifts here is not my concern, though."

The mildest barring I've experienced was at the Marina, when the casino manager came up to the table and said, "Rather than playing, why don't you and your girlfriend have dinner on us at our new restaurant?"

The techniques can be more forceful, and may include ejection from the casino. The bosses have said, "OK, buddy. We don't want your action here. Hit the front door."

At the Sands, I was asked to step into a back office where I was interrogated by a plainclothes policeman. My picture was taken with a polaroid camera and I was frisked. Then, a security guard read the "Trespass Act," which stated that if I returned to the Sands or any other Hughes Hotel, I would be subject to arrest.

One teammate was hustled into the security office of the Hilton Hotel and physically attacked by the head of security; he was then arrested. That same player was detained in the back room of the Riviera and subsequently arrested. We've been followed out of the casino by casino employees and by Griffin agents. On several occasions, automobile license plates have been recorded, and our cars and taxicabs have been tailed.

The only time I was physically assaulted occurred at the Mapes Moneytree in Reno in August 1978, an incident which I'll relate.

I'd been playing at the Mapes (in a "cowboy" disguise) for four days as a comped guest. I'd won a few thousand dollars and most of the casino people seemed quite cordial throughout the stay.

On the last night, while waiting for my table at Mr. M's, the gourmet restaurant on the mezzanine level of the Moneytree, comped there for the third dinner in a row, I went down to the casino to play. At a head-on game, I asked if the limit could be raised from $300 to $500; the pit happily complied.

The maitre d' called down to inform me that my table was ready. I preferred to continue to play under conditions that were favorable, and, acting the bon vivant, requested a bottle of expensive French wine.

Shortly thereafter, a formally-attired headwaiter descended the escalator holding a bucket, a towel over his arm. He uncorked a $30 bottle of wine at the blackjack table and handed me the cork. I sniffed it, approved the wine and tipped the waiter ten dollars as he poured the wine and placed the bottle on the green felt. To say the least, it seemed the Mapes liked the action.

Then the pit personnel changed. I continued to play since I'd played against the shift before with no heat; however, I soon noticed a chill in the pit. Someone in the new shift apparently recognized me. Shortly thereafter, I was asked to leave. Incredulous, I was escorted out the door of the casino.

A friend had been eating at Mr. M's. I decided to inform him that I'd be waiting at the Sahara for him. I went back up to the restaurant, taking the *side* door to avoid having to go through the casino.

At the top of the escalator, the tall shift manager, decidedly unfriendly, grabbed my jacket by the collar and pushed me onto the down portion of the escalator. At the bottom, we were joined by a large plainclothes security guard. The shift manager told him, "Get rid of this f____ing punk."

They pushed me out the door, and in the street outside, they both called me a "f____ing punk" about six times.

I tried to explain to the shift manager that I was just trying to play some blackjack, that I was a "comped" guest at the Mapes Hotel (across the street, but affiliated with the Moneytree), asking what on earth I'd done wrong.

This was to no avail. Their epithets continued. Finally, I realized my urging was fruitless and I turned to leave, foolishly saying, "Well then, you're a f____ing punk, too."

That was a mistake. It violated a strict rule to leave as quickly and unobtrusively as possible. It was a mistake for another reason. The next thing I knew, I was on the ground. I reached up and felt a sickening crinkling sensation around my left eye. The security guard, a former coast guard boxer, had shattered my left cheek bones, resulting in my having plastic surgery a few days later.

*   *   *

Barring techniques vary widely, from comping a player to a lavish dinner so he won't play, to having him arrested, or putting him in the hospital with broken bones. The successful counter must know how to avoid losing his job, i.e., getting barred, by taking extensive cover measures to avoid heat and by reacting quickly to heat when it does come down.

How To Avoid Getting Barred

When you play day in and day out, as we have for the past six years, and extract significant amounts from the casinos, it's inevitable that eventually the "heat will come down." The process of getting barred, while perhaps a necessary fact of life to the high intensity full-time team player, need not be inevitable to the individual player or smaller group. Our barring experiences have led us to understand what actions make a floorman "snap" and what types of behavior draw heat. The one most important single piece of advice is: *put yourself in the boss' place.*

Most bosses envision a standard stereotype they apply to spot counters. They often watch for:

— A serious player who may look like a graduate student or professor.

— A player who looks at all the cards.

— A player who doesn't talk much.

— A player who doesn't drink.

— A player who doesn't get disturbed when he loses—the counter knows he should win in the long run.

— A player who doesn't tip much, if at all.

Dress.   Most of the blackjack books start off by saying, "Dress like a tourist." This is good advice as far as it goes, but it's an oversimplification. Look around a crowded casino. In Atlantic City, you'll see men dressed in double-knit suits with sports shirts; in La Coste, polo shirts with slacks; elsewhere in denim jackets and denim pants; or in Ivy League business suits. The women's dress varies even more. In Las Vegas, the above outfits will be seen, but the dress gets more garish with tailored suits and Gucci shoes, and gold chains also become prevalent. During the Vegas summer, you'll see T-shirts, sometimes only with bathing trunks.

The important thing is: blend in and don't dress out-of-line with the amount you're betting. Don't look collegiate or professorial; if a boss spots a button-down shirt, a collegiate sweater or an austere pair of sunglasses, he may pause to take a second look. If you don't feel self-conscious, consider sporting an item of apparel that is associated with a person who enjoys life, who likes to have fun and who is more interested in play than in work; such items as a bright golf cap, or a T-shirt inscribed with "Hawaii," "Las Vegas" or with some sports message is suggested. Other stereotyped attire that can be effective are such articles as cowboy hats, motorcycle jackets and ski jackets (particularly effective in Lake Tahoe in the winter). Dressing "grubby" is okay, too, as long as you don't come across like a broke counter desperately trying to eke out a living. "Grubby" denotes "loser" in many bosses' minds; you don't care if they think you're dirty, as long as they don't think you're smart.

If you're betting small, avoid attention-getting jewelry or dress. If you're betting high, look like you can afford it; if you don't, they may take for you for a member of a team, especially if you're young-looking.

If you do look young, try to look older. Younger counters *do* tend to get more heat, especially if betting high. But even if not, the pressure comes because many counters *are* young. Also, the bosses may be more likely to try to intimidate you if you look young and inexperienced.

General Casino Comportment. The act we've developed has brought exceptional rewards over the past six years. It's one you might emulate. In a casino, I'm continually trying to guess what each boss wants to see. As I said before, he's looking for a serious, non-talking, non-drinking, non-tipping player who looks at all the cards. He relaxes when he sees a hunch player, a "steamer" trying to recoup past losses or a wealthy guy who enjoys throwing his money around.

Show Them What They Want To See. When they check you out, they're trying to "get into your head," that is, figure out what motivates you, what turns you on, why you are there. Get into their heads first; make every little gesture, glance, comment and reaction prove to them that you're what you want them to believe you are: the nervous loser, the careless "partier," the rich girl-chaser, the confounded card player. We call it the "act" because *you are acting* in every sense of the word, every single minute; in an hour, you might "lay down" a hundred or more little hints that you are what you want the pitboss to believe that you are.

If it suits your personality, be a little loud and careless in the way you handle you money. Talk with the other players or the dealer. There are times, particularly during the shuffle and after you've made your play in what is obviously the last round of the deck, that you don't keep the count and can talk away to your heart's content. But, if you're not comfortable with it, don't try too much conversation. On many occasions, I've flinched as I've heard counters trying to lay it down by saying, "Boy, I can't play this game," or (to the dealer) "You sure are lucky," with a little smirk on their faces. That's a dead giveaway.

It sometimes helps to let the bosses think you're a drinker. This can be done by getting a drink before the play, pouring most of it out and walking (or staggering a little bit) toward the table (difficult to do in Atlantic City since, by law, a player may not carry a drink from the cocktail lounges into the casino).

In either Nevada or New Jersey, while at the table, you can ask for "cocktails." When the waitress comes, order the drink so the bosses can hear, if possible. To spread it on thick, ask for a double. During a subsequent negative deck or shoe, take a break, take the drink with you and dispose of most of it in a drinking fountain or in the washroom.

Try to act relaxed and casual: shrug your shoulders, check out the cocktail waitresses, look distracted from the game. If you're losing, show that it bothers you; appear to get flustered or "steam;" act angry, particularly at yourself for letting your "gambling" get out-of-hand.

When you put your chips out, try to throw them out sort of recklessly, rather than placing them precisely. For some reason, this "body language" goes a long way in leading the bosses to believe you're a reckless gambler rather than a methodical player.

If you plan to play more than one session at a club, save the chips from the previous play. A player starting at a table with chips attracts less attention than one who comes in with cash. The boss must watch while the dealer makes the cash-to-chip conversion and, in so doing, will often check you out. If you have chips, you can just sort of slide unobtrusively into the play; the bosses, if they notice you at all, will often take you for just another guy who's been playing in that club over a period of time; therefore, you must be "all right."

When you're counting cards on the table, always try to be aware, through peripheral vision, of where the bosses are. If you feel they may be staring at you just as some cards are revealed, look away from the table. When I suspect a boss is checking me out just as the dealer turns over his holecard, I often look away, purposely not seeing the holecard. I've sacrificed seeing one card for seeing a lot more in future games. If it's the last round, of course, we haven't lost a thing.

One trick that is very effective in taking heat off head-on games: after you've played for a while, arrange to have a friend sit at your table, pretending he doesn't know you, if possible. As your friend plays, the chances are that the bosses will now be watching you to see if you're looking at the other player's cards. Do not show ANY interest in his cards. After a few hands, the boss may walk away, reassured that you're a normal player. Soon after, signal your friend to leave the table and resume your head-on game.

Tip the dealer modestly. Try to do so when the boss is watching to get "more bang for your buck." If a dealer starts dealing a little further into the deck, try tipping toward the end of the deck. Sometimes dealers, in a subconscious Pavlovian way, will relate the tip to the depth in the deck, and, you may find the quality of the game improving.

Betting for the dealer can make it appear you're tipping more than you actually are. If the dealer wins, give him the win and let the original bet ride (sometimes, to do this, you must place the dealer's bet on top of your bet, due to club rules). If you win three or four hands in a row, you've tipped the dealer several times, but only with one bet. After each hand, the dealer will bang his tip on the metal rim of his tray and may say, "Thank you." The bosses may hear some of this.

Don't try to get too friendly with the bosses, until they act friendly toward you. As one boss once told me, "I suspected Jim (a teammate) because he tried to be too friendly with me." If you're betting high, you should exercise the privilege of asking for comps to shows; it shows you're a high-roller who's "been around" and indicates that you're interested in more things than just blackjack. If you don't go to the show, that's okay; in fact, it's good cover as you say, "'I lost track of the time, gambling."

Avoid having too many chips in front of you, even if you've cashed in for a lot and are "digging out," pocket chips periodically to avoid huge stacks on the table (whether black, green or red in color). But, do it obviously, as if you're keeping a reserve in your pocket; many "normal" players do this. I usually say, "Just saving airfare home." If you do it furtively, be sure you're not seen; that will arouse much suspicion.

To repeat, put yourself in the boss' place. Each pitboss varies in temperament and outlook, and each has his own ways of trying to spot counters. Thus, it's impossible to generalize on how to act. Try to get a feel for the "vibes" of the bosses in the pit. Show them exactly what you think they want to see to be convinced you're a loser. The player who can improvise effectively will be most successful in getting a good game and avoiding heat. The good act gets better bet ratios, and thus, higher expected value.

TV stars aren't the only ones who get paid good money to act!

What To Do If Barred

With good cover, you should be able to play extensively before getting heat. You'll know if your act is working. The bosses will extend themselves to you, acting friendly, making small talk or even offering you "comps." In Nevada, if they whisper to the dealer to "convert" you, that is, to upgrade the value of the chips you're playing with, you know you're "in." They think you're a loser and want you to be tempted to bet more.

You'll be able to detect heat from the pit far before they decide to bar you. They'll watch you closely, with grim or suspicious looks on their faces. If you place a big bet, they may pick up the cards on the discard pile and scan through them to determine if the discards are full of low cards. They may whisper to each other, periodically glancing in your direction. A boss may pick up the phone as he turns his back to you (probably calling the sky to check you out). If the pit is suddenly empty, or if no one is watching your game, beware. Some clubs, particularly Harrahs, the Sands and Hilton, use this approach to give the counter "plenty of rope to hang himself"—they're hoping you'll drop your act as they watch you from the sky.

If you feel heat, it's best to get up from the table and head for the door without looking back or cashing in your chips. In Atlantic City, you may be able to play other pits later. In Nevada, chances are, in a month or so, these same bosses will have totally forgotten who you are—they see hundreds of faces each day. They may even remember your face and think you were a good customer. We've returned to the same shift, time after time, able to play once again.

In Nevada, it's important that you *always carry identification* in a casino. While it's not likely, you *can* be arrested in Nevada for not carrying ID. The original intent of the law was to prevent suspicious characters from wandering around wealthy neighborhoods in the middle of the night, but this law can be and has been used to harass and arrest counters. Arrest is not likely unless the bosses really have it in for you.

You do not, by law, have to show identification to casino security guards or other casino employees. They may try to convince you that the sanctity of their uniforms (and sometimes their pistols) entitles them to see your identification. If you choose, you may say, *courteously,* "I don't feel I have to show you ID," and leave the casino.

Don't be intimidated. You needn't be sheepish or defensive, if detained. You've broken no law, either in Nevada or New Jersey. Despite this, they'll sometimes treat you like a criminal. Swallow your pride, be restrained, act politely if they insult (as I forgot to do at the Mapes) and get out of there as soon as you can. Chances are you'll be back, playing in that casino before too long.

The Griffin Detective Agency

It's difficult for me to write objectively about the Griffin group. They've cost us thousands of dollars over the past six years. I even hesitate to say that, because it implies that they've been partially successful in their highly questionable role of keeping counters out of the casinos.

The Griffin Agency fulfills some functions which I feel are worthwhile. Many dishonest casino employees—from dealers to shift managers—have been caught with their hands in the till. There are numerous slot cheats and cheaters at other games.

The Griffin people maintain a dossier of these people, as well of card counters. It's called the "brown book" or "Mug Book." The book has pictures of the "undesirables;" in some cases, they use Las Vegas Police Department mugshots. (Does this constitute illegal dissemination of information by a government agency?) Opposite the pictures are descriptions of the "suspect:" his date of birth, history and a list of his associates, if any.

I've seen the book several times. At the front is an alphabetic index of the suspects. It has hundreds of pages. The book is unwieldy since a pitboss must know the suspect's name in order to verify his appearance from a picture in the book. Griffin also circulates fliers to its member-casinos if a cheating or counting team is discovered operating in town.

About half of the major casinos in Vegas and Reno employ Griffin's services to some degree. Services include providing a copy of the Mug Book (it has loose leaf pages for periodic updating), being on call to identify people and to patrol casinos full time. Griffin agents work in three shifts, day, swing and graveyard, just like casino people (and, for that matter, the call girls).

We've had our share of entries in the Mug Book. Several dozen teammates are listed. I've seen my own entries; they've got several pictures of me, clean-shaven, bearded and in various disguises. One of our teammates is accused of being an "associate of known cheats." Some entries from the Mug Book are reproduced on pages 264-265.

We believe that the Mug Book may be illegal. At the front of it are several admonitions, including:

> — "No one is to be told that he is in the Mug Book."

> — "No one is to be asked not to play or to leave the Casino, using the fact that he is in the Mug Book as a reason for that action."

> — ". . .the contents (of the Mug Book) shall not be copied or reproduced." (Sorry about that, fellows.)

Thus, people are secretly written up in the book—sometimes referred to as crooks—and they have no right even to see the entry, let alone to try to refute it. Even with consumer credit, persons are allowed by law to review their records and respond if they feel the information is faulty.

Through private sources, we received a video-tape of key pages in the book, taken by one of the sky's video-machines. The producer who put together a *60 Minutes* TV segment on barring of counters reviewed it (more about this at the end of the chapter), with the hope of including it in the program. Unfortunately, it was not reproducible. I was anxious to have this film seen on national television—it might have helped in our efforts to secure an injunction against the use of the Mug Book, which we're trying to accomplish through the courts.

The Griffin headquarters in Las Vegas is in Maxim's, appropriate because Maxim's is particularly intolerant of card counters. In Reno, the headquarters was at the Cal Neva for years and is now at the Comstock. It's difficult to supply an up-to-date list of which casinos employ Griffin because the list changes so rapidly. In fact, I'm happy to say, a number of casinos have recently dropped Griffin. Further, their agent turn-over has been high—several experienced agents have left them.

As far as we can tell, as of this writing, Griffin is employed by the Sands, Frontier, Desert Inn, Castaways, Silver Slipper, MGM, Maxim, Dunes, Hilton, Flamingo, Sahara, Mint and Riviera. In Reno, Harold's Club, Cal Neva, Sahara, Shy Clown and the Mapes apparently use them. Harrrah's and Caesars do not, nor to my knowledge do any casinos at Lake Tahoe.

Griffin had a softball team which played in a casino league. We toyed with the idea of getting a telephoto camera and compiling a pictorial dossier of Griffin agents for card counters. We didn't, but for your information, I can describe two of their mainstays for you:

- Bob Griffin, the founder: About 6'1", built like a football player; dark and gray hair, about 50, well-dressed; known to personally patrol casinos.
- Richard Gonzales: About 5'10", dark hair, built like a weightlifter; small eyes, straight white teeth, high forehead; usually works swing shift.

Sorry. I don't have their pictures.

EXCERPTS FROM THE GRIFFIN MUG BOOK

1. No one is to be told that he is in the Mug Book.

2. At no time will any person be advised that he cannot be employed because he is in the Mug Book.

3. No one is to be asked not to play, or to leave the Casino, using the fact that he is in the Mug Book as a reason for the action. (The trespassing law does not require that the person be given a reason.)

4. No pages or photographs shall be removed from the Mug Book by anyone other than persons authorized by Griffin Investigations or Argy, Inc., and the contents shall not be copied or reproduced.

The material on this page has been reproduced exactly as it appears in the Griffin Mug Book. We neither endorse nor repudiate the alleged veracity of the material contained therein.

Figure 17a

What Is The Fair Solution To The Problem?

The paradoxical thing about casino barrings is that they're not necessary. There is a workable solution, both in Nevada and in Atlantic City.

Nevada. The problem can be solved more simply in Nevada than in Atlantic City because the casinos in Nevada have more latitude in running the game. The solution: forbid barring of skillful players and continue the present practice of allowing the casinos to shuffle when they choose, either by breaking the deck or placing the cut-card further from the end of the shoe—Caesars Palace, for example, hasn't barred a card counter for years—it's simply not necessary. I believe it unrealistic to suggest that the Gaming Commission control shuffling points and blackjack rules as in Atlantic City. Casinos have had full prerogative over these procedures for years.

Under this solution, known counters like me will have trouble getting a good game. Other counters, especially those with good acts, will be able to play undetected. Thus, as in other areas of the American economy, the fittest will survive. If the counter is skilled, he will find a game; if the pitboss is effective, he will detect the skilled players and effect the necessary counter-measures.

Atlantic City. The commission, in my opinion, actually reached an equilibrium solution to the barring issue in its December 1979 experiment, but was misled by the casinos into believing that counters were winning more than they really did.

By the end of the experiment, after three modifications to tighten the original rules, a set of rules was established which I believe largely solved the problem in New Jersey. These rules were:

- The casinos could shuffle if a player more than doubled his bet.

- The casinos could shuffle if a player joined a game after the cut-card had been inserted.
- The casinos could cut off up to one-half of the cards in the shoe.

This set of rules was in effect only two days when the experiment was called off. On those last two days, our team, the largest, didn't make a dime. The other few counters in town—many had left because of the tough rules—won minimally. As I continually stressed to the commission, blackjack profits were lower primarily because the casinos insisted on keeping the cut-card at half-a-shoe at *all* the tables, even though the counters were playing at perhaps 10% of the tables at most. The half-shoe cut-card reduced total playing volume by 13%, since more shuffling was required.

The above three rules, combined with the cutting off of half of the six or eight decks, should solve the problem by seriously reducing counters' profitability. Other players would be affected only slightly.

Status Of Litigation Against Casinos

A number of lawsuits have been initiated against the casinos, but, to date, none has been resolved conclusively. The first lawsuit was filed by Chris Peters, a non-counter who was mistakenly asked to leave the Hilton Hotel. He claimed a violation of his civil rights (he is black) and the Hilton settled the case for $5,000.

The Hilton was also sued by Mark Estes, who was accused of spooking the casino with a confederate. Mark was beaten up and thrown in jail. Videotapes of that evening have since proven that he was merely observing the play of a friend, and it appears that his case may be settled favorably.

I initiated lawsuits against the Dunes, Sands, MGM, Marina and Hilton. Initially, we tried to have these suits heard in California Federal Court, since I was a California resident. We were not successful and the suits were thrown out.

We re-filed in Nevada Federal Court; Judge Foley dismissed two of them, but, "without prejudice;" we re-filed several in Nevada State Court, including the Hilton case. Frankly, I feel we failed in Nevada State Court because of poor legal work; the cases have since been reassigned to more competent counsel.

In New Jersey, Attorney Morris Goldings and I filed a claim against Resorts International with the New Jersey Control Commission after the January 30, 1979 barring. After lengthy hearings, the commission concluded that the casinos, according to New Jersey law, did have the right to exclude counters (Commissioner Al Merck dissented), but, they felt it was undesirable for the State of New Jersey to institute this policy. Thus, they established the "experiment" (described in detail in Chapter 13) which took place in December 1979. As I mentioned, the experiment was concluded after two weeks because casino profits were seriously eroded. The commission met and concluded that the exclusion policy should be continued until a computerized study of blackjack counting and its effect in Atlantic City was completed. They commissioned Econ. Inc. of Princeton, New Jersey to study the playing expectations of the average and Basic Strategy player and the card counter in Atlantic City.

The study, which was completed in the fall of 1980, simulated millions of blackjack hands. It was concluded from the study that, using eight decks and cutting off four decks, the perfect Basic Strategy player has a .04% edge over the house; the *conservative* counter has a .25% edge.

At any rate, after the termination of the experiment, we filed an appeal with the Superior Court in Trenton, New Jersey. Our lengthy brief was submitted to them in March 1980. The commission applied for, and was granted, permission to provide the court with a brief stating their position on this issue.

In our brief, we petition the Superior Court for four remedies:

1. A reversal of the commission's original decision.

2. A ruling that the Casino Control Act has abrogated the common law right to exclude patrons at will.

3. An order enjoining, restraining and prohibiting the commission from approving any policy of exclusion.

4. An order enjoining, restraining and prohibiting all New Jersey casinos from excluding any patron from playing because of skill or the use of a counting strategy.

Attorney Goldings is optimistic. Walter Tyminski, the respected editor of *Rouge Et Noir*, the gambling newsletter, feels we have a 60% chance of winning the appeal.

The popular television show, *60 Minutes,* recently did a story on this issue. We're hoping the national TV exposure will garner public support against the arbitrary exclusion of skilled players. The *60 Minutes* crew accompanied me to the Flamingo Hilton and the Holiday casinos where, recorded by hidden camera, I was prevented from playing. Harry Reasoner later returned to those casinos with the crew and attempted to get explanations from their management. As you might expect, their answers were vague and evasive.

Parenthetically, we also shot a blackjack match at VegasWorld. The owner offered a single deck game, $300 to $1,200, dealing five rounds. I played, with Harry Reasoner at the table while the crew filmed from the pit. At one point, I was down $6,000 of the $20,000 I'd brought with me and had visions of tapping out in front of 35 million viewers (there was only about a 59% chance of winning). But the cards turned and I won slightly more than $6,000.

Currently, the legal battle continues. As of this writing, casinos in Nevada and Atlantic City are still barring counters at will. Dozens of non-counters are also being barred in both states. If we win in New Jersey, we plan to try to extend to Nevada any legal precedents established.

Perhaps, some day, finally, skilled players will no longer be arbitrarily prevented from playing, and, rather than being viewed as quasi-criminals, will be looked upon with respect.

Chapter Eighteen

Being the House and Caddy Blackjack
(A Peek Inside the Underworld)

Casino gambling is legal in only a few states. But, Americans love to gamble, and illegal private card games proliferate from coast to coast. From Maine to California, thousands of "friendly," and theoretically illegal, poker games take place on any given Friday night. Interest in blackjack, due in large measure to the expansion of casinos to New Jersey, is growing exponentially. Casino-type blackjack games are conducted in private locations all across the country.

Homestyle blackjack games, in which the deal rotates from player to player, are also popular. This game is often called "Caddy Blackjack," since it supposedly originated in golf caddy shacks as the caddies idled away the day waiting to be called out. Caddy blackjack is far more prevalent in the East; it's also widespread in Oregon, where social blackjack is permitted by law and occurs in many bars in that state—the maximum bet allowed is $10.

We'll talk first about conducting a private casino-type blackjack game, how to protect the game, how to set betting limits and how much can be earned. Then, we'll discuss Caddy Blackjack, including its rules, how to play it, and a rather unusual way to gain a long-run advantage playing this game.

Being The House

It's usually not difficult to start a private blackjack game, acting as the house. Sure, the players know you have the mathematical advantage, for the most part, but, they still like the action. On several occasions, I've dealt blackjack games, acting as the house. It seems there's always an abundance of players, even in states where casinos are accessable. If you don't believe it, try the following experiment:

Go to a neighborhood bar with (1) a deck of cards and (2) a friend. Sitting at the bar, deal blackjack to your friend, using match sticks for chips (or dollar bills, if the bartender will let you get away with it). The chances are good that within 10 or 15 minutes, other players will be asking to join the game, buying in for match sticks or throwing out dollar bills. Your long-range earnings potential is low in this game, since few bartenders or owners, except in Oregon, will allow a full-scale blackjack game to be conducted in their bar. But the game can be continued elsewhere. We've played for hours in a backroom of one San Francisco watering hole, supported largely by the after-work drinking habits of the Pacific Stock Exchange executives.

The point is—there are gamblers out there everywhere, longing to throw their bucks into a private blackjack game. While with the Pacific Stock Exchange, at the annual outing of Exchange specialists and management, I began to deal a blackjack game to a few of the fellows who worked on the Exchange floor. Within ten minutes, we had a full-scale game in operation; the "house" won $500 after six hours of dealing. The game became an annual tradition—I dealt the game each year, generally winning around $1,000 or so. Finally, some of the specialists wised up and began asking for the deal themselves. At the last outing I attended, I couldn't even get the deal.

On a recent trip to New York, a friend, John, who lives in Larchmont, urged me to deal a game to his friends. He said, "These guys are crazy. They'll bet on anything and half of them owe their lives to their bookies. Hey, they're gonna lose it anyway—I'd rather see them take a shot with you than fight the bookie odds. We'll call it 'Las Vegas Night' and hold it at my place."

I had mixed feelings. First, the game would be illegal—if word got around that small town, the game could be busted, or perhaps some disgruntled loser would blow the whistle on the game. Second, the game could be "hijacked," to use gamblers' parlance, that is, ripped off by someone finding out about the time and location of the game. But, John assured me that his friends were all "salt of the earth." He allayed my other fear by saying, "If any cops around here got the word, you'd have trouble keeping them out of the game."

I finally agreed to deal the game. I had $12,000 with me, and after a few calculations, concluded that a $50 upper limit would remain within a 5% element-of-ruin. I had no knowledge of the expertise of the players, although John continually reassured me, "They're horrible players; they just want a chance to gamble."

I assumed the average player would be at a 2½% disadvantage. Thus, the house would have a 2½% advantage, requiring 75 units for a 5% element-of-ruin (from Table 9-1). With a $12,000 bank, I could handle $12,000/75, or $160 in betting action per round. Since there would be six hands played, greater action could be handled, because with six spots, the house risk is dispersed over six hands. Statistically the multiplier calculates to about .7 (as in Table 9-5), that is, I could cover $160/.7 in action spread over the six spots, or $228, an average of $38 per spot. Since some players would undoubtedly be betting small, from $2 to $10 per hand, I concluded that a maximum bet of $50 would keep the total safely within $228 per round. I planned to adjust the $50 maximum as the game progressed, after assessing the skill of the players and depending upon whether the "house" was winning or losing.

The game began. About half the players bet low, up to $10 per hand; the other half varied between $20 and $50. The "house" was never behind, and, after six hours, was up about $1,000. Most of the players lost. Some won, which was good since it allayed any suspicions that I might have been a cheater; it was also good "advertising" if a subsequent game were to be dealt. As it turned out, about a week later, I was asked to deal again, and did, once again winning about $1,000.

Setting The Limits Of The Game If You're The House.

Anyone who plans on being the house should make element-of-ruin calculations. First, one must estimate the house advantage—it's probably around 2½%, but, could be more or less, depending on the expertise of the players and the rules of the game. Then, it's necessary to derive an acceptable element-of-ruin percentage. Given these two factors, it's possible to determine the number of units required (see Table 9-1). Divide the available bankroll by the units, increase the result by about one-third to account for the .7 multiple-hand factor mentioned earlier (1.00 divided by .7) is about the same as adding one-third) and you've got the total amount of action that can be handled per round. Translate this to a maximum per hand betting limit. The following table will help you determine the limits:

Table 18-1
Limits Of Privately Dealt Blackjack Games*

A. House Bankroll	B. Max. Bet Dealing Head-on Game (One Hand Per Round) (A/75 units)	C. Total Action You can handle Assuming Six Hands Per Round) (B x 1.33)	D. Average Bet Per Player (C/6)	E. Probable House Maximum	F. Average Earnings Per Hour (50 Rounds Per Hour) Full Table
$ 1,000	$ 13	$ 17	$ 3	$ 5	$ 21
5,000	67	89	15	25	111
10,000	133	178	30	50	222
15,000	200	267	44	75	333
20,000	267	356	59	100	444

*Assumes 2½% advantage, 5% element-of-ruin; 75 units needed.

271

As the table above shows, one cannot become the house on a shoe-string. A bankroll of $1,000 is needed just to deal to six $3 bettors. On the other hand, as the size of the bankroll increases, the limits can be extended. The table maximum can be increased beyond that shown in Column D, since probably not all players will play the maximum. To take the $15,000 bankroll example, it is doubtful that all players would bet up to the $44 maximum per hand; thus, a $75 maximum would probably keep the house within the maximum of $267 that can be bet on any one round. Possible maximum limits, assuming several small bettors at the game, are shown in Column E.

Determining Average Hourly Earnings. Column F of Table 18-1 estimates the house's hourly earnings for various average bet sizes, assuming a 2½% house advantage. These are average expectations—actual results will fluctuate (probably widely) around these numbers. The numbers reveal why Nevada and New Jersey casinos are opening more and more blackjack tables—the potential profits are awesome. With only a $1,000 bank, the house will average $21 per hour. With $10,000, the house should earn $222 per hour—a 2% hourly return on investment. Of course, there are risks—like getting arrested or "hijacked." Further, it *is* possible to lose—with a 5% element-of-ruin, the house will lose its total bankroll 1-out-of-20 times, on average.

How To Enhance House Earnings. The house should normally enjoy a healthy advantage if average players are participating. There are legitimate steps that can be taken to increase the house edge. First, the use of two decks increases the house edge by .35%. There are other reasons for using two decks, reasons which should be explained to the players. The use of one deck of blue-backed cards and one deck of red-backed cards, intershuffled, will assure the player that second dealing is not taking place (if the top card has a blue back and a red-backed card is dealt, something's obviously wrong). Using two decks also speeds up the game, since fewer re-shuffles are necessary (which augments the house profits).

It's to the house's advantage to speed up the game. This not only increases earnings expectations, but makes it more likely, as more hands are dealt, that expected value will be achieved. Chips should be used if possible. In dealing games using currency, I find the game is slowed down significantly because of the need to make change and keep the piles of bills in separate denominations. Chips also provide an element of safety too—in the event of a bust or hijack, there's no money on the table.

If the house hits soft 17, its edge is increased by .2%. Generally, it seems that when the blackjack options—insurance, doubling-down on any two cards, splitting pairs—are offered, they tend to benefit the house; more players seem to misuse these options rather than to capitalize on them properly.

Conducting The Game. It's essential that precautions be taken when dealing a game. The house edge isn't that great, and a cheating player, or only several mistakes per hour on the dealer's part, could completely wipe out the edge. The dealer should watch for many of the things professional dealers are taught to be alert to, including:

— Holding out. Peripheral vision should be used to ensure that no players are holding out cards and substituting them from hand to hand, to their advantage. The use of two colors of cards helps here.

— Capping Bets. The dealer should watch for players increasing or decreasing their bets *after* they've seen their hand. The dealer should never turn his back on the table or allow any of the hands out of peripheral vision for more than a second or two, especially with a tableful of players.

— Hole Carders. When the dealer checks for blackjack (with a 10 or ace upcard), he should make sure that no one can see the hole card. Only the corner of the hole card should be flipped up, so the dealer can read the index on the corner of the card. The hole card should be shielded with the two hands and the deck to hide it from any potential spooks.

If you deal a game, I strongly urge you *not* to do anything illegitimate. Your normal edge should yield you handsome profits—there's no need to enhance your edge through questionable means (taking aces or 10's out of the deck, second-dealing, "rolling" the deck, or any of the other techniques described in Chapter 16, "Cheating"). Take pains not to take advantage of the player—if there's a dispute over whether the player wanted a hit or not, give the break to the player. You'll gain their respect and perhaps an opportunity to continue dealing longer—or on subsequent occasions. Also, they outnumber you. Do nothing that might be suspect, however tempting. (I once dealt myself a 10 upcard. No one noticed that the card was the last one in the deck. The card gave the house a healthy advantage. However, I picked it up, announcing "last card," shuffled and dealt myself a new card.)

Prevalence Of Private Casino Games. Private casino games are far more prevalent than one would assume, although it generally takes contacts to get invited to one. Several games in Manhattan and Long Island are surprisingly open and easy to get invited to. I personally know of games in Philadelphia, Hollywood, Austin and Odessa, Texas, and Alaska.

Caddy Blackjack

A Peek Inside The Underworld. A friend of John's, call him Dan, told me he had lined up some "heavy hitters" to play at a second game I would deal at John's apartment. Dan had a number of "connected" friends, including his own bookie and other bookies.* I expressed concern at their "connection"—would it be healthy for me if word got out that a competitive blackjack game was being held in town?

Dan responded, "No problem. You're not doing it on a recurring basis. Hey, I know these guys—everything's fine."

I decided to agree to have them come, not knowing where this chain of events would lead. It led somewhere interesting.

At the game, Dan explained that the "heavy hitters" weren't coming to the game. "They had the same concerns you did—they weren't sure of you. Also, they can play big anytime they want. There's a game in town several times a week. In fact, there's one tonight."

My ears perked. "Where?"

"Somewhere in the 'North,' Dan responded, referring to the north side of a neighboring town, a run-down section of the city once predominantly Italian, now partially black.

"Any chance I could go see it?"

"Sure. Sure," Dan said with his typical bragadoccio. "No problem at all. Wanna come? I'll take you. No problem."

Later, Dan and I drove to a bar in the "North." We talked briefly with the owner, who said, "If there's a game tonight, it's at Charlies," and gave us directions. Charlie was Dan's former bookie, obviously connected.

Five minutes later we were walking into a basement hall; it had a concrete floor, was brightly lighted and furnished with old, worn furniture. Eight old Italian gentlemen sat at a table, playing gin rummy. A younger fellow, also Italian, came up, shook hands with Dan and was introduced to me. This was Charlie, the owner of the establishment.

Dan said, "Ken's a friend of mine. He's in town for a while. Looking for a blackjack game. Know where he can play?"

Charlie gestured for Dan to join him in the back room. The two disappeared for ten minutes. I sat in front, watching the gin rummy game, fantasizing which players were bullet men, which *consiglioris* and which mafia lieutenants.

Dan emerged. I bid goodbye to Charlie and we left. Dan said, "There's no game tonight, but there's one tomorrow night run by friends of Charlie's. He said he'd bring us."

---

*"Connected" is the euphemism for being a member of organized crime. I was told on several occasions that one does not remain a bookie in New York for long without being connected. The syndicate doesn't like competition.

I said, "Shouldn't we tell Charlie something about the fact that I play blackjack for a living?"

"No problem, Ken. None of those guys would have any idea of what you'd be doing. Believe me, I know them."

"But what if they found out? There's a Wall Street Journal article on me coming out. Wouldn't it be healthier for me not to come into a game with these guys under false pretenses?"

"Well, I'll tell Charlie. Maybe he'll want a piece of your action."

I couldn't believe it. I had visions of my going joint bank with a connected bookie to a connected blackjack game. Who would believe all this?

Dan told me a little about Charlie. He was busted for bookmaking several months prior, had achieved great notoriety—from the front pages of newspapers and through extensive TV and radio coverage—and was "hotter than a pistol." He was once Dan's bookie before he caught the heat, and in the backroom he had asked Dan once again to place his bets through him. "But, you'll have to call me just once a week and place all the bets then. There's too much heat on me to take more frequent calls."

Dan explained to me, "There's no way I can bet that way. I gotta be able to call in every day or nothing at all. Tho' I feel sorry for Charlie. He's hot as hell and is just trying to re-establish himself. By the way, for tomorrow night, Ken, you gotta 'guinea up;' you can't wear that ridiculous sport jacket you had on tonight. Charlie wondered about you."

The next day, I "guinea'd up" with a black turtleneck and leather jacket. Dan phoned Charlie, asking about the game. I heard Dan say, "Yea, a long time" and knew Charlie was asking Dan about me. Then, "He's good as gold. A friend of mine."

I thought, "A great recommendation; but, really, Dan's only known me for a few days." I wondered if Dan's recommendations about Charlie and friends were as soundly based.

A few more minutes of conversation and we agreed to meet at a discotheque later that night.

My mind was whirring with questions: How much cash to bring to the game? Do I dare count cards in a connected game? If I win a lot, will I get out safely? Will they cheat me, since, clearly, I'm not connected? Should I just forget all this foolishness and fly back to California, while I'm still in one piece?

Charlie was at the disco bar, sucking up a martini. We shook hands again; he eyed me suspiciously. Dan said to him, "Do you mind if your friends get beat for some money?", as I cringed.

Charlie replied, "No one's gonna steal nuthin' in this game. I play as good as anybody and believe me they're sharp. It's not a game like in a casino—the deal rotates."

Charlie didn't want a piece of my action. Then, Charlie described the game to me. It was similar to the standard rules for a private blackjack game.

Rules Of Caddy Blackjack. The deal rotates from player to player, with the player who gets a blackjack or natural getting the deal (the players cut for the deal at the start of the game).

A single deck is used, the cards dealt face down. All ties go to the dealer. Blackjack pays 2-to-1 to the player. The player wins double his bet if he has five cards totalling 21 or less (called "five-card Charlie"). No insurance is offered to the players. The dealer can hit or stand, as he chooses, after dealing to all the players. (This rule makes blackjack more like a poker game in which knowledge of individual player's idiosyncracies is helpful.) The player can double-down on hard totals of 10 or 11 only, but can do so after any number of cards has been dealt to him. Pairs, other than aces, may be split. (I later found these are the standard rules played in most Caddy Blackjack games in the East.)

When a player gets the deal, he declares how much he wants to put in his bank. He deals until that amount has been depleted (or until another player gets a blackjack). If the dealer gets a blackjack, he can restate the size of the bank he's willing to risk. If the dealer and a player both get a blackjack, the dealer keeps the deal. If two players get a blackjack, the first blackjack (the one closest to the dealer's left) gets the deal. If a player doesn't want the deal, he can sell it by auctioning it off to the other players.

As Charlie explained the rules, I realized there was no way that I could immediately gain the advantage. I knew none of the players and had no computer-tested rules for when the dealer or player should hit or stand with these rules. But, I decided to go to observe, perhaps playing until I lost a few hundred dollars, intrigued by the thought of observing an illegal, but regularly scheduled private game.

I wasn't sure of the bankroll I'd need. Were the games attended by only wealthy *mafioso*, with thousands of dollars to throw around? I asked Charlie about the limit.

"$100 limit."

"Max or minimum," I asked.

Charlie gave me a weird look. "Maximum, but," he went on, "when you get the deal, you declare how much you want the bank to be."

"Is a couple of thousand enough?"

"Hell. They don't play that big. A couple of 'thou' is more than plenty."

I was relieved and now really wanted to participate in this intriguing game. I certainly couldn't get hurt too badly, or so it seemed. Even Charlie suggested, "Why not go for a while, bet small, see how it goes and then maybe go bigger."

"Good idea. Are you going to play?"

"I'm a little short now. The last three times I played, I lost $200, won $1,500 and lost around $700. But believe me, these guys know how to play—you're not going to steal nuthin' in this game."

"Hey, I don't want to steal anything, believe me." (I hoped he did.) "I just want to play a little cards."

We got into Dan's car. Dan, knowing I was apprehensive about being left alone, generously agreed to accompany me to the game. We parked in front of an older multi-storied building, just off a main street. I felt relieved that the game was so close to civilization—that I could get a cab quickly if necessary.

The three of us emerged from the car and rang the buzzer on the outside of the ground floor doorway. A young Italian, without a shirt, came down and opened the door, nodding a greeting to Charlie. We walked up the stairway and went down a long hall where several men were waiting for us. A sign said, "Grace Social Club." The men escorted us through an outer room into another room. There was a large, round wooden table with nine men sitting around it. Some were in their 20's; others were older and well-dressed. A fat fellow, about 40, and reminiscent of *The Godfather's* Tessio, was playing in the game also.

One middle-aged Sicilian, with a large pot belly and attired in a tight-fitting polo shirt, appeared to be in charge of the game. He rotated the two single decks of cards used in the game, to ensure that the game moved along rapidly and smoothly; he also made sure the money pay-offs between the players were accurate. The table was a sea of cards and currency, mostly $10 and $20 bills. I tried to observe the game, but for the first several hands, couldn't understand what was taking place. People were betting on each other's hands; sometimes the dealer would only deal to one person; some cards would be thrown in face up, others face down. After a few minutes, I figured out what was happening and tried to keep the count as the deal progressed. Since the dealer dealt to eight players, only occasionally did the deal progress beyond one round with the same deck, which seemed at the time to obviate a good portion of the advantage of counting.

A seat opened up and the fat owner, who Charlie introduced to me as Joe, said, in a friendly way, "You wanna sit in?"

"Yeah, don't mind if I do; tanks a lot," I said, in my best Brooklynese.

I sat down and put down a $5 bet, as a loud middle-aged guy dealt the hand. The cards were carefully dealt face down to all the players. It was explained to me that if any of the players' cards were exposed, the dealer must pay the amount of the bet to the player with the exposed cards. After dealing both cards, the dealer stopped.

He said, "Okay now, any wrong cards? Speak now or forever hold your peace. There's no misdeal now—I warned you."

277

He turned over his upcard—a 4. When my turn came to play, I stood with my 13, gesturing with my hand as in a casino. The dealer said, "Talk, please. I don't wanna misunderstand what you want."

I said, "Wait," the expression I'd heard the other players use to indicate "stand." The dealer turned over his bottom card, a 6, drew a 10 for a total of 20.

"Pay the point," he said. There were no "points" (21's) and he collected all the money on the table, including my $5. I noticed that one of the players had split 10's on this play—clearly the wrong play; the count hadn't come close to warranting that play. Maybe there was some potential here after all. "It's a zero sum game," I thought, "except for the $2 charge paid to the house at the exchange of each deal. The good players must win in the long run at the expense of the bad players."

The players were quite emotional, slapping their cards down emphatically, barking loud profanities in both English and Italian. After 15 minutes, I was dealt a blackjack and found myself with the deal. It had become obvious to me that the clear advantage in this game was when the player had the deal. Thus, it was best to declare a large bank when assuming the deal, so that you stood no chance of losing the deal because your bank had been depleted. Yet, no one had banked more than $300. So I said, "$300." This seemed to surprise several of the players.

Each player declared the amount of his bet against me and I carefully dealt the round, being cautioned several times by Joe not to turn over any cards.

He said, "Deal slower, Kenny. There's no rush."

I busted and Joe, who was holding my $300, paid the players. I noticed that there was always a separate cashier for each dealer. I later found out that the players usually went partnership in the deal, one dealing, the other handling payouts. I had no one to handle payouts for me, so Joe assumed the chore, for which I was grateful—temporarily.

Joe announced, "$13 left in the bank." I had lost $287 on the one round. The first player on my left bet the $13; no other players could play. I lost the hand and the deal.

Joe said, "That was a quick $300." I silently cursed myself for losing the deal needlessly, i.e., for lack of declared bank. But, had I established a larger bank, I certainly would have raised more eyebrows. (I had about $2,000 in cash and $3,000 in traveler's checks, although the latter would not be acceptable in this cash-only game.)

I played a minimal $5 per hand as a player, counting as I could and observing the play of the other players. Most dealers tended to hit until 17, although on occasion, some stood on totals below 17. The players also seemed to be playing a rough approximation of Basic Strategy.

One hand I was dealt caused comment. With a three card soft 18 versus a 10, I took a hit in accordance with Basic Strategy. I drew another ace. As I went to tuck my cards under the $5 bill, the player on my left said, "Go for the five-card Charlie—you can't lose."

Joe looked over at my hand and said, "Pay him double." In other words, with my four-card soft 19, I couldn't bust with the next card and had an automatic five-card total of 21 or under, which pays 2-to-1. Thus, in this game, the four-card soft hand should be hit for an automatic winner.

After a few minutes, I was dealt another blackjack and was given the deal again.

I said, "I'll try $400."

Joe said, "You're really taking a flier."

"Yeah, well, I got to get my $300 back plus some," as if the rationale for the $400 bank was the old "good money chasing bad." It was due, of course, to the realization that the dealer had a decided edge in this game and that any player who is dealing should get as much money out as possible.

Joe said, "$400. Take your shot boys."

I lost the first hand and found myself with about $50 left. The players put out their money for the next round and, after only three players bet, my $50 bank was totally covered. The remaining players had to sit out. I won that hand and several after it. Joe soon had a wad of bills in his hand—my bankroll—around $500 or so.

On the next round, I had hard 18. Joe collected some bets for me; he paid some bets, including a $20 bet he had made for himself. I wondered if his cashiering was "accurate" and whether he took due diligence in being sure to segregate his betting funds from my dealing funds. I made a mental note to audit him on the next round.

I won the next round. Joe lost his hand. Joe collected the money in what appeared to be a legitimate way. He moved his right hand (he was on my right) behind him and my eyes followed his motion. I saw he had about five $20 bills in his hand. Two other men had been helping run the game; they looked very much like Joe and I assumed that all three were brothers. One of the brothers was standing behind Joe at that precise instant, with his hand extended toward Joe's back. As they saw my glance, the brother dropped his hand and Joe dropped the bills into his back pocket, as if his hands had been in the process of doing that anyway.

I froze, probably turned white and looked around the table, wondering if the other players were in on the rip-off of this new player. I had purposely been acting a bit naive, dealing hesitantly, listening "wide-eyed" to the coaching from Joe and the others. Did they assume I was a sucker ripe for a rip-off?

The fat guy saw my expression. "What's a matter? You won the hand."

I said, with a sardonic smile, "Nothing, I guess."

I glanced at Joe. He was dead-pan. It looked as if Joe was just doing a little private ripping off. Obviously, there was no way I could call him on it.

I dealt another round, determined to watch Joe closely and let him know I was watching him. I had a 10 up. Checked the hole card. A blackjack! Joe collected my bets—correctly this time—and the fat player announced, "You can change your bank when you get a blackjack."

Joe handed me my bank. I counted it. About $800. I pocketed $700 and said, "Let the $100 ride."

Joe, pointing to another player, said, "Let him handle it," referring to my cashiering. "He can do it."

I gave my $100 to another player, concluding that Joe knew that I knew, didn't want me to make a scene (no way would I have) and wanted to avoid embarrassment in front of his friends. He apparently felt that the best way to handle it was to get rid of the cashiering job. The next round covered my $100 easily. I busted and was actually relieved to lose the deal. I played a few hands of $5 each. One of the players asked what time it was. "Just after two."

That was my excuse. "Jees. I've got a 2 o'clock date. Gotta go, but I'll be back tomorrow."

I rose, said goodbye to several of the players who were friendly to me and asked Joe where the phone was.

As I went to the phone, one of the brothers came up and said, "Here," reaching for the phone, "we have a special number for the taxi. I'll call for you."

I held onto the phone. "It's OK. I'll dial it—don't want to bother you. What's the number?"

I didn't want him dialing some unknown number for a "cab" to pick me up. He gave me the number. To my relief, the voice on the other end answered, "Luxor Cab."

Joe escorted me to the door. As I was let out the door, he said, "If you ever want to come back again, just ring the buzzer." I jumped into the cab and returned to the motel, my mind buzzing with the possibilities of the game I'd just played.

How To Win At Caddy Blackjack.

By far, the single most important factor in winning at caddy blackjack is the bet spread, that is, the ratio between how much you bet as a player and how much action you get as a dealer. The dealer has a high edge over the players. The tie-goes-to-dealer rule is the key factor; it adds 9% to the dealer's edge.

Then, too, the dealer is helped by the limited doubling (10 and 11 only) and the exclusion of ace-splitting; the offsets are the 2-to-1 payout for blackjack and the five-card Charlie. Overall, the dealer has about a 10% edge over the average player.

Being The Dealer. The player should try to get the deal as often as possible and bet as much as he can get away with when he's the dealer. He should bet as little as possible when he's the player. The greater the "ratio," the greater the long-run edge. The adequately financed player, then, is at an advantage; other caddy blackjack players undoubtedly understand the "ratio" factor, but their risk aversion keeps them from offering large banks.

As in the casinos, you should employ cover. If you bet $5 each time as a player, and then offer a $5,000 bank as the dealer, your strategy will be all too clear before long. It's the same old cat-and-mouse game.

As a dealer, try to play with a partner. You will need someone you can trust to cashier for you. With the partnership playing two hands, you will double the frequency of your winning the deal. Being with a partner will give you a more credible rationale for setting a large bank, since two of you are contributing to the bank. The principle of joint bank once again applies, as *each* of you will be able to offer, and capitalize on, a higher bank when you get the deal. You should *never* lose the deal because of lack of funds.

Try not to sit to the left of high rollers. They will freeze you out from play when the dealer's bank is limited, decreasing your chance of winning the deal.

Deal slowly and deliberately. If you expose a player's card, you lose that hand to him. Just a few such errors and your edge will evaporate.

Count cards and aces while dealing. In most games, you have complete control over whether to deal another round or to shuffle up (if there are enough cards for subsequent rounds). Shuffle the positive decks; deal the negative ones.

In playing as a dealer, follow casino rules. Stand on hard 17. Hit soft 17; you will benefit slightly, just as do the casinos. Periodic deviations may be in order if you detect patterns in the hitting or standing patterns of certain players.

Being The Player. Your goal as a player is to lose the least you can, until you once again get the deal. Bet the smallest amount you can get away with and not draw attention. If you count, and it's not important to do so as the player in this game, consider betting a little higher if the deck is positive *and* ace rich (the 2-to-1 blackjack payout will help here). You've got almost 10% to overcome, so it's unlikely you have the edge as the player except in rare instances. But, the slightly larger bets may provide cover, so you're not betting the minimum all the time.

As a player, the play of the hands is not too important since you've got small bets out. But, because of the tie-to-dealer rule, you obviously will tend to hit less, since you are risking busting and will have less opportunity to win if you do make a hand. You should also double-down and split pairs less because of the tie rule.

Counting as a player is probably not worth it with many other players and thus, few rounds per deck; it is more helpful with fewer players in the game and more rounds per deck. If you do count, to reflect the tie rule, deduct five points (an approximation) from the Uston APC plus standing numbers and from the minus hitting numbers (e.g., stand on 14 against a 10 with a +4 or higher; hit 12 against a 6 with a −6 or lower). Using the Uston Advanced Plus/Minus system, deduct two points from the numbers.

Essentially, the key to winning at caddy blackjack is to become the dealer. It should not be necessary to memorize a special playing strategy in order to win. However, you should take into consideration the variations mentioned above, coordinating them with the particular rules of any given game and the idiosyncratic patterns of the other players. Generally, though, play Basic Strategy.

How Much Can You Win At Caddy Blackjack? Average earnings will depend upon the number of players in the game and the player-dealer betting ratio. I've calculated average earnings for a hypothetical but realistic situation, similar to what you are likely to encounter. You can utilize the same factors to calculate your potential earnings from other games.

Assume there are eight players in the game and that you are in partnership with one other player, sharing equally in your playing and dealing bank. You each bet $5 as a player, offer a $1,000 bank when dealer, and the other players' bets average $15 each. Assume 50 hands per hour are dealt. Assume also a 5% disadvantage to you as a player and a 10% advantage to you when you are the dealer. The average hourly earnings of your partnership calculates to $94, or $47 each.

If the players bet higher against you when you deal, the game becomes much more worthwhile. If you bet at the same $5 level as a player and the players' average bets are $50 when you are dealing, your partnership earnings increase to $355 per hour, or $175 per partner per hour. Each partner might expect to average around $1,000 in the course of a six-hour session—not a bad night's work.

Chapter Nineteen

Blackjack Abroad—
Where It Is
and
How to Play It

For years, our team members (as well as other players) have literally combed the globe in the continuing search for blackjack opportunities. It's difficult to maintain an up-to-date list of locations where good games are offered, since conditions change so rapidly. Further, when a good location is finally found, it is often "burned out" after it suffers losses at the hands of skilled players.

This chapter discusses some of the locations where we've found favorable blackjack games and the proper way to capitalize on these opportunities. We'll discuss what factors to look for in attempting to identify other profitable situations and include places that are *not* recommended for play.

As we've discussed, potential blackjack profits are affected by a number of factors: the number of decks used, the rules for doubling-down, pair-splitting and surrendering, the location of the cut-card in the shoe (determining when the cards will be shuffled) and the bet variation that the player can employ without drawing heat. These factors vary widely around the world.

It's essential that the player be discriminating, playing only where conditions are favorable and reasonable profits can be made. The search can be pain-staking and frustrating. A distressingly high proportion of our time on foreign soil is spent travelling from town to town and country to country, seeking out casinos, and, determining rules and playing conditions. This research can take weeks of time (and considerable expense money) before the player even turns a card. We hope that this chapter will save you some time and expense. We'll include information gleaned from months of research in foreign lands and summarize the best way to play casinos where favorable conditions still exist. An up-to-date list of casinos around the world is published by Gaming Industry Information Service (a division of Gambling Times, Inc.) in the *International Gambling Directory.*

How To Evaluate A Blackjack Game

Generally speaking, foreign blackjack games have rules which are statistically less favorable to the player than the games in the United States. This often can be offset, however, by the use of a bigger bet spread, usually far greater than a player could get away with in this country. In evaluating a blackjack game, there are five primary factors to consider:

1. *What are the rules?* The player should evaluate the factors on the following check-list:

   — How many decks are used?

   — Can the player double-down on any two cards, or just with certain totals?

   — Can the player double-down after he's drawn one or more cards?

   — Can any pair be split; can non-identical 10's be split (e.g., a jack and a king)?

   — Can pairs be re-split? Can aces be re-split? Can the player draw to split aces?

   — Does the dealer take a hole card? If not, does the player lose the full amount of a double-down or split pair if the dealer has a blackjack (European no hole card), or, just the amount originally bet (as in Atlantic City)?

   — Can the player take insurance? (The answers are generally yes; only if the player has a blackjack; and no.) Can the player insure for more than half his original bet?

   — Is surrender available? Can the player surrender before the dealer checks for blackjack (early surrender) if the dealer has a 10 upcard? How about an ace upcard? Can the player surrender after hitting his hand, doubling-down or splitting pairs?

   — Does the dealer stand on soft 17?

284

— Are there any bonus options, such as:

—Automatically winning with 5, 6 or more cards and not busting.

—Receiving 2-to-1, 3-to-1, etc., with three 7's or with 6, **7** and 8 in the same suit?

—Any other options?

As in the U.S., it's best not to display too great an interest in the options. Rather than blatantly asking what the rules are, which may draw heat, it's best to play low stakes and gradually try various plays until most of the rules are known. Some of the bonus options may not be revealed this way, but if you get a "five-card Charlie" or three 7's, ask if it means anything. Also, watch what other players do.

Once you've discovered the rules, calculate what the house edge is off-the-top. Start with "zero," assuming Las Vegas Strip single deck, and add or subtract from that, using the figures in Table 4-1, adding for the rules listed under "favorable to the player" and subtracting under the rules listed as "unfavorable to the player." Don't forget to adjust for the number of decks played.

2. *Where is the cut-card?* Is it a half-deck from the end? Three-quarters of a deck? One deck or more? (Any more than one deck is generally not playable in a four deck game unless the rules are exceptionally good, that is, not worse than about —.5% off-the-top.) Does the dealer complete the round when the cutcard comes out, or does he stop right at the cutcard and re-shuffle before completing the round? You obviously prefer the former practice.

Be sure to watch more than one dealer in a given casino; cut-card placement can sometimes vary quite widely from dealer to dealer. If possible, check different shifts, too; shift managers can have different philosophies about the cutcard.

3. *What bet variation is allowed?* The player accustomed to playing in the U.S. will be surprised at the bet variation sometimes permitted in foreign casinos. In fact, this is generally the factor that makes the foreign games attractive. Ratios of 300-to-1, 500-to-1 and even 700-to-1 are sometimes encountered abroad (these often require large banks). Foreign casino operators tend to have less expertise about card counting (although they're learning fast); many also assume their multiple decks and limited rules protect them from counting.

4. *What are the limits?* If you're playing to a small bank, the house minimums may be too high for you to get an acceptable bet ratio without betting too high relative to your bank. If you're playing abroad primarily to make money, you should have worked out a betting strategy given the size of your

285

bank, as shown in Chapter 9. If your trip is primarily a vacation, remember that with a 1% edge over the house on a given hand, you can bet 1/150 of your bank and have a 5% ruin factor; with 2%, it's 1/75. For other percent edges, and for other ruin factors, check the chart in Table 9-1. Thus, at casinos such as the "Big Casino" at Monte Carlo and Cannes, with minimum bets of 50 francs, it's impossible with a small bank to get the 50- or 100-to-1 bet ratios necessary to enjoy an acceptable edge over the house.

If you're playing to a large bank, the house maximums may be too small to make it worth your time. Some clubs, such as those in Austria and parts of Germany, may have maximums of $50 (U.S.) or so. Hourly earnings rates here with banks of $100,000 or so are just not worth it; find higher games.

5. *What are the conditions?* Are the tables always full? Is it necessary to wait before getting a seat? How many hours a day are the blackjack tables open? How fast is the play? Can an acceptable number of hands per hour be played? Is it possible to change tables periodically when a really negative shoe is encountered? If you have a fairly large bank, you may want to be able to arrange a private game; we've done this in numerous places, including the casinos in Nederbraun and Dieppe, France, at Loews' Monte Carlo and in Korea.

Summary. You've compiled a lot of information, but basically, you're interested in only one number: *how much you can make per hour.* All the factors we've discussed impact that figure (the rules, the bet ratio, the hands per hour, the limits, the cutcard). Calculate the house edge off-the-top; then, determine your average bet size given the betting ratio. Factor in number of hands per hour to get your total action per hour. Apply your overall percentage edge and your expected value per hour results. (Refer to the section entitled "How to calculate expected value" in Chapter 9.)

Europe

Currently, the most attractive places to play blackjack in Europe are at Loews' Monte Carlo and at selected casinos in France.

The Big Casino At Monte Carlo. The well-known Monte Carlo casino referred to in books and movies, while an interesting place to visit, is no place for the card counter. The casino, referred to locally as the "Big Casino," is located in an attractive square, adjacent to the opulent Hotel de Paris.

Six decks are used and the cutcard is usually placed at more than a deck from the end, often 1½ decks. The player may double-down only on 9, 10 and 11 and may not double-down on split pairs. European no hole card applies. The big problem here is the 50 franc minimum bet.

With their rules, the player must put down a 75-to-1 or 100-to-1 ratio to make the game marginally worthwhile, betting up to 4,000 or 5,000 francs per hand. Thus, the minimum is too high for all but the most well-financed counter with a bank of 500,000 francs or more.

Playing the European six deck game is quite different from playing the games in the U.S. Just under 10% of the shoes become significantly favorable to the player. Thus, the counter must wade through shoe after shoe with small waiting bets before favorable situations develop. When they do develop, the player must jump in with huge bets to offset the losses on the many waiting bets. It's a real grind.

The Big Casino deals blackjack only during certain periods of the day, usually from late afternoon until closing. This is because this casino tends to cater to Europeans, who prefer *chemin de fer,* roulette and *trente et quarante* (a baccarat-type card game popular in France). Nevertheless, the visitor to Monaco should visit the Big Casino, if only to see the museum-like trappings, the tuxedoed croupiers and, unlike Nevada, both clocks and windows in the casino. He'll observe countless Europeans, many successful, intelligent, well-dressed businessmen, faithfully keeping track of each roll of the roulette ball or each *trente et quarante* outcome on the scorecards provided by the management for that purpose—with obvious disdain for the Law Of Independent Trials.

The "Salons Ordinaires" for the common folks costs 10 francs admittance, offers blackjack games and closes at 1 a.m. The "Salons Privés" remains open until the action dies down, costs 20 francs and is reminiscent of the Yale or Harvard clubs in New York City, with polished oaken bars, waiters in neat white uniforms, and quite properly dressed clients—the men often in formal attire, attractive and sometimes unescorted young women in evening gowns. For those of you so inclined, beware—the European hustler, unlike the Vegas "working girl," requires wining, dining and polite conversation, to give her an opportunity to tell you about the revolution in the Near East which wiped out her fortune, her husband the Count (who recently disappeared), or some other disaster, which is designed to make it easy and natural for you to offer her financial assistance.

Loews' Monte Carlo.

Loews' Monte Carlo is a different story. There are currently no better blackjack rules in all of Europe. Loews deals a four deck game and offers Las Vegas rules, including soft doubling and doubling-on-split-pairs. They offer insurance, the dealer stands on soft 17 and the player may split any pair.

The one unfavorable rule is that the dealer, as in all of Europe, does not take his hole card until all the players have played their hands. Unlike Atlantic City, if the player doubles-down or splits pairs and the dealer turns up a blackjack, the player loses his *total* bet. The European no hole card rule costs the Basic Strategy player .13%.

Loews' dealers are instructed to place the cut-card at one deck from

287

the rear of the shoe. Many dealers, probably to minimize the tedious task of shuffling, tend to cut off about 35 to 40 cards. When the cut-card comes out, the dealer completes the round before shuffling. Overall, Loews' rules are about comparable to a four deck game on the Las Vegas Strip, the no-hole card rule nearly offset by the double-on-splits option. The Basic Strategy player is at a .58% disadvantage.

Loews resembles a Vegas casino more than it does a European casino. It has American roulette, Bally slot machines and even a Big Six game with American bills of various denominations under the glass betting area. The original casino manager, John Licini, came from Caesars Palace; he returned there, replaced by an executive from the Aladdin. Of all the clubs in Europe, Loews is the most similar to Las Vegas in set-up, operation, and, alas, in pitboss knowledge of card-counting.

I first played Loews immediately after it opened in the fall of 1975. Despite their Vegas expertise, the bosses were so concerned with ensuring that their novice dealers avoided elementary mistakes and incorrect pay-offs (by Monaco law, all dealers must be locals) that we were able to play unharassed, enjoying betting ratios of up to 700-to-1, from one hand of 25 francs to seven hands of 2,500 francs! Using both team play and individual play, four of us won 126,000 francs on that trip.

The bosses didn't know we were together until the final day, when we sat together in the coffee shop, with our hand calculators, breaking the bank.

Basic Strategy. Basic Strategy for play at Loews' Monte Carlo is identical to that used in Atlantic City, except for surrender (presented in Table 5-2), with only two exceptions:

With A A:　　— split against 2 through 10. Not against an ace.

With 11:　　— Double against 2 through 9.

Both of these changes are required because of the European no hole card rule. You want to avoid putting more money on the table against a dealer's 10 or ace upcard since you'll be losing the total amount if he turns up a blackjack. As in Atlantic City, 8's are split against 2 through 9 only, but for a different reason. In Atlantic City, the reason is because against 10 and ace, the player invokes the early surrender rule; at Loews, the reason is due to European no hole card.

Obviously, the player does *not* surrender at Loews, since that option is not available.

The Numbers. The Uston APC and Advanced Plus/Minus matrix numbers are exactly the same as those used in Atlantic City (again disregarding early surrender) with only three exceptions:

| With A A: | — Do *not* split against a 10 if the true count is −8 or lower (Uston APC), or −3 or lower (Advanced Plus/Minus). |

With A A: — Do *not* split against a 10 if the true count is −8 or lower (Uston APC), or −3 or lower (Advanced Plus/Minus).

With 11:   — Double against 10 if the true count is +3 or higher (Uston APC), or +2 or higher (Advanced Plus/Minus).

13,14,15,16:   — The numbers for standing against an ace are higher: They are +14, +11, +9 and +7, respectively (Uston APC) and +6, +5, +3 and +3 (Advanced Plus/Minus).

The Basic Strategy and matrix numbers exceptions above apply also to all casinos in England, and to the casinos in France and other European countries that permit doubling-down-on-splits. The vast majority of the rules are identical to Atlantic City. Nevertheless, if you play in Europe frequently, you may find it helpful to prepare a separate set of Basic Strategy and numbers flashcards for practicing.

Other Advice. The best time for play is when the casino first opens at 1 p.m. Although only several tables are open, it is often possible to get a head-on game, averaging 200 hands per hour, or more. During busy periods (after 9 p.m.), more tables open up. Since conditions are moderately crowded, modified team play may be used to advantage (as outlined in Chapter 12). The BP may play at one table, with a counter or two stationed at other tables (or back-counting) to signal him in when hot shoes develop.

You can save money on foreign currency conversions if, when cashing American traveler's checks, you tell the cage to hold the checks for you in the event that you have the French currency to buy them back at the end of the day. If you do buy them back, you'll be allowed to convert at the same exchange rate as when you cashed the checks, thus saving an exchange rate differential.

Loews offers junkets to players, usually from the East Coast. Airfare, room and meals are comped if the player puts up $3,000 to $5,000 in front money. If the bosses suspect you're a skillful counter, however, they will not hesitate to deduct the expenses from your front money, effectively rescinding your comp. When the bosses suspect a card counter, they often move the cut-card up, cutting off two decks or more; they have barred counters there as well.

France. Except for Loews' Monte Carlo, some casinos in France offer the most favorable blackjack games in Europe. There are about 150 casinos in France; not all of them offer blackjack.

The French casinos all use six decks, but the rules vary from club to club. Some clubs allow doubling on 9, 10 and 11 and splitting any pair, but only identical 10's (i.e., two jacks, but not a jack and a king). These include the Casino Ruhl in Nice and the casinos in Biarritz, Cannes and Menton.

Other casinos offer double-down-on-splits, resplitting of aces and the splitting of all 10's, such as the Palais de la Méditerranée in Nice and the casino in Dieppe.

French casinos stand on soft 17, offer insurance and pay 3-to-2 for blackjack. All employ European no hole card.

The big advantage in France is that huge bet ratios are often allowed, up to 300-to-1 and even greater. The player must look for good cut-cards, not too crowded conditions and favorable betting limits. Many clubs, such as the Lido on the Riviera, have maximums in the 500 franc range, which may not be high enough for some players.

Clubs with playable conditions in France include St. Raphael, Canêt Plage and Antibes on the Riviera. Other good clubs include Biarritz (good ratios) on the Western Coast, Dieppe and Trouville on the Northern Coast, and Nederbraun, near Strasbourg by the German border.

Two teammates went to the casino in Dieppe. The owner noticed that big bets tended to be placed near the end of the shoe. Wanting the action, he obligingly moved the cut-card back to 5 or 6 cards from the end. It cost him $180,000 before he called it off! (He went out of business and welched on a portion of the loss.)

How To Play The French Casinos. If doubling-on-splits is permitted, use the same Basic Strategy and matrix numbers as shown for Loews' Monte Carlo. If doubling-on-splits is not offered, use the Las Vegas multiple deck Basic Strategy and matrix numbers shown in Chapters 5, 6 and 8, modified by the Loews' no hole card changes in this chapter.

Working The Cut. In some French clubs, dealers shuffle in a manner that allows the observant player to know where the high and low cards are located. With this knowledge, the player who is offered the cut can ensure that the 10's rich portion will come out at the beginning of the shoe and thus, he can place big bets during those favorable situations.

At the Palais de la Méditerranée in Nice, for example, dealers separate the six decks in the discard pile into six equal stacks of roughly one deck each and shuffle each separately, neatly placing the shuffled decks in one pile (the one unplayed deck is cut into halves and placed in separate sections of the discard pile, confusing the issue somewhat).

Thus, it is possible to note what types of cards have been dealt in each deck by noting variations in the count; watch the shuffle carefully to detect the location of clumps of high and low cards. As a crutch, I use chips, which in France are different sizes for different denominations. A big chip represents big cards (that is, the count dropped during that deck); a little chip, small cards (the count went up); and an average size chip for an average deck (little variation in the count). As the dealer shuffled the decks, I would "shuffle" the chips so that they were an exact replica of the shoe. When the deck was cut, I "cut" the chips in the same location. I knew when the little cards would tend to come out (and bet small) and when the 10's rich portions would be dealt (betting big).

The player can use this information to his advantage when he is offered the cut. The player can cut immediately before a 10's-rich portion. He knows a 10's rich section is coming out and can bet big off-the-top. (This technique is sometimes usable in Vegas, particularly at the MGM and the Mint.)

England.

The blackjack games offered in England are marginally profitable. The rules are average, but good cut-cards can be found. Some English bosses, particularly in London, seem aware of card counting. If a suspected counter starts winning, the cut-card may be moved up. London bosses are not reluctant to bar high-rolling counters, using the euphemism: "Your membership is no longer active."

The casinos require a 48-hour waiting period between the time you apply for membership and the time you're admitted. But, a large bankroll may get around this. I've been able to gain immediate entrance to the Curzon House in London and the Silhouette Club in Southampton. Apparently, even in sedate England, "money talks."

English casinos use four decks, permit doubling-down on 9, 10 and 11, and doubling-down on split pairs. Re-splitting of pairs is not allowed, only identical 10's may be split and the player may insure only if he has a blackjack. Cut-cards are sometimes located quite favorably at a half-deck or so from the rear.

The Playboy Club in London is a nice place to play. The cut-cards vary widely, but, they stand for wide variation if you put on the "act." The Playboy ambiance is pleasant and the bosses are fairly liberal with comps to the excellent gourmet restaurant downstairs. They also give international Playboy membership cards, with no expiration dates, to high-rollers.

The Silhouette Club in Southampton is an excellent place to play for low stakes. The club is not crowded and the two blackjack tables are often vacant. The cut-card is at about half deck and the bosses allow wide bet variation. I played from the minimum (50 pence, or roughly $1) to the maximum of 50 pounds (about $100) with no problem.

The Silhouette is located in a convenient spot. Southampton is the town where the ferry traversing the English channel docks (the French port is Le Havre, not far from Dieppe). The European traveller, starting in England and making his way to France, might well try this club.

One caution: the club has a sign saying, "We reserve the right to issue a check for amounts exceeding 200 pounds." I cashed out each time I reached 200 pounds, which became a bit ludicrous. Yet, a pub-owner friend of mine who knew the Silhouette owner claimed his debts were "good as gold." But, play at your own risk there. There are other casinos in Southampton as well, but I didn't play them and can't evaluate them for you.

In summary, chances are you won't make a killing in England, but, there is money to be made. If you play, use the Loews' Monte Carlo Basic Strategy and numbers—the European no hole card and double-after-split rules make the playing rules identical. A number of scandals in England have led to drastic changes in casino ownership. A number of casinos have lost their licenses and the state of the gaming industry is subject to possible reform.

Italy. There are a few casinos in Italy, but none is of interest to the blackjack player. The Italian casinos are:

- San Remo, on the Italian Riviera, just over the French border. No blackjack.
- Campione D'Italia, north of San Remo. Blackjack is seasonally offered.
- St. Vincent. No blackjack, although this may be seasonal.
- Venice.

There are two casinos in Venice which offer blackjack—the Municipal, open in the winter, and the Lido, open in the summer. I wish I could report that conditions were good, because I can't think of a more beautiful city in which to spend time.

The Municipal uses two decks, allows doubling-down only on 11, and has a minimum bet of 5,000 lire and a low maximum of 50,000 lire (about $60). The cut-card is randomly shuffled in with the rest of the cards, so, on average, the decks are shuffled after one deck is played. With these rules, you're sure to lose money in the long run. We lost 100,000 lire checking the place out, picked up our souvenir ashtrays and gambling chips, and left. Pity.

Belgium. In 1979, several Belgian casinos offered four deck games, dealing down to a half-deck and even less. The player could double on 9, 10 or 11, double-after-splits and insure. The dealer stands on soft 17 and pairs cannot be re-split.

The bosses, particularly at Oostende, permitted wide bet variation, up to 100-to-1 and greater. Counters burned this and other clubs out in late 1979, and the Belgian games are currently not recommended. When a counter is suspected, the cut-card is moved to halfway from the end of the shoe.

Germany. There are numerous casinos in Germany offering blackjack; they are located in Hamburg, Frankfort, Baden-Baden and elsewhere. In late 1979, I found good games in Hamburg, especially at the Intercontinental Hotel: four deck, double-down-after-splits, a half-deck joker, 100-to-1 ratios. The game was slow because the tables were almost always full. You really hear it if you hit stiffs, even if the dealer has a 9 or 10 upcard; never have I been so roundly criticized for playing my hands so stupidly, although somehow I managed to win about 15,000 marks.

A team toured Germany in the spring of 1980, won heavily and burned out many of the games. Many German clubs now use six decks, with an unfavorable cut-card.

Holland. Several years ago, there were several illegal casinos in Amsterdam which offered four decks, doubling-on-splits and a half-deck cut-card. The maximum was about $80, but four or five hands could be played. The game was beatable, although I don't know if these casinos are still open.

There are legal casinos in Zandvoort and Valkenburg, with similar rules. The games were played heavily during the summer of 1979. The cut-card's been moved up and the games are now marginal.

Austria, Spain, Portugal. Forget it. We combed the many casinos in these countries and found crowded conditions, low limits and poorly placed cut-cards. Good for vacations, but not for blackjack.

Yugoslavia. We consciously avoid playing here. Rumors of questionable gaming practices (such as the "short shoe") in this country are rampant.

The Grand Bahamas

El Casino in Freeport offers rules which, overall, are slightly more disadvantageous than those in Northern Nevada. The player may double-down on 9, 10 or 11; the dealer stands on soft 17; the player may split any pairs, including any 10's. Four decks are used, with the cut-card usually placed at just under a deck. When the cut-card appears, the dealer deals until the round is completed. The Basic Strategy player is at a .65% disadvantage.

The bosses don't seem as "hep" as the Vegas bosses, most originating from elsewhere in the world. Ratios of 25-to-1 and higher are usually permitted, enough to make play profitable. During the busy periods of the day, usually from 8 p.m. to 2 a.m., many tables are open; if the casino is not too crowded, it lends itself to modified team play.

The Resorts casino on Paradise Island is a different story. While the rules are identical to those in Freeport, several factors make this spot less attractive than El Casino:

- The dealers shuffle immediately upon encountering the cut-card, rather than finishing the round (Resorts tried, without success, to get this rule established in Atlantic City).

- On a blackjack of $5, rather than paying the extra $2.50, the pay-off is even money, with a second $5 placed "en prison" for the next round.

- The bosses are more likely to pick up on card counting or team play.

- Some bosses have told me that they feel card counting per se

293

is cheating. On more than one occasion, we've been in-carcerated in their security office, our hotel rooms have been searched and we encountered threats (idle, so far) of lengthy detention in the Nassauvian jail.

Conditions at the Playboy casino are similar to those at Resorts. Your trips to Paradise Island are best limited to swimming and water-skiing.

Other Countries In The Caribbean

Outside of Freeport, there is little opportunity in the Caribbean. Un-favorable rules prevail in Puerto Rico, the Dominican Republic, Aruba and Curacao.

In Puerto Rico, four decks are used and just under a deck is usually cut off. The player may double only on 11, may double on 11 after split-ting (not as statistically valuable as double-on-splits) and may draw to split aces. The Basic Strategy player is at a disadvantage of about 1¼%. If counting is suspected, the cut-card is moved up to half the shoe or so.

Aruba is poor also. They offer four decks there, double on 10 or 11, no re-splitting of pairs and they hit soft 17. Here, too, the Basic Strategy player is at more than a 1% disadvantage. Early in 1979, Aruba offered early surrender, à la Atlantic City! One team beat them fairly heavily in April 1979 and the rule was discontinued.

The rules in Curacao vary, but are all unfavorable. All casinos offer four deck games; some allow doubling on only 10 and 11. One casino allows doubling on any two cards, but, cuts off two decks from the end of the shoe.

Panama

Conditions in Panama change periodically. Several years ago, they offered one of the most highly favorable games outside the U.S. They had four decks and allowed doubling-on-splits, re-splitting of aces, drawing to split aces and wide bet variation; and, the cut-card was placed way back in the shoe. Only the European no hole card and hit-ting soft 17 rules worked against the player.

One team beat them for $52,000 in six weeks. Six decks were soon in-troduced, several of the liberal rules were discontinued and the cut-card was moved up. About a year later, the original game was restored, but that game was once again hit heavily.

Conditions in Panama seemed very temporary, depending upon whether they've been severely beaten recently. If so, they tighten up; if not, they relax.

Macao

This Portuguese colony, a 45-minute hydrofoil ride from Hong Kong, has three main casinos, the largest of which is located in the

Lisboa Hotel. The unique rules make profitable individual and team play possible. The single deck games (offered at about half the tables) cannot be beaten, since the deck is shuffled after *every* hand; a shuffler is assigned to each single deck table. The rules:

— Double-down only on 11, split any pair (one card on split aces), insurance, and the dealer stands on soft 17.

— The player may surrender, giving up half his bet, on any number of cards and after doubling-down. He may *early* surrender when the dealer has a 10 upcard (that is, before the dealer checks for blackjack); with an ace upcard, conventional surrender applies.

— With five cards under 21, the player has the option of winning half his bet, or, he can continue to play for the full win. Three 7's and the 6, 7 and 8 in the same suit pay 3-to-1.

— The player may bet on *any* spot on the table, whether it's being used or not (as long as the house maximum is not exceeded). The player with the largest bet on the spot calls the play of the hand.

— The cut-card is placed at a quarter to a half-deck from the end of the shoe.

— The table limits vary from $10 to $1,000 HK (about $2 to $200 U.S.) to $500 to $5,000 HK (about $100 to $1,000 U.S.). Higher limits are available.

The game is beatable, due primarily to the surrender options and the favorable cut-card and the wide bet variation that is allowed. To play the surrender properly, use the Las Vegas surrender Basic Strategy and matrix numbers against the ace and the Atlantic City surrender playing rules against the 10.

The play-on-any-spot rule can lead to an interesting bet spread opportunity for the well-financed player. Theoretically, the BP, with sufficient bank, could spread the table in favorable situations, since he can play all the spots on the table, placing bets large enough to enable him to call all the plays. In practice, he would obviously not spread so aggressively to avoid irritating the other players and drawing undue attention from the bosses.

A serious drawback to the game in Macao results from the habit of most Chinese players of "squeezing" out their hands. They pick up their hands slowly, place one card in front of the second, and *very* slowly peek at the value of the second card as they slide back the first card, exposing the face of the second card. If they draw additional cards, they "squeeze" out these cards, too. The result: it takes, on average, about 22 minutes to deal a shoe in Macao. At less than three shoes per hour, the player's earnings rate is seriously curtailed.

Korea

Several years ago, both single deck and four deck games were offered, with favorable rules, including conventional surrender and double-on-split pairs. Currently, only four deck games are available. The game was quite beatable; wide variation was allowed and the cut-card was placed near the rear of the shoe.

In late 1979, however, a team beat Korea for over $250,000 and effectively burned out the game. It may eventually be restored, since about 18 months prior to that another team won heavily there and the favorable conditions were subsequently restored. Warp play (see Chapter 15) won $51,000 from the casinos in Seoul (Walker Hill) and Inchon, one of the very few practical opportunities in playing the warps.

A serious disadvantage of playing in Korea is getting your winnings home. First, it may be necessary to pay an exorbitant fee to convert your Korean "win" to dollars; one team paid 10%. Secondly, it's illegal to leave the country with more than a minimal amount of currency. One team brought money out by hiding American $100 bills in their shoes ($6,000 per shoe). If they'd been caught by customs, they'd still be in a Korean jail.

Summary

As of this writing, the most profitable foreign games are:

Monte Carlo	—Loews (not the Big Casino).
France	— At perhaps one-tenth of the approximately 150 casinos.
England	— If your "act" permits a wide bet spread.
Bahamas	— The El Casino in Freeport.
Macao	— Any of the three large casinos, but particularly the Lisboa.
Panama	— Possibly, depending upon whether conditions and rules happen to be currently favorable; it varies frequently.
Korea	— Same as above.

It's difficult to present a "snapshot" of favorable games around the globe. Conditions are continually changing, particularly as casinos are burned out by good players. But, the vast demand for blackjack by people of all countries, and the competition between casinos in various countries, keeps them experimenting and occasionally liberalizing the rules.

The material in this chapter should provide the travelling blackjack player with all the factors he need consider in evaluating the attractiveness of blackjack games around the world and should enable him to recognize (and capitalize on) a good game when he finds one.

Bon voyage!!

Chapter Twenty

Living the American Fantasy Without Spending A Dime

The Portland Playboy

Let me tell you about a fellow I met not too long ago who is living what many would perceive to be the "good life." Let's call him Howie Goss. Howie stands 5'5" and is 40-ish, has an aquiline nose, a squeaky voice which often emanates egotistic "I this's" and "I that's," and a full-grown beard and moustache. In addition to his thick glasses and beady eyes, he has a pot belly and "love handles" and is partially bald. He also dates (and beds) some of the most gorgeous girls in America.

Howie works part time as a consultant to businesses in Portland, Oregon and makes $35,000 per year, working three or four days a week. The rest of the time, he plays.

About every three weeks, Howie flies from Portland to Caesars Palace in Las Vegas. Upon arrival, he turns in his airline stub at the casino cage for a full refund. He also gets a refund for his date's ticket if he chooses to bring one; he usually doesn't, because he doesn't want to be tied down. He stays in a $150-a-day suite, which always has a large, round bed, mirrors on the ceiling, and a sunken tub; sometimes, his living room has a grand piano. He freely orders bottles of booze from room service (the tab is often over $100), eats gratis at Caesars' best restaurants (the Palace Court, the Bacchanal and the Ah So) as well as at other restaurants on the Strip, and has never paid to see Sammy Davis, Frank Sinatra or Paul Anka, even though he almost always has a ring-side seat (and he never, of course, stands in line).

He dates several of the prettiest girls in the cashiers' cages at Caesars and the Dunes, a couple of cocktail waitresses on the Strip and one or two downtown dealers. Occasionally, he chooses to bring good-looking gals to Vegas from out-of-town.

Howie told me he received $50,000 in "comps" in Vegas last year, an exaggeration, perhaps, because I think he has a tendency to stretch the truth, but I would guess that at least half that figure *is* likely. He also travels—free—to Aruba, Monte Carlo and to other casino locations out of the country.

Howie says that he's a good blackjack player. Indeed, he's told me that he's won considerable amounts over the past years. He may be telling the truth, though I tend to doubt it—I've watched him play. One time, in 30 minutes, he made several errors in playing strategy alone, which, together with his conservative 2-to-1 betting ratio, would make it difficult for him to win a lot in the long run.

The point is: Howie probably plays about even with the house. He uses a count and varies his bets accordingly. He doesn't vary his playing strategy; he plays what he calls "Basic," which is actually an approximation of correct Basic Strategy. He also plays an occasional hunch, either in betting or in playing his hand.

Yet, with Caesars' surrender and double-on-split options, he's still playing about even with the house. Howie was once told that he couldn't play there any more—by Mike Velardo, the Caesars' blackjack expert who made appearances on all three shifts, before being transferred to Lake Tahoe. Howie coddled up to another high-level Caesars executive and managed to get reinstated.

Under normal circumstances, Howie would probably have trouble dating most of the gals in Portland. But, with his Vegas comps, which put suites, shows and the best gourmet restaurants at his disposal, Howie "freely" escorts some of the world's most gorgeous ladies. Since Howie can play about an even game (and has a $20,000 credit line with Caesars), he puts in a decent amount of play each trip, always betting black chips. He'll probably be able to do this for years to come, if he's careful (I've changed some identifying facts for his protection). Most Strip casinos have been continually tightening up their comp policies, but for steadily "losing" old customers, the RFB comp is always available.

Why does Caesars put up with this? Because they think Howie's losing more than he is. Here's how that works. When Howie gets to town, he draws "markers" against his $20,000 credit line, let's say in $1,000 increments. He plays for a while. If he loses, fine—he leaves the table and the bosses have his marker, thinking he's lost all or part of the $1,000. If he wins, he'll stash a black chip or two in his pocket, or change tables several times, pocketing a black chip or two each time.

Let's say he wins $400 and stashes six chips. The bosses think he has only eight chips left and that he can't "buy back" his marker. So, he is noted as "walking with" $800. The bosses in this case are instructed to make notes on high-rollers for their "high-roller computer program;" the bosses note that "Goss left with 8 black," and the computer figures he lost $200. If the bosses somehow neglect to note how many chips Howie leaves with (and this can happen at casinos with a number of high-rollers—Caesars has $500 and $1,000 bettors), the computer will record that Howie lost the entire $1,000. Howie needs to repeat this little routine just several times per trip to make his losses appear much greater (or his wins smaller) than they really are.

How does Howie get rid of the chips? There are several ways. Howie's dating of the gals in the cage helps. During a busy period, they will cash his black chips for him unobserved by the cashier cage managers. Howie told me that once he had a full rack of black chips ($10,000) in his safe deposit box. A gal in the cage unobtrusively slipped him the packages of $100 bills in exchange for the chips and Howie was home free. He makes it a point to "toke" them after each trip as well—perhaps a quarter ($25) or so; not much is required to make a "splash" since rarely are cage employees tipped.

At the end of the trip, Howie may have accumulated $3,000 in markers. He initially would write a check against his Portland bank and give it to the casino to cover his "loss." In the meantime, he's converted his chips to cash, bought a cashier's check, and mailed it to his bank in Portland to cover the check. As his credit became established, he wouldn't write the check to the casino until the beginning of his next trip. Thus, he had the use of the cash in between trips, a cash flow technique that has not been lost on many others as a method of short term financing for businesses, other gambling or whatever. Howie claims it's not a loan, but a gift, saying "I'll owe it to them when I die."

When Howie checks out of the hotel, he signs his comped bill, which may run from $750 to $2,000, and pays for his tips and phone calls—usually with chips. Then, he flies back to Portland until the next trip.

How many people do this? One would think many. But, for some reason, there aren't many non-losing players who capitalize on this. There are many losers who get comped trips, of course, until they run out of money or decide to stop making periodic deposits in Vegas. But most gamblers, by definition, aren't methodical enough to be willing to adhere to a disciplined approach such as Basic Strategy, to say nothing of card counting.

I'll relate two more cases, one player who actually does count and one who thinks he does. Then, we'll discuss how you can capitalize on this opportunity for the "good life."

The Los Angeles Lawyer

Tommy Tucker is from Los Angeles, claims to be a lawyer and I believe he is. Tommy comes to Vegas monthly, he told me, but I suspect it's far more often. He checks into several casinos using a different name at each one. It looks more natural to emulate the typical week-end gambler who stays at a specific hotel and plays there—it seems most have their favorite clubs; each hotel thinks Tommy is its "fish" exclusively.

He has credit lines of $10,000 at each of several casinos. He has bank accounts in different names in Los Angeles and accompanying business cards. Each bank account is paired with a specific casino. Even though identification is required when opening bank accounts, it's not difficult to secure the necessary ID.

The use of different names accomplishes several things. Each time a marker is drawn and paid back, the casinos notify "central credit," a centralized record-keeping agency that records marker activity for players with credit. Having too many entries on a single record would raise suspicions—why is he drawing so many markers on the same week-end in different clubs? Worse yet, the agency would have a written record of the frequency of his trips to Vegas, which are suspiciously greater than those the most hooked of gamblers take. Separate names avoid discovery. There's also a larcenous reason for the multiple identities, as we shall see.

Tommy often brings a girl with him on his trips. It's good cover—he's just another guy in town with his date to see a few shows and do some gambling. And, he doesn't overdo it. He plays blackjack three or four hours a day, varying the casino and varying the shift. He might play graveyard at the Dunes, day shift at Caesars and swing at the MGM Grand or the Flamingo.

I've watched him play on several occasions. He's a good player. He varies his bets well, makes the appropriate deviations from Basic Strategy according to his count and uses conventional surrender appropriately when available, which few players do.

At one club, he poses as an amateur counter, saying things like, "Knew I wouldn't get a blackjack. There were 13 aces out."

He'll also discuss the hands with the pitbosses, particularly when he makes plays that are correct, but seem strange to the pit. For example, he'll say to a floorman (at a single deck double-on-split club), "You won't believe this hand. With $400 out, I split 7's against an 8. Got another 7. Drew three 10's for three 'dead man's hands.' Dealer has a 6 in the hole and busts. Can you believe I won?"

He's way ahead of the game. Yet they let him play. Why? The old chip ruse. He has an unusual way of pulling black chips off the table. He wears denim pants with lots of little pockets sewn in at the seams, almost like a dealer's "sub," discussed in Chapter 16. A chip can be subtly slipped into each pocket undetected. One chip per pocket per session can add up to enough to change a winning session into a losing one.

Tommy has been doing this for about seven years. It's a nice way to make a living—income of several thousand a week and all expenses paid. In one year, he reportedly made $65,000 at a single casino. Very recently, he was finally barred at one casino. But, he got the last word in; he "stiffed" them for a $28,000 marker—the other reason for the multiple names and multiple bank accounts. What's one bad credit rating out of five or six?

The Canadian Doctor

One more story and then I'll explain what steps you should take to arrange free trips to Vegas, with the comps. There's a fellow named Sherwood, a doctor in Montreal, who comes to Vegas. He's convinced that he, too, can beat the game. Sherwood always plays sober, has a serious attitude about the game and is totally disciplined. He rarely has a gal with him; his reason, "Let's face it, you're likely to say something you shouldn't. I date back home. Here, it's business."

Good philosophy. There's only one problem: Sherwood can't play the game. I asked him what count he used. He mumbled something about 2's are minus 1, 3's minus 4, 4's minus 1 and on and on. Even disregarding the fact that the signs are in the wrong direction, the card values are way out-of-line with known weighting.

Sherwood agreed to have me watch him play, but furtively, he insisted, "No reason for us counters to be seen together—bad for cover."

After only 15 minutes, I estimated he was playing at about a 3% disadvantage to the house. He often varied his bet the wrong way and made many common playing errors and some uncommon ones (standing on soft 18 versus a 10, standing on 12 versus a 10, and so on).

He was totally convinced, however, that he could beat the game and he was putting it over on Caesars by getting comped every third week or so. He often flies in on the hotel's private plane, "Caesars' Chariot." Casino managers would do well to fly him in any day of the week. He disappeared from the scene after about eight months; I was surprised that he lasted that long.

The point is that for every good player, there are many who think they can beat the game, but really can't. This is why the casinos are so generous in their hospitality, even though the skillful player with a good act can slip through. The good player can try to look and act like a Sherwood.

How You Can Live The American Fantasy For Free (On Average)

If you're willing to settle for enjoying this treatment while breaking even with the house, on average, you should take a few hours to learn

Basic Strategy. Use the flashcards and practice as I suggest in Chapter 5 so you'll know when you're ready. Concentrate on Las Vegas single deck strategy, because to break even, it's necessary to play single deck. (Single deck clubs with the best shows and restaurants are Caesars, the Sahara, Frontier and Stardust. Other single deck games are at Circus Circus, Maxim's, Silver Slipper, Holiday, Castaways, Royal Americana, Royal Las Vegas and Bingo Palace.)

Although the effort should yield you a break-even in the long run, you need some wherewithal to get it going—about $10,000 in front money. Put the $10,000 in some bank account so that when the casino credit manager calls, your banker will say, "His account is in the low five figures." The $10,000 will give you pretty good protection against the inevitable swings which you will encounter, particularly if your average bet is not more than $100. If you do happen to win on early trips, leave your win in your blackjack fund as further protection against future losing trips—remember, despite these wins, you're playing even with the house.

Now it's time to apply for casino credit. Ask for a "$10,000 line," as they call it. If you go there, dress well and ask with authority. You'll give the bank account number on the credit application they'll provide you. Be sure your banker has time to process the $10,000 deposit. If you do business with a small bank, you might advise your banker of the impending call to check your credit just to make sure there's no slip-up.

Or, you can apply for credit over the phone. Call Murray Gennis at Caesars, Bob Stella, Jr. at the Stardust, Dick Kaydas at the MGM or just ask for the casino manager. You could also go on a formally organized junket, by calling Julie Weintraub of the Dunes in New York City or any of a number of other junket organizers—or call the hotel directly and ask for the junket manager.

Your credit line should take only a few days to clear. Chances are you'll be granted a lower limit of, say, $5,000. Then, call your contact, or ask for a "21" shift manager of the casino manager, and say something like, "I'm John Doe from New Haven. I've got a $5,000 line with you and want to come out next weekend. Can you take care of me?"

Chances are the answer will be an enthusiastic "yes," and your room will be immediately arranged. Because the hotels are tightening up somewhat, they may hedge and say, "Come on in. I'll get you a room. We'll take care of you if you show us the action to warrant it."

Be sure you've practiced Basic Strategy, know it perfectly and fully intend to play it perfectly with *no* deviations and no hunch bets.

When you get to the casino, approach the blackjack table and ask the pitboss for a marker. He'll probably ask your name and date of birth (or mother's maiden name), make a phone call and return with a draft for you to sign. Then, you'll be given chips to play with.

Don't play five hands and run—an often-tried ruse to avoid giving the action, but getting the comps. If you've practiced, you will break even with the house in the long run. You're protected with 100 units and should be able to play safely for extended periods. When you bet $100, do it with black chips, rather than four green ones—it gets more attention and you fall into the "black action" category.

Change tables and take trips to the men's room, each time taking your chips and putting slightly fewer chips on the table when you return. If you bet black, play with other black chip players if possible; you might be able to slip a few black chips into your pocket without being detected. But, be careful and make sure they don't spot this move.

Each time you play, take out another marker, even if you have chips from prior plays. The more chips you have that they don't know about, the more they will over-estimate your loss (or under-estimate your win).

Initially, you'll be able to cash in your chips during crowded periods, such as when the shows break, without being known or spotted—be careful with black chips; they attract attention. Go over to a craps table and break a black chip down, placing a $5 bet on the layout. If you put it on the line, your overall expected loss is only seven cents. Take the resulting red and green chips and cash them out. You can have a friend or someone you trust cash out your chips for you. It's also possible to go to the Horseshoe casino in downtown Vegas, play a few hands and cash in your home chips there—the Horseshoe takes foreign chips.

During your trip, as an RFB guest, you can charge all show, restaurant and bar tabs to your room. If you add tips, you'll be billed for them at the end of the trip. You'll also be charged for phone calls and are expected to pay for any pictures you may have taken in the showrooms. You're a high-roller so you have every right to charge the best meals that are offered and fine wines within limit, perhaps in the $30 to $40 per bottle range. Don't abuse your privileges by taking six people out to dinner or by ordering many bottles of booze through room service. It may come back to haunt you. (One of our BP's put 15 bottles of booze on his tab at the Hilton; he used them for Christmas presents!!! They stood for it because he was a $1,000 per hand player.)

At the end of your trip, take the trouble to thank your host. You might drop a hint that you lost quite a bit; in this case, I wouldn't worry about exaggerating. Even if he knows, a lot of people exaggerate in Vegas, winners and losers, so you'll fit right in. Check out, paying the residual amount of your bill.

When you get home, deposit the cash into your blackjack account (or wire it to your bank if you're not returning directly). Promptly send the casino a check for the amount of markers you drew. You are now on file as a player who showed good action and who (presumably) lost. With your check, you might also drop a note, asking that your line be increased to $10,000. Keep a record of all markers and deposits so the

IRS will know they're "wash" entries.

Before your next trip, call your host. You'll probably find a much warmer reception. After you've repeated the process a few times, you'll find your rooms will turn into suites and your host may even start suggesting that you turn in your airline ticket at the cage for a refund. If your line reaches $20,000 or so, most casinos will be willing to pick up two tickets, one for your spouse or whomever.

A few more tips:

When you ask for comps, act as if you deserve them. Remember, you're a high-roller, the lifeblood of most casinos. Come across like a nice guy—don't be overbearing. Show the bosses some consideration—perhaps a card at Christmas, a box of cigars, something indigenous to your home town (lobsters from Maine, for example), shirts, golf balls and so on. I used to give $100 gift certificates from the fancy men's shops located in the casinos; avoid cash; it's sort of bad form and many casinos forbid its acceptance (although more than one boss, when I asked them what I could do, has said, "You could slip me something.")

Howie carries it a bit farther. He plays golf, ping pong and tennis with casino "execs." He often buys them gifts; his latest gifts were watches from his recent (comped) trip to Aruba.

Be friendly with the dealers and tip them a reasonable amount. If you happen to be counting (more on this in a minute), they may tend to deal a little further into the deck if you're a tipper (of course, you don't want them to know that it matters). Rather than tipping them directly, place bets for them; if your bet requires a double or a split, occasionally do it for the dealer, too. Most people don't, and thus, your gesture will make a favorable and perhaps lasting impression.

Cop chips whenever possible—there will be many opportunities. But, *don't get caught*! That's probably the surest tip-off to the bosses that you're trying something. Once, I suspected that I was observed slipping some chips into my pocket. I waited a while, and when I was sure the boss was looking at me, I pulled out the chips, threw them on the table, and said, "Well, it's time to use the reserves." I was hoping to convince the boss that I was salting away chips for my own idiosyncratic reasons, rather than trying to mislead the pit.

You can keep chips in a safe deposit box—for months if you want. Good customers sometimes have permanent safe deposit boxes in the cage. Be careful how you use the box though. Bosses can and do check the frequency of your visits to your box, since you must sign in every time you use it and the date and time are noted. However, if, like Howie, you get in "tight" with the cage employees, you may not have to sign in.

Become friendly with other high-rolling losers (innocence by association). Howie used to patronize a South American who had a huge credit line with Caesars. The Latin was allowed to bet three hands of $3,000 at blackjack and $4,000 per roll at craps. They even let him turn over the dealer's hole card himself, after he'd played his hand. He now owes Caesars just over a million dollars in unpaid markers, but, is still allowed to play—for cash only.

You can sometimes use your comps to buy yourself more comps. During a Jimmy Conners-Chris Evert tennis match, there was much haggling and strategizing for box seats. Sherwood ended up with two extra tickets—comped, of course. What did he do with them? He graciously bestowed them on one of the shift managers! Now he's owed yet another favor by the boss. The possibilities get almost ludicrous.

Don't feel self-conscious about being seen in Vegas every two or three weeks or so. As you come more often, you'll see an amazing number of familiar faces—losing high-rollers who are simply hooked on gambling. You'll fit right in.

Sometimes, you might feel a little sorry for the bosses or feel guilty about continually getting comped while breaking even or winning. If you do suffer guilt pangs, read Julie Weintraub's story, *Big Julie Of Vegas*, which explains how willingly the bosses cater to the high roller as long as he's losing. Julie tells stories of guys who have literally lost millions in Vegas, were wiped out financially, and then tried to get on another junket. They were met with, "Why should we put up with that free-loader?" The bosses can be tough and ruthless when it comes to running their business.

If you decide you want to earn some money rather than break even, you've got several alternatives. You can take a few hours to learn the ace-five count in Chapter 6. It'll give you a slight edge, perhaps ½%, over the single deck games, which is respectable—the house odds at baccarat are just above 1%. Or you can spend more time and learn the Simple Plus/Minus (also in Chapter 6).

Girls are not hard to find in most lounges unless it's close to election time, when the gendarmes clean up the town temporarily. Read all about them in *The Gals Of Nevada* (38). Some bosses will fix you up and their standards are generally high; however, you're expected to "take care of" the gal yourself. Bellmen at all the major hotels can help you out; the average fee is $100 (less when times are slow in Vegas), of which the bellman gets 40%. Many California gals come to Vegas. The pro's, called "week-end warriors," detested by the local girls, are often far from hard-core; they're secretaries, teachers and other typical gals you might encounter at home. There are, of course, regular non-professional visitors as well; they usually travel in pairs. Stewardesses stay at the Marina Hotel and the Royal Las Vegas.

It's usually not too difficult, especially with black chips, a suite and offers of the best shows in town, to talk many a cocktail waitress, keno runner, cashier or gal dealer into a date—on a nonprofessional basis. Then, there are the dates you can bring to Vegas; her expenses, of course, will be defrayed by your RFB (and eventually her airline ticket, if you work it right). Your social life at home may pick up—a weekend in Vegas to see Sammy Davis, Jr. is a hell of an icebreaker.

A final caution. If you're the Basic Strategy player, adhere to it strictly. Every time you deviate, it will cost you money in the long run. Don't chase your money if you're losing. In your case, the standard advice offered applies: bet bigger when you win and less when you lose. If you're using one of the count methods, exercise the cover precautions discussed in Chapter 17. Make sure that they think you're a loser.

And, the next time you're living the American fantasy in Vegas, say "hello" to Howie for me. You'll recognize him immediately—he'll undoubtedly have a beautiful companion on each arm.

Chapter Twenty-One

Tournament Blackjack
and
Additional Aid

This final chapter deals with two subjects. The first is "tournament blackjack," which is a new phenomenon in the blackjack world, and it is growing rapidly. The second subject is a guide to receiving additional books and instruction in the game of Twenty-one.

Tournament Blackjack

A new concept in blackjack play was introduced in December 1978, at the Las Vegas Sahara Hotel, by an organization called "World Championship of Blackjack, Inc." (WCB). Ed Fishman, the dynamic president of WCB, after some difficulty, persuaded the management of the Las Vegas Sahara to hold a tournament.

The tournament turned out to be highly successful, drawing about 1,400 entries, due in part to the endorsement of Stanley Roberts, and to the support of *Gambling Times Magazine*. Since the tournament was held during one of Las Vegas' slower periods, many additional gamers were drawn to the Sahara, including customers from other casinos. After the tournament, the Sahara officials were anxious to hold additional events of this nature. Tournaments were then held in July 1979 (1,900 entries), in December 1979 (2,500 entries), and at four other times in 1980. $250,000 in prizes was offered for the December 1980 tournament, with $75,000 of it going to the winner. This tournament has also been extended to casinos throughout the world, including Loews' Monte Carlo, which held a tournament in November 1980, with 200,000 francs going to the winner. Aruba was also the site of a blackjack tournament.

While the tournament does not offer a positive expected value to the player, even for the most skilled player, the event has become quite popular because of the excitement the competition offers, and the ego gratification the players derive from family, friends and onlookers who cheer them on. It should be noted that authors of books on the subject, or instructors of blackjack systems, are not eligible to play in a tournament. The entry fee has ranged from $250-to-$275. The Nevada tournament is held simultaneously at all three of the Sahara hotels in Las Vegas, Lake Tahoe and Reno.

Another organization managed to stage a tournament at the Dunes, but it was not well attended. Some other tournaments were scheduled by organizations in Nevada (Circus Circus, Reno), but they could not draw sufficient amounts of players to hold the tournaments.

Should You Play Tournament Blackjack? If you are an active professional blackjack player, it is probably better for you to avoid these tournaments since you could be exposing your identity. The aspiring professional also runs the risk of exposure. The chances you have of winning in these tournaments are more dependent on luck and money management than on skill. However, in the long-run, a skill factor can influence the results to turn in your favor. One of the winners (March 1980) was a graduate of the Stanley Roberts School of Winning Blackjack. He is Avery Waisbren, a Los Angeles businessman. The runner-up in the first tournament, Norman Hem, an airline pilot, was also a Stanley Roberts graduate. Two others of the six finalists in that tournament also claimed to be card counters. You will have to make the judgment as to whether or not the possible exposure is worth the potential rewards. Since everyone who reads this book is not a professional, those who are should have the benefit of the best advice available on how to play.

WCB Tournament Procedures. The players are randomly assigned tournament blackjack tables and starting times. All tournament rounds last two hours and have one ten-minute break.

At the beginnning of each round, the players buy in for $500 in chips; no additional buy-ins are allowed. Special tournament chips are used. The player at each table who holds the most money at the end of the two-hour period is declared the winner for that table, and he is entitled to advance to the next round.

There are three rounds, then a semi-final round, then the final round. Although it depends on the total number of players enrolled in the tournament, usually six players play at the first three rounds, and usually seven players compete at each table in the semi-final round. In the final round, only three players compete with each other. The player who holds the most money at the end of the final round is declared the "Champion," and he is awarded the prize money.

Rules Of Play. Las Vegas Strip rules apply for the tournaments. The player may double-down on two cards, split any pair or re-split pairs. The dealer must stand on soft 17. In Nevada, single decks are dealt face-up; in Monte Carlo, four decks are used. A rotating marker is used to determine the betting and dealing order. The player who is sitting in front of the marker begins the betting and the other players bet in turn. The minimum bet is $5, and the maximum bet is $500.

How To Play Tournament Blackjack.

The material that follows is a condensed version of a lecture which Stanley Roberts gave just prior to the first WCB Blackjack Tournament. A considerable amount of research by Roberts' staff preceded the discussion. Those who attended the class indicated that the principles expressed did, indeed, bear out in tournament play. Further interviews with the tournament winners, which appeared in *Gambling Times Magazine*, further indicated that the following approach holds merit:

Persons who enter the tournament should adopt a focused view of their purpose, i.e., they should realize that there is only one reason to be there and that is to win. If you want to play blackjack you can do it at your own pace, in your own time, without the constraints of the rules of the tournament. Since you are there for that purpose, you should be prepared to risk your entire stake, or whatever you may have in front of you, at the appropriate time, if there is any feasible way that you can win your round. If it is clear to you that you're out, you should withdraw from play, and save your remaining chips for a later time.

There are three major factors that will affect the outcome. These are: luck, betting strategy (money management), and skill—in that order. Since luck is not a factor we can measure, we can deal only with the other variables.

Although there are seven levels, ranging from totally unskilled to expert, for the purpose of this discussion we can refer to tournament players as unskilled, Basic Strategy players, or skilled player. It is unlikely for someone who does not play close to Basic Strategy (or better) to win the tournament. This statement is borne out by the results. So, I suggest that all of the readers of this book refrain from entering a tournament—at least until they have the Basic Strategy from Chapter Five under their belts. If you happen to be a skilled player, then you can use your best-learned strategy for your play.

There are times when the correct strategy, be it basic or expert, becomes subject to exceptions to the rule. These exceptions will invariably involve the last hand or two. For example, in one dramatic play, a heads-up player was dealt a blackjack on the final hand. Her payoff would have left her without sufficient sums to beat one other opponent. She alertly doubled-down on the blackjack, thereby wining the hand, and the round. Of course, one doesn't need a blackjack to do this. You can double-down on any two cards, even a hard 19, should that be your only way to win.

Tournament Conditions. When playing in the first round, one can anticipate between 50 and 75 hands per hour. If there are early "bustouts," then that number can be increased. The game is generally dealt in two rounds, then the deck is shuffled. Thus, you will only have available information for betting purposes on the second of the two rounds. Including the dealer's hand, the average number of hands dealt will vary between 700 and 1,000 during the less-than-two hours of play. The exact number will depend upon the speed and skill of the dealer and the relative skill level of the players. Good players will play more quickly than poor players, as a rule. Knowing the approximate number of hands you will play can influence your betting strategy as you move toward the final few rounds.

General Guidelines. A few general rules on casino comportment during the tournament should be observed. First, do not drink alcoholic beverages before or during your round of play, or during any following rounds you may be in. You want to be as alert as possible, so, it is well to refrain from all excesses—that includes not overeating the delicious gourmet foods available.

Remember that you are out to devastate the other players. They are your opponents in the tournament, so friendships should be reserved for after the game. Do not do anything to interrupt your concentration; this includes excessive conversation with other players or dealers. Be pleasant, smile, say hello, relax and try to be an all-around nice person. But remember, you are out to win.

Refrain from commenting on the play or actions of other players. The one exception might be if you are sufficiently behind near the end of play and would like to get the leaders to try to play loosely in hopes they will have their bankrolls reduced to your level. In that case, quietly point out how much each of them has or, at least, who is leading. Use gamesmanship to get the others to challenge the leader. This, of course, can backfire if one of the players should get lucky. On the other hand, if you are far behind, the chances of winning are remote.

Do not toke the dealer until the round is over, after all the chips have been counted. You could toke yourself right out of the prize.

Be aware of the time since you will have to stop when the bell rings. This is particularly important in the final hour.

If you stay in the contest until the end, you should be very aware of the amount of money each of the remaining players has. You must know your own count as well. Keep your checks messy, if you can get away with it, to keep the other players from estimating how much you have. Such a move will not be allowed in the finals, since the chips are placed in one of three appropriately colored circles ($5, $25, $100). Your final bets must anticipate the end result. This requires an alert mind and a keen eye. Many people have lost their rounds by making an insufficient bet or by making too large a bet at the end.

310

Know when you are scheduled to play for each round you may be in. If you can, get a good night's rest or a brief nap prior to your round. Be careful not to oversleep or you will be out. Use the hotel's wake-up service *and* an alarm clock to insure you will not miss out.

Playing Theory. There are two opposite playing postures: aggressive and conservative. Playing theory rides on the supposed "luck" of the dealer. If one plays a conservative game and the dealer is "hot," the other players will all lose more money, leaving the winner with smaller losses than the rest.

One who assumes the aggressive posture bets more money when the dealer is "cold," therefore winning more money than the other players, and, thus, winning the round. Aggressive play has invariably been the most productive, based upon the results of the tournament. It has been shown that most table winners end up with more than their original $500 stake. This percentage is well over 75%. Since you must go through four-to-six rounds of play to win, it is unlikely that a conservative posture will out in the end, or that you will make it to the finals. Further, the distribution of winning hands does not usually dictate that every player will beat the dealer or that every player will lose to the dealer in the short span of time of the tournament round. It is clear that an aggressive posture, or at least a moderately aggressive posture, is proper for the tournament.

Betting Strategy. Tournament blackjack contains many of the elements of poker. How you manipulate your opponents, causing them to make mistakes in betting and playing, can result in a victory for you. The best way to confuse your opponents is with your own bets. Be sure to bet in turn, in accordance with the position of the marker. Use your position, with relation to your closest opponents, to advantage. You may also try to fool them, toward the very end, by fingering your chips, making them think that you are going to make a smaller or larger bet than you really intend, prior to your actually making that bet.

Think of the time involved as four distinct periods: the first hour, the third half-hour, the fourth half-hour and the last three hands. The chart below shows a proposed posture and bet range based upon skill level. Also shown is a desirable goal, should you be fortunate enough to achieve it, where you can feel reasonably ahead of the pack and can afford to play a conservative game.

If you are not a card counter, generally, a good strategy is to bet more on the second round of cards than on the first. This is because the deck may become favorable on the later round, whereas it is nearly even on the first round.

311

Table 21-1

Tournament Blackjack Suggested Betting Ranges

Time	Basic Strategy Player		Skilled Player		Desirable Goal
	Posture	Bet Range	Posture	Bet Range	
1st hour	Moderate	$25-$50	Easy	$5-$50	4x closest opponent
3rd quarter	Strong	$25-$100	Paced	$10-$100	10x closest opponent
4th quarter	Caution	$5-$25	Strong	$5-$500*	2x closest opponent or $3,000 + $5/hand left
Last 3 hands	Plunge if necessary (or sit back and pray)				$3,000 + $15

*unless ahead with good lead

In the last three hands, you will want to consider making exceptions to proper play. These exceptions include not doubling or splitting when you are ahead, to avoid the risk of losing additional capital, or doubling and splitting when it is not indicated, if you are behind (in hopes that the dealer will lose). You may also make your decision regarding insurance with consideration of your eventual bankroll, as opposed to using properly indicated play.

Naturals cannot be predicted; they come only once in every 21 hands, on average. You may consider making your last bet with the understanding of the possible effect of a natural on your opponents' bets. Remember, if you cannot possibly win, then you should withdraw at the end. If there is any way that you can win, bet everything that you can.

Brochures and entry blanks for the WCB tournaments may be obtained by calling toll free (800) 462-0469 from Pennsylvania or (800) 523-4621 from any other state.

Additional Aids And Learning Material

Several recommended items are available to the reader. These may be purchased by writing to the addresses provided or by calling the telephone numbers indicated.

FLASHCARDS

A complete set of flashcards, covering every system described in this book, is available on index cardboard stock. This kit contains Basic Strategy flashcards for the following places:

1. Harrah's, Sahara, Harvey's (Reno-Tahoe)
2. MGM Grand (Reno-special rules)

3. Sahara, Circus Circus, Stardust
   (Vegas single deck)
4. Caesars (Vegas single deck)
5. Sands, Frontier, Aladdin, Hilton,
   Tropicana (Vegas multiple deck)
6. MGM Grand (Vegas)
7. Dunes (Vegas)
8. Freeport and Paradise Island
   (Bahamas)
9. Atlantic City
10. Double exposure (Vegas-Reno)

The kit also contains flashcards for the following Uston systems:

11. Uston Simple Plus/Minus
12. Uston Advanced Plus/Minus
13. Uston Advanced Point Count

To purchase this kit, send $9.95 (includes postage and handling) to:

SRS Enterprises, Inc.
Attn: Uston Flashcards
1018 N. Cole Ave.
Hollywood, CA 90038

INSTRUCTION

Uston Institute of Blackjack—tuition $495. This class on blackjack is taught by Ken Uston or one of his teammates. The course includes Basic Strategy, and Simple and Advanced Point Counts. The class enables the serious student to become a competent professional card counter. Courses are taught in most major cities by scheduling. Class size is usually from 3-to-5 students. Additional information about the course may be obtained by calling the Uston Institute of Blackjack TOLL FREE number at (800) 523-4621. In Pennsylvania, call (800) 462-0469.

Stanley Roberts School of Winning Blackjack—tuition $595. This course in advanced level blackjack lasts for several days and is designed to teach winning skills to the average person. The course includes Basic and Advanced Strategy. Courses are taught from fixed school locations in Los Angeles, San Diego, San Francisco, Sacramento, Reno, Las Vegas, Dallas, Fort Lauderdale, New York, New Jersey, Chicago and Detroit. . .or by fly-in sessions. Class size varies from 2-to-7 students. Additional information about the course may be obtained by calling TOLL FREE (800) 421-3102. In California, call (800) 252-2089.

> **The following items may be obtained from the**
> **Uston Institute**
> **P.O. Box 1949**
> **Philadelphia, PA 19105**
>
> **or**
> **Call Toll Free (800) 523-4621.**
> **In Pennsylvania,**
> **Call Toll Free (800) 462-0469.**

The Big Player—$10.95 (includes postage). This is Ken Uston's first book. The story is the exciting drama of how the world's first major blackjack team won a million dollars by using team play. It is being made into a major motion picture by Dale Crase-Frank Capra, Jr. Productions. See below for further movie details.

The Uston—$10.95 (includes postage). This device, which is the "ultimate" in blackjack Basic Strategy, will make a beginner or a non-player into a perfect Basic Strategy player after only a few minutes of practice. It is a heavy duty, circular plastic calculating device pinpointing the optimum strategy for blackjack play. It easily fits into a breast pocket or handbag. This device actually will give the player a slight edge over the casinos in Atlantic City. It is accompanied by a booklet, *Dollars and Sense*, which explains how to use THE USTON. Versions for other than Atlantic City are currently under development.

Blackjack Video Cassette. "Beat the house at Blackjack," by Ken Uston, is recorded in full color. When ordering, specify VHS or Beta format. Side 1 is 1¼ hours long and includes Basic Strategy for Reno, Las Vegas and Atlantic City. Side 2 is ¾ of an hour long and includes the Uston Simple Plus/Minus count, and a simple counting system designed for the part-time, non-professional player. This is a Video presentation, by Ken Uston, of the material contained in this book as stated above.

Ken Uston's Blackjack Newsletter—$30 per year. This is a bimonthly newsletter that identifies new developments, rules changes and timely topics. Subscribers may send a self-addressed stamped envelope for Ken to answer questions concerning blackjack. Up to five questions per subscription are allowed.

GAMBLING TIMES MAGAZINE
($29 per year for 12 issues)

This is the world's foremost periodical on gaming. It contains regular articles by such authorities as Edward O. Thorp, Stanley Roberts, Ken Uston, and all of the other well-known experts. The Gambling Times Bookshelf and Systems Shop offers most recommended books and systems to subscribers at a 10% discount. 1018 N. Cole Ave., Hollywood, CA 90038.

MOTION PICTURE

"The Big Player," a major motion picture based on the life of Ken Uston, the world's premier blackjack player, was announced at the 1980 Cannes Film Festival by producers Dale Crase and Frank Capra, Jr. Award-winning screenwriter Howard Rodman is now completing the screenplay of "The Big Player." The part of Ken Uston will be played by an international star. The independently-financed feature will be filmed in mid-1981, and has a budget of $10 million. Principal photography will include scenes in Las Vegas, Reno, Atlantic City and San Francisco and international locations in Monaco (Monte Carlo), France, England and the Bahamas.

Uston has been banned from the blackjack tables in Atlantic City, because of his proficiency as a winning blackjack player. Prior to that, he was barred from a majority of major casinos in Las Vegas. Subsequently, he has filed lawsuits of $85 million against these casinos. While litigation continues, Uston still plays blackjack discreetly, with the aid of makeup disguises and aliases.

Dale Crase Productions has acquired all film rights to Uston's biography. For further information contact Dale Crase Productions, 850 Townsend Street, San Francisco, CA 94107.

Appendix A

A Dictionary of Terms and Jargon in the Blackjack Business

As in other professions, a language unique to blackjack, to card counting, to team operations and to hole card play has evolved through the years. The terms below, used in this book and defined when first introduced, are also defined in this glossary for ready reference by the reader.

Ace Adjustment—Adjusting for the proportion of aces remaining to be played, in order to determine bet size.

Ace Adjustment Factor—The number specified by advanced card-counting systems to be multiplied by the number of aces rich or aces poor, in order to adjust the running count for betting purposes.

Ace-Poor—When there is a lower than average proportion of aces remaining to be played; favors the house.

Ace-Rich—When there is a higher than average proportion of aces remaining to be played; favors the player.

Action—The total dollar amount bet by the player(s) on all hands played.

Adjusted Running Count—The value of the running count, adjusted to reflect the number of aces rich or poor.

BP—"Big Player." The member of a team who "bets the money," or makes the big bets. Often supported by ancillary members who may bet small amounts, or not play at all.

Back-Counting—Counting down a deck or shoe, but not playing the table; usually standing in back of the players.

Bank—The playing stake of a player or team.

Bar—To exclude a player from a casino, or prevent him from playing a table game, almost always blackjack.

Basic Strategy—The optimum way for the blackjack player to play his hands if he's not counting, given a prescribed set of house rules; also called "Basic."

Betting Ratio—The mathematical ratio between the highest and the lowest bets placed by a player.

Betting True Count—The value of the true count, adjusted to reflect the number of aces rich or poor.

Black—$100 chips, generally black in color.

Blackjack—An ace and ten-valued card on the first two cards dealt; also called a "natural" or "snapper."

Bop—To jump from table to table, as decks or shoes become favorable to the player. The hot deck is signalled by a counter at each table.

Break It Down—To cut chips into countable piles, or to separate them into colors.

Break The Bank—To distribute the net monetary results of a blackjack effort to the members of a blackjack team.

Burn—(verb) The dealer's act of removing the first (or more) cards after the shuffle and placing it (them) in the discard pile or at the bottom of the deck.

Bust—To exceed a playing total of "21."

Caddy Blackjack—A private blackjack game, popular in the Northeast, where the deal rotates from player to player. Under the proper conditions, it can offer a more attractive opportunity for the skilled player than can casino blackjack.

Cage—Location of the casino cashier.

Call Bet—A bet made without money or chips (usually allowed only to customers with excellent casino credit, or with money in the cage).

Call-In Numbers—Pre-determined numbers representing the running count (adjusted for aces in counts which require a side count of aces) used by the counter to summon a Big Player to his table.

Call Plays—To count and signal a blackjack player how much to bet and how to play his hands.

Card Eat—To spread to multiple hands in order to cause more cards to be dealt (usually done with small bets in minus counts).

Check—Gambling chip; used primarily by casino employees.

Chunk—To bet large; sometimes, to over-bet.

Cold Deck—A deck or decks unfavorable to the player, that is, with a high minus count. Also, a deck(s) in prearranged sequence inserted into play by cheating players (also called a "cooler.")

Comp—(noun) The privilege of using casino-hotel services free-of-charge (complimentarily). (verb) To give a player, usually a high-roller, complimentary services in a hotel-casino.

Conversion Factor (CF)—The number by which the running count is divided (sometimes multiplied) to derive the true count. It is generally equal either to the number of full decks or half-decks that have not been put into play.

Count—(noun) Usually used to refer to the running count, which is the cumulative value of all cards played at any given time, based on a set of preassigned values for each card denomination.

Counter—A player who uses a counting system to keep track of the type of cards played, in order to determine whether the deck is favorable or unfavorable to the player.

Cover—Measures used by counters to disguise from casino personnel that they are counting.

Cover Bet—A bet made by the counter to disguise from pit-bosses the fact that the player is counting (such as a large bet off-the-top, a small bet with a favorable count, or a large bet with an unfavorable count).

Cover Play—A play of the hand (usually a strategy error) made by a counter to disguise from the pitbosses the fact that he is counting.

Cutcard—A card, usually a solid colored piece of plastic, which is inserted into the cards in a deck or shoe to determine when the pack will be shuffled.

Dealer—An employee of the casino who deals the cards, makes payoffs, sees the rules are followed at his table and plays the house cards in accordance with a fixed specified set of instructions.

Double Deck—A blackjack game played with two decks of cards.

Double-Down—An option that allows the player to double the value of his bet after looking at his (usually) first two cards. He is dealt one additional card.

Double Exposure—A blackjack game in which both dealer cards are shown to the player before the player plays his hand; other rules are changed to restore to the house the overall edge in most such games.

Double The Bank—The goal of most card counters or teams: to double the original playing stake. The bank is often broken at this point.

319

Drop—The total amount of cash plus the value of markers drawn at a table game (or for a shift, or an entire casino).

Dumping Off—The act, by a cheating dealer, of causing house money to be given to a player, usually a confederate or agent, by overpaying bets and other techniques.

Early Surrender—The player option of giving up half of the bet before the dealer checks to determine whether he has a blackjack.

Element-Of-Ruin—The percentage likelihood that the player(s) will lose his (their) bank.

Expected Value—The dollar amount that the player(s) should win (or lose) if encountering "average luck," that is, in exact accordance with the statistical advantage or disadvantage to the house.

Fill—The act of bringing additional checks to the table to replenish the dealer's rack.

First Base—The far right-hand seat on the blackjack table. (First player to receive cards.)

Five-Card Charlie—A bonus popular in caddy blackjack where a five card total equal to or less than 21 pays the player 2-to-1.

Flash—To show a card, usually a dealer's hole card.

Flat Bet—(verb) To bet the same amount on each hand played. Usually done for cover purposes or in a hole card game.

Floorman—The lowest echelon of pit personnel supervising a casino table game.

Foreign Checks—Checks from another casino.

Front-Loader—A careless dealer who exposes the hole card in the process of dealing.

Front-Loading—Observing the value of the dealer's hole card as it is inadvertently exposed during the process of dealing by a careless dealer.

Gorilla BP—A non-counting player who receives signals from a counter. He's a "gorilla" because he need not know how to win at blackjack, yet he's playing with an edge over the house.

Green—$25 chips (usually green in color).

Griffin Agent—An employee of the Griffin Detective Agency who is hired by numerous casinos to detect slot cheats, dishonest employees, and, alas, card counters.

Hard Hand—A hand without an ace that can be counted as "11."

Heat—Actions or statements by casino personnel that lead the player to believe he is suspected of being a counter; also applicable to hole card players and cheats.

Hit—(verb) To request another card from the dealer.

Head-On—(adverb) Playing alone with the dealer as the only player at the table. Also, head-up.

Hold—The ratio between the win (amount won by the house) and the drop.

Hole Card—The dealer's bottom card, usually dealt face down and not exposed until after the players have played their hands.

Hole Card Play—(noun) A blackjack play, often involving more than one person, which is based on the player having knowledge of the dealer's hole card, such as, but not limited to, front-loading and spooking.

Hot Deck—A deck or shoe favorable to the player.

Hustling—Hinting, or asking a player, for a tip or a gift (done by some dealers and also by girls who make their living at this).

Index—The number in the upper left-hand and lower right-hand corners of a playing card which designates its denomination.

Insurance—A side bet when the dealer has an ace upcard that (usually) equals up to half of the player's original wager. If the dealer has blackjack, the house pays 2-to-1; if the dealer does not have blackjack, the player loses.

Insurance Counter—A player who uses a special count, perfect for the insurance bet. He often signals the correct insurance play to another counter, who is playing a different system.

Joint Bank—An arrangement where two or more players combine resources and play jointly off the total amount, sharing in the win or loss.

Leak—(noun) A dealer weakness, such as exposing a hole card or overpaying the bettor.

Loader—A front-loader; a careless dealer who exposes the hole card in the process of dealing.

Marker—A special casino check or draft used by the gambler to draw chips against his credit or money on deposit in the casino cage.

Mechanic—A cheating dealer; generally one who deals seconds.

Minus Count—A cumulative negative count of the cards placed in play; tends to be to the disadvantage of the player.

Multiple Deck—A blackjack game played with two or more decks of cards; usually four or six decks.

Natural—A blackjack or "snapper:" that is, an ace and a ten-valued card.

Negative Swing—A period, usually extended, during which the player(s) shows a loss.

Nickels—$5 chips.

Off-the-Top—At the beginning of a deck or shoe, immediately after the shuffle.

Office—A signal in a casino or during a gambling game.

On-The-Rail—Observing a gambling game, but not playing it; in blackjack, usually from behind the players (in poker, usually behind a rail that separates the players from the spectators).

On-The-Square—On the up-and-up; fair.

Outside Man—A casino employee who surreptitiously observes from outside the pit, usually pretending to be a patron. To casino employees: a non-casino employee, usually a cheat.

Paint—A jack, queen or king (sometimes, also a 10).

Pair Splitting—Two cards of the same value, or two ten-valued cards when they may be split.

Pat—A hand totalling 17 through 21.

Peek Freak—A disparaging term used by casino personnel to describe a hole card player.

Pips—The suited designs on a playing card that indicate the denomination of the card.

Pitboss—A casino official who supervises play at a group of gaming tables; often supervises the activities of several floormen.

Preferential Shuffling—The action by a dealer of shuffling up decks positive to the player, and dealing out decks negative to the player.

Pull Up A Play—To call off a play in the casino, usually a counting or hole card play. Usually accomplished by one player furtively signalling another.

Push—A tie or stand-off, in which the player neither wins or loses.

Quarters—$25 chips.

Readable Dealer—A dealer whose hole card can be spotted by a player or other person in a casino.

Red—$5 chips.

Relay—A person who relays signals from one person to another, in a casino.

Rubber Band—A system of assigning dealers to table games when the dealers are not assigned a specific table during their shift (so-called because a rubber band is often placed around a clip-board under the name of the last dealer assigned).

Running Count—The cumulative value of all cards played at any given time, based on a set of preassigned values for each card denomination.

Scam—A method for bilking a gambling (or other) opponent.

Seconds—Not dealing the top card from the deck; a form of cheating.

Shill—A casino employee who plays to generate business for a casino game; in baccarat, called a starter.

Shoe—A container used to hold undealt cards, usually used when four or more decks are used.

Short Shoe—A pack of cards dealt from a shoe which is not composed of complete decks; usually 10's have been taken out (or 4's or 5's added) to the benefit of the cheating house.

Silver—Silver dollars or $1 gaming tokens.

Single Deck—A blackjack game played with one deck, almost always hand-held by the dealer.

Six Deck—A blackjack game played with six decks, dealt from a shoe.

Sky—An area above the main casino where play is observed through one-way mirrors. Also, the employee(s) assigned to work in such an area; also called "eye-in-the-sky."

Snapper—A blackjack, or natural.

Soft Hand—A hand with an ace which can be valued as "11."

Split—An option allowing the player to make two cards of identical value into two hands, betting an amount equal to the original wager on the second card.

Spook—A person who reads the hole card in a spooking play.

Spooking—Spotting the dealer's hole card from the rear, when the dealer checks to see if he has a blackjack, and signalling that information to a player at the dealer's table.

Spread—To bet more than one hand, as "to spread to three hands of $500."

Stacked Deck—A pre-arranged sequence of cards used to cheat players.

Stand—A player's decision not to draw additional cards.

Steaming—Betting higher and higher, usually after a series of losing hands. The out-of-control steamer is the pitboss' delight.

Stiff—A hand which has a small chance of winning, usually one totalling 12 through 16.

Strike Number—The plus or minus count in a counting system at which the size of the bet or the play of the hand is varied.

Take It Off From The Inside—The act of stealing from the house by casino personnel.

Take-Off Man—The player, usually in a spooking or cheating operation, who bets the big money.

Tap Out—To lose one's total bank.

Third Base—The far left-hand seat on the blackjack table. (Last player before the dealer.)

Toke—A tip to the dealer, or to other casino employees.

True Count—The running count adjusted for the number of cards or decks remaining to be played. Also called the "true."

Upcard—The dealer's card which is exposed to the player.

Upsidedown 7—A 7 card, of which only the portion of the face without the center pip is visible; it thus resembles a 6. Used in hole card play.

Window—The space, usually between the left side of the (right-handed) dealer's body and his left upper-arm, through which the value of his hole card is seen when he checks to see if he has a blackjack. A spooking term.

Wired—To have a good hand, usually a 20.

Appendix B

Evaluation of Blackjack Literature and Schools

The variation in the quality of books on blackjack has led to widespread reader confusion. Because of this, I am including a section on books that I recommend to the student of blackjack. I have commented briefly on each. The reader is cautioned that I have also listed books and systems which I emphatically do *not* recommend, either because the Basic Strategy is incorrect or the betting strategies recommended constitute some form of fallacious progressive betting system. Following this is an evaluation of other references that were either referred to in this text or which may be of general interest to the student of blackjack or of gaming in general. Finally, an evaluation of most blackjack schools is included.

Recommended Books On Blackjack
(listed chronologically)

Serious students of blackjack should probably have the following in their library:

1. Thorp, Edward O. *Beat The Dealer, A Winning Strategy For The Game Of Twenty-One.* New York: Random House, 1966 (earlier version: 1962).

    The book that started it all. Interesting anecdotes about conditions in the 1960's. The 1966 version has a practical point count, later revised by Braun. The book is outdated, but it's still enlightening reading.

2. Wilson, Allan N. *The Casino Gambler's Guide.* New York: Harper and Row, 1970 (earlier version: 1965).
    The first knowledgeable treatment of element-of-ruin and betting strategy; many of the formulas are still valid.

3. Revere, Lawrence. *Playing Blackjack As A Business.* Secaucus, N.J.: Lyle Stuart, 1971 (revised versions: 1973, 1975, 1977, 1979).

   A definite advance in the state-of-the-art. Informative statistical tables and color-coded Basic Strategy tables that some find helpful. Now out-of-date (later versions have only minor changes). For years, it was "must reading" for the serious student of the game.

4. Roberts, Stanley. *Winning Blackjack.* Los Angeles: Scientific Research Services, 1971.

   An effective counting system and good advice on cheating and conduct within the casino. No. 1 best seller in this field in terms of dollars—has grossed over $2,000,000 in sales.

5. Staff of "Rouge Et Noir." *Winning At Casino Gaming.* Glen Head, N.Y.: Rouge Et Noir, Inc., 1975.

   Basic coverage of blackjack and in-depth coverage of other gambling games. Extensive review of gambling in foreign countries which is somewhat out-of-date.

6. Andersen, Ian. *Turning The Tables On Las Vegas.* New York: Vanguard, 1976.

   An excellent, readable book. Helpful recommendations for establishing cover and the "act." The system per se is weak. Good coverage of Las Vegas poker games.

7. Uston, Ken. *One-third Of A Shoe* and *How You Can Win At Blackjack.* P.O. Box 1949, Philadelphia, PA 19105: Uston Institute of Blackjack, 1979. ($10.95)

   A narration of the January 1979 Atlantic City "counter convention," a primer of Basic Strategy and an ace-five count, and a discussion of the legal issues in the barring-of-counters litigation. The technical data relating to the material in these two books are contained in *Million Dollar Blackjack.*

8. Braun, Julian H. *How To Play Winning Blackjack.* Chicago: Data House, 1980.

   A clear exposition of Basic Strategy and the Braun count. Effective graphics. An intellectually honest book.

9. Humble, Lance, and Cooper, Carl. *The World's Greatest Blackjack Book.* New York: Doubleday, 1980.

   Good coverage of the game. Loses credibility because it is overtitled. Hi Opt I is over-rated and the extent of cheating is over-stated. But, in sum, an accurate book. Recommended.

Books And Systems—Not Recommended

The following books or systems give incorrect Basic Strategy or betting advice. Be careful!

Books

10. Chin, S.Y. *Understanding And Winning Casino Blackjack.* New York: Vantage, 1980.

11. Donatelli, Dante A. *Blackjack—Total Profit Strategy.* Greenburg, Pa.: Mar Lee Enterprises, 1979.

12. Goodman, Mike. *How To Win At Cards, Dice, Races and Roulette.* Los Angeles: Holloway House, 1963.

13. Goodman, Mike. *Your Best Bet.* Northridge, Calif.: Brooke House, 1975

14. Guild, Leo. *The World's Greatest Gambling System.* Los Angeles: Holloway House, 1970.

15. Riddle, Major A., and Hyams, Joe. *The Weekend Gambler's Handbook.* New York: Random House, 1963.

16. Scarne, John. *Scarne's Complete Guide To Gambling.* New York: Simon and Schuster, 1961, 1974.

Systems

17. *Atvada Proven Method Of Play,* Atvada Associates, San Francisco, Calif.

18. *Aus The Boss Blackjack System,* Computerized Systems Institute, Century City, Calif.

19. *Win At Blackjack,* Mel Grant, Alhambra, Calif.

There is a host of others—not worth mentioning— which are deservedly out of business, but may appear again at another time or in another form. *Caveat Emptor!*

Other Books And Systems Of Interest

20. Archer, John. *The Archer Method Of Winning At 21.* Hollywood, Calif: Wilshire, 1978.

    Information is basically accurate as far as it goes. Discusses the Roberts or Insurance Count (ten's—2 and non-tens +1). Not useful for Atlantic City.

21. Baldwin, Roger, et. al. *Playing Blackjack To Win: A New Strategy For The Game Of 21.* New York: M. Barrows, 1957.

    The first published version of a Basic Strategy, the precursor to Thorp's book. Now out-of-print, a collector's item.

22. Canfield, Richard A. *Blackjack, Your Way To Riches.* Secaucus, N.J.: Lyle Stuart, 1979.

    An interesting book by a former pitboss in association with

others. The author is currently running a blackjack school in the Sacramento, Calif. area.

23. Collver, Donald L. *Scientific Blackjack*. New York: Arco, 1977.
    Contains a 3-register counting system. The author used hand calculations to arrive at his strategy. The material is difficult to use and the casino information is out-of-date.

24. Einstein, Charles. *How To Win At Blackjack*. New York: Cornerstone, 1971.
    First publication of the Hi Opt values. Out-of-date.

25. Epstein, Richard A. *The Theory Of Gambling And Statistical Logic*. New York: Academic Press, 1977.
    An exhaustive, theoretical exposition of the statistics of blackjack and other gambling games.

26. Friedman, Bill. *Casino Management*. Secaucus, N.J.: Lyle Stuart, 1974.
    Comprehensive discussion of casino administrative procedures. Must reading for the aspiring casino manager.

27. Griffin, Peter A. *The Theory Of Blackjack*. Las Vegas: GBC Press, 1979.
    A technical and theoretical discussion of the mathematics underlying blackjack interlaced with an occasional practical gem. An honest, responsible text. To follow it, you must understand higher mathematics.

28. Humble, Lance. *Blackjack Gold*. Toronto: International Gaming, 1976.
    Basic coverage of the game, with computer support by Julian Braun. Extensiveness of cheating is way over-stated and cover tips are a bit naive. No advanced strategy is included.

29. Humble, Lance. *Blackjack Super Gold*. Toronto: International Gaming, 1979.
    Same as *Blackjack Gold*, with some new material.

30. Ita, Koko. *21 Counting Methods To Beat 21*. Las Vegas: GBC Press, 1976.
    Includes methods to physically keep track of the count; some intentionally humorous methods not meant to be taken seriously.

31. Mitchell D. Howard. *DHM Professional System*. Available though Gambling Times Systems Shop.
    A sound, professional-level system, particularly good for multiple deck play.

32. Mitchell, D. Howard. *DHM Simplified System*. Available through Gambling Times Systems Shop.
    A simplified and less expensive version of the above.

33. Noir, Jacques. *Casino Holiday.* Berkeley, Calif.: Oxford Press, 1968, 1970.

    Simple one-two count included. Quality of advice to players is mixed. Excellent graphics.

34. Patterson, Jerry L. *A Winner's Handbook.* Vorhees, N.J.: Echelon, 1977.

    An evaluation of available blackjack systems, books and periodicals.

35. Patterson, Jerry L. *Blackjack's Winning Formula.* Vorhees, N.J.: Casino Gaming Specialists, 1980.

    A responsible book written for the beginning player, with a simple high-low count and tens count.

36. Smith, Harold S. *I Want To Quit Winners.* Englewood Cliffs, N.J.: Prentice-Hall, 1961.

    A revealing insight into the life of a gambler and casino owner. Totally non-technical.

37. Uston, Ken, with Rapoport, Roger. *The Big Player.* New York: Holt, Rinehart & Winston, 1977.

    A non-technical narration of Team 1 and the team approach. (To be made into a major motion picture by Frank Capra, Jr. and Dale Crase, producers.)

38. Vogliotti, Gabriel R. *The Girls Of Nevada.* Greenwich, Conn.: Fawcett, 1975.

    The title tells it all. Enjoyable reading and informative.

39. Wong, Stanford. *Professional Blackjack.* Las Vegas: GBC Press, 1977, 1980.

    Correct Basic Strategy, an adaptation of the Thorp point count subsequently refined by Julian Braun (8), and a multi-level "halves" count.

40. Wong, Stanford. *Winning Without Counting.* Pi Yee Press, 1978.

    Misleading title; most techniques do not give the player an edge without counting. Warping is over-rated and over-emphasized. Discussion of front-loading and spooking is superficial. Book is over-priced.

Evaluation of Blackjack Schools

Because of the mounting interest in blackjack—it's the most popular casino table game and the most widely played card game in the world—and due to the opening of casinos in Atlantic City (in the midst of the largest megalopolis in the world), more and more blackjack schools are being formed. This section discusses some of the larger schools in existence and evaluates them.

The Uston Institute of Blackjack. With two teammates, I have
been teaching over the past six years, as time permits. We cover
both the Simple Count and the Uston Advanced Point Count; if a
student has started down the road using Hi Opt I or II or some
other responsible system, we instruct him as well (only the card
values and table numbers differ; the techniques are identical).

The seminar has from three-to-five students, lasts as long as
necessary to cover all the material in one session (usually four-to-six
hours), and costs $495. We teach on Tuesdays in Los Angeles and on
the first week of each month in cities around the country (usually in
Chicago, New York and Atlantic City).

Address: P.O. Box 1949, Philadelphia, PA. 19105.

Stanley Roberts School of Winning Blackjack. The Roberts
School teaches the two-level count (tens are—2; all other cards are
+1), contained in Roberts' book, *Winning Blackjack*. The class includes two days of instruction in small groups—cost is $595. The
school is conducted in Los Angeles, San Francisco, San Diego,
Sacramento, Calif., Las Vegas, Reno, Detroit, Chicago, Atlantic
City, and Fort Lauderdale, Fla.   Additional schools are being
opened regularly.   The largest and most successful blackjack
school operation; established in 1976.

I recommend the school. Over 2,000 people have graduated from
this program.

Address: 1018 North Cole Avenue, Hollywood, CA 90038.

Jerry Patterson's Blackjack Clinic. This school teaches a one-
level count (2 through 6 is +1, tens and aces are—1), which effectively is the Braun (Wong) High-Low count. The class has four sessions
of three hours and subsequent review sessions. It costs $395. Jerry,
a dedicated instructor, sometimes teaches the course himself; he
also has other instructors. I recommend this school, which is located
in Cherry Hill, New Jersey. Other locations are planned.

Address: P.O. Box 796, Cherry Hill, N.J. 08003

Canfield Expertise School Of Winning Blackjack. This
school was opened in the spring of 1980, in the Sacramento, Calif.
area, by the people who wrote *Blackjack, Your Way To Riches* (22).
They teach the one-level count contained in their book. Cost is $200
for eight hours (one day) of instruction.

Scientific Systems. This school, held in Chicago, comprises a weekend of intensive training. A two-level count (tens are—2, all others,
+1) is taught. The cost of $695 includes a notebook of material. Bad
feedback has been received and while I don't feel this school is in
the irresponsible category, I can't recommend it.

The Revere School. Since Revere's death several years ago, this school has been taught by his daughter-in-law and past associates of Revere. Attempts are made to teach one-level and advanced counts, but the instructors don't have the in-depth knowledge necessary to teach blackjack. I must say that *all* the feedback I've received from their students over the past two years has been negative.

The Golden Eagle Gaming Institute. Located in Philadelphia, this school claims to teach students to win without counting. It teaches a so-called "sequence system," where the player is taught to look for "patterns" in the cards to determine how to play the hands. The charge is $65 per hour and the course lasts for seven-to-eight hours. It's popular with people having trouble learning to count. Definitely not recommended.

Arnold Van. This school opened in the San Francisco Bay Area in mid-1980, amidst extensive television coverage. The charge is only $30, but in the long run, the student will pay more. Incorrect Basic Strategy is taught (example: "1 wouldn't hit 12 against a 10 with a gun at my back") and a fallacious progressive betting system is encouraged. I hope blackjack schools will someday be licensed, so the public won't be sucked in by operations like this.